REVOLUTIONARY AMERICA
1763–1815

Revolutionary America describes and explains the crucial events in the history of the United States between 1763 and 1815, when settlers in North America rebelled against British authority, won their independence in a long and bloody struggle, and created an enduring republic. Placing the political revolution at the core of the story, this book considers:

- the deterioration of the relationship between Britain and the American colonists;
- the War of Independence;
- the creation of the republican government and the ratification of the United States Constitution;
- the trials and tribulations of the first years of the new republic.

Revolutionary America also examines those who paradoxically were excluded from the political life of the new republic and the American claim to uphold the principle that 'all men are created equal'. In particular, this book describes the experiences of women, who were often denied the rights of citizens, Native Americans, and African Americans. *Revolutionary America* is an important book for all students of the American past.

Francis D. Cogliano is Lecturer in American History at the University of Edinburgh.

REVOLUTIONARY AMERICA 1763–1815

A political history

Francis D. Cogliano

Routledge
Taylor & Francis Group

LONDON AND NEW YORK

First published 2000
by Routledge
2 Park Square, Milton Park, Abingdon, Oxon OX14 4RN

Simultaneously published in the USA and Canada
by Routledge
270 Madison Ave, New York, NY 10016

Reprinted 2002, 2003, 2004 (twice)
Transferred to Digital Printing 2007

Routledge is an imprint of the Taylor & Francis Group, an informa business

Typeset in Garamond by Taylor & Francis Books Ltd
Printed and bound in Great Britain by
Biddles Ltd., King's Lynn, Norfolk

British Library Cataloguing in Publication Data
A catalogue record for this book is available from the British Library

Library of Congress Cataloging in Publication Data
Cogliano, Francis D.
Revolutionary America 1763-1815; a political history / Francis D. Cogliano.
p. cm.
Includes bibliographical references (p.) and index.
1. United States-Politics and government-1775-1783. 2. United States-
Politics and government-To 1775. 3. United States-Politics and government-
1783-1865. I. Title.
E210.C56 1999
973-dc21   99-27130

ISBN-10: 0-415-18057-0 (hbk)
ISBN-10: 0-415-18058-9 (pbk)
ISBN-13: 978-0-415-18057-3 (hbk)
ISBN-13: 978-0-415-18058-0 (pbk)

FOR EDWARD AND SOFIA

CONTENTS

ACKNOWLEDGEMENTS

One of the great pleasures of writing a book is derived from acknowledging the debts incurred in producing the work. My most obvious debt is to the hundreds of scholars past and present who have made the study of the American Revolution and the early republic such an intellectually rewarding experience. The literature on the Revolution is remarkable not only for its quantity but for its quality. The preparation of this book has allowed me the pleasure of engaging with this literature. I was introduced to the historiography of the Revolution by excellent teachers – particularly John Brooke and Alan Taylor – who set a superior example for me by the quality of their own scholarship.

I am grateful for the advice and support of many friends and colleagues, including Paula Coonerty, Derek Edgell, Jane McDermid, John Oldfield, and Adrian Smith at the University of Southampton and Charles Hanson of the Collegio del Adriatico. Colin Nicholson of the University of Stirling provided me with valuable advice relating to Chapter 2. I have had the benefit of working with excellent colleagues at the University of Edinburgh whose advice and friendship I have come to appreciate in the preparation of this study, including Alan Day, Robert Mason, and Philip Cullis. I am grateful to Rhodri Jeffreys-Jones for his counsel with respect to the structure of the book, especially Chapters 9 and 10. Owen Dudley Edwards deserves special thanks for his close reading of the manuscript. Some of my best critics at Edinburgh have been my Senior Honours students. Their insightful questions and comments have influenced my own thinking on the Revolution, and I am grateful to them.

This book grew out of a conversation on a sunny afternoon in Southampton, England between myself and Heather McCallum of Routledge. Since that day, Heather has been a friend to this project. I am very grateful for her support and guidance. I have incurred institutional debts in the course of writing this book. I began writing this book at the University of Stockholm library. While writing, I enjoyed a research fellowship from the David Library of the American Revolution, where I completed much of Chapters 3–5. There is no better place to read, think, and write about the Revolution

ACKNOWLEDGEMENTS

than in Sol Feinstone's "Big House" on the banks of the Delaware River. All who have visited the David Library know what a joy it is to work there. I benefited not only from the convivial and collegial atmosphere fostered there by David Fowler and his colleagues, but also by the advice and insights of Dave and Greg Knouff. My greatest institutional debt is to the University of Edinburgh. The Faculty of Arts provided support for the completion of the manuscript and I conducted most of the research for the book at the university's main library, and I am grateful to the staff of the library for their assistance.

I owe more to my wife Mimi than I can express here. Without her support this book would not have been possible, nor worthwhile. She has juggled the demands of her own career in order to make it possible for me to write this book. The present work is but the smallest token of my gratitude and esteem. This book is lovingly dedicated to my children, Edward and Sofia. Without their presence this book would have been completed sooner. I'm glad it wasn't.

Needless to say, while all of the people named above have made this a better book for my contact with them, any faults or errors are mine alone.

F.D.C.
Edinburgh, Scotland
March 1999

ABBREVIATIONS

The following abbreviations are used throughout the text:

AHR	*American Historical Review*
JAH	*Journal of American History*
WMQ	*William and Mary Quarterly*, 3rd Series

INTRODUCTION

In the past two decades there have been three very good overviews which consider the period of the founding of the United States: Robert Middle-kauff's *The Glorious Cause*, Edward Countryman's *The American Revolution* and Colin Bonwick's book, also titled *The American Revolution*.[1] Each of these works made a significant contribution to the literature and advanced our knowledge of the subject. Middlekauff provided a detailed political, military, and diplomatic account of the American struggle for independence. Countryman's more concise treatment had as its major theme the impact of the Revolution on American society. Bonwick presented a detailed synthesis of the literature on the rebellion of the American colonies and the creation of the United States. Given the strengths of these works one might ask: why another book on the American Revolution?

In part, the nature of the exercise itself provides the answer to the question. It has been nearly a decade since the most recent of the studies noted above, Colin Bonwick's *The American Revolution*, appeared. Early American history remains one of the most active fields in American historiography. The discussion groups on early America sponsored by H-Net are among the most active academic discussion groups on the Internet. The annual output of significant articles in journals such as *The Journal of American History*, *The Journal of the Early Republic* and especially *The William and Mary Quarterly* is testimony to the strength of the field. Each year, aspects of the revolutionary and early national period are the subject of high-quality monographs such as those published by the University of North Carolina Press under the auspices of the Omohundro Institute for Early American History and Culture. Given the quality and quantity of the scholarship on the period, it is necessary to take stock of the literature periodically. At a basic level, this work endeavors to present a synthesis of the secondary literature on the Revolution with particular attention to the scholarship of the past decade.

As Middlekauff, Countryman, and Bonwick have demonstrated, such a synthesis is a worthy and challenging undertaking. In the course of writing the present work, I have often questioned my own worthiness for such a

1

task. The present literature on the American Revolution is so vast that it would be impossible to digest in a lifetime. As noted above, more works pour off the presses monthly. Given such circumstances, to undertake a synthesis of such a literature relatively early in one's career seems foolhardy at best and presumptuous at worst. At the conclusion of his own book. Professor Countryman wrote: "This book has tried to summarize what historians now think. But it will be successful only if readers argue with it, and if some decide to go to the sources and encounter the Revolution for themselves."[2] As one who read and was inspired by Professor Countryman's book as an undergraduate, I have taken up his challenge. What follows is one scholar's attempt to explain and assess the remarkable events of two centuries ago which gave birth to the United States. I hope that this work, like that of my predecessors, will inspire present and future students to turn their attentions to early America.

Both Countryman and Bonwick were British-based when they published their studies of revolutionary America. They contributed to a long and distinguished historiographical tradition of British-based historians writing about the revolutionary and early national periods of American history.[3] Like Professor Countryman when he completed his study, I am an American based at a British university. I believe these circumstances have been of inestimable value in terms of my approach to this subject. This book had its genesis in my experiences teaching British undergraduates about the American Revolution. Like their American counterparts, I have found that British students have a keen interest in the events which led to the creation of the United States. Unlike their American counterparts, most British students bring little foreknowledge and few or no preconceived notions to their study of the subject. This experience convinced me of the value of producing a work which provides a clear, concise description of the early history of the United States. Residence in Britain during the writing of this book has brought home to me the fact that the American Revolution was a British as well as an American event. Although this book focuses on the American aspects of the story, it has a trans-Atlantic theme as a premise.[4]

My point of departure in this book is the assumption that the fundamental question between 1763 and 1815 in the American colonies, latterly the United States, concerned relations with Europe. Between 1763 and 1783, the most important issue facing most Americans was their relationship with Britain. After 1783, American relations with and attitudes toward Britain and France were of primary importance. This was especially true during the period from 1789 until 1815 when the French Revolution and Napoleonic Wars posed a series of diplomatic, economic, and ideological challenges to the new republic which fundamentally shaped its development. During these years, the question of trans-Atlantic relations assumed an importance in American life to an extent which would not be replicated again until after

1945. Of course in 1945 the United States approached trans-Atlantic relations from a position of strength. Between 1763 and 1815, however, the colonies/United States were, in most respects, weaker than their European adversaries and allies. Approaching early American history from a trans-Atlantic premise leads to another theme of this book. The book contends that between 1763 and 1815, Americans were compelled to *react* to external events and decisions: changes in Parliamentary legislation, the French and Haitian revolutions, and so on. These reactions eventually led Americans to seize the initiative and undertake a revolution. I am certain that the trans-Atlantic theme and the thesis which emerges from it in this book might not have emerged as clearly had I approached this subject from the perspective of the United States. As such, I feel my presence in Britain was essential to the writing of this book.

My desire to address the question of how trans-Atlantic relations affected early American development has led me to adopt a relatively wide chronological approach. Most works on the American Revolution, including those of Middlekauff, Countryman, and Bonwick, conclude with the ratification of the Constitution in 1788 or with the triumph of the Federalists in 1789. When the subject is approached from a trans-Atlantic perspective, then one is compelled to consider the period until 1815. No sooner had the colonies won their independence and erected a national government than the sovereignty and independence of the new nation faced fundamental challenges from the French, British, and Spanish. Only by considering how the revolutionaries addressed these questions can the extent and implications of the American Revolution be properly examined. The adoption of a broader chronological approach does have significant limitations. In order to present a coherent narrative, I have focused primarily on the political history of the American Revolution. At times this means that I have paid careful attention to academically unfashionable high politics in order to tell the story of the creation of the United States. I have, where possible, also tried to tell the story of the Revolution from the perspective of America's common people, whose sacrifices and efforts made the United States possible. Among these, one particular group, white males, were empowered by the events of 1763 to 1815. By drawing on the literature of the "new" political history, I have been able to tell their story as well. It is my hope that I have been able to weave the two together in a coherent fashion.

Such a politically oriented narrative of the Revolution is in danger of ignoring those groups which were marginalized within American society at the turn of the nineteenth century, notably women of all races and African Americans. No history of the Revolution, political or otherwise, could be written without considering these segments of American society. Indeed, much of the most important scholarship of the past generation has focused on recovering the revolutionary experiences and contributions of these two

3

groups. In consequence, my final two chapters consider the experiences of women and African Americans by way of illustrating the limits of the Revolution. I had originally eschewed the idea of such distinct chapters; I felt that separating the histories of female and black Americans from that of the white males of all classes who dominated the Revolution would be to contribute to the intellectual Balkanization of American history into a variety of sub-specialisms. My intent had been to integrate groups on the political margins into the overall narrative. Intellectually, such an approach still seems to me to be correct. In practice, however, it proved nearly impossible to achieve. As I wrote my narrative, I felt that the treatment of women and African Americans would be too superficial and contrived.[5] Consequently, I resolved to dedicate discrete chapters to both groups. Because political power in the eighteenth-century America was confined to white males, a political history of the Revolution must, of necessity, focus primarily on them. Nonetheless, Chapters 9 and 10 demonstrate that the ideology of the revolution was impossible to contain. The attempts by those in power to exclude those without power constitutes one of the most profound and distressing aspects of the early (and later) history of the United States.[6]

Due to my focus on the political history of the American Revolution, other areas such as military affairs, diplomacy, and economic developments are addressed insofar as they influenced the political struggle at the heart of the independence movement. Constraints of space and organization prevent detailed discussion of other themes such as religion or culture. These remain crucial areas in which excellent scholarship is being conducted, but they fall outside of the remit of this study. This organizational difficulty arose because the American Revolution was fundamentally a political and ideological struggle. As such, the history of the political struggle is crucial to an understanding of these other areas. Put another way, while it is possible to write a history of the American Revolution which pays scant attention to religious or cultural developments, it would not be possible to write a religious history of early America without considering the political implications of the Revolution. The lowest common denominator in the early history of the United States was the political struggle for independence and the creation of a national republic. I have endeavored to write a history which concentrates on those events.

This book is intended for advanced undergraduates and inquisitive general readers (though I hope that my colleagues, past, present and future, will be engaged by its interpretations). I have attempted to let my readers glance over my shoulder by providing citations which acknowledge the sources of quotations, interpretations, and facts which are not my own; and to expand upon historiographical issues. I have tried to keep my citations to a minimum so that they would not intrude upon the text. In the main I have relied on published primary and secondary sources so that readers possessing sufficient curiosity and access to an academic library can follow my intellectual path. In order to assist them, I have provided a detailed bibliographic essay at the conclusion of my text. Like the nation that it created, the American Revolution remains a fascinating bundle of contradictions. In terms of the questions it raises, and the richness of the primary and secondary sources, it remains one of the great historical events since the Renaissance. I hope this book will be a suitable introduction to the topic and might inspire some of its readers to contribute to the literature summarized in the bibliographic essay.

THE THIRTEEN COLONIES
IN 1763

Pontiac's uprising and its aftermath

On May 7, 1763, a small detachment of British soldiers and sailors was taking soundings on Lake St. Clair, near Detroit, when it was attacked by a band of Chippewa warriors. Two days later, Ottawa war parties under the leadership of a war chief named Pontiac attacked and killed British settlers near Detroit. By May 14, the British garrison at Detroit was besieged by more than 600 warriors representing various Native American tribes. Over the next two months Indians attacked every British fort north of the Ohio and west of the Susquehanna rivers as well as outlying settlements and farms. All told, the Indians from a variety of western tribes captured nine British forts; only the largest, including Detroit, Niagara and Fort Pitt withstood attack. This pan-Indian attack, remembered by historians as Pontiac's uprising, represented a direct challenge to Britain's newly-won authority over the trans-Appalachian west. The conflict had its roots both within Native American culture and in the results of European diplomacy.[1]

In February of 1763 the major European powers, including France and Britain, agreed on a peace treaty at Paris which brought an end to the Seven Years' War. That conflict, known in Britain's North American colonies as the French and Indian War, was the culmination of a prolonged struggle for imperial mastery between France and Britain which persisted throughout the eighteenth century. In its North American dimension France had initially enjoyed success during the war, inflicting a series of humiliating defeats on British and colonial forces with the help of her Indian allies. Eventually the British recovered, capturing Quebec in 1759 and Montreal in 1760 as well as a number of French possessions in the West Indies. Under the terms of the Treaty of Paris, France ceded to Britain all of its territory in North America east of the Mississippi River (with the exception of New Orleans). In return, France retained fishing rights on the New-foundland Banks as well as the small north Atlantic islands of St. Pierre and Miquelon. In addition, Britain returned captured French colonies in the

West Indies including Martinique and Guadeloupe. Spain, which fought unsuccessfully as an ally of France, ceded Florida to Britain but was compensated by France with all French territory west of the Mississippi, and New Orleans. The geopolitical results of this diplomatic settlement were profound. After nearly two centuries, France had been removed from North America and Britain was nominally the master of all the vast territory of eastern North America, from the Atlantic west to the Mississippi and from Hudson Bay in the north to the Florida Everglades in the south. Winning this territory at the negotiating table would prove less difficult than governing it. Pontiac's uprising revealed in a particularly bloody fashion the difficulties empire in America would hold for a succession of British governments.

During the early years of the French and Indian War the British sought, with limited success, to cultivate the Indians of the trans-Appalachian west. They offered favorable trade relations and gifts of weapons, ammunition, and liquor, while restricting land grants to settlers. Once the British conquered Canada this policy of accommodation and cultivation ceased. In 1761, General Jeffrey Amherst stopped the policy of gift-giving, and British traders raised their prices for manufactured goods. As Native American dissatisfaction increased, Anglo-American settlements sprang up around the British (formerly French) forts in the west. To anxious western Indians, the defeat of France represented a profound change in their relations with Europeans. British hegemony in the transmontane west seemed to represent a serious threat to Indian autonomy. When news of the Peace of Paris spread throughout the west, many Native Americans concluded that their very survival was endangered by the diplomatic settlement.

The threat posed by Britain in the wake of the Peace of Paris is not sufficient to explain Pontiac's uprising, which as a pan-Indian movement represented a significant development in the cultural and diplomatic circumstances in the west. Pontiac's uprising was one of the earliest expressions of a militant pan-Indian identity which emerged during the latter eighteenth century in the trans-Appalachian west. The notion that Indians of different tribes should cooperate in response to common problems and against their common enemy had its origins among the polyglot Native American communities of the Ohio River valley. The movement for Native American unity had an important religious dimension. One of the earliest proponents of pan-Indianism was a Delaware religious prophet named Neolin. Beginning in the autumn of 1761, Neolin began preaching a message of spiritual and cultural reform and renewal among Indians. His message was simple: Indians should reject their dependence, both cultural and material, on Europeans. He was especially critical of Indian dependence on the alcohol trade. Neolin was not the only religious figure who advocated such cultural resistance. The message spread, and by 1763 when Anglo-Indian relations were deteriorating, the pan-Indian movement was gaining strength. The message of Indian autonomy and intertribal cooperation in the preaching of Neolin and the other Indian prophets gave strength and unity of purpose to the Indian uprising during the summer of 1763. Indeed, it is not a coincidence that the attacks were concentrated in the same region where Neolin's message was most popular. Pontiac's uprising was more than a postwar spasm in response to the diplomatic settlement. Over the next two generations, pan-Indianism would be at the heart of successive attempts by Native Americans to resist first British and then American encroachments in the Ohio River valley.[2]

In response to the uprising, General Amherst planned a series of punitive raids against the western tribes. Under his successor, General Thomas Gage, the British army found itself hard pressed to recover its lost posts, let alone punish the Indians. The Indians, meanwhile, found that while they could successfully attack small settlements and lightly garrisoned forts, more substantial forts like Niagara, Detroit, and Pitt withstood their sieges. By the summer of 1765 the two sides reached an uneasy accommodation and peace was temporarily restored in the transmontane west.

While the native followers of Neolin and other Indian prophets were attacking British forts and settlements, nearly four thousand miles to the east, British officials discussed how the vast new territory should be governed. On June 8, 1763 the Board of Trade recommended to King George III that three new colonies should be created: Quebec (confined to the eastern portion of the previous French colony), East Florida and West Florida (encompassing much of present day Florida and southern Alabama, Mississippi and Louisiana, excluding New Orleans). The remaining land should be designated Indian territory and settlement by whites should be prohibited. Colonial settlement, according to this plan, should be limited to the watershed of the rivers that flowed into the Atlantic Ocean, roughly to the east of the Appalachian Mountains. On July 14, George III approved the plan and instructed his ministers to make suitable preparations. Government officials worked out the details of the plan throughout the summer, against the backdrop of the conflict in the Ohio River country. On October 7, 1763 the king issued a proclamation creating the new colonies and setting aside the Indian reserve in the west. Because the policy was enacted by means of a proclamation, the line separating white settlers from Indian territory came to be known as the Proclamation Line.[3]

Despite the best efforts of the British army and government to restore order along the frontier, many settlers in the region were dissatisfied with circumstances in the wake of Pontiac's Rebellion. They felt that the army did not provide them with adequate protection, and that the Proclamation Line was intended to protect Indians at the expense of white settlers who coveted the newly conquered territory. The situation was especially acute in western Pennsylvania, where large numbers of Scots-Irish settlers were exposed to attack during the summer of 1763 and felt that the pacifist-inclined Quaker-dominated colonial government in Philadelphia was unsympathetic to their peril. As a consequence, frontier settlers took up arms to defend themselves against perceived dangers. On December 14, 1763, a group of roughly sixty settlers from Paxton Township, unable to find any hostile Indians, descended upon a small settlement of peaceful Christian Indians in Conestoga. The so-called "Paxton Boys" murdered six of the Conestoga Indians. In response to the outrage the governor of Pennsylvania, John Penn, ordered the remaining Conestoga Indians, fourteen in number, taken into protective custody and held in the jail at Lancaster. On December 27, a party of approximately fifty vigilantes broke into the jail at Lancaster and massacred the fourteen Indians. A much larger group of 250 disgruntled frontiersmen then marched on Philadelphia, determined to kill other Christian Indians who had taken refuge there and to demand fairer representation from the colonial government. In February 1764 they were confronted at Germantown by a delegation of the colony's political leaders. In return for laying down their arms, the Paxton Boys were allowed to present a remonstrance of their political grievances. The officials in turn promised: to take stronger measures to protect the frontiers; more equal representation for western districts in the colonial assembly; and amnesty for all involved in the murders at Conestoga and Lancaster.[4]

Events along the frontier in 1763–4 presaged the difficulties which would undermine British–American relations over the next thirteen years. Over the next decade the British government would have increasing difficulty in exercising authority not only over its newly acquired territory but over long-established colonies as well. It was one thing for politicians in London to draw a line on a map and proclaim that Native Americans should remain on one side and settlers on the other. It was quite another, as the Indians and settlers demonstrated when they took up arms, to make such a policy reality. Neolin recognized more clearly than Prime Minister George Grenville that keeping Americans off western lands would be a very difficult task. Grenville and his successors would soon learn that bringing the Americans to heel would prove equally difficult in a range of different areas. An important explanation for American recalcitrance toward Britain after 1763 was the extraordinary growth of Britain's North American colonies during the course of the eighteenth century.

The colonies and their people

The Indians who took up arms in 1763 recognized that the outcome of the Seven Years' War had fundamentally altered power relations in eastern North America. With the defeat of France, the unchecked growth of the British North American colonies seemed a real possibility. In the wake of the peace of Paris and the Proclamation Act, Great Britain had twenty-six colonies in the New World, including seventeen in North America.[5] Despite the number of colonies, the population of British North America was concentrated in the thirteen seaboard colonies that would declare their independence from Britain in 1776, especially in the coastal region running from Portsmouth, New Hampshire in the north to Savannah, Georgia in the south. In these colonies, the population was growing at a remarkable rate which threatened not only the Indians of the west but also unnerved imperial officials in London.

The population of the thirteen British colonies that became the United States grew at a prodigious rate during the eighteenth century. The population doubled nearly every generation (see Table 1). Thus when Benjamin Franklin was born in 1706 the population was approximately 300,000; when he died in 1790, the American population was nearly four million people. By 1800 the population exceeded five million souls. It is likely that Britain's American colonies had one of the fastest growing populations on earth during the eighteenth century. Indeed between 1763, when the Anglo-American dispute commenced, and 1815, when it was finally resolved, the American population increased from more than 1.5 million to more than 8.4 million people. During the eighteenth century, population growth was seen as a measure of power. Consequently, many commentators in America and Britain welcomed this growth as an indicator of future American and British greatness. Some British observers were wary of American growth, fearing it might lead to a desire for autonomy and possibly independence in the colonies.[6]

Table 1   American population growth, 1700–1800

Year	Population
1700	250,888
1710	331,711
1720	466,185
1730	629,445
1740	905,563
1750	1,107,676
1760	1,593,625
1770	2,148,076
1780	2,780,368
1790	3,929,625
1800	5,297,000

Source: U.S. Bureau of the Census, Historical Statistics of the United States, Colonial Times to 1970, 2 vols., (Washington: U.S. Bureau of the Census, 1975) 2: 1168.

Although the American population was concentrated along the eastern seaboard, it was not evenly distributed. In 1770, on the eve of the Revolution, the New England colonies (Massachusetts – including what is today the state of Maine – New Hampshire, Rhode Island, and Connecticut) had a population of 581,038, which was 27 percent of the American population. The Middle Colonies (New York, New Jersey, Pennsylvania and Delaware) had 555,904 residents, which constituted 25.9 percent of the total population. It follows that slightly less than half (47.1 percent) of the American colonists lived in the South (Maryland, Virginia, North Carolina, South Carolina, and Georgia). With its longer growing season and fertile soil, the South was attractive to migrants from other colonies as well as Europe. As the region where slave-based agriculture had proven profitable, the southern colonies were the destination for most African slaves brought unwillingly to American during the century. These factors, combined with the very high American birth rate gave the South, as a region, the largest percentage of the American population. The southern population was divided between the older more populous colonies along Chesapeake Bay, Virginia and Maryland, which had 649,615 residents in 1770, and the newer, less populous colonies of the Lower South, North Carolina, South Carolina, and Georgia, which had a combined population of 344,819 on the eve of the Revolution.[7]

American population growth during the eighteenth century was the result of two important factors: natural increase and immigration. The overwhelming majority of eighteenth-century Americans lived in households which were dependent upon agriculture. American society was characterized by relatively large amounts of land and a shortage of labor. Since the family was the essential economic unit, as well as social unit, large families were a valuable source of labor. Thus economic necessity combined with demographic factors – an increase in life expectancy during the eighteenth century by comparison with the seventeenth century, as well as early marriage – to produce a high birth rate. The average American woman during the eighteenth century could expect to marry in her late teens or early twenties (the average age of marriage for men was slightly higher). She could expect to become pregnant quickly, and was likely to repeat the cycle of pregnancy, birth, and lactation every two years for the duration of her childbearing years. For most eighteenth-century American women maternity, with its attendant risks, was a fact of life for the first two decades of married life. The result was a rapidly growing population, with families averaging six to eight children, as well as a definition of womanhood which was indistinguishable from motherhood.[8]

The American population swelled not only through an increase in the birth rate but as a result of a large influx of immigrants during the eighteenth century. All told, nearly 600,000 immigrants from Europe and Africa, voluntary and involuntary, migrated to British North America between 1700 and the Revolution.[9] The rate of immigration increased as the century progressed. In the fifteen years between 1760 (when fighting between the British and French effectively ended in North America) and the outbreak of the War of Independence in 1775, more than 220,000 immigrants arrived in America, at a rate of approximately 15,000 per annum. As a result of this influx, almost 10 percent of American colonists were foreign-born when the War of Independence began.[10] Eighteenth-century immigrants had a profound impact on the development of pre-Revolutionary America. They came from two places, Europe (including the British Isles) and Africa.

According to a recent estimate, more than 300,000 Europeans migrated to British North America between 1700 and 1775. Unlike their predecessors who settled the colonies during the seventeenth century and were mostly of English origin, the immigrants of the eighteenth century were remarkable for their heterogeneity. Indeed, the 44,100 English men and women who migrated during the eighteenth century made up only about 14 percent of the migrants.[11] The remaining European immigrants were drawn from throughout northwestern Europe and the British Isles. However, the two largest immigrant groups were German-speakers from central Europe and Scots-Irish. About 85,000 Germans, many from small radical Protestant sects, were attracted by the religious toleration and fertile soil of Pennsylvania. Most of the German migrants came in family groups and approximately one-third of the migrants came as redemptioners, or contract workers, who pledged their labor (or that of their children) to pay for their trans-Atlantic passage. Philadelphia was the first destination for many of these migrants, who established numerous German-speaking settlements in eastern and central Pennsylvania. Within Pennsylvania, where the German population was concentrated, the immigrants maintained an important degree of religious and cultural autonomy and exercised considerable political power and sustained a German-language press until after the Revolution. By the eve of the Revolution there were also congregations of German pietist immigrants in North Carolina, Maryland, New Jersey and New York as well as Pennsylvania.[12]

The other major group of European emigrants to American before the Revolution were the Scots-Irish, Protestants from Ulster. Estimates vary widely as to how many Scots-Irish migrated, but it is likely that the figure is around 200,000.[13] These migrants, mostly descended from Scottish Presbyterians who emigrated to Ulster in the seventeenth century, resented discrimination at the hands of the English who gave primacy to wealthier Ulster Episcopalians. Many were hard-pressed tenant farmers, who were attracted to America as much by the promise of cheap land as religious toleration. They, like the Germans, arrived in Philadelphia as their first port of call. Most then migrated to western Pennsylvania and then up and down the Appalachian region. By the eve of the Revolution, Scots-Irish settlers not only predominated in western Pennsylvania but also in the frontier regions of Virginia and the Carolinas. Just as their forebears found themselves guarding the frontier between the English and Catholic Irish in Ulster, the Scots-Irish in America found themselves along another frontier between the coastal settlements and territory occupied by Native Americans. The Paxton Boys gave expression to the difficulties faced by the settlers, who felt threatened by the Indians and ignored by political authorities along the coast.

The arrival of vast numbers of Scots-Irish and German, as well as lesser but still significant numbers of Irish, Scottish, Welsh and other European immigrants, made the white population of America much more ethnically diverse than it had been in 1700. No longer could it be assumed that all white Americans were of English descent. Thus during the revolutionary period, Pennsylvania was a complex ethnic mosaic with a white population that was only 19.5 percent English, 33.3 percent German, and 42.8 percent Celtic (Scots-Irish, Irish, Scottish, and Welsh) in origin. Similarly in South Carolina, only about a third of the white population was of English extraction. Such diversity was not uniform. The white population of New England was 75 percent English. Nonetheless, in the remainder of the colonies, the majority of the population was not of English extraction. When the revolutionary crisis erupted, the English officials and English-dominated Parliament which ran the British Empire could not assume that cultural affinity between the colonists and their rulers would promote unity.[14]

Slaves

The largest single group of migrants to eighteenth-century British North America were African slaves. Although the first African slaves in British America arrived in Virginia in 1619, chattel slavery evolved slowly during the seventeenth century. During the eighteenth century, importation of black slaves from the West Indies and directly from Africa increased as planters sought a cheap alternative to indentured servants as a source of labor. As a result, nearly 280,000 Africans were forcibly transported to North America to endure the rigors of perpetual racial servitude. As a consequence of colonial imports of slaves, the number of people in North America who were either African-born or of African descent increased steadily throughout the eighteenth century (see Table 2). Indeed, by the beginning of the American Revolution approximately one in five Americans was black.

Table 2 Africans as percentage of population

	New England	Middle Colonies	Chesapeake	Lower South	Total
1700	2	7	22	17	11
1730	3	8	23	43	14
1770	3	6	39	45	21

Source: U.S. Bureau of the Census, *Historical Statistics of the United States, Colonial Times to 1970*, 2 vols. (Washington, D.C., 1975), 2: 1168.

The slave population was not evenly distributed throughout the colonies. While, broadly speaking, there were few slaves in the northern colonies and quite a large proportion in the southern colonies, there were wide variations within the regions and even within individual colonies. For example, although New England had a slave population of only 3 percent at the time of the Revolution, 6 percent of Rhode Islanders were slaves of African origin. Similarly, the Middle Colonies taken as a region had a slave population of 6 percent on the eve of the Revolution, yet New York's slave population was 12 percent. Most slaves were concentrated in the southern colonies, yet even among the settlements where the practice of slavery on a large scale was economically viable there were important regional variations. Thirty-one percent of the Marylanders, for example, were enslaved in 1770 compared to 61 percent of South Carolinians. (South Carolina was the only mainland British colony with a population the majority of which was enslaved.) Within colonies themselves, there was an uneven distribution of slaves.[15] Most of Rhode Island's slaves were concentrated around Narragansett Bay, and New York's slaves largely lived and worked in New York City and its environs. Within the South similar concentrations occurred, although on a much larger scale. In the Chesapeake colonies of Virginia and Maryland, most of the slave population was concentrated in coastal tidewater where tobacco cultivation was centered. South Carolina's black majority largely resided in the coastal lowlands of the colony. Across the South there were relatively few slaves in the frontier regions.

The experiences of slaves varied widely by region and over time. Northern slaves, few in number, were concentrated in the maritime trades and were also employed as manual workers in cities and towns. Some were kept as personal servants by wealthy urban merchants as a mark of status. The few slaves in the rural north usually worked as farm laborers in close contact with their white masters, in isolation from other slaves. In the southern colonies there was a comparable diversity of experience. Slaves in Maryland and Virginia were generally scattered on hundreds of small farms and plantations given over to tobacco and cereal production. Most slaves in the region toiled as agricultural workers performing a variety of tasks, although on the larger plantations numbers were concentrated enough to allow for a degree of specialization and the employment of some slaves as personal servants. In South Carolina slaves enjoyed a degree of autonomy under the task system but were confronted by an unhealthy climate and difficult conditions cultivating rice and indigo.

Regardless of where they lived or the labor they performed, the overwhelming majority of African Americans (with the exception of a small number of free blacks in the northern colonies) shared a common status as chattel slaves. As a result they were, in the eyes of the law as well as custom, property to be bought, sold, punished, and forced to labor without pay in perpetuity. Slaves were not the only unfree migrants to eighteenth-century America. Tens of thousands of German redemptioners, indentured servants, and convicts found their way to the colonies. Indeed, unfree migrants constitute the majority of the immigrants to eighteenth-century America. Slaves were set apart, however, by their race and the permanence of their status. Other unfree migrants could aspire to freedom, economic, social, and political, which was denied to African slaves. Their status as slaves, moreover, would be transmitted to their children. As a result, slavery as practiced in eighteenth-century America rendered one-fifth of the population, identifiable by race, as a permanent class of unfree laborers. The presence of slave labor on such a wide scale had profound implications for American society during the era of the Revolution. When colonists of European origin protested the existence of a British conspiracy to enslave them, they did so with a clear and intimate knowledge of what slavery was. In practical terms, many of the men who would lead in the revolutionary struggle – most notably figures like George Washington and Thomas Jefferson – relied on slave labor to provide them with the status, time and wealth which made them effective leaders. Ultimately, slavery was a constant presence and problem in the American struggle for independence.[16]

Colonial society

Before the American Revolution, slavery was accepted by most Americans (at least those who were not enslaved) as a normal part of the social order. People in eighteenth-century America, as in Britain, accepted that they lived in a society which was unequal and hierarchical. While social position in a society in which the majority of heads of household were small property owners was not as fixed in America as it was in Europe, there was a definite and recognizable social order among the colonists.

The chief distinction was between those who worked with their hands and those who did not. At the top, perhaps five percent of the population, were those men – urban merchants, large planters, and some successful professionals – who did not work with their hands and had the wealth and leisure time to distinguish themselves as gentlemen by their learning, conversation, habits of consumption, and public service. These were men who served as councilors to the colonial governors. The upper tier of colonial society provided indigenous political and military leaders, educated their sons at American and British colleges and universities, and expected deference from those below them. Although not aristocrats in the formal British sense (by either title or wealth), these men were the closest eighteenth-century America would produce to fit the term. Below this elite were those professionals – ministers, lawyers, doctors, schoolmasters – who were educated and did not toil (primarily) with their hands but with their intellect. Although not enjoying the wealth of those above them (and upon whom they frequently depended for their livelihoods), these were men who, in many cases, could achieve elite status by hard work and luck. These men were respected in their communities and would be expected to hold lesser offices and positions of public responsibility, perhaps serving as members of colonial assemblies.[17]

Below the would-be aristocrats and the professionals were the vast majority of Americans who supported themselves by the labor of their hands and the sweat of their brows. At the top of this group were those who owned their own property. This was a large group. About four out of five free males were farmers and most of these owned their own land, usually between 60 and 100 acres. Prior to the Revolution, approximately 70 percent of land in the mainland colonies was owned by freehold families. Although property ownership was common, thanks to a large supply of land – obtained at the expense of Native Americans – and a relative shortage of labor, it was by no means universal. Most property owners held title to their own farms, which might vary in size from small plots to substantial holdings. The more successful among this group found themselves socially on a par with the professionals. Most probably worked their own land with labor provided by themselves, their families, and possibly a servant or slave or two. Steady population growth coupled with a social and economic expectation to acquire land led to a surge of westward settlement and land speculation after 1763, which the Proclamation Act did little to stem.[18]

Below the property-holders were those who labored for others. This was a diverse and complex group, ranging from sons of property-holders who could expect to inherit land, to African slaves who enjoyed no such possibility. The key distinction within this social group was between the apprentices, some servants, and younger sons who had a reasonable chance of acquiring property and economic autonomy and the slaves, long-term tenants, and the chronically poor who did not have such prospects. Approximately 30 percent of the land in America was farmed by tenants. Tenancy, however, took a variety of forms. In New England, tenants were often young men awaiting inheritances or families who sought to increase their holdings. Even in New York's Hudson River Valley, where long-term manorial tenancy was implemented, tenants often were given long-term leases and the right to sell their produce. The shortage of labor which characterized pre-revolutionary America, when coupled with the availability of inexpensive frontier lands, limited the incidence and extent of tenantry and prevented growth of a large class of landless agricultural workers (with the obvious exception of slaves). A similar situation did not prevail in the towns and cities.

In the cities and towns of America, the situation was very different. In the urban setting, the property-less included artisans' apprentices, sailors, servants, and laborers. Among this group, the proportion who were poor increased to about one in five by the time of the Revolution. At the same time that poverty was increasing, an increasingly small urban elite was controlling a greater proportion of urban wealth. On the eve of the Revolution, the top 5 percent of inventoried estates in Boston controlled 46 percent of the wealth. In the late seventeenth century the comparable segment of the population had owned 26 percent of the assessed wealth. In Philadelphia, which emerged as the major metropolis in eighteenth-century America, the figures were more stark. In 1700, the richest 5 percent of Philadelphians owned 25 percent of the city's wealth; by the eve of the Revolution that figure had increased to nearly 56 percent. Although the distribution of wealth in the American colonies as a whole remained constant during the eighteenth-century, economic stratification occurred in the cities. This social and economic polarization was offset somewhat by the fact that a very small proportion of Americans lived in towns and cities. On the eve of the Revolution, fewer than 5 percent of Americans lived in cities (and the proportion was declining). Nonetheless, given the importance played by the major towns, especially Boston, in the early resistance to Britain, this increasing inequality was a significant development.[19]

American society was hierarchical on the eve of the Revolution, ranging from very wealthy planters and merchants to propertyless slaves. The great bulk of the population, however, lived and worked on family-owned land. For many of those who did not own property, the acquisition of land remained a reasonable aspiration. Such aspirations remained beyond a significant proportion of urban dwellers, a smaller number of rural folk and all African American slaves. Because the colonies were still relatively new even in the mid-eighteenth century and because inherited titles and offices were not prevalent, wealth, public office, and genteel behavior were the prerequisites for entry into the provincial elite. The case of John Adams is instructive. Adams's father had been a shoemaker and farmer in Braintree, Massachusetts. The elder Adams eventually acquired significant amounts of land as well as local offices, serving as a Selectman and a church deacon. He was able to send his son to Harvard College. After receiving his degree and a short stint as a schoolmaster, John Adams read law and was admitted to the Massachusetts bar. By dint of hard work and self-promotion, Adams was one of Boston's most prominent lawyers and a member of the city's elite by the eve of the American Revolution. His steady rise was testimony to the potential fluidity of provincial society during the eighteenth century.

The economy

The key to social advancement in colonial America was wealth. The American economy experienced a steady, at times spectacular, growth of about 0.5 percent per annum during the eighteenth century. As a result, by 1775 Britain's North American colonies had an economy that was approximately two-fifths of the size of that of the mother country. The growth of the American economy and the role it played within the overall British economy are essential to understanding why British policy makers were eager to raise revenue in, and assert Parliament's authority over, the colonies after 1763. American economic growth was the result of both domestic production and colonial participation in trans-Atlantic trade.[20]

The domestic sector of the colonial economy, which encompassed subsistence agriculture as well as the local production and distribution of goods and services, comprised approximately 90 percent of colonial economic production. The engine of domestic economic growth within the colonies was the rapid expansion of the population. The steady increase in the American population during the eighteenth century necessitated the creation of new farms. Given the relatively wide availability of arable land in the colonies, the burgeoning colonial population was able to find and settle new farms, thereby creating a steady increase in overall production. The domestic economy was largely oriented towards domestic needs. Most farmers raised cereals, vegetables, and livestock for their own consumption, with any surpluses set aside for the local marketplace where goods and services could be obtained. According to a recent estimate, colonial households, depending on local factors like fertility of the soil and climate, could divert as much as 40 percent of their total output to the marketplace. Local transactions, in farm produce, goods, services, small-scale manufactures and land, were the mainstays of the domestic economy. As long as there was a supply of relatively cheap arable land, the increasing population would drive domestic economic growth.[21]

The second major area of American economic enterprise before the Revolution was the trans-Atlantic trade. Early modern theories of imperialism dictated that colonies should produce raw materials for export to the mother country, which in turn would export its manufactured goods to eager colonial consumers. Within the British empire this system was organized around a body of laws, the Navigation Acts, which dictated that colonists could only trade certain enumerated staple products via British vessels within the empire. This colonial economic model was most successful (from a metropolitan standpoint) in the British West Indies, where armies of African slaves toiled to produce sugar which was exported to Britain by colonial planters. The planters in turn purchased British manufactured goods with their immense profits. In British North America the staples model was only partially successful. Staple-producing plantations were established in the Lower South, which produced rice and indigo for export, and the Chesapeake, which exported tobacco. Even in these regions, agriculture was more diverse than in the West Indies. Indeed, Chesapeake planters were giving more of their land over to wheat on the eve of the Revolution. North of Chesapeake Bay the colonies did not produce staples for export. This is not to say the northern colonies did not play an important role in the trans-Atlantic economy; Pennsylvania and the middle colonies were a major source of wheat and flour products for export. New England agriculture did not contribute much to the trans-Atlantic trade, but the region's shipyards produced many of the vessels which carried British and colonial trade, its sailors manned them, and its fishermen plied the Newfoundland banks for cod which helped feed the slaves of the West Indies and the peoples of southern Europe.[22]

As the eighteenth-century progressed, colonial trade played an increasingly important role in the British economy. As British affluence increased, so too did dependence on the colonies. At the beginning of the century, imports from the colonies (including the all-important West Indies) constituted about one-fifth of British imports and the colonies were the destination for about one-tenth of British exports. By 1773, more than a third of Britain's imports and exports crossed the Atlantic. The major exports of the mainland colonies were (in order of importance) tobacco, bread and flour, fish, rice, and wheat.[23] The colonies in turn imported luxury items, manufactured goods, clothing, and books, among other items, from the metropolis and other British colonies. This trade brought prosperity to British and colonial merchants, shippers, planters, and bankers. It helped to create an affluent colonial elite while providing labor and an increasing range of manufactured goods to less wealthy colonists. The trade left many colonists in debt to British merchants and bankers. The importance of the trans-Atlantic trade would be among the factors which convinced British policy-makers that closer control should be exercised over the colonies during the 1760s.[24]

Southerners, with their reliance on slave labor and the production of staple crops like tobacco and rice, were more directly engaged in the trans-Atlantic economy than their northern counterparts. In all regions, however, a mixed economy based on both domestic and trans-Atlantic production and exchange prevailed. Indeed the boundary between the two was blurred, as exemplified by the hundreds of rural storekeepers who sold imported items to their farming colleagues.[25] Despite the wide regional variations in economic practice, average per capita wealth was roughly comparable throughout the colonies. In 1774, average per capita wealth was £36 in New England and the South. The Middle Colonies were slightly more prosperous, with an average per capita wealth of £40. These figures must be placed in the context of regional economic practices. Southern slaves were denied access to the region's wealth which they contributed so much to producing. When average wealth per free wealth-holder is computed (including the value of slaves and servants), the figure for New England is £161, the Middle Colonies £186, and the South £394. The imbalance in the figures reflects the inequality in the plantation system where slaves were denied the fruits of their labor. As one historian has written, "White southerners had more wealth than white northerners only because black southerners had none." Despite the inequitable distribution of wealth, most eighteenth-century Americans enjoyed a economic opportunity and a level of prosperity greater than that of their European counterparts.[26]

Family and government

The basic unit of eighteenth-century American economic and social life was the household, which was a venue for production and consumption. Like American society, the household had a hierarchical structure. At its head was a white male who represented the household to the outside world. The rest of the family included the head of household's wife, his children, and his servants and slaves. In eighteenth-century America the family included all those for whom the head of household had responsibility (and who were answerable to him). Thus bonds of servitude were as significant as those of blood in determining family membership. Hierarchy prevailed among dependent family members as well. The male head's wife, while subordinate in law and custom to her husband, had wide authority within the household as her husband's "help-mate." While the male head of household was responsible for managing the farm and its production, his wife was usually responsible for the day-to-day management of the home including food preparation, cleaning, laundry, clothing manufacture, child-rearing and the management of any servants and slaves involved in these tasks. Within the household, children were subordinate to their elders, females were likewise subordinate to males, as were servants to those members of the household united by blood, and blacks to whites. The labor required to make a household function properly was considerable. As a result, most eighteenth-century Americans, even those who were prosperous, worked long and hard. Only a very small and wealthy minority were spared physical labor of some sort on a regular basis.[27]

The household functioned not only as a unit of social organization and economic production, but also as a political institution. Four out of five

Americans were dependent members of households, which meant that for them political authority was vested in the male head of household. The head of household served in the militia and fulfilled other public duties for his family. If the family could meet property requirements, he cast its vote and was eligible to hold office. The head of household managed the family's finances and exercised legal authority over the other members of the family. For the overwhelming majority of Americans – women, slaves, servants, dependent males – government and politics were literally domestic concerns.[28]

Beyond the household, a wide variety of political practice prevailed in pre-revolutionary America. In New England, local government was organized around the town, where annual elections were held to select a range of local officials. In the annual town meeting, all of a community's voters came together to deliberate upon issues of local importance. In the Middle Colonies, a wider variety of practices prevailed at the level of local government. New York City was governed by a mayor, who was appointed by the colony's governor, and elected aldermen and councilors. In the rural regions of the colony, some communities had New England-style town governments while in others government was organized by county. Philadelphia was governed by a closed corporation. The rest of Pennsylvania was organized into counties whose officials were appointed by the colony's proprietor. In some of the townships which comprised the counties, local voters could nominate local office-holders. The southern colonies were organized by parishes, which were governed by vestries comprised of members of local gentry. Above the vestries were county courts, whose members were recommended by the vestries and appointed by the governors. Only in New England, therefore, can local government be characterized as fully representative.[29]

During the eighteenth century, all of Britain's mainland North American colonies (as well as its major Caribbean colonies) had elected assemblies. The right to vote for representatives in the assemblies varied from colony to colony, the key requirement being a property qualification. Although historians disagree as to how widespread the franchise was, it is likely that the majority of white males could vote in these elections. The colonial assemblies made local laws and acted as protectors of local colonial interests. The assemblies usually met in the spring or autumn for a session of four to six weeks. The main item on their agendas was to vote taxes to pay the expenses of the colonial government, such as the salaries of the governor and other permanent officials. Most colonists viewed the assemblies as having rights and privileges comparable to those of Parliament, including the right to determine their membership, choose a speaker, audit expenditure, and adjourn when they wanted. Although the British saw the assemblies as privileges granted to the colonies by charter (which could in extreme cases be revoked), the colonists viewed the assemblies as the legal guardians of their rights and interests.

The assemblies could not govern the colonies alone. Each colony had a governor who acted as its executive. In most colonies the governor was appointed by the king. Exceptions were the proprietary colonies (Pennsylvania, Maryland, and Delaware), where the proprietors who ran the colonies appointed the executive, and the corporate colonies (Rhode Island and Connecticut), where the governor was popularly elected. The governors were assisted by a council whose members were appointed by the governor (except in Massachusetts where, by charter right, the council was elected by the assembly). The councils functioned as both the upper house in the legislature and the highest court of appeal within the colony. Ideally the governor, assisted by the council, should work in harmony with the assembly in a governmental system that balanced local and imperial interests to provide stable government in the colonies. In practice, the system did not function so smoothly. Governors frequently found themselves at loggerheads with their assemblies. Although colonial governors had considerable power in theory – they could veto acts adopted by the colonial assemblies; they determined when and where the assemblies could meet and they could dissolve assemblies and call new elections – in practice they were hamstrung by the assemblies which controlled their budgets, including their salaries. The result was persistent conflict between local and imperial authorities.

The discrepancy between the theoretical and actual powers of the colonial governors reflected the limits of central authority within the British empire during the first half of the eighteenth century. During much of the century, responsibility for the supervision of the colonies fell to the Lords Commissioners for Trade and Plantations (commonly known as the Board of Trade) which answered to the Parliamentary Committee on Plantation Affairs, which in turn made recommendations to the Privy Council which exercised ultimate authority over the colonies. All acts passed by the colonial assemblies, for example, required not only the assent of the local governor but also that of the Privy Council. The situation was further complicated by the Secretary of State for the Southern Department, whose brief included colonial affairs. The Secretary of State was the principal minister responsible to Parliament for American colonial government until 1768. Both the Board of Trade and the Secretary communicated with governors on policy and routine administration until 1768. The most controversial issues were occasional instructions from the Secretary of State directing the governor to make requisitions of the colonial assemblies, to veto certain categories of provincial legislation, or to enforce specific acts of Parliament and orders-in-council. Governors submitted regular reports to the Secretary of State on colonial affairs generally, and to the Board of Trade on matters relating to the corpus of trade laws.

In addition to the Board of Trade and the Secretary of State for the Southern Department, the colonies were of course subject to legislation adopted by Parliament. In order to follow developments respecting colonial affairs as well as to lobby Parliament and the Board of Trade on behalf of their interests, most of the colonies employed agents. These agents were sometimes Members of Parliament or prominent colonists such as Benjamin Franklin. Sometimes special interest groups, such as the West Indian planters and their London-based business associates, cooperated to exert pressure on the government. The result was a cumbersome, inefficient group of institutions which was responsible for administering the colonies. When coupled with the communications difficulties posed by far-flung colonies during the age of sail, it is not surprising that colonial governors frequently found themselves isolated and impotent in the face of local intransigence. As a result, the North American colonies were largely left to their own devices for much of the first half of the eighteenth century. During this period of "salutary neglect," the colonies flourished economic- ally and enjoyed a wide degree of autonomy over their internal affairs. By mid-century, officials in London had become concerned at the growth of American independence and began to discuss ways to assert metropolitan authority over the colonies. War with France then intervened. It was not until the conclusion of the war that ministers had the time and resources to re-evaluate the relationship between the metropolis and the colonies.

Before 1763, few Americans gave serious thought to the constitutional relationship between the colonies and the empire. The colonial governmen- tal structure with its governors, councilors, and assemblies bore a resem- blance to the British constitutional arrangement with its tripartite division between the monarch, the House of Lords, and the House of Commons. Colonial Americans, who believed that the British constitutional arrange- ments were the main bulwark of their liberties, contended that their local political arrangements played a comparable role in the colonies. Only when government officials sought to strengthen central control over the colonies did the colonists embark on the ideological journey which would culminate in the Declaration of Independence. To understand that journey, it is necessary to appreciate what colonial Americans believed about politics and power before the Revolution.

Over the past generation, no question has occupied historians of the American Revolution more than the ideological origins of the resistance to Britain. An army of historians, chief among them Bernard Bailyn, have scoured the books read and pamphlets written by colonial Americans to recover the intellectual world of the eighteenth-century American elite. In his seminal 1967 book, *The Ideological Origins of the American Revolution*, Professor Bailyn persuasively argued that colonial Americans drew on a variety of intellectual traditions, from the Classical historians to John Locke to the common lawyers to the seventeenth-century Commonwealth writers and their descendants in the eighteenth century, to create a libertarian political ideology which stressed the danger which government power posed to liberty. According to Bailyn, this ideological outlook predisposed Americans to be acutely sensitive to all threats, perceived or real, to their liberty. This ideology has been termed the "Real Whig Ideology," because it drew closely on the opposition, so-called "Real Whig" literature of eighteenth-century England. It was because they identified with the traditions of the English opposition that opponents of British rule in America identified themselves as "Whigs" and their opponents as "Tories."[30]

More recently, other historians have identified more diverse intellectual and emotional sources for American political resistance including feelings of jealousy and resentment between Britain and the colonies and colonial anxiety over commercial dependence on the mother country for manufactured goods. Just as large numbers of historians have examined the intellectual world of the American elite, others have examined the actions of crowds to find political expression in the actions of more common Americans. They have demonstrated that the common people gave expression to their political sentiments by their actions in demonstrations and riots. It is possible as a result of these historiographical efforts to make some generalizations about American political attitudes before the Revolution.[31]

In general terms, those Americans who had, or aspired to, some political rights believed they were British and consequently enjoyed the same rights and privileges as other Britons. Despite their diverse origins, the colonists believed that by history and charter they enjoyed the vaunted "rights of Englishmen." Before the 1760s few colonists actually attempted to enumerate precisely what those rights were, but most would have agreed that they included the right to self-government, petition for redress of grievances, trial by jury, freedom of speech, and a measure of religious toleration (usually limited to Protestants) as delineated in the Bill of Rights of 1689. The colonists believed that they possessed these rights and that it was in the exercise of them that their liberty was preserved. Threats to liberty could originate from various quarters, including monarchical tyranny and standing armies. The greatest protection to liberty was the virtue of a free people who did not allow themselves to be corrupted. When a people lost their virtue, when they gave in to selfishness and avarice, they undermined the public good and were liable to lose their liberty. Only the maintenance of virtue and public vigilance could guarantee the survival of liberty. The political culture which prevailed in the colonies predisposed the colonists to be suspicious and vigilant with respect to threats, perceived and otherwise, to their liberty. Colonial political culture also recognized a variety of tactics which could be employed in the defense of imperiled liberty, ranging from drafting petitions to violent protest. Within colonial political culture were the ingredients of a republican culture. These political beliefs, which were not fully enunciated by the colonists until the crisis with Britain, are crucial to understanding how and why the colonists reacted as they did to ministerial attempts to exercise greater control over the colonies.

If Americans gave relatively little thought to their political beliefs before the 1760s, the same could not be said of their religious beliefs. The American colonies were strongly Protestant during the eighteenth century. The largest denominations were the Congregationalists (based in New England) followed by the Presbyterians, Quakers, Baptists, Anglicans, Lutherans, German Reformed, Dutch Reformed and a host of smaller groups spread throughout the colonies. At the time of the Revolution there were nearly 3,300 churches and congregations in America (one for approximately every 850 Americans) and a majority of the population attended church regularly. The decades immediately before the Revolution had witnessed a pan-colonial series of religious revivals, known to historians as the Great Awakening. The Awakening fostered a sense of religious egalitarianism, as all souls were eligible for salvation, while challenging the social hierarchy in colonial society. The plethora of diverse religious groups in their midst forced Americans to acknowledge a degree of religious toleration. This toleration was largely confined to Protestants – of 3,286 churches and congregations in 1780, only 56 were Catholic – nonetheless a desire to preserve religious as well as political liberty would be an important element of the movement to resist British encroachments.[32]

Conclusion

By 1763, Britain's North American colonies were thriving. After a fitful development during the seventeenth century, the eighteenth century had witnessed a steady increase in American population and prosperity. Most of the colonies had mature, stable, social and political institutions which were controlled by indigenous local elites. The colonies had developed largely without direct interference from imperial authorities. The success of the colonies, in short, was as much in spite of the British government as because of it. Consequently the colonists, while they considered themselves British, also enjoyed a remarkable autonomy in their day-to-day lives. Their ties with Britain were based as much on affection and culture as political obedience.

In the wake of the Seven Years' War, the relationship between the colonies and the mother country would undergo a massive transformation. Like the colonies, Britain was more prosperous and vigorous in the wake of the defeat of France. Government ministers believed Britain now had the political, financial, and military strength to exercise more direct control over the colonies which, to their minds, existed to serve the needs of the metropolitan center. In seeking to alter the relationship between the colonies and Britain, it was the succession of government of ministers who sought to raise revenue and assert British control over the colonies who were the innovators. As a result, the American protest movement would begin as a defense of traditional autonomy. However, within thirteen years of the Peace of Paris the thirteen most populous colonies would declare themselves independent of Britain. What would begin as a defense of traditional rights would culminate in revolution.

2

THE IMPERIAL CRISIS

The Sugar Act

George Grenville had a problem. In 1763, the fifty-one-year-old left his post as First Lord of the Admiralty to become Prime Minister. Grenville discovered that the recent victory over France had not only been glorious but costly. Britain's budget deficit, which stood at £73 million before the war, had ballooned to £137 million by 1763. The annual interest on the debt alone was £5 million at a time when the government's income was £8 million per year. The acquisition of new territory in America would only increase the financial pressures on the government. Addressing the government's financial problems would be one of the foremost concerns of the Grenville ministry. As a result, Grenville would undertake a program of reform with an eye towards raising revenue in America. This program was intended fundamentally to alter the relationship between the colonies and the metropolis. Thus at the outset of the sequence of events which would result in American independence, it was not the future revolutionaries who advocated change but their imperial masters.

Soon after he entered office, Grenville asked the Treasury to estimate the cost of maintaining a garrison force in North America. The Treasury reported that it would cost £225,000 per year to maintain 7,500 troops in North America. (This was a low estimate. The actual cost of the troops was £384,000 per year between 1763 and 1775.) The Prime Minister, who had had little previous experience with the colonies, looked to America to bear some of this burden. The Americans, after all, had benefited from the defeat of the French; hence it was only just, he felt, that they should pay something towards their own defense. Ordinary Britons, moreover, were overtaxed by comparison with their American counterparts. One source of potential revenue was to tax imports and exports via the Navigation Acts, which stipulated that Americans could send their goods only to British ports and only on British vessels. The purpose of these acts, first adopted in the seventeenth century, was to compel the colonies to send their unfinished staple products – tobacco, wheat, furs, and so on – to Britain in exchange for finished products. Under the system, taxation in the form of customs duties was used to compel the colonies to comply. If made more efficient, then the same duties could also be used to raise revenue.

In 1763, the British government undertook a series of measures which laid the foundation for a more aggressive policy of taxation in America. In March, Grenville, who was then First Lord of the Admiralty, sponsored a bill approving the use of the Navy on peacetime duty to collect customs revenue and suppress smuggling. The bill was enacted by Parliament in April. In May, Prime Minister Grenville wrote to the Board of Customs Commissioners asking for advice on how increased revenue could be collected in America. In July the Customs Board recommended that customs collectors be required to go to their American posts (rather than remaining in Britain and collecting their salaries which was a common practice), and that they should be paid a commission on the duties they collected. These measures addressed the major problems with a revenue plan based on custom duties: inefficiency and corruption. The Customs Board estimated that the total duties obtained from America in 1763 would be a paltry £1,800, which would cost more than £7,000 to collect. The reason that customs revenues were so low was because smuggling was rife and the customs officers were frequently lax or corrupt. For example, under the terms of the Sugar Act of 1733, Americans should have paid approximately £200,000 annually in duties on imported sugar and molasses. The actual total was £700. If George Grenville hoped to use the Navigation Acts to raise revenue in America, he would have to see that they were properly enforced. The actions taken by the government in 1763 signaled a new determination to extract revenue from the colonies.

When the Customs Board made its recommendations to the Prime Minister during the summer of 1763, it suggested that the duty on molasses be collected more rigorously. Under the terms of the Sugar Act of 1733, Americans should pay a duty of 6d per gallon on molasses and sugar imported from non-British colonies in the West Indies. This duty, which was due to expire, had largely been ignored by American merchants and British customs officials. The Board advised the government that a revised duty of 3d per gallon, rigorously collected, would yield £78,000 per annum while protecting the interests of British West Indian planters. Grenville introduced this revised duty in the Sugar Act, which he presented as part of his budget in March of 1764. As part of the legislation associated with the Sugar Act, Grenville added products to the list of enumerated items – including wine, silk, calico, and coffee – which, according to the Navigation Acts, would be subject to a increased duties if not traded via Britain. Grenville also proposed that the customs service be strengthened and that acts be enforced not by local colonial civil courts but by an admiralty court to sit at Halifax, Nova Scotia, far from local interference. Simultaneously, under the terms of the 1764 Currency Act, Grenville forbade the colonies from issuing paper money, thereby making it more difficult for Americans to pay the new customs duties. The whole program was adopted by Parliament over little opposition. In so doing, Parliament had taken the hitherto unprecedented step of taxing the American colonies to raise revenue. This step represented a fundamental revision in the relationship between Britain and the colonies. Spurred on by a legitimate desire to raise revenue in America, George Grenville had undertaken a policy which, if fully implemented, would severely curtail the autonomy previously enjoyed in the colonies.[1]

The Sugar Act would have its greatest immediate impact in southern New England. Of the 113 rum distilleries in British North America which used molasses as their main raw material, sixty-four were in Massachusetts and forty were in Rhode Island and Connecticut. There were no molasses distilleries south of Pennsylvania. Nonetheless, rum was of immense importance in eighteenth-century America. It was a favored spirit of many Americans, as well as a significant article of trade in the Atlantic trade and in relations between British Americans and Indians. The extension of the list of enumerated items and stricter customs enforcement could severely curtail the coasting trade which was vital to colonies lacking sufficient roads. Moreover, the enforcement of the new legislation by admiralty courts represented a challenge to the colonial legal system and the common law tradition in America. As a consequence, when word of the act reached America in May 1764, some of the more perspicacious colonists saw ominous tidings in the legislation.[2]

The colonial reaction to the Sugar Act was inchoate and largely ineffective. As would happen so often over the next decade, the people of Massachusetts took the initiative in formulating a colonial response. On May 24, 1764 the Boston Town Meeting instructed its representatives in the Massachusetts assembly, known as the Great and General Court, to request that the colony's agent in London should defend the right of the Massachusetts assembly to levy its own taxes. The assembly took the course of action suggested by the Town Meeting at the end of May. A month later, the assembly issued a circular letter to the other colonial assemblies calling for a united response to the Sugar Act. At the end of October a special session of the assembly asserted its right to levy taxes within the colony – internal taxes – implying that Parliament had the right to levy customs duties such as the Sugar Act. Throughout the summer and autumn of 1764 other colonial assemblies voiced their own protests against the Sugar Act. Connecticut, for example, condemned internal taxes but accepted the propriety of Parliament's levying customs duties for the purpose of raising revenue. The New York assembly, by contrast, petitioned Parliament and the king asserting that duties intended to raise revenue were unjust. Virginia's House of Burgesses endorsed the Massachusetts circular letter in

October and claimed freedom from both internal taxation and taxation intended to raise revenue. Pennsylvania, New Jersey, and South Carolina each instructed their agents in London to protest against the act. Rhode Island, which would be especially hard hit by the Sugar Act, called for an inter-colonial conference on the subject and complained about the impact of the act on colonial trade and the use of admiralty courts to enforce the act, and condemned internal taxes. Only North Carolina, with little direct interest in the Sugar Act, took the position which would become the standard colonial reaction to British taxation within a few years. The Carolinians petitioned George III asserting that the colonies were not subject to taxes to which their representatives had not given their consent.

Americans did not only object to the Sugar Act through their assemblies. Many also took up their pens to object to Parliament's high-handed treatment of the colonies. Among them was James Otis of Barnstable, Massachusetts. Otis was an outspoken and idiosyncratic member of a prominent Massachusetts family. Elected to the Great and General Court in 1762, he was a prominent critic of royal government in Massachusetts. In 1761 he achieved notoriety when he challenged the Writs of Assistance – general warrants which enabled British customs officials to search the homes of colonists for contraband – arguing unsuccessfully before the Massachusetts Supreme Court that illegal acts of Parliament need not be obeyed. In the wake of the Sugar Act, Otis published the most famous of the early pamphlets, *The Rights of the British Colonies Asserted and Proved*, which criticized Parliament's new aggressiveness towards the colonies. The confusion and contradiction of the colonial response to the Sugar Act is reflected in Otis's pamphlet. On the one hand Otis asserted, along with North Carolina's lawmakers, that "Taxes are not to be laid on the people but by their consent in person or by deputation." Despite the revolutionary implications of such an assertion, Otis also proclaimed that Americans must obey Parliament. For, he wrote:

> The power of Parliament is uncontrollable but by themselves, and we must obey. They only can repeal their own acts. There would be an end of all government if one or a number of subjects or subordinate provinces should take upon them so far as to judge of the justice of an act of Parliament as to refuse obedience to it.[3]

Otis's response, that Parliament could not tax Americans without their consent and that Parliament must be obeyed, epitomized the confusion and contradiction which bedeviled the colonial reaction to the Sugar Act. Despite their ineffective protests, the Sugar Act and its corollary measures sharpened colonial awareness with respect to taxation and parliamentary intentions *vis-à-vis* the colonies. The determination of some colonies to declare, despite the Sugar Act – an external customs duty – that Parliament had no authority to levy internal taxes, indicates that some colonial politicians feared that the Sugar Act would be the first of several taxation measures designed to raise money from and exert control over the colonies. They were correct.

The Stamp Act crisis

Despite the objections of the colonial assemblies and the grumbling of colonial merchants and politicians, Americans mainly complied with the Sugar Act (though coastal smugglers, often the very merchants who protested about the legislation, profited from illicit trading). This compliance gave George Grenville the confidence to proceed with a far more ambitious program of colonial taxation, the Stamp Act. When he presented his budget in March 1764, Grenville not only introduced the Sugar Act and related measures, but also announced his intention to devise and introduce a stamp duty in the American colonies. Such a duty, which was already in place in Britain itself, would apply to almost anything formally written or printed. Parliament endorsed the idea of such a tax without much debate or discussion on March 9, 1764. It was this resolution which led the colonial assemblies to object to internal taxation when they protested and petitioned against the Sugar Act.

In August 1764 the Earl of Halifax, the Secretary of State for the Southern Department, sent a circular letter to colonial officials soliciting information about the proposed stamp duty. Halifax, unlike the Prime Minister, had extensive experience in colonial administration and sought information concerning how the tax could be collected and what level of revenue could reasonably be expected from the duty. By December, a provisional plan for a stamp duty had been approved by the Board of Trade. Under its terms, a wide range of fifty items including wills, deeds, diplomas, almanacs, advertisements, bills, bonds, newspapers, dice, and playing cards would have to be on special stamped paper. Unlike the Sugar Act, which affected a relatively small number of colonists, the stamp duty would be paid by a majority of Americans. Halifax and his peers took steps to insure that the duty would be palatable to the colonists. The level of duty was to be much lower than in Britain, and of the fifty items subject to the tax, only nine would have a stamp duty in excess of £1; those most likely to be paid were 1s or less. The revenue from the act, moreover, would be earmarked for the army to help defray the cost of the troops in America.

Prime Minister Grenville met with the colonies' London representatives, the colonial agents, the most prominent of whom was Benjamin Franklin, on February 2, 1765 to discuss the duty before he presented it to Parliament. Grenville hoped to obtain their consent to the Act and set a precedent for future acts. When some of the agents suggested that the colonies tax themselves, Grenville rejected the proposal. Similarly, when the agents suggested that the colonies offer financial requisitions in lieu of the duty (a common practice during wartime), the Prime Minister indicated that such a settlement would also be unacceptable. In the wake of colonial protests, petitions, pamphlets, and remonstrances concerning the Sugar Act and the proposed Stamp Act, Grenville came to see the Stamp Act not only as a source of revenue but as an assertion of parliamentary sovereignty over the colonies. This was the clear message that the colonial agents took away from their meeting with Prime Minister. Four days later, on February 6, 1765, Grenville introduced the Stamp Act to Parliament as part of his budget program. In debating the issue, Parliament decided that three new vice-admiralty courts should be created, in Boston, Philadelphia, and Charleston, to help enforce the act. The act was adopted by the House of Commons by a margin of 245 to 49. It was passed by the House of Lords on March 8, and given royal assent on March 22. The Stamp Act was to take effect on November 1, 1765. The new tax raised, as Grenville had intended, the basic issue of parliamentary sovereignty over the colonies. When the Americans paid the duty, they would not only contribute to the defray the cost of their own defense but they would also acknowledge Parliament's authority to tax and govern the colonies.[4]

The Stamp Act forced Americans to articulate their view of the colonial relationship with Britain. News of the act reached the colonies in April of 1765. Initially there was little reaction in the colonies to this unprecedented legislation. It was not until the end of May that a young firebrand in the Virginia House of Burgesses ignited the storm of protest against the act, beginning a sequence of events that would culminate in revolution. Patrick Henry was a twenty-nine-year-old self-taught lawyer, who had been a member of the House of Burgesses for all of nine days when he rose to present a series of resolutions condemning the Stamp Act on May 29, 1765. Henry, a renowned orator, passionately attacked the Stamp Act and he proposed that the assembly (which had only one-third of its members in attendance because it was the end of the session) adopt a series of seven resolutions in defense of liberty. The burgesses adopted the four most mild of Henry's resolutions, asserting that: they possessed the rights of Englishmen; their rights were guaranteed by royal charter; they could only be taxed if they had proper representation; and colonists had the right to give their consent to their laws. They debated and rejected a set of more radical resolutions which asserted that: the House of Burgesses had the sole right to tax Virginians; Virginians were not obliged to obey any law designed to tax them without their consent; and support for such taxes rendered the supporter an enemy to the colony. Although the rump session of burgesses only adopted the resolutions which were roughly congruent with the previous year's objections to the Sugar Act, many colonial newspapers printed all of the resolutions, which made the actions of the Virginians seem more radical. As a consequence, the Virginia Resolves energized the movement against the Stamp Act. By the end of 1765 the assemblies of eight other colonies had passed resolutions condemning the Stamp Act for reasons similar to those debated in Virginia.

American colonists employed a variety of methods to resist the Stamp Act. Their resistance had two objectives: to prevent the implementation of the act on November 1, and to convince Parliament to repeal the measure. In general they pursued three different yet related strategies to achieve these objectives: they protested through their assemblies and political institutions, they exerted pressure through popular crowd actions and riots, and they applied economic pressure via formal and informal boycotts. The combination of these methods served not only to realize the objectives of the colonists but to lay the foundation for future colonial resistance.

In the wake of the Virginia Resolves, other colonial assemblies began to discuss the Stamp Act and draw up petitions to the king and Parliament appealing for its repeal. Rhode Island went the furthest, endorsing all seven of the Resolves in September. By the end of the year the assemblies of Pennsylvania, Maryland, Connecticut, Massachusetts, South Carolina, New York and New Jersey had also adopted resolutions and petitions protesting the Stamp Act. Such resolutions were similar to the unsuccessful actions some of the colonies had taken with respect to the Sugar Act during the previous year. By contrast with the Sugar Act, the Stamp Act would affect all the colonies, and as a consequence some colonists advocated closer cooperation in expressing their grievances. In June the Massachusetts assembly suggested that an inter-colonial meeting be held in order to draft a set of resolutions which expressed a common colonial position.

This meeting – known as the Stamp Act Congress – took place in October in New York City. Twenty-seven delegates from nine colonies sent delegates to the conference. New Hampshire eschewed participating in congress but later endorsed its work, and three colonies – Virginia, North Carolina, and Georgia – were unable to send delegates because their governors refused to call their assemblies into session in order to elect delegates. The representatives spent a fortnight drafting a set of fourteen resolutions which set out the colonial view on the Stamp Act and the relationship between the colonies and Parliament. The congress resolved:

- that the colonies owed the same allegiance to the crown and Parliament as British-born subjects;
- that the colonists had all the rights of British-born subjects;
- that among those rights was the right not to be taxed without their consent;
- that it was impossible for the colonies to be properly represented in Parliament;

- that no taxes could be levied against the colonies except by their own assemblies;
- that it was contrary to the British constitution for the British people as represented in Parliament to take the property of Americans;
- that trial by a jury of their peers was an "inherent and invaluable right of every British subject in these colonies";
- that the extension of admiralty court to enforce the Stamp Act contravened the rights of the colonists;
- that given the scarcity of specie it would be impossible for the colonists to pay the Stamp Duty;
- that since the profits of American trade eventually went to Britain and were taxed, the colonies already contributed to the cost of running the empire;
- that the Stamp Act would undermine the ability of Americans to purchase manufactured goods from the British;
- that the future success of the colonies depended on the enjoyment of their rights as well as unfettered trade between America and Britain;
- that British subjects in America had the right to petition the king and both houses of Parliament;
- that it was the duty of the colonies to seek the repeal of the Stamp Act, the abolition of admiralty courts, and "of other late Acts for the restriction of American commerce."

Essentially, the congress put forward ideological and economic arguments in opposition to the Stamp Act: Parliament had no right to tax Americans, and besides, to do so would not make economic sense for either the colonies or the mother country. These views were expressed in the many pamphlets which issued from American presses during the summer and autumn of 1765. There was an important contradiction within the ideological argument made by the delegates. On one hand they asserted that they were loyal British subjects who owed allegiance to the king and Parliament; on the other, they denied Parliament's right to exercise practical authority over the colonies. Americans would spend the next decade trying to resolve this contradiction.

Ultimately, the battle over the Stamp Act moved from the assembly halls to the streets. Americans, after all, had made similar protests to no avail with respect to the Sugar Act. At the same time that political leaders and pamphleteers were making the intellectual case against the Stamp Act, other Americans nullified the act by their actions. During the late summer and autumn of 1765, crowds throughout the colonies made the act impossible to enforce. As a result, by November 1 the Stamp Act was a dead letter in the thirteen colonies.

The street protests began in Boston. Here, the common people opposed the measure which would lead to an increase in taxation at a time of economic stagnation. The elite was divided between those who opposed the act and those merchants who, although not entirely supportive of the measure, did not oppose it. Opposition to the act was led by populist politicians like Samuel Adams, who sought to galvanize the crowd in opposition to the act. The popular initiative to resist the act originated among a group of leading artisans and shopkeepers known locally as the "Loyal Nine". It was their desire to harness the energy of the people and channel it toward realizing their own political ends. In the course of the Stamp Act crisis, this group evolved into a larger organization known as the Sons of Liberty. The Sons of Liberty operated as a semi-secret political organization, committed to opposing Britain. For them, as well as for rank and file Bostonians, the most treacherous people were men like Andrew Oliver, a politically well-connected local merchant who not only supported the act but, it was widely believed, would profit from it as the colony's Stamp Distributor.

With the encouragement of Sons of Liberty, resentment grew towards the Stamp Act and purported supporters of the act like Oliver as well as the governor, Francis Bernard, and the Chief Justice (and Oliver's brother-in-law), Thomas Hutchinson. Boston had a long tradition of rioting, especially where the public interest was concerned. In August, Bostonians drew on that tradition in opposition to the Stamp Act. On the morning of August 14, Bostonians awoke to find effigies of Andrew Oliver and the Earl of Bute, reputed to be the king's foremost advisor, hanging from a huge tree known as the Liberty Tree, in the town's South End. Chief Justice Hutchinson ordered the sheriff, Stephen Greenleaf, to cut the effigies down. A crowd formed and Greenleaf was prevented from carrying out his orders.

At the end of the working day, a mass of working men gathered under the leadership and prepared for the mock funeral of Andrew Oliver. Oliver's effigy was cut down and carried by the mob toward the South End wharves where Oliver had built a brick office in July, rumored to be the place from which stamps would be distributed. In thirty minutes the crowd tore down the building. The timbers were used to start a bonfire by Oliver's house. Oliver was not at home, but Thomas Hutchinson appeared and tried to reason with the crowd. Hutchinson's presence served to infuriate the crowd. He was chased off in a hail of stones and the crowd proceeded to destroy Oliver's stable house and coach, symbols of upper-class affluence and the widening gap between the rich and the poor in Boston. Having finished with these the crowd then turned to his home, breaking windows, smashing furniture, tearing up the gardens, and emptying the wine cellar.

On August 15 Oliver publicly resigned from the office he never actually entered into. His brother, Peter Oliver, described Andrew Oliver's humiliation: "He was carried to the Tree of Liberty by the Mob & a Justice of the Peace provided to swear him; and there he was obliged, on pain of Death, to take an Oath to resign his office."[5] The solution was infectious.

Without distributors, the act could never take effect. The Sons of Liberty became a more general phenomenon and similar disturbances occurred throughout the colonies. On August 27, Newporters took to the streets and forced their stampman to resign. By the end of October mass uprisings, real or threatened, won resignations in Massachusetts, Rhode Island, New Hampshire, Pennsylvania, Delaware, Virginia and Connecticut. North Carolinians and Marylanders followed suit in November. Of the mainland colonies, only in Georgia did the stampman briefly take office before he was forced to resign. While the delegates at the Stamp Act Congress articulated the ideological opposition to Parliament's action, more common Americans made that opposition reality by their forceful actions. Parliament would not be able to legislate its authority in America without coercion.

American crowds may have made the Stamp Act impossible to implement, but they could not secure its repeal. Leading merchants, who opposed the Stamp Act as well as the Sugar Act, believed that commercial pressure could force Parliament to change its mind. On October 31, 1765, two hundred leading merchants in New York City signed an agreement not to import from Britain until the Stamp Act was repealed. Two weeks later, four hundred Philadelphia merchants signed a similar pledge, as did two hundred Boston merchants on December 9. Elsewhere, non-importation was adopted as a tactic without resort to formal agreements. The Sons of Liberty appealed to the public to be virtuous in defense of liberty and eschew buying imported goods from merchants who violated the agreements. Because of their relatively short duration – the non-importation movement lasted only a few months – it is unlikely that colonial boycotts had a direct economic role in the repeal of the Stamp Act. Nonetheless, opponents of the act on both sides of the Atlantic *believed* the boycotts were instrumental in securing its repeal and would employ the tactic in the future.[6]

The political and economic situation in Britain as much as American opposition accounted for the repeal of the Stamp Act. In July of 1765 the Grenville ministry was replaced by that of the thirty-five-year-old Marquis of Rockingham. The new government inherited a crisis in imperial authority over the Stamp Act. While not necessarily committed to the policies of its predecessor, the Rockingham government wanted to see the authority of Parliament upheld. Members of the government believed that Americans would have to relent and accept the act if they wanted to do business. Rockingham was willing to compromise and modify the act after the Americans acquiesced and paid the duty. Unfortunately for the Prime Minister, he was overtaken by events when the colonists effectively nullified the act. Influenced by a postwar recession which exacerbated fears of the colonial boycott, merchants pressured the government to repeal the act. By December 1765 the government found itself with a choice between making concessions to the colonists or attempting to coerce them into complying with the Stamp Act.

Despite American claims that the Stamp Act was the first step to tyranny in America, the Grenville government was unwilling to use force in the colonies to uphold the measure. On December 27, 1765 the cabinet made a preliminary decision to recommend that Parliament repeal the Stamp Act for the "relief" of America while adopting another measure, the Declaratory Act, which asserted Parliament's authority over the colonies. Parliament debated the repeal of the Stamp Act on February 21, 1766. In making the case for repeal, ministers and supporters of the government ignored the political implications of repeal and stressed the deleterious economic impact of the act. The House of Commons voted for repeal by 275 votes in favor to 167 against. On March 4, 1766, almost a year after the adoption of the Stamp Act, Parliament adopted the Declaratory Act which asserted that the colonies were subordinate to the "Crown and Parliament of Great Britain" and that "Parliament assembled, had, hath, and of right ought to have full power and authority to make laws and statutes of sufficient force and validity to bind the colonies and people of America, subjects of the Crown of Great Britain, in all cases whatsoever." Here was a seemingly clear statement of Parliament's authority with respect to the colonies. With the Declaratory Act, Parliament reserved the right to govern at will without the approval of the colonies. Americans viewed the declaration somewhat differently. Since the act did not specifically cite Parliament's right to tax the colonies, many Americans read the act, in the context of the repeal of the Stamp Act, as a statement of Parliament's right to legislate for but not tax the colonies, a distinction many colonial commentators made in 1765. This ambiguity would be the source of future confusion and conflict between the colonies and Parliament. On March 18, 1766, George III gave his assent to the Declaratory Act and the bill for the repeal of the Stamp Act.[7]

As a revenue-raising measure, the Stamp Act had been a disaster. Under its terms a mere £3,292 had been collected, at a cost of £6,863. The failure of the Stamp Act obscured the relative failure of the Sugar Act. Rather than anticipated £78,000 per annum in revenue, £5,200 in duties were collected under the act in 1764 and £4,090 in 1765. As a consequence, in another climbdown the Rockingham ministry recommended that a flat duty of 1d be implemented on all molasses and sugar imported by the mainland colonists, whether it be of British or foreign origin. Grenville's program had generated very little revenue and considerable ill-will.[8]

The Stamp Act crisis marked a crucial turning point in imperial–colonial relations. As George Grenville had recognized, there was more at stake in the controversy than revenue. The fundamental issue, better recognized by the British than the Americans, was Parliament's sovereignty over the colonies. In denying Parliament the right to tax them, the Americans were implicitly denying Parliament's right to govern them. Though few Americans would have gone so far in 1766, such was the logic of their position. When Parliament acquiesced to American resistance and repealed the Stamp Act, it relinquished a measure of its authority over the colonies which would prove impossible to recover. Observers on both sides of the Atlantic learned important lessons from the crisis. Americans learned that they must be vigilant in defense of their liberties, and that the London government – regardless of who was in office – was not to be trusted. They believed that the popular activities of the Sons of Liberty coupled with the economic coercion of non-importation had compelled Parliament to restore American liberties by repealing the Stamp Act. Benjamin Franklin articulated this position when he testified before the House of Commons during the debate over the repeal of the Stamp Act. So too did the Boston loyalist Peter Oliver, who provided a perceptive analysis:

> In 1766 the Act was repealed. Illuminations & Sky-rockets pro-claimed the general Joy. But it was not the Joy of Gratitude, but the Exultation of Triumph. *America* had now found out a Way of redressing her own Grievances, without applying to a superior Power. She felt her own Superiority...[9]

In London, imperial and government officials concluded that the Americans were obstreperous, willful, lacking in respect for and subordination to authority, and too selfish to contribute to their own defense and mainten-ance. If future governments were to raise needed revenue in America and reassert Parliamentary authority, they would have to adopt more subtle means than those pursued by George Grenville.

The Townshend program

In July 1766, after a year in office, the Rockingham government fell. Rockingham was replaced by William Pitt, now Earl of Chatham, a traditional friend of the American colonists. Due to declining health and increasing hypochondria, Pitt would take little active interest in the administration. Pitt's Chancellor of the Exchequer, forty-one-year-old Charles Townshend, would serve as *de facto* Prime Minister during the Chatham government. Townshend had extensive experience in colonial administration: he served a long apprenticeship as a member of the Board of Trade between 1749 and 1754, and he later served as President of the Board, Secretary of War, Paymaster of the Army and First Lord of the Admiralty. Townshend's experience not only gave him insight into colonial affairs but also the financial demands of imperial administration. He was firm in his conviction, which he first expressed in 1753 as member of the Board of Trade, that colonial officials should be independent of local authority and that the only way this could be achieved was through taxation, the revenue from which could be applied to support royal officials in America.

During the winter of 1766–7, Townshend crafted his "American program" which was intended to raise revenue and tighten imperial control over the colonies. Townshend's program consisted of three elements: legislation to compel the colonies to support the army in America, reform of the customs service, and – the key to the program – a series of customs duties. Under the terms of the American Mutiny Act of 1765 (commonly referred to as the Quartering Act), colonists were required to help house and supply British soldiers stationed amongst them. The burden of this act fell disproportionately upon New York, which served as the headquarters for the British army in America. In December of 1765 the New York Assembly refused to comply with the act, fearing that to do so would be to undertake an open-ended commitment which was the equivalent of a tax. In May of 1766 the assembly modified its position somewhat, agreeing to provide the troops with some supplies but not alcohol, as stipulated in the act. In August the Chatham government ordered New York to comply completely with the act. The assembly refused. Faced with such outright defiance, Townshend proposed the New York Restraining Act, which Parliament debated and adopted in March. Under its terms, the New York Assembly was prohibited from taking any legislative action until it complied with the Quartering Act. On June 6, 1767 the Assembly relented and appropriated the funds to support the troops. Although the Restraining Act only applied to New York, the implications of the measure were clear: any colonies that did not comply with the Quartering Act faced the reduction of their right to govern themselves.

The other elements of the Townshend program would have a more general impact. In anticipation of introducing a package of new customs duties, the chancellor proposed yet another overhaul of the customs service. In January of 1767 the British Board of Customs examined the problems it faced in collecting revenue in America. It recommended the creation of an American board based in Philadelphia to oversee the collection of customs revenue. During the debate over the New York Restraining Act, Townshend introduced the plan to create an American Board of Customs Commissioners, which Parliament endorsed. In August 1767, two months after the final adoption of the act, the Treasury decided that the American Board of Customs Commissioners should have five members on salaries of £500 per year, and that the board should be located in Boston, not Philadelphia. The rationale for the decision to locate the board in Boston, the epicenter of resistance to the Stamp Act, is not clear. Such an action was bound to be inflammatory. At the same time that the Treasury decided to locate the customs board in Boston, the cabinet also approved a measure to create new vice-admiralty courts in America, located in Boston, Philadelphia, and Charleston, to complement the work done by the court in Halifax. Parliament approved this proposal in March of 1768.

Such institutional reform was necessary because the centerpiece of the Townshend program was a series of new customs duties on a range of articles. Since Americans had objected to internal taxes but grudgingly complied with the Sugar Act, Townshend planned to expand the range of items upon which Americans would have to pay import duties. His objective was to raise enough revenue to pay imperial officials such as customs officers and governors so that they would be free from local interference, and to help defray the cost of the army in America. Townshend sought duties on a wide range of items which would prove difficult or impossible for Americans to produce themselves. As a consequence, Parliament levied duties on wine, china, glass, paint, and tea among other items. Townshend believed that because the duties were spread over a range of items, were not especially heavy, and would be collected externally, Americans would pay them. Once they did so, the revenue to govern and administer the American colonies would be guaranteed, *and* an important precedent would be set: Parliament would not only possess the right to tax the colonies as stated in the Declaratory Act, it would have exercised that right, thus settling the question of colonial sovereignty once and for all. Charles Townshend did not live to see his plan come to fruition. He died suddenly on September 4, 1767. Chatham was still too ill to undertake the responsibilities of government; consequently it fell to the Duke of Grafton to act as Prime Minister and collect the Townshend Duties.[10]

Unlike the Stamp Act, the Townshend Acts elicited an immediate response from Americans, who were now predisposed to see in each new act of Parliament a threat to the liberties. As in 1765, intellectual, political, and economic protests were made. Resistance took a variety of forms, from pamphleteering to legislative action to rioting. The resistance to the Townshend Acts differed from that to the Stamp Act not only in the rapidity of the colonial response but also in its duration and in the number and types of people involved. Resistance to the Townshend Acts would require the participation of groups such as women and African Americans who were normally excluded from public discourse, although they were sometimes consulted – or harangued – in private with respect to public matters.

On an intellectual level, the resistance was led by a wealthy Philadelphia lawyer named John Dickinson. As a member of the Pennsylvania assembly who had previously been a delegate at the Stamp Act Congress, Dickinson was well versed in colonial grievances against the Parliament. In November 1767 he began writing a series of twelve anonymous letters, which first appeared in the *Pennsylvania Chronicle & Universal Advertiser* between December 1767 and February 1768. Dickinson's letters were reprinted in most colonial newspapers and appeared as a pamphlet, *Letters from a Farmer in Pennsylvania*, which was widely published in America and Europe. Dickinson argued that Parliament could regulate the trade of the colonies but it did not have the right to tax them without their consent, either through internal taxes or external duties. Moreover, he suggested that loyalty to the crown and mutually beneficial trade relations bound Britain and America, not Parliament's authority. By contrast with the confused and contradictory position expressed by James Otis four years previously, Dickinson's *Letters* demonstrate how far the colonial opposition had come. Dickinson advocated that the colonies revive non-importation and directly petition the king to secure redress of their grievances.[11]

On the political level, Massachusetts was again at the forefront of resistance. For nearly three weeks in December 1767 and January 1768, the colony's assembly discussed the Townshend Acts and prepared a remonstrance. The result was a circular letter to the other colonial assemblies condemning the legislation. Samuel Adams, who had been one of the leaders of the Sons of Liberty in Boston, was, in his capacity as clerk of the assembly, primarily responsible for drafting the circular letter. The letter, which appeared on February 11, 1768, urged the other colonies to resist the Townshend Acts, arguing that no colony could enjoy liberty if the monarch had full control over the salaries and appointments of colonial officials. Adams repeated the now familiar claim that Parliament had no right to tax the colonies for the purpose of raising revenue. When the Earl of Hillsborough, Secretary of State for the newly-created American Department, learned of the letter in April he ordered that colonial governors should prorogue their assemblies rather than allow them to endorse the letter. He further ordered the royal governor of Massachusetts, Francis Bernard, to require the Massachusetts assembly to rescind the offensive epistle. In late 1768 the legislature rejected Bernard's instruction that they recall the letter by a vote of 92 to 17. Bernard immediately dissolved the assembly, and other governors followed suit when their legislatures debated the letter.

At the same time that the assemblies were involved in political disputes with the imperial authorities respecting the Townshend Acts, other colonists sought to revive boycotts as a tactic to compel Parliament to repeal the noxious legislation. After word of the acts reached America, radicals within the Boston Town Meeting proposed the revival of non-importation as a tactic. By January 1768, twenty-four Massachusetts towns had endorsed the proposal. In March, ninety-eight Boston merchants voted in favor of restricting trade until the acts were repealed. In April, New York merchants adopted a restrictive non-importation agreement. Philadelphia's merchants delayed endorsing non-importation until 1769. Similar agreements were adopted in the southern colonies as well. In May 1769, the prorogued members of House of Burgesses met in a Williamsburg tavern and adopted the Virginia Association, a colony-wide non-importation agreement. Similar actions were taken in Maryland, North

Carolina, and South Carolina. By the end of 1769, every colony but New Hampshire had organizations which were pledged to non-importation or non-consumption. These groups normally appealed to virtue and the values of sacrifice, independence, and selflessness as central to the protection of liberty. Thus non-importation was valuable not only because it would bring economic pressure to bear on Parliament, but because it would strengthen the moral resolve of the colonists as they struggled to preserve their liberty in the face of what came to be seen as plot to subvert their freedom. American protesters were putting the precepts of the Real Whig ideology into action.

Resistance to the Townshend Acts was, by necessity, a popular (though by no means universal) phenomenon. Although the non-importation usually originated among the colonial social and political elite – merchants and political leaders – resistance could only succeed if it enjoyed popular support. Indeed, popular support was crucial to the opposition to the Townshend Acts. As an immediate reaction to the Townshend Acts, the Sons of Liberty were revived throughout the colonies in order to coordinate popular opposition. They played a key role in organizing and participating in popular protests and crowd actions against the acts and enforcing the non-importation agreements. Just as some American colonists demonstrated their willingness to take the law into their own hands during the Stamp Act crisis, some did so again in the wake of the Townshend Acts. In September 1767, a crowd in Norfolk, Virginia attacked the crew of a Royal Navy vessel that came ashore in search of deserters. In June 1768, Bostonians rioted when customs commissioners seized the sloop *Liberty*, owned by the patriot merchant John Hancock, on suspicion of carrying smuggled goods. The disturbance forced the customs commissioners temporarily to take refuge in Castle William in Boston harbor. Such disturbances, and the threat of such disturbances, encouraged support for non-importation even among those who otherwise might have complied with the Townshend Acts.

Many who may have been unwilling to riot could oppose the Townshend duties by supporting the non-importation agreements. Colonists could demonstrate such support in a variety of ways. At the most basic level, all colonists should eschew buying imported goods and paying the duties. Indeed, non-importation would only work if a majority adopted this course. The Virginia Association, for example, appealed to "all Gentlemen, Merchants, Traders *and* other Inhabitants of this Colony" to support the boycott.[12] Violators of the agreements should be ostracized and shunned, at least until they acknowledged the error of their ways. This too required an important level of popular participation. An important corollary of non-importation was the necessity of colonists going into production themselves to provide an alternative to boycotted imported goods. Many non-importation agreements stressed the importance of American manufacturing as a substitute for imports. This was welcomed by many urban artisans, who saw in the boycotts an opportunity for them to market their own handiwork at the expense of their British counterparts. Not surprisingly, artisans and tradesmen frequently formed the core of the urban crowds which were instrumental in enforcing the non-importation agreements.

By their various actions between 1767 and 1770, many Americans took important steps which led to revolution. The Stamp Act and Townshend Act controversies introduced lower-class whites, blacks and women into the realm of imperial politics through non-importation and protest movements. This was the source of the movement's success, and also a source of tension. Elite leaders of the protest movement were troubled by the implications of such a mass movement; indeed, one reason for the formation of the intercolonial Sons of Liberty was to channel resistance into acceptable forms. Thus the Sons of Liberty, usually led by popularly-inclined political leaders, existed as much to control colonial resistance as to encourage militancy. But the Sons could not control all reactions in the new climate of protest. For example, in October 1765 a crowd organized by the local Sons of Liberty in Charleston, South Carolina (a group whose origins lay in the city's fire company), chanted "Liberty, Liberty, & Stamp'd Paper" before the home of a rumored stamp distributor. Then in January 1766, amidst rumors of planned slave insurrection, local African slaves paraded through the streets chanting "Liberty, Liberty," seemingly mimicking the Sons of Liberty. The freedom-loving citizens of Charleston who took to the streets in defiance of the Stamp Act willingly accepted a week of martial law after the latter demonstration.[13]

Women were more directly politicized by their support for the non-importation movements. Both as producers and consumers, white women were instrumental to the success of non-importation movement. American women were called upon to produce more clothing, as wearing homespun garments became both a necessity and a political statement in the absence of imported British cloth and clothing. Daughters of Liberty held spinning bees to produce cloth and yarn. Women came to appreciate the political significance of their actions. When more than three hundred Boston "Mistresses of Families" pledged to abstain from tea in February 1770, they did so in order to "save this abused Country from Ruin and Slavery." Resistance to the Townshend Acts taught some American women that they could make a vital, if indirect, contribution in the public realm.[14]

Resistance to the Townshend Acts was not uniform. The non-importation agreements adopted in various colonies differed greatly in their structure and implementation. Moreover, some of the boycotts broke down in 1770. Yet despite the unevenness of colonial opposition, the acts had failed to generate enough revenue to support imperial officials in America. It appeared that Parliament had yet again stirred up opposition in America while failing to make sufficient financial gain. In 1769 the Grafton cabinet decided that the duties should be repealed. Grafton himself resigned in January, and the task of overseeing the repeal of the Townshend duties fell to his successor, Frederick, Lord North. Ironically, North had succeeded Townshend as Chancellor upon the former's death and had been responsible for the implementation of the unpopular duties. On March 5, 1770, North recommended the repeal of all the duties save that on tea, which would be maintained as a symbolic statement of Parliament's authority to tax the colonies. In April the repeal was passed by Parliament and received the royal assent. Parliament had yet again been forced to acquiesce to colonial pressure.

The Boston Massacre

The repeal of the Townshend Duties did little to reconcile the colonists to British authority. On the very day that Lord North proposed the repeal of the duties, a clash between civilians and British soldiers led to the death of five Americans in Boston. The origins of the events Whigs called the Boston Massacre lay in repeated clashes between customs officers and the people of Massachusetts. The creation by the Townshend Acts of an American Board of Customs Commissioners had been an error enough; to base it in Boston severely compounded the problem. The board was intended to make the collection of tax revenue more efficient, but it could have been located in New York or Philadelphia rather than Boston. From the time they arrived in November of 1767, the commissioners were frequent targets of popular wrath. The riots in turn helped convince the ministry in London that troops were needed to maintain order in the unruly port. By October 1768 there were five regiments of British troops in the city.

Bostonians, who had been accustomed to leading their lives with a minimum of interference from government, now found themselves hemmed in at every turn. Guards on Boston Neck checked all travelers and their goods. Redcoat patrols roamed the city day and night, questioning and harassing passers-by. Military parades were held on Boston Common, accompanied by loud martial and derisive music during the Sabbath. Deserters were hidden by local citizens. The greatest potential for violence lay in the uneasy relations between the soldiers and Boston's working people. Many redcoats sought to supplement their meager incomes by moonlighting in their off-duty hours, competing for unskilled jobs with the working men and poor of the city. Moonlighting soldiers depressed wages and added to the tension between the working people of Boston and the king's forces. Brawls in the taverns and streets of the city were quite common. (These conditions were not unique to Boston: on January 19, 1770, New Yorkers and British regulars engaged in a brawl which was remembered as the "Battle of Golden Hill.") Meanwhile, the local courts were especially harsh in their treatment of the soldiers who came before them. It seemed only a matter of time before a serious incident took place.

Despite the presence of the soldiers, the Boston crowd, often under the direction of the Sons of Liberty, remained very active. Tension was very high in the late winter of 1770. On February 22, 1770 a suspected customs informer killed an eleven-year-old boy, Christopher Seider, during a riot. The Sons of Liberty organized Seider's funeral, which was attended by 5,000 Bostonians and was as much a political demonstration as funeral. On March 2, 1770, workers at a ropewalk (ship-rigging factory) attacked some redcoats seeking jobs, and a pitched battle ensued. On March 5, a crowd began to throw hard-packed snowballs at a sentry guarding the Customs House. Reinforcements were summoned and eight soldiers found themselves confronted by a taunting, heckling crowd. The crowd threatened to kill the soldiers and pelted them with stones, snowballs, and pieces of ice. One of the soldiers was struck by a club and fired his weapon: whether out of fear, anger, or accident, it is impossible to know. His fellows, thinking their commanding officer, Captain Thomas Preston, had given an order to fire, also discharged their weapons. When the shooting stopped, six male civilians were wounded and four were dead. Within two weeks one of the injured men died from his wounds. The men killed by the British on March 5 represented a cross-section of the crowds resisting the Townshend Duties and enforcing the non-importation agreements: James Caldwell was a young sailor; Samuel Maverick was a seventeen-year-old apprentice; Crispus Attucks was a West Indian sailor who may have been of mixed Indian and African descent; Patrick Carr was an Irish immigrant who worked as a tailor; and Samuel Gray was a ropemaker who was a veteran of the battle on March 2. Without the efforts of men such as these, non-importation would have been impossible.

In the hours and days after the shootings, public order threatened to break down completely in Boston. A crowd estimated at least a thousand swirled through the streets almost immediately after the killings. Preston and the soldiers were jailed immediately, in part for their safety. Governor Thomas Hutchinson removed the troops from the town to Castle William in Boston harbor. The Sons of Liberty, especially Samuel Adams, sought to maintain control while encouraging anti-British sentiment in the wake of the killings. As with the death of Christopher Seider, the funerals of the deceased were occasions for mass political demonstrations. Whig leaders wanted a quick trial for the soldiers, but the Superior Court judges delayed the hearing until the autumn. Prominent Whigs John Adams and Josiah Quincy defended Preston and his men. On December 4, 1770, six of the soldiers were acquitted; two were found guilty of manslaughter and had their thumbs branded. As a symbolic event, the outcome of the trial did not matter. British soldiers were slaughtering Americans on their own streets.[15]

After nearly six years of tension and conflict between Parliament and the colonies, a superficial calm characterized their relations by late 1770. Patriot leaders took advantage of the quietude to organize for what they believed would be an inevitable return to conflict. In September of 1771 the Boston Town Meeting, at the behest of Samuel Adams, formally created a committee of correspondence which was to communicate colonial grievances to all the towns of Massachusetts, as well as to people throughout the mainland colonies and in the West Indies and British Isles, and to serve as the catalyst for the creation of similar committees throughout the colonies. More than half of the towns in Massachusetts responded positively to the call to create their own committees of correspondence. The spread of the committees ensured that the Whigs, whose resistance had been concentrated in the cities, could now cultivate support in the countryside where the majority of colonists lived. The movement was so successful that in March of 1773, the Virginia House of Burgesses recommended that each colony establish a committee of correspondence to insure the rapid dissemination of information and a unified response in the event of another trans-Atlantic crisis. The committees served as the propaganda and information-gathering counterparts of the Sons of Liberty.[16]

The Boston Tea Party and its consequences

The inter-colonial committees of correspondence established in the spring of 1773 would not have long to wait before they took action. In May, 1773, Parliament passed an act designed to save the East India Company from bankruptcy by changing the way that British tea was sold in the colonies. Under the Tea Act, certain duties paid on tea were to be returned directly to the company. Furthermore, tea was to be sold only by designated agents, which enabled the East India Company to avoid colonial middlemen and undersell any competitors, even smugglers. The net result was cheaper tea for American consumers. The result was ironic. Since the repeal of the other Townshend Duties many Americans had been drinking tea and paying the duty on it. Nonetheless the Tea Act, designed to save the East India Company rather than assert parliamentary sovereignty over the colonies, revived the dispute over taxation. Whig activists and the committees of correspondence did their jobs well, and many colonists interpreted the new measure as a pernicious device to make them admit Parliament's right to tax them. Recent experience had taught them how to respond to such a challenge.

During the summer, the East India Company dispatched shipments of tea to Charleston, Philadelphia, New York, and Boston. In New York and Philadelphia crowds turned the ships back before they could unload their tea. In Charleston, the tea was unloaded, stored under the direction of local tradesmen, and later destroyed. In Boston, as ever, confrontation occurred. Both sides, the Town Meeting, dominated by the Sons of Liberty and supported by nearby towns, and Governor Thomas Hutchinson – two of whose sons were appointed tea agents – rejected compromise. The first of three tea ships, the *Dartmouth*, entered Boston harbor on November 28. According to law, the ships had to unload their cargoes and pay the duty within three weeks. After a series of mass meetings, Bostonians voted to prevent the tea from being unloaded and to post guards on the wharf. Hutchinson for his part refused to permit the vessels to leave the harbor. On December 16, 1773, with time running out, a special Town Meeting convened in the Old South Church. The meeting, chaired by Samuel Adams, made a final half-hearted attempt to persuade Hutchinson to send the tea back to Britain. The governor was adamant. That evening about sixty Sons of Liberty, crudely disguised as Indians, assembled at the wharf, boarded the three ships and dumped the cargo into the harbor. By 9 p.m. the "Mohawks" had destroyed 342 chests of tea worth approximately £10,000.[17]

Parliament was furious at this challenge to its authority and the willful destruction of private property. One Member of Parliament said of Boston, "I am of the opinion you will never meet with that proper obedience to the laws of this country until you have destroyed that nest of locusts."[18] Even the friends of America in Parliament would not support the action. In March 1774, after failing in an attempt to charge the resistance leaders with high treason, Lord North proposed four bills that became known as the Coercive Acts, which were intended to punish Boston. The first bill, the Boston Port Act, called for the closure of the port of Boston until all the ruined tea was paid for. The Massachusetts Government Act altered the province's charter, substituting an appointed council for an elected one, increasing the powers of the governor, and forbidding special town meetings. The Justice Act provided that a person accused of committing a capital offense while in the course of suppressing a riot or enforcing the laws could be tried outside the colony where the incident occurred. Finally, the Quartering Act gave broader authority to military commanders seeking to house their troops in abandoned private dwellings. These acts were all adopted in the spring of 1774. In June, Parliament turned its attention to much-needed reforms in the government of Quebec. The Quebec Act granted religious freedom to Catholics within the former French colony, alarming the Protestant colonists, especially in New England, who regarded Catholicism as the mainstay of political despotism. The act also extended the southern border of Quebec to the Ohio River in an effort to protect northern Indians from white encroachment. Taken together, the Coercive Acts and the Quebec Act seemed to proof positive of a deliberate plot to oppress Americans.

The Coercive Acts were intended to punish and isolate Massachusetts, especially Boston, as the center of colonial resistance. The Boston committee of correspondence had done its work well. Most country towns (which were affected both directly and indirectly by the Coercive Acts) in the province expressed support for the people of Boston. When the Boston committee drafted a Solemn League and Covenant which called for the non-consumption of British goods effective August 1, 1774 (an easy pledge to keep given that the colony's major port was closed), many communities held special town meetings to endorse the document. Whigs created committees to enforce the embargo, and militia units began to drill in preparation for war. In protest against the Coercive Acts, the courts were closed by angry crowds who threatened judges seeking to enforce the unpopular laws. By the latter half of 1774, British authority had broken down completely in Massachusetts. The newly appointed military governor of the colony, General Thomas Gage (who was also commander-in-chief of British forces in North America), found that his power extended only as far as his troops could march. The troops themselves were as much a source of resentment as of power. On September 1, 1774, Gage sent a detachment from Boston to nearby Charlestown and Cambridge to seize patriot munitions. An alarm was sounded when it was reported that the British had slaughtered civilians along their line of march. Although the rumor proved untrue, thousands of militiamen descended upon Boston believing that the apparently inevitable armed conflict had begun.

What of the other colonies? Would they stand by Massachusetts or view its problems as a local difficulty which was not their concern? In the face of threatened starvation due to the Port Act, committees of correspondence throughout New England, and beyond, sent food and money to Boston throughout the summer and autumn of 1774. On May 27, 1774 a meeting of the Virginia burgesses in a Williamsburg tavern (the House of Burgesses had been prorogued by the governor, Lord Dunmore) declared that "an attack, made on one of our sister colonies, to compel submission to arbitrary taxes, is an attack on all of British America, and threatens the ruin of all," and proposed that an intercolonial congress be called to seek redress of American grievances.[19] During the summer of 1774, open meetings were held in the towns, cities, and counties throughout the colonies to discuss the Coercive Acts. Most of the congressional delegates were selected by extra-legal provincial conventions, which were held in seven colonies where the royal governors had forbidden the regular assemblies to conduct formal elections. In some cases the provincial conventions were simply the colonial assemblies meeting without sanction. In others, the conventions had a much broader membership than the old assemblies. Thus the very act of designating delegates to attend the congress involved Americans in open defiance of British authority. As British rule collapsed, these provincial conventions began to assume the role and functions of government.

The First Continental Congress

Fifty-five delegates, representing twelve colonies (Georgia was not represented), journeyed to Philadelphia for the grandly-named First Continental Congress, which convened on September 5, 1774. Because of the means of their selection, the delegates felt they enjoyed broad support. The congressmen represented the colonies' leading political figures. Most were lawyers, merchants or planters who had played prominent local roles in opposition to Britain over the previous decade. Among those in attendance were the cousins Samuel and John Adams of Massachusetts, and lawyer John Jay of New York. Pennsylvania sent the conservative lawyers Joseph Galloway and John Dickinson as its representatives. Nearly a decade after the Virginia Resolves, Patrick Henry was still ardent in his opposition to Britain when he represented Virginia at the conclave. He was joined by fellow radical Richard Henry Lee and prominent planter and colonial soldier George Washington. Though selected by a more open and democratic (if *ad hoc*) process than most colonial representatives had been, the congress was still comprised of substantial men of the type in whom Americans had usually entrusted public responsibility.

The congressmen faced three tasks when they convened in Philadelphia. First, they had to define American grievances. Second, they sought to define their constitutional relationship with Britain. Finally, they sought to develop a plan to achieve redress of their grievances. The delegates readily agreed on a list of the laws they wanted repealed (notably the Coercive Acts). They held widely differing views on the relationship between the colonies and Britain. The most radical congressmen, like Lee of Virginia, Roger Sherman of Connecticut, and of course the Massachusetts delegates, believed that the colonists owed allegiance only to George III, and that Parliament was nothing more than the legislature of one part of the empire. As such, it could not exercise legitimate authority over the American provinces which had historically been governed by their own assemblies. The conservative position was represented by men like Joseph Galloway of Pennsylvania and his ally James Duane of New York, who insisted that the congress should acknowledge Parliament's supremacy over the empire and its right to regulate American trade. Galloway argued that Britain had spent millions to support and protect the American colonies.

A compromise position, largely the work of John Adams, was eventually agreed. The crucial clause in Congress's Declaration of Rights and Grievances, which appeared on October 14, 1774, read:

> The foundation of English liberty, and of all free government, is a right in the people to participate in their legislative council: and as the English colonists are not represented, and from their local and other circumstances, cannot properly be represented in the British parliament, they are entitled to a free and exclusive power of legis-

lation in their several provincial legislatures, where their right of representation can alone be preserved, in all cases of taxation and internal polity, subject only to the negative of their sovereign, in such manner as has been heretofore used and accustomed. But from the necessity of the case, and a regard to the mutual interest of both countries, we cheerfully consent to the operation of such acts of the British parliament, as are *bona fide* restrained to the regulation of our external commerce, for the purpose of securing the commercial advantages of the whole empire to the mother country, and the commercial benefits of its respective members excluding every idea of taxation, internal or external, for raising a revenue on the subjects in America without their consent.[20]

In other words, Parliament had no authority over the colonies except in the case of trade legislation. That legislation, subject to colonial consent, could only be used to regulate commerce and not to raise revenue. Americans would govern themselves with the approval of the king (as exercised through the royal governors). That such a position was a compromise position in 1774 is vivid testimony to the rapid development of colonial opposition to Parliament in the nine years since the Stamp Act Congress had met.

The congressmen did agree on their method of resistance. They agreed that a comprehensive trade embargo should be implemented until Parliament repealed the Coercive Acts. To that end, the Congress adopted an agreement called the Continental Association, which called for nonimportation of all goods from Great Britain and Ireland beginning on December 1, 1774. A total ban on exports would begin on September 10, 1775. The reason for the delay on the export ban was to allow the staple-producing colonies of the South to export their crops one more time before the ban took effect. Unlike previous boycotts, the Continental Association was to be one inter-colonial effort rather than a congeries of local initiatives. Support for the effort was nearly unanimous in New England: in Massachusetts alone, 160 town meetings endorsed the plan. County conventions in 62 out of 77 counties in Maryland and Virginia likewise gave their approbation. While support was more mixed in the middle colonies, New York and Philadelphia endorsed the plan. Congress also called for the creation of local committees of inspection to enforce the boycott, and such committees were established in cities and towns throughout the colonies. Their members were usually elected locally, and they used a range of methods from public humiliation to threats and intimidation to enforce the boycott. Unlike service in the Continental Congress, membership of the committees of inspection, which may have had as many as 7,000 members across the colonies, represented a broader spectrum of colonial society. As the months passed, the committees in many localities began to act in place of defunct local governments. In so doing, many more common American men – farmers, artisans, and shopkeepers – gained valuable experience in self-government.

Conclusion

In the decade between the adoption of the Sugar Act and the Coercive Acts, relations between the Parliament and the North American colonies had undergone a profound change. In 1763, the overwhelming majority of white male colonists would have considered themselves loyal British subjects while asserting a somewhat vague right to self-government. By 1774, many questioned their relationship with Britain and had an increasingly clear notion that self-government meant that Parliament had little authority to interfere in the daily lives of Americans. This remarkable transformation was the result not of any American initiative but of that of successive British governments. Faced with mounting debts and a desire to compel Americans to pay for their own defense, successive Prime Ministers and Chancellors of the Exchequer from George Grenville to Lord North attempted to devise acceptable means to tax the Americans. The government also sought, in the wake of the Seven Years' War, to better organize and rule the British Empire. When Americans resisted these plans, the issue quickly shifted from one of financial solvency to that of Parliament's authority. Each time Parliament acquiesced to American pressure, it undermined its claim to exercise control over the colonies. As a result, with each successive crisis in British–American relations, the colonial resistance grew in strength and authority, until by late 1774 British authority was on the brink of collapse in the colonies and Americans were effectively governing themselves.

Just as the conflict transformed the imperial–colonial relationship, it also had profound implications for American society. In mobilizing opposition to Britain, American Whigs, through the Sons of Liberty and committees of correspondence and inspection, employed a language of liberty which stressed rights – the right to self-government, the right of representation, the right to trial by jury – and decried the tyranny and slavery which resulted when these rights were violated. In so doing, they gave voice to a traditional British political language in ways which could potentially transform their unequal society. When colonists decried the threat of slavery in the face of parliamentary taxes, their own slaves, who understood bondage and unfreedom in ways most colonist could not fathom, could not but hear them. When the Sons of Liberty appealed to frugality and economy and called for domestic manufactures in support of colonial boycotts, it was inevitable that American women, Daughters of Liberty, would be called upon to contribute to those efforts. In so doing, they were bound to experience increased political awareness and empowerment as a result of their contributions. Similarly, when the working men of America, sailors, artisans, traders, and small farmers, were called on to support boycotts, demonstrate, riot, participate in extra-legal conventions and serve on committees, and prepare for war in militia units, their conceptions of life and politics in an unequal society were bound to change. American society was pregnant with the possibility of change by late 1774.

This crucial turn of events was the result of British actions and American reactions. Beginning in 1775, Americans would begin to take the initiative in their relationship with Britain. In so doing, they would initiate one of the most profound and significant periods of change in American history.

3

REVOLUTION, 1775–1776

Introduction

During the decade from Parliament's adoption of the Sugar Act to its adoption of the Coercive Acts, the relationship between the colonies and the imperial center underwent a dramatic transformation. In the main, the initiative for change originated in London rather than the colonies. Beginning with George Grenville, successive ministers sought to transform the relationship between Britain and the colonies in order to extract revenue from America. When the colonists resisted these initiatives through crowd action, political protest, and economic coercion, the main question at issue ceased to be revenue and became one of sovereignty. During this crucial period, it was not the governed but the governors, Whitehall officials and Parliament, with the agreement of George III, who were the innovators in the imperial–colonial relationship. It was they who sought to revolutionize that relationship in a manner which would result in increased metropolitan authority over and revenue from the colonies. Colonial resistance, fitful and unfocused at the outset, was concerned with preserving traditional liberties and restoring the previous relationship between the imperial center and the colonial periphery.

Given their backward-looking objectives, it is not surprising that the initial colonial resistance was conservative in nature. In general, the colonists *reacted* to the actions of their governors. From this cautious beginning, revolutionary change would develop. As discussed in the previous chapter, the resistance to Britain required the political contributions and awareness, even if limited, of groups which were traditionally marginalized in the colonial power structure, especially poor whites and women. Eventually the unforeseen and, to many politically powerful colonial leaders, unwelcome changes in American society which characterized the American Revolution would spring from the original limited and conservative resistance to British initiatives.

A crucial transition in the colonial resistance took place in the years 1775 and 1776. During these years, the initiative in the struggle between the colonies and the metropolis shifted across the Atlantic. By 1776 it was the colonists who were setting the agenda, and officials in London were compelled to react to American actions. This two-year period is perhaps the most significant in American history. It witnessed the outbreak of war between the colonies and Britain, the declaration of colonial independence which created the United States, the establishment of republican government in America, a failed attempt to export the Revolution by force of arms, and the near collapse of the rebel war effort. 1775 and 1776 witnessed, in short, the transformation from American resistance to revolution.

In the face of the emergence of extra-legal governing institutions in the colonies which were created to enforce the Continental Association, the government in London was determined to assert its authority over the America colonies. The abstract, at times confusing, constitutional issues of the previous decade were much clearer by late 1774. As George III commented to Lord North on November 18: "the line of conduct now seems chalked out ... the New England governments are in a state of rebellion, blows must decide whether they are to be subject to this country or independent."[1] While few Americans then contemplated independence and colonial dissatisfaction had spread beyond New England, the king perceptively recognized that the fundamental issue had become one of sovereignty. As 1775 began, neither the king nor his ministers nor Parliament were willing to compromise with the colonists. For their part, the colonists were prepared to protect their broadly defined rights. In late 1774 and early 1775, the Whigs not only pursued economic and political resistance, they also stockpiled arms and munitions and drilled their militias in anticipation that armed resistance might be necessary.

Thomas Gage, the king's new governor of Massachusetts and the commander-in-chief of British forces in North America, sat impotently in Boston while the colony's assembly met illegally and governed the colony as a Provincial Congress. Rebellious colonists, subjects of the crown who owed him their allegiance as the king's representative in colony, defied the governor, using threats and violence to prevent the operation of laws duly adopted by Parliament, and to close the courts. Ominously, the Americans were preparing for war not against the French but the soldiers of Gage's own command. On December 14, 1774, several hundred New Hampshire militiamen stormed Fort William and Mary in Portsmouth, overpowered its garrison, struck the royal colors and seized the arms and munitions stored in the fort.

In response to these challenges to British authority, General Gage made preparations of his own. In late 1774 and early 1775 he sent spies throughout eastern Massachusetts to assess the strength of colonial resistance and determine where the Whigs had stockpiled their arms and munitions. Several times he ordered detachments of his soldiers to march into the countryside to seize these supplies. These expeditions met with mixed results. On September 1, 1774 his soldiers seized 250 barrels of gunpowder that the colonists had stored near Boston. On February 26, 1775 Gage sent troops under Lieutenant Colonel Alexander Leslie to Salem to seize munitions and stores. Local people denied Leslie and his troops entry to the town by refusing to lower its drawbridge. As hundreds of militiamen from surrounding communities descended on Salem, Leslie was forced to withdraw after a making a perfunctory gesture of searching for the munitions. Americans not only defied Parliament's laws, they openly resisted British soldiers performing their duty.[2]

While General Gage struggled with events in Massachusetts, Lord North pursued a program in Parliament intended to defuse the crisis. On February 9, 1775 Parliament adopted a resolution which declared Massachusetts to be in a state of rebellion. As a consequence, the legislation prohibiting the trade of Boston was extended to all of Massachusetts. (In March the prohibition would be extended to all of New England, and in April to Pennsylvania, New Jersey, Maryland, Virginia, and South Carolina.) On February 27, Parliament endorsed a conciliation plan proposed by the Prime Minister. According to Lord North's proposal, if the colonies undertook to tax themselves and to make provision for the support of the army and navy, Parliament would only levy external taxes. These measures demonstrate an effort on the part of the government to isolate and punish New England, especially Massachusetts, while offering to return to the *status quo ante* with regard to the other colonies. This program revealed the government's complete misunderstanding of the American situation. By 1775, most Americans had rejected Parliament's right to levy either internal or external taxes. Moreover, the committees of correspondence had successfully convinced the colonists that the cause of Massachusetts or New England was also their cause. Perhaps the most astute British analysis of the situation came from the king. Several months before Parliament endorsed North's plan of reconciliation, George III wrote of the Americans: "We must either master them or totally leave them to themselves and treat them as aliens."[3]

War

On April 14, 1775, General Gage received a letter from Lord Dartmouth, the Secretary of State for the Colonies, instructing him to arrest the leaders of the Massachusetts Provincial Congress and authorizing him to use force in order to disarm the population and end the incipient rebellion in Massachusetts. Gage planned to send a column of 600 troops to nearby Concord, where the Provincial Congress was meeting, to arrest its leaders.

Concord also served as a depot where the Whig militiamen had stored arms and munitions. Gage's troops would not only arrest the leaders of the putative rebellion, but would seize and destroy the arms necessary to carry out the rising. When Gage's soldiers departed from Boston on the evening of April 18, Massachusetts Whigs were well-apprised of their intentions. Hundreds of sailors thrown out of work by the Port Act observed the preparations for the expedition. Express riders, including Paul Revere and William Dawes, brought word of the expedition to Concord and its environs.

The British troops arrived in the town of Lexington early in the morning of April 19. As they passed through the village they encountered approximately seventy "minutemen", militiamen who had pledged to turn out at a moment's notice in the event of an emergency. The minutemen were a cross-section of New England society. Half of Lexington's adult males turned out that morning. They ranged in age from 16 to 65, and eight father-and-son combinations stood on the green in the misty dawn. An African American, Prince Eastabrook, stood shoulder to shoulder with his white neighbors. Captain John Parker, commanding the Lexington minutemen, ordered his men onto the town green in a show of resistance to the British, who would pass on the road to Concord. A forty-five-year-old veteran of the French and Indian War, Parker was aware that his men could not fight highly trained British troops. Sylvanus Wood, a twenty-three-year-old minuteman at Lexington, described the scene many years after the fateful morning:

> The British troops approached us rapidly ... with a general officer on horseback at their head. The officer came up to within two rods of the center of the company ... The officer then swung his sword and said "Lay down your arms you damned rebels, or you are all dead men. Fire!" Some guns were fired by the British at us. ... Just at this time Capt Parker ordered every man to take care of himself. The company immediately dispersed, and while the company was dispersing and leaping over the wall, the ... British fired and killed some of our men.

This may not be true. It is unclear who fired the first shot at Lexington. It is clear, however, that once the shooting began the British soldiers, after months of frustration and boredom punctuated by abuse and defiance at the hands of Americans, proved difficult to control. The soldiers were "so wild," reported Lieutenant John Barker, "they could hear no orders and they ignored their commander, uselessly cutting the air with his sword as the signal to cease firing."[4]

Eight Americans lay dead, mostly shot in the back. Among the dead was Captain Parker. Having spent no more than half an hour in Lexington, the

British had begun the American Revolution. Fighting continued when the British arrived in nearby Concord. Here they managed to destroy 500 pounds of musketballs and 60 barrels of flour. They remained in Concord until noon, inflicting property damage. When they left, they were assaulted by thousands of massing militiamen who fought and harassed the British with deadly fire from concealed places along their route of march. The fighting was so fierce and the progress of the column so slow that Gage was compelled to send a relief column from Boston to rescue the expedition. Although a British veteran of the fighting described the fighting as a "little fracas," the events of April 19 resulted in 73 redcoats killed and 200 wounded or missing. The rebels, whom the same officer described as "the most absolute cowards on the face of the earth," sustained 49 dead, 39 wounded and 4 missing in the fighting. Most significantly, the events of April 19 transformed the political dispute between the colonists and the British into a military struggle. In the next eight years there would be many more casualties. Significant human suffering would be the price of American independence.[5]

Word of the fighting in Massachusetts spread rapidly throughout the colonies. As many as 17,000 militiamen from around New England poured into camps around Boston. Faced with an impromptu siege, General Gage was under pressure to take action. On May 25 he was joined in Boston by three ambitious major-generals, William Howe, Henry Clinton, and John Burgoyne, who were sent to Boston to advise him. They demanded action, and they had the support of London to do so. Gage declared martial law on June 12, and agreed to occupy the surrounding heights of Dorchester and Charlestown outside of Boston before the rebels did. On June 15, the Massachusetts Committee of Safety, which received intelligence of Gage's intentions, called for the occupation of Bunker Hill on the Charlestown peninsula. On the evening of June 16 about 1,600 Americans under Colonel William Prescott and General Israel Putnam began to fortify positions on Breed's (not Bunker) Hill. Rather than outflank the rebels, which he could easily have accomplished, General Howe led a bloody frontal assault on the rebel defenses on June 17. The rebels were forced to relinquish their positions when they ran out of gunpowder. The Americans suffered 100 dead, 271 wounded and 30 taken prisoner. Among the American dead was Dr. Joseph Warren, President of the Massachusetts Provincial Congress and a leading radical. Warren would become one of the earliest heroes of the rebel cause. The British endured their worst casualties of the war, 228 dead and 826 wounded, or 42 percent of the 2,500 troops engaged that afternoon.[6]

Bunker Hill was a Pyrrhic victory for the British. Thomas Gage gave his assessment of the American situation a week after the battle, based on his long experience in the colonies in both peace and war:

> These people shew a spirit and conduct against us they never shewed against the French, and everybody has judged of them from their formed appearance and behaviour when joined with the Kings forces in the last war, which has led many into great mistakes. They are now spirited up by a rage and enthusiasm as great as ever a people were possessed of, and you must proceed in earnest or give the business up. A small body acting in one spot will not avail. You must have large armys, making diversions on different sides, to divide their force. The loss we have sustained is more than we can bear.

Gage had accurately described the situation. Unfortunately for Gage his perspicacity was not enough to redeem his reputation or his career. In October he was replaced by William Howe.[7]

Congress takes over

When the Second Continental Congress began sitting on May 10, 1775, its members found that their brief did not require them to coordinate political and economic resistance to unpopular acts of Parliament, but rather to coordinate a war against one of the foremost military powers on earth. The congressmen convened in an atmosphere of militant resistance. In the months after Lexington and Concord, enthusiasm for war was widespread and the colonies were swept by what came to be known as the *rage militaire*. Despite the enthusiasm for military action, however, Congress was inclined to act cautiously. Although the confrontation between the British and the colonists had resulted in bloodshed, in the spring of 1775 most congressmen, and indeed most Americans, advocated reconciliation between the parties. As a result, Congress attempted to pursue an ambivalent policy of directing a war while attempting to secure a peaceful resolution to the conflict. Consequently, Congress advocated that the rebels only pursue a defensive struggle until a proper resolution to the conflict could be negotiated.

The difficulties and contradictions of the congressional policy are best represented by the actions it took with respect to Canada. Americans, especially those in the northern colonies, had traditionally viewed Quebec as a military threat. More than a century of antipathy between the French and British colonies had not been erased with the peace of 1763. The Catholicism of Quebec's inhabitants made them suspicious to Americans, especially in the wake of the Quebec Act. The province, moreover, posed a military threat to the rebellious colonies as the British could invade down the Champlain corridor and isolate New England. In order to prevent such an attempt, on May 9 a small number of rebellious militia in the New Hampshire Grants region of New York (present-day Vermont), known as the Green Mountain Boys, seized the lightly defended Fort Ticonderoga at the juncture of Lake Champlain and Lake George. Although the Green Mountain Boys acted on their own initiative, their actions were endorsed by the Massachusetts Committee of Safety, which had authorized Colonel Benedict Arnold to lead the assault. (The Green Mountain Boys preferred their own leader, Ethan Allen.) Confronted by what was clearly an aggressive and offensive action on the part of the colonists, Congress adopted a series of fictive resolutions which asserted that because they feared an imminent invasion from Quebec, the rebels had acted in a defensive manner.

In 1775, the Quebecois were fellow colonists of their rebellious southern neighbors. Although the province might be used as a base for a military assault, congressional leaders hoped that Quebec would join them in resistance. The First Continental Congress had invited the Quebecois to join their resistance and send representatives to Congress in October 1774. On May 29, 1775 its successor renewed that invitation. On June 1, Congress seemingly made its intentions towards Quebec clear. "As this Congress has nothing more in view than the defense of these colonies," the representatives resolved, "no expedition or incursion ought to be undertaken or made, by any colony, or body of colonists, against or into Canada." This pledge lasted less than a month. On June 27, concerned at the military threat posed by Quebec, Congress ordered General Philip Schuyler of New York to seize St. Johns and Montreal as long as his actions were not "disagreeable to the Canadians." In September, a second rebel expedition under Benedict Arnold entered the Maine wilderness intending to capture Quebec City. If Canada could not be convinced to join the rebels, it would be conquered to prevent its use against the wayward colonies. Military necessity compelled Congress to move away from its stated policy of defense and to take aggressive actions which would make reconciliation between Britain and the colonies impossible. Slowly, almost imperceptibly, the rebellious colonists were beginning to take the initiative.[8]

The ambivalence of the congressional policy with respect to Canada also characterized its other actions during the summer of 1775. The most urgent task facing the Second Continental Congress was to take charge of the rebel war effort. For the first few months of the struggle, the rebels had carried on their struggle in an *ad hoc* and uncoordinated manner. On June 14, Congress voted to create the Continental Army out of the motley throng of militiamen besieging Boston. In a critical decision, Congress appointed George Washington of Virginia to command the rebel forces. Washington, who had represented Virginia in the Congress, had more military experience than any other patriot leader. A very wealthy Virginia planter, he was also was a committed supporter of the rebel cause. Crucially, Washington was a Virginian: since most of the fighting to date had been done by New Englanders in New England, it was important that in establishing a national army to wage the struggle against Britain, all regions be represented. Otherwise, the pan-colonial movement that patriot leaders had carefully built over the previous decade might come to naught. John Adams of Massachusetts recognized the importance of appointing a non-New Englander to command the army, and threw his support behind Washington. The appointment of Washington as commander-in-chief constitutes one of the first sectional compromises in American history. Events would also prove that the appointment of Washington was among the most important decisions made by the Second Continental Congress.

George Washington could not wage a war, defensive or otherwise, against the might of Britain alone. Over the next two weeks, Congress made a series of significant military decisions. It appropriated funds to send rifle companies from Maryland, Virginia and Pennsylvania to Boston to join the New England forces. Simultaneously, Congress voted to create brigadiers and major-generals as Washington's subordinates. It also took responsibility for rebel activities in the Champlain region, and made the aforementioned decision to invade Canada. The exigencies of war were compelling Congress to adopt the attributes of a national government.

Congress may have begun to act as a national government, but during the summer of 1775 it was reluctant to formally accept such a role. Despite the fighting in New England, most Americans and most members of Congress still longed for a reconciliation between Britain and the colonies. On July 6, Congress issued a Declaration of Causes and Necessity of Taking Up Arms. The declaration asserted that the colonists had been forced to choose between "an unconditional submission to the tyranny of irritated ministers, or resistance by force." Although the colonists had been compelled to use force to defend their rights, Congress assured Americans and other British subjects "that we mean not to dissolve that union which has so long and so happily subsisted between us and which we sincerely wish to see restored." Two days later, on July 8, Congress adopted a petition to George III which was mainly the work of John Dickinson. Although Dickinson had been an early defender of colonial rights, he had come to represent the conservative position in the Congress which sought to defend American rights through political and economic protest rather than military force. Dickinson's appeal, known as the Olive Branch Petition, was a direct appeal to the king to intervene and address colonial grievances and restore peace in the empire. The petition was important not only to convince conservatives within Congress but also the American people, that Congress did not intend to pursue independence except as a last resort.[9]

When the Second Continental Congress ended its first session on August 2, its members had accomplished much. They had organized the rebel war effort while attempting to stay within their stated defensive aims, and they had appealed directly to the king to intercede on their behalf to end the crisis. That they prepared for war before adopting their appeal to the monarch indicates that most congressmen were not optimistic about the fate of their petition. Nonetheless, the advocates of conciliation could take some comfort from the actions of the Congress. If George III and his ministers would only listen to American appeals, then peace could be restored. Events over the next few months would prove to people on both sides of the Atlantic that reconciliation was impossible. By the summer of 1775, the Olive Branch Petition was as unlikely to meet with success as Lord North's reconciliation proposal of the previous February.

The sovereign of Great Britain was not inclined to hear appeals from an illegal body which was waging war against his troops and persecuting his loyal subjects in America. George III refused to receive or consider the Olive Branch Petition. Indeed, on August 23 the king declared the colonies to be in a state of open rebellion and he called upon all civil and military officials as well as his loyal subjects to assist to suppress the uprising. Some of the king's servants were happy to follow the orders of their monarch. On October 18, 1775, after declaring that the residents of Falmouth (present-day Portland), Maine were guilty of "the most unpardonable rebellion," the captain of H.M.S. *Canceau* ordered a day-long bombardment of the town which resulted in the burning and destruction of most of the community. In the wake of the fighting in New England and the proposed invasion of Canada, such a response is not especially surprising. Over the next six months, the British government and its forces would make a series of pronouncements and actions which would convince the majority of colonists to embrace independence.

At the opening of Parliament on October 26, 1775, George III made his most forceful statement yet with regard to the crisis in America. He noted that a conspiracy of unnamed malcontents in the colonies had misled the majority of colonists and assumed authority by raising troops, stealing public revenue and arrogating legislative, executive, and judicial powers. The king noted that the stakes were rising in the conflict: "The rebellious war now levied is become more general, and is manifestly carried on for the purpose of establishing an independent empire." If the rebels were as yet unwilling to declare independence, the king had no doubt that they had such an end in mind. He was unwilling to allow such a development:

> The object is too important, the spirit of the British nation too high, the resources with which God hath blessed her too numerous, to give up so many colonies which she has planted with great industry, nursed with great tenderness, encouraged with many

commercial advantages, and protected and defended at much expence of blood and treasure.

The government would use force to suppress the rebellion. To that end, the monarch announced that he was increasing the land and naval forces in America to bring the insurrection to an end and restore British authority. The dead of Lexington, Concord and Bunker Hill precluded compromise. The colonists must submit. The king promised that "if the unhappy and deluded Multitude, against whom this force will be directed shall become sensible of their Error, I shall be ready to receive the Misled with Tenderness and Mercy," and that he would authorize his commanders in America to issue pardons to contrite rebels. The king's speech was the clearest public signal to those among the rebellious colonists who were reluctant to pursue the war that they would receive little sympathy from the throne. No longer could conservatives argue that the king might intervene on their behalf with his ill-guided ministers.[10]

Although Americans would not learn of the content of the king's speech until January 1776, events in the meantime convinced them to expect a robust British response to their armed resistance. On November 7 the royal governor of Virginia, Lord Dunmore, in a desperate measure to undermine support for the rebellion in the colony, issued a proclamation promising freedom to any slaves who fled their rebel masters and supported the British war effort. At the time of his proclamation, Dunmore's authority in Virginia had all but disappeared; indeed, the governor issued his decree from the safety of a British warship off the Virginia coast because he had been forced to flee from Williamsburg. That a British official would offer freedom to slaves who took up arms against their masters was anathema to most white southerners. Dunmore's proclamation, while it served to encourage the aspirations for freedom among Virginia's bondsmen and women, solidified rebel support in the colony among white Virginians. On December 22, Parliament adopted the American Prohibitory Act which excluded all American commerce, subjecting all of the thirteen colonies to a naval blockade and the seizure of their shipping. On January 1, 1776 Royal Navy vessels burned Virginia's largest port, Norfolk. Each of these actions served to convince Americans that the struggle with Britain was not confined to New England. Rather, these actions encouraged the thirteen colonies to unite in their opposition to British rule.

Independence and revolution

In 1776, the men who led the colonial resistance to Britain made two daring decisions of enduring importance to American history. First, they declared that the colonies were an independent nation. Second, they committed the new nation to republicanism, which is to say a government whose sovereignty was derived from the consent of the governed as expressed through the vote. Popular input was to be limited to white men with property. Nonetheless, these decisions transformed a rather narrow dispute over the constitutional relationship between the British Parliament and the North American colonies into a revolutionary struggle.

From the time the Second Continental Congress began sitting in May of 1775, it confronted the ultimate question the controversy with Britain had spawned: how could American rights best be protected? Within the British empire or without? The war both complicated and simplified the situation. How could one remain a subject to a government with which one was actively engaged in combat? The moderate position was that it was acceptable to raise an army and engage in armed self-defense of colonial rights. For example, the Provincial Assembly of Connecticut declared that its troops besieging British soldiers in Boston were enlisted in "His Majesty's Service ... for the preservation of the Liberties of America." Similarly, when rebel forces seized the royal outpost of Fort Ticonderoga in May of 1775, Congress ordered that the colonists carefully catalogue the fort's ordinance so it could be returned to the crown when peace was restored. This step was taken to cast what was patently an offensive action as a defensive measure. In a similar vein, Congress authorized the invasion of Canada on the condition that Canadians approved the action. While such decisions appear inconsistent and contradictory, they reveal the strength of feeling in favor of reconciliation even after the war began. As the war spread and intensified in the latter part of 1775 and it became clear that George III would not intervene to affect a reconciliation, sentiment in favor of independence began to grow in America.

Independence represented a massive leap into the unknown for the colonists. To declare the colonies independent, opponents of such a step argued, would not only invite an unrestrained military assault by the British, but *if* the colonies were to win their independence on the battlefield, they would probably be conquered by another European power with interests in the New World such as Spain or France. Independence would mean severing ties which had grown over six generations. The colonies were linked to Britain not only by politics and economics but by bonds of language, religion, and culture. Despite the war, there were still many Americans, probably a majority of the population at the beginning of 1776, who hoped for a reconciliation between Britain and the colonies. They would need to be convinced that American interests would best be served by severing their ties with Great Britain.

On January 10, 1776 Robert Bell, a Philadelphia printer, published a pamphlet with a simple title, *Common Sense*. Although published anonymously, the author of *Common Sense* was an obscure English immigrant named Thomas Paine. An unsuccessful tax-collector and staymaker, Paine emigrated to Philadelphia in late 1774 at the age of thirty-seven. Although a late arrival on the colonial scene, Paine became involved in the radical politics of Philadelphia's artisans and was an articulate supporter of the resistance to British rule. The radical Philadelphia physician Benjamin Rush recognized Paine's abilities as a writer, and encouraged him to prepare a pamphlet which considered the question of independence. Paine set to work during the autumn of 1775; the result was *Common Sense*, which had the widest circulation and greatest influence of all the hundreds of pamphlets published during the era of the American Revolution.[11]

Unlike most eighteenth-century pamphlets, which were written in a learned style replete with classical allusions, legal citations and high-flown elitist language, Paine wrote *Common Sense* in a forceful, direct vernacular style which was readily accessible to the common people of America's shops, taverns, and farms. These were the people among whom Paine lived, and whose support he recognized was essential if the colonies were to achieve their independence. Paine eschewed classical imagery and ornate language for biblical allusions and simple language to make his point: the colonies must declare themselves independent. Paine began *Common Sense* by stressing the Lockean theme that government was a contractual (and regrettable) relationship made necessary by human selfishness. "For were the impulses of conscience clear," Paine wrote, "uniform and irresistibly obeyed, man would need no other lawgiver; but that not being the case, he finds it necessary to surrender up a part of his property to furnish means of protection of the rest." Government being a necessary evil, Paine was eager to demonstrate to the American colonists that the vaunted British constitution which they had revered as the bulwark of their liberties was deeply flawed. The balance of interests which Americans believed they saw in the British constitution was a sham. The House of Commons was the only republican element in the British system, and it had been corrupted and compromised by the monarchical and aristocratic elements embodied in the crown and the House of Lords.

Since the colonists had made a long-standing case against Parliament's authority over them, Paine concentrated his attack on the British monarchy. Paine argued that the hereditary kingship and aristocratic titles were inherently unfair. According to Paine, "Government by kings was first introduced into the world by the heathens, from whom the children of Israel copied the custom. It is the most prosperous invention the Devil ever set on foot for the promotion of idolatry." Hereditary succession compounded the inequity of monarchical government, for not only did kings set themselves up as superior to their subjects but they insured that their descendants would enjoy the benefit of the same unfair relationship. "For all men being originally equals, no one by birth could have a right to set up his own family in perpetual preference to all others forever," declared Paine, "and though himself might deserve some decent honors of his contemporaries, yet his descendants might be far too unworthy to inherit them." For his part, Paine was not convinced that many of the kings who initiated dynasties were worthy of their titles. In one of his most famous rhetorical thrusts, Paine assailed the Norman origins of the British monarchy, "A French bastard, landing with an armed banditti and establishing himself king of England against the consent of the natives, is in plain terms a very paltry rascally original. It certainly hath no divinity in it." Rather than fear independence, Paine demonstrated, Americans should welcome the opportunity to sever their ties with an oppressive, unequal system of government which had no basis in scripture or natural law.

Having demolished the basis for colonial loyalty to the British monarchy, Paine turned his attention to the situation in America. He based his comments on "simple facts, plain arguments and common sense." Paine argued that independence would free American from involvement in European wars. He asserted that free trade would make an independent America the friend of all nations and that American agriculture "will always have a market while eating is the custom in Europe." Freedom in economics would complement the political freedom Paine envisioned in an independent America. In *Common Sense*, he sketched a plan for a republic based on a broad franchise, annual assemblies, and a rotating presidency. Rather than fear independence, common sense dictated that Americans should welcome it, for national independence would lead to increased prosperity and liberty. More immediately, independence would allow the rebels to seek foreign assistance with which to carry on their struggle. In any event, Paine believed that events made independence a foregone conclusion. The war had made reconciliation impossible: "The blood of the slain, the weeping voice of nature cries," he wrote, " 'Tis time to part." *Common Sense* was an instant success. In 1776 it sold in excess of 100,000 copies. It was reprinted and excerpted in newspapers, and republished throughout the colonies and in Britain and France. Paine himself brought out revised editions which addressed the inevitable charges of his opponents. Thanks to Paine's direct writing style, the pamphlet could be read aloud to those who could not read. It inspired both imitators and critics. The pamphlet certainly convinced many wavering colonists that independence was a reasonable course to pursue. If nothing else, *Common Sense* placed the question of independence at the center of American life.[12]

Although the Continental Congress, as the only institution which could purport to speak for the colonies as a whole, would have to be the body to formally declare independence, such a momentous step required wide popular support. Because the various delegations within the Continental Congress were bound by instructions from their provincial assemblies, they could not declare their colonies independent without prior authorization. By necessity, therefore, the political momentum for independence originated at the local level in the various colonies, where the issues raised by the war and by *Common Sense* were debated and discussed throughout the early months of 1776. Between April and July 1776 various bodies and institutions – from voluntary associations to provincial congresses – debated the merits and risks of independence. Over ninety of these organizations issued their own declarations of independence by changing statutes, issuing new instructions to their congressional delegations, or adopting resolutions asserting their independence. These "other declarations of independence" preceded and laid the foundation for the formal Declaration of Independence adopted by Congress in July.[13]

North Carolina was the first colony to act. On April 12, 1776, the North Carolina Provincial Assembly authorized the colony's delegation at the Congress in Philadelphia to concur if the other state delegations voted in favor of declaring independence. Massachusetts provided the most thorough response on the issue of independence. On March 10 the assembly resolved:

> that the inhabitants of each Town in this Colony ought, in full meeting warned for that purpose, to advise the person or persons who shall be chosen to represent them in the next General Court, whether that, if the honourable Congress should, for the safety of the said Colony, declare them independent of the Kingdom of Great Britain, they the said inhabitants, will solemnly engage, with their lives and fortunes, to support them in the measure.

The assembly was asking voters to make a personal pledge when they endorsed independence. Between May and July, special town meetings were convened throughout the colony to debate the issue. Although some communities were deeply divided on the question and a few opposed it, the majority of towns endorsed independence. In so doing, the voters of Massachusetts were putting the principles of republican government vaguely outlined by Thomas Paine into practice.[14]

Massachusetts was not alone. Independence would not be foisted on the American people by a small cabal of radical congressmen. Rather, during the spring and early summer of 1776, individuals and groups throughout the colonies would pressure Congress to declare the colonies independent. Between April 22 and 24, conventions in the Virginia counties of Cumberland, Charlotte and James City endorsed independence. On May 15, 112 members of the Virginia Provincial Convention unanimously resolved:

> that the delegates appointed to represent this colony in General Congress be instructed to propose to that respectable body to declare the United Colonies free and independent states, absolved from all allegiance to, or dependence upon the crown or parliament of Great Britain; and that they give the assent of this colony to

such declaration, and to whatever measures may be thought proper and necessary by the Congress for forming foreign alliances and a confederation of the colonies, at such time, and in such a manner, as to them shall seem best.[15]

On June 7, Richard Henry Lee introduced the Virginia resolution to Congress, and on June 8 the Congress debated the proposal. The moderates, who opposed acting "till the voice of the people drove us into it," were led by John Dickinson and James Wilson of Pennsylvania, Edward Rutledge of South Carolina and Robert R. Livingston of New York. They argued that the time was not yet right for a declaration of independence because "the people of the middle colonies (Maryland, Delaware, Pennsylvania, the Jersies & N. York) were not yet ripe for bidding adieu to British connection but that they were fast ripening & in short time would join the general voice of America." By June 1776 the moderates had given up hope of achieving reconciliation. They questioned the timing of independence, not the sagacity of it. Indeed, they endorsed the republican principle that the people of their colonies must support independence before they could act. Their hesitancy is testimony that the initiative for independence came from the American people themselves, not Congress. The radicals, led by the delegations from Virginia and Massachusetts, favored an immediate declaration of independence but recognized that unanimity was necessary for such a momentous decision. Consequently, Congress decided to delay a decision on independence by three weeks. In the meantime, a committee would work on a draft declaration in the event Congress agreed on independence in July.[16]

The proponents of independence put the delay to good use. On June 14 the Connecticut assembly instructed its delegates to support independence. The next day the assemblies of New Hampshire and Delaware followed suit. Also in mid-June, radicals in New Jersey ousted the royal governor William Franklin (the son of Benjamin Franklin). The new government of New Jersey sent a new delegation to Congress on June 22 with instructions to support independence. The Maryland assembly refused to endorse independence as late as May; however, after a series of conventions in Frederick, Ann Arundel, Charles, and Talbot counties called for independence, the assembly instructed its delegates to support independence on June 28. As in New England and Virginia, popular pressure was beginning to tell in the Middle Colonies.

The two most important colonies which had yet to give their approval to independence were New York and Pennsylvania. In Pennsylvania, the colonial assembly elected before the outbreak of the war continued to sit. This body, which was dominated by the old Quaker proprietary elite, refused to change its instructions, adopted on November 9, 1775, which opposed a declaration of independence despite a growing popular clamor in favor of such a measure. On June 14 the assembly was overthrown by the radical Committee of Safety. Elections were called for a constitutional convention to reform the government of Pennsylvania. These elections were to be based on a broad franchise, and would result in one of the most radical governments of the revolutionary era. In the meantime the colony was ruled by the Committee of Safety, which authorized Pennsylvania's delegates to vote for independence. The situation was still more complicated in New York, which faced an imminent British invasion. Despite entreaties from General Committee of Mechanics in New York City and communities around Albany in favor of independence, the New York Provincial Congress refused to instruct its delegates in Philadelphia to vote for independence. Rather, it argued that it would wait until Congress made a decision on the issue and then issue a response.

When Congress considered the question of independence on July 1, the momentum seemed to favor the radicals. Although, according to John Adams, "The Subject had been in Contemplation for the more than a Year and frequent discussions had been had concerning it. At one time and another, all the Arguments for it and against it had been exhausted and were become familiar," John Dickinson rose and gave a lengthy speech against independence which "combined together all that had before been written in Pamphlets and News papers and all that had from time to time been said in Congress by himself and others." Adams responded to Dickinson in a lengthy delivery which repeated the arguments in favor of independence.[17] When the vote was taken on the motion for independence, the radicals were disappointed. Nine colonies voted in favor of the measure but four did not support it. South Carolina and Pennsylvania voted against the measure. The Delaware delegation – two men who could not agree – was split, and the delegates from New York were prohibited by their instructions from participating. Realizing that nine out of thirteen was not sufficient for such an important decision, the congressmen decided to revisit the question the next day. After a night of frantic lobbying, the radicals got the vote they wanted on July 2. Caesar Rodney, a third delegate from Delaware rode all night to change that delegation's vote in favor of independence. South Carolina's delegates changed their minds and their votes. Pennsylvanians John Dickinson and Robert Morris who opposed independence did not attend the next session, and James Wilson of the same delegation changed his vote. On July 2, twelve of thirteen colonies voted in favor of independence while New York abstained. (The New York Provincial Congress subsequently endorsed Congress's decision on July 9.) Having decided to declare the colonies independent, Congress turned its attention to the declaration itself.

When Congress voted to postpone consideration of the question of independence on June 10, it created a committee to draft a declaration of independence. The members of the committee, Thomas Jefferson of Virginia,

John Adams of Massachusetts, Benjamin Franklin representing Pennsylvania, Roger Sherman of Connecticut, and Robert Livingston of New York, represented a broad geographical and political spectrum with respect to the question of independence. The committee in turn delegated the task of preparing the draft declaration to Thomas Jefferson. A wealthy Virginia planter, Jefferson was a thirty-three-year-old member of Congress who had previous experience as a penman of the colonial cause. In 1774 he had written *A Summary View of the Rights of British America*, which was an articulate and influential statement of the American case. As a member of Congress, Jefferson had drafted the official response to Lord North's reconciliation plan in 1775, and he had contributed to its later Declaration of the Causes and Necessity of Taking Up Arms. Jefferson worked on the draft declaration of independence for two weeks while consulting informally with Adams and Franklin on its content. His draft was then discussed by the full committee, which suggested some changes. The result was a work that, although the product of group effort, was largely the work of Jefferson. The committee submitted the draft declaration to Congress on June 28.

After it voted on independence Congress carefully considered the draft declaration on the afternoon of the second, third and part of the fourth of July. While Jefferson fumed, the members of Congress made a series of stylistic and substantive changes to the text of the declaration. As a result, Congress eliminated a quarter of Jefferson's original draft. The most important change made by the Congress was the elimination of a clause in which Jefferson indicted George III for the trans-Atlantic slave trade. Given the willing participation of so many Americans, especially many members of Congress – including Jefferson – in the system of chattel slavery, such an accusation was not only historically untenable but hypocritical in the extreme. As a result of Congressional editing, the draft declaration, while no longer solely Jefferson's handiwork, was greatly improved. The revised Declaration of Independence was formally adopted by Congress on July 4, 1776. It was not formally signed until August 2, after New York had approved the document.

The Declaration of Independence as adopted by Congress began with an eloquent assertion of the right of revolution:

> We hold these truths to be self-evident, that all men are created equal, that they are endowed by their Creator with certain unalienable Rights, that among these are Life, Liberty, and the pursuit of Happiness. That to secure these rights, Governments are instituted among Men, deriving their power from the consent of the governed, That whenever any Form of Government becomes destructive to these ends, it is the Right of the People to alter or abolish it, and to institute new Government, laying its foundation on such

principles and organizing its powers in such form, as to them shall seem most likely to effect Safety and Happiness.

Congress asserted a notion of universal rights in this statement. In order to secure their rights, people voluntarily created governments. If their governments violated their rights, then the people had a right to overthrow their governments and create new ones better suited to their needs.

Having asserted that the American people had a right to change their government if it violated their rights, Congress proceeded in the body of the Declaration of Independence to demonstrate that "The history of the present King of Great Britain is a history of repeated injuries and usurpations, all having in direct object the establishment of an absolute Tyranny over these States." The Declaration presented a list of eighteen charges ranging from interfering in colonial government and justice to waging war against the colonies as proof that the revolution against royal authority was justified. Although to the modern reader many of the charges against George III seem specious, the focus on the monarch was crucial to legitimate the rebel cause. By 1776, few Americans accepted Parliament's right to govern the colonies. The tie which bound the colonies to Britain was the monarchy. In order to sever that tie, Congress had to demonstrate the king's culpability in subverting American rights. Even though George III sought to impose tyranny on the colonies, Congress continued in the declaration, the colonists sought redress by peaceful means through repeated petitions to the king, Parliament, and the British people, all of which were rejected. As a result, the Americans were but reluctant revolutionaries driven to take up arms as a last resort and to declare "that these United Colonies are, and of right ought to be Free and Independent States." In a few eloquent sentences, Congress articulated the principles of revolution and republican self-government for which Americans had been searching for more than a decade. These words transformed what had been a narrow dispute over taxation and authority into a revolutionary struggle over principles of self-determination, rights, and equality. In adopting the Declaration of Independence, Congress adopted a manifesto which presaged revolutionary changes in American life which would extend far beyond the question of relationship between the self-proclaimed states and Britain.

Conclusion

During the congressional debate over independence, John Adams wrote, "We are in the very midst of a Revolution, the most compleat, unexpected , and remarkable of any in the History of Nations."[18] Adams, who was as intimately involved in the campaign for independence as anyone, knew whereof he spoke. The political controversy between Britain and the American colonies bred a new political philosophy, at the center of which was a belief in the rights of man. Human liberty, in this conception, was derived from natural rights, not the British Constitution. The Declaration of Independence was based upon the Lockean notion of a contractual society between the governed and their governors. When the British government, specifically the king, broke its contract and violated the rights of the colonists, the Americans were justified in resorting to armed resistance once all means to achieve a peaceful redress had been tried. At the heart of the new philosophy was republicanism. Defined at its most basic level, republicanism was government by the consent of the governed. To be sure, many of these ideas had been circulating in the trans-Atlantic world throughout the eighteenth century; indeed, many of them had been discussed and debated by Americans and Britons in the period from 1763 to 1776. The Declaration of Independence initiated the first systematic attempt to implement republican principles. Over the next fifteen years Americans would experiment, debate, and grapple with the implications of republicanism. They would disagree over who should be included in the republican polity, what form a republican government should take, and just what rights must a republican government guarantee. Each of these questions was crucial to the outcome of the political revolution set in motion by the Declaration of Independence.

The "compleat" revolution initiated in 1776 was not confined to politics. The popular politicization and mobilization which began with the Stamp Act resistance culminated in a popular clamor for independence. Indeed, the momentum in favor for independence originated among the common men of America who attended town meetings and county conventions which pressured the provincial governments to endorse a separation between the colonies and Britain. These were the men who would have to win independence on the battlefield. In return, they would demand a greater voice in American society. Ultimately the revolutionary credo of equality and natural rights would be embraced and appropriated by other groups, notably women and African slaves, who also would demand a new role in a republican America. Their campaigns would meet with mixed results. The political revolution of 1776 would quickly evolve into a social revolution far beyond what the congressmen in Philadelphia anticipated or hoped for when they adopted the Declaration of Independence.

Declaring independence was one thing, winning it on the field of battle quite another. As Americans celebrated the Declaration of Independence during the summer of 1776, they prepared to counter the largest European invasion force ever sent to North America.

4

WINNING INDEPENDENCE

The wars of the American Revolution

Introduction

The American War of Independence lasted eight and a half years, making it the longest armed conflict in the history of the United States with the exception of the Vietnam War. The war lasted twice as long as the Civil War or American participation in the Second World War, both of which have made a deeper imprint on the popular historical consciousness than the struggle for independence. Nonetheless, the War of Independence had a crucial impact on the outcome of the Revolution and the development of the United States. Indeed, eastern North America was characterized by a congeries of violent conflict between 1775 and 1794 which should properly be termed "the wars of the American Revolution".[1] These concurrent struggles reveal the complexity of the American Revolution. After a summary of the military conflict, this chapter will assess these "wars" by considering the fight against Britain as: a civil war, a war of conquest, and a struggle for liberty.

Overview of the conflict

When George Washington arrived in Cambridge, Massachusetts in July of 1775 to take command of the grandiloquently named Continental Army, he was confronted by seventeen thousand poorly trained, poorly equipped, and poorly disciplined soldiers. His soldiers, primarily New England militiamen, were not yet prepared by training or inclination for a prolonged conflict with British regular soldiers. A British surgeon who visited the rebel camps around Boston in late May wrote of his adversaries, "This army ... is truly nothing but a drunken, canting, lying, praying hypocritical rabble, without order, subjection, discipline or cleanliness, and must fall to pieces of itself in the course of three months."[2] Although American writers extolled the virtues of their militiamen as the avatars of liberty, in contrast to the tyrannical automatons to be found in the ranks of European standing armies, Washington recognized at the outset that a more disciplined, stable force – an American standing army – would have to be created if the rebels were to succeed. It is one of the paradoxes of the American Revolution that the rebel struggle for liberty could only be achieved through the creation of an institution, the Continental Army, by curbing the democratic excesses of its members. As Washington complained in August 1775:

> the officers of the Massachusetts *part* of the Army are *nearly* of the same kidney with the Privates ... there is no such thing as getting of officers of this stamp to exert themselves in carrying orders into execution – to curry favor with the men (by whom they were chosen, and on whose smiles possible they may think they may again rely) seems to be one of the principal objects of their attention.[3]

The effort to transform the Yankee militia before Boston into an American army was a daunting task for the Virginian.

Washington and his officers set about instituting and enforcing a disciplinary code. Incompetent officers were removed, and those who remained were distinguished from enlisted men by special insignia. In mid-July, an American chaplain wrote of the impact of these changes:

> There is a great overturning in camp as to order and regularity. New lords new laws. The Generals Washington and [Charles] Lee are upon the lines every day. New orders from his Excellency are read to the respective regiments every morning after prayers. The strictest government is taking place, and great distinction is made between officers and soldiers. Everyone is made know his place and keep it, or to be tied up and receive not 1000 but thirty or forty lashes according to his crime. Thousands are at work every day from four till eleven o'clock in the morning. It is surprising how much work has been done.[4]

Although bedeviled by manpower shortages as militiamen returned home when their enlistments expired, Washington's efforts paid off. By late 1775 the Continental Army had begun to live up to its name: its members were drawn from throughout America as recruits arrived from other colonies, and its siege of Boston was conducted in a more regular manner. While Washington recognized that discipline was essential to creating an army, he also appreciated that a victory would bind the army together in common cause. Unfortunately for the general, victories were hard to come by for much of 1775 and 1776.

As discussed in the previous chapter, in June 1775 Congress authorized an invasion of Canada. The invasion would be two-pronged, with forces from New York under the command of Major-General Philip Schuyler to proceed from Fort Ticonderoga northwards via the Lake Champlain region to capture Montreal. A second force composed of volunteers from among Washington's troops at the siege of Boston under Colonel Benedict Arnold was to march through Maine, liaise with Schuyler's troops, and attack Quebec, thereby denying Canada to the British as a base of operations from which to strike the rebellious colonies. Schuyler's army, which was commanded by Richard Montgomery, a former British officer, captured Montreal on November 13, 1775. Arnold's expedition set out in mid-September. After an arduous journey through the Maine wilderness, which earned Arnold the sobriquet "America's Hannibal," Arnold led the remnants of his force, less than seven hundred exhausted, hungry, and sickly men to the banks of the St. Lawrence River opposite Quebec on November 9. Arnold and his men spent several weeks recovering from their trek and instituting a rather desultory siege against the forces of the British governor Guy Carleton in the city. In early December, three hundred soldiers under Montgomery arrived from Montreal. Faced with the prospect that their army would disintegrate on January 1, 1776 when the enlistments of many of their soldiers would expire, Montgomery and Arnold led an assault on Quebec during a snowstorm on December 31. Carleton's forces, a motley combination of British regulars, sailors, and settlers repulsed the attack, killing, wounding and capturing many of the rebels; Montgomery was killed, and Arnold was badly wounded. In the spring of 1776, the last remnants of the rebel army were driven from Canada.

While the effort to take Canada came to grief, the main rebel effort was concerned with driving the British from Boston. General Washington had been eager to attack the city, but had been restrained by more cautious officers and politicians who feared the destruction of the region's largest town. In November 1775, Washington ordered that the captured artillery from Fort Ticonderoga be transferred to Boston. Responsibility for shifting the ordnance fell to Washington's artillery chief, Henry Knox, a two-hundred and eighty pound, twenty-six-year-old Boston book-seller who had read widely in military science but was lacking in battlefield experience when he was made a colonel in charge of the Continental artillery. Under Knox's direction, rebel teamsters transported the ordnance by sledge and wagon more than three hundred miles through the ice and snow from Ticonderoga to the outskirts of Boston, arriving in February of 1776. Under the cover of a diversionary barrage, the rebels occupied Dorchester Heights which overlooked Boston during the evening of March 4, 1776. As the rebels set about placing the cannons from Ticonderoga, the British commander William Howe (who had succeeded Gage the previous October) weighed his options. Howe's initial instinct was to attack the rebel positions on Dorchester Heights. Upon consideration, perhaps with the memory of Breed's Hill in mind, Howe elected to abandon Boston, which had become untenable. On March 17, 1776, eight years after troops had been first sent to the city to protect customs officers, the British army abandoned Boston. After looting the abandoned homes and shops of rebels, the last British soldiers and loyalists boarded Royal Navy vessels bound for Halifax, Nova Scotia.

William Howe took his troops to Halifax to prepare for the 1776 campaign season. In anticipation of the campaign, the British government had sought to hire trained troops in Europe to augment its forces in America. In late 1775 and early 1776, Britain entered into agreements to pay the rulers of the German principalities of Hesse-Cassel, Hesse-Hanau, Waldeck and Brunswick for 18,000 soldiers. In 1777, subsequent agreements with additional princes would yield an additional 3,000 German troops for the British war effort. All told, approximately 30,000 German mercenaries served with the British in America. These German soldiers, generically referred to as Hessians by the Americans, provided vital manpower to the British effort to suppress the rebellion in America. Not only did they provide the British with trained and disciplined troops who could immediately be sent to America, but when the war spread beyond America in 1778 the presence of the Hessians in America freed British troops for service in the West Indies, the Mediterranean, and India. After 1776, the British army would derive approximately one-third of its strength from German auxiliaries. Although the Hessians provided essential support to the British war effort, their presence came at a cost beyond the £4.7 million paid by the British government to the various German princes. The hired German soldiers who went to America brought with them a fearsome reputation for rapacity. Their presence frightened and angered many Americans, convincing many neutral and even loyalist-inclined colonists to support the rebels. The Hessians exemplified the fundamental difficulty the British faced in prosecuting the American war: in order to defeat the rebels, the British had to resort to methods which were sure to alienate the Americans, thus making the ultimate objective, the restoration of British authority, more difficult.[5]

The major British objective in 1776 was the capture of New York and its environs. With its deep harbor, central location, and its melange of citizens, many of whom were reputed to be loyalists, New York seemed a far more attractive site than Boston had been. William Howe hoped to lure Washington into a decisive battle, defeat the Continental Army, occupy the city, and negotiate a peaceful resolution to the rebellion. General Howe would have at his disposal 30,000 soldiers as well as the resources of the Royal Navy in American waters under the command of his brother, Admiral Richard Howe. Howe's expeditionary force – the largest the British had ever sent abroad – arrived off New York in June. Washington had anticipated that the British would attempt to capture New York, and after the evacuation of Boston he shifted his forces to defend the city in April. The rebel commander had approximately 17,000 troops at his disposal – ten thousand Continentals and seven thousand militiamen – to defend the city. In order to defend the city adequately he divided his troops among Long Island, Manhattan and the mainland. This deployment would give the British, who had overwhelming naval superiority, a decided advantage in the battle for New York.

As a preliminary to their attack on New York, British forces occupied Staten Island on July 2. As the rebels celebrated news of the Declaration of Independence, Howe awaited the arrival of the reinforcements from Europe which he believed would give the lie to American pretensions to independence. When the additional soldiers arrived on August 12, General Howe prepared for what he hoped would be the final campaign of the war. On August 22, British troops landed on Long Island intending to confront the main rebel positions on Brooklyn Heights. During the evening of August 26–7, British forces under Henry Clinton successfully outflanked the rather feeble rebel defenses at Flatbush and routed the rebel army, which performed poorly and suffered nearly fifteen hundred killed, wounded or captured. By midday on the twenty-seventh, the British were before the main rebel defenses at Brooklyn Heights and poised to destroy the rebel army. Howe, possibly with Breed's Hill in mind again, eschewed a head-on attack on fortified rebel positions, just as he had at Dorchester Heights in March. Howe's caution would prove costly. On the evening of August 29, Colonel John Glover's Continental soldiers, mainly fishermen from Marblehead, Massachusetts, ferried the remainder of Washington's army – approximately 9,000 men – to Manhattan. Though badly beaten at Long Island, the rebel force had not been destroyed. Some of Howe's subordinates were critical of his cautious approach. One captain felt that if the general had been more resolute in following up the initial British successes on Long Island, "we might easily have put an End to the Rebellion."[6]

The Battle of Long Island and its aftermath set the pattern for much of the rest of the 1776 campaign. Howe drove Washington's forces out of New York City, which the British occupied on September 15. Over the next several months Howe pursued Washington's forces north into Westchester County and southwest across New Jersey. Although the British won notable victories, defeating Washington at White Plains on October 28 and capturing Forts Washington and Lee on the Hudson River (on November 16 and 18, respectively), Howe was never able to strike the final blow and destroy the rebel army. Indeed, the rebels were in something akin to full flight across New Jersey in late 1776, making the prospect of a decisive battle all but impossible. When the Continental Army crossed the Delaware into Pennsylvania in early December, Washington's forces had dwindled to 3,000 men – by then hard-bitten veterans, who had known little but defeat, retreat, and privation over the previous five months. Despite the Declaration of Independence, the United States looked to be stillborn. Thousands of Americans in British-occupied New Jersey – including Joseph Galloway, who had been an advocate of conciliation at the First Continental Congress, and Richard Stockton, who had signed the Declaration of Independence – renounced their support for the rebels and applied to General Howe for pardons. On December 18, a disconsolate Washington wrote, "I think the game is pretty near up."[7]

The game was not over yet. Despite the orders of General Howe, British and Hessian troops had been heavy-handed in their treatment of American civilians. Plunder had been common during the campaign in New York and New Jersey. General James Robertson testified before the House of Commons in 1779: "A number of officers who lately came into the country, and entertained a notion that Americans were enemies, perhaps did not take enough care to prevent soldiers from gratifying themselves at the expense of the people, so that plundering was very frequent." Rape was also a common feature of the campaign. The remarks of Francis, Lord Rawdon with respect to the treatment of women on Staten Island reveals a level of arrogant contempt for the Americans among some British officers: "A girl cannot step into the bushes to pluck a rose without running the most imminent risk of being ravished, and they are so little accustomed to these vigorous methods that they don't bear them with the proper resignation, and of consequence we have the most entertaining courts-martial every day."[8] While this ill-treatment caused some Americans to petition the British for guarantees of safety and succor, it also created rebels. When Washington halted his footsore and dwindling army in Pennsylvania in early December, hundreds of Pennsylvania and New Jersey militiamen temporarily joined the Continental forces to strike a blow at the British. Washington, ever sensitive to the political implications of the military struggle, recognized the importance of ending the campaign on a positive note. On Christmas night he crossed the Delaware with his force and launched a surprise attack on the Hessian garrison at Trenton, which resulted in the capture of nearly 1,000 Germans. On January 3, 1777 the rebels defeated the British garrison at nearby Princeton. With the British hold on New Jersey no longer as secure as it once appeared, Washington settled into winter quarters at Morristown keeping a wary eye on Howe, who wintered in New York City. The victories at Trenton and Princeton buoyed rebel spirits after what had been a very poor campaign. Late 1776 represented low ebb for the rebel war effort. The victories at the conclusion of the campaign, while of minimal military significance, bolstered rebel morale and encouraged recruiting for what, in many respects, would prove the most crucial year of the war.

The British undertook two separate and uncoordinated campaigns in North America in 1777. During the winter of 1776–7, General John Burgoyne had won approval in London for a plan to lead a combined force of British regulars, Hessians, Indians, Canadians, and loyalists south from Montreal through the Champlain and Hudson valleys to join with the main British forces in New York. The objective of such a campaign would be to isolate the New England colonies, already subject to a British naval blockade, and thus snuff out the rebellion. William Howe, meanwhile, planned to use the main body of British forces in North America to attack the rebel capital at Philadelphia and thus force Washington and the Continental Army into a decisive struggle. Both plans were intended to bring about a timely end to the American rebellion, yet both failed in the end. Without significant assistance from British forces in New York City, most of which were en route to Philadelphia with Howe, Burgoyne's expedition came to grief in the forests of New England and New York. Howe for his part managed to capture Philadelphia by defeating, but not destroying, the Continental Army.

After the experiences of the previous year, William Howe decided not to undertake an overland march from New York to Philadelphia. Rather than march across New Jersey exposed to the wrath of vengeful patriot militiamen, Howe elected to take advantage of British naval superiority and to make a seaborne movement towards the colonial metropolis in Pennsylvania. After delaying several months while provisions ran low and his men endured the summer heat of New York, Howe loaded 13,000 men, their horses and supplies, and put to sea on July 23. The soldiers endured nearly six stultifying weeks crammed on board the transports. The expedition put in briefly at Delaware Bay, but moved on when the commander deemed a landing there too dangerous. Eventually Admiral Howe landed his brother's sickly army at the head of Chesapeake Bay, barely forty miles closer to Philadelphia than they had been when they departed New York. As Congress and civilians fled and loyalists prepared to greet their liberators in the City of Brotherly Love, Washington's Continentals unsuccessfully tried to stop Howe's advance at Brandywine Creek on September 11. On September 26, the British occupied Philadelphia. Washington counter-attacked and was defeated by Howe at the Battle of Germantown on October 4. As in 1776, despite what appeared to be a successful campaign, the British had not managed to destroy the Continental Army, which had acquitted itself well despite its battlefield defeats. The loss of Philadelphia did not lead to a collapse in the rebellion as Howe had hoped. The experience of the first years of the war had given the rebels new symbols and institutions, especially the army and its commander, George Washington. As long as Washington could keep his forces in the field, he could rely on local militia to turn out in times of crisis to augment his forces and resist the British, and the rebellion could continue.

The impact of the loss of Philadelphia was lessened because the city fell at almost the same moment that the rebels received good tidings from the north: Burgoyne and his entire army had surrendered to General Horatio Gates at Saratoga, New York. Burgoyne and his force of 8,000 regular and irregular soldiers departed from Montreal in mid-June. Initially the campaign went as planned, as Burgoyne's army floated down Lake

Champlain in flat-bottomed boats and easily recaptured Fort Ticonderoga. Once the troops left Lake Champlain and sought to traverse the wilderness of the Hudson River valley, the force ran into difficulty. Burgoyne's men were heavily laden with materiel and supplies (including the general's extensive baggage train) which were better suited to the plains of north-western Europe than the American forest. Moreover, the troops were subject to harassment by rebel militiamen who attacked stragglers and placed obstacles in the way of the advancing army. Several fierce skirmishes took place, delaying Burgoyne's advance. His army had covered more than one hundred miles during the first three weeks of the expedition; during the subsequent three weeks it made progress of barely more than a mile a day.

Like so many British commanders during the American war, Burgoyne had hoped that loyalists would flock to his standard, augmenting his troops and undermining rebel authority. On June 23, 1777, as he set out, Burgoyne issued a proclamation which stated that his purpose was to restore royal authority and liberate Americans from the tyranny of Congress. If Americans did not support and assist Burgoyne's army, then the general promised that "Devastation, Famine, and every concomitant Horror" would be visited upon them. Given the suffering of loyalists in New Jersey the previous year – both at the hands of the rebels *and* the British – it is unlikely that many Americans would identify themselves as supporters of the crown in northern New England. Indeed, as in New Jersey, the presence of British forces did much to create rebels out of neutral-inclined Americans. Burgoyne's Native American allies were particularly problematic in this regard. In several instances during the expedition's advance Burgoyne's Iroquois warriors attacked outlying farms, killing several families. In a much-publicized incident a young woman, Jane McCrea, who was engaged to a loyalist soldier, was killed by two of Burgoyne's Indians. Once Indians and whites came into conflict along the frontier, political considerations took second place to racial enmity. In the wake of the killings, hundreds of militiamen from the northern New England and New York turned out to oppose the British advance.

In August, things began to go dreadfully wrong for the northern campaign. As Burgoyne descended from Lake Champlain a second, smaller British force was to approach Albany from Fort Oswego on Lake Ontario to support Burgoyne. This force was turned back in a hard-fought battle with rebel militiamen at Oriskany, New York on August 6. Meanwhile Burgoyne's troops, bogged down in the wilderness, were running out of supplies. The general dispatched a force of nearly 900 Hessians, Canadians, and Indians to search for supplies for his hungry army. On August 16 the foraging party was destroyed in a battle with New England militia at Bennington, Vermont. Burgoyne was running low on supplies, he had lost a significant portion of his army, he could not expect relief, and he had yet to cross the Hudson and confront the main body of Continental troops under

Horatio Gates in northern New York. He did not cross the Hudson and head for Albany until mid-September. His forces clashed with the Continental forces in successive battles at Freeman's Farm on September 19 and October 7. Having failed to defeat the rebels and sustained significant casualties (1,200 to less than 500 for the rebels), Burgoyne was surrounded. He recognized that he could expect no assistance from the small garrison remaining at New York. On October 17, 1777 he surrendered the remnants of his army, approximately 6,000 men, to Horatio Gates. For the first time, the rebels had defeated the British in a sustained campaign.[9]

Saratoga immediately changed the nature and scope of the American War of Independence. Frenchmen had been providing covert assistance to the American rebels, via dummy companies trading in the West Indies, since the beginning of the conflict. By late 1777, representatives of the United States, led by Benjamin Franklin, were seeking a treaty of alliance with the French government. When news of Burgoyne's defeat reached Paris in December, the balance was tipped within the French government in favor of a formal alliance between France and the United States. Treaties between the United States and France were signed in February 1778. With the conclusion of the Franco-American alliance, the American War of Independence became a European conflict in which the colonial war in America was but one theater. Eventually Britain found itself at war simultaneously with the American rebels, France (1778), Spain (which entered an alliance with France in 1779 but not with the United States), and the Netherlands (1780). While Britain sought to retain its North American colonies, after 1778 suppressing the American rebellion was one of several objectives, including British protection and enlargement of their holdings in the West Indies, Africa and India, and protecting the British Isles from a Franco-Spanish invasion. In consequence, the government could not devote the military resources to the North American theater of the war that it had during the period from 1775–7. In 1778, 65 percent of the British army was in North America. By 1780, only 29 percent of British troops were in North America, with 55 percent guarding Britain against invasion. Similarly, while in 1778 41 percent of the Royal Navy's ships of the line were in American waters, in July 1780 that figure was reduced to 13 percent and by April 1782 to 10 percent. After 1778, London would have far fewer resources to devote to the American rebellion, while the rebels benefited from additional assistance in the form of arms, materiel, and men from the French, distraction of the British by the Spanish, and money from the Dutch. Crucially, the presence of the French navy would challenge British naval superiority in American waters.[10]

The globalization of the American war required a change of strategy by British policy makers. In March 1778 Lord George Germain, the American Secretary, ordered General Henry Clinton (William Howe's successor) to prepare for a more limited campaign against the rebels. The government

Faced with war against the Americans, French, Spanish and Dutch as well as a mounting national debt to pay for the conflict, there was little enthusiasm for pursuing the American conflict in the wake of Cornwallis's surrender. On February 27, 1782 Parliament voted to discontinue offensive operations in America. Although some parliamentarians wanted to pursue the war with the French, Spanish, and Dutch (and conflict between these powers, as well as American privateersmen, and the British would continue until the final peace treaty of 1783), the government of Lord North – and its wartime policies – had become untenable. On March 20, Lord North resigned and was replaced by the Marquis of Rockingham. The most powerful member of the Rockingham government was the Colonial Secretary, the Earl of Shelburne, who was amenable to negotiations with the representatives of the United States. (When Rockingham died in July 1782, Shelburne became Prime Minister.) Despite a commitment to France not to make a separate peace and orders from Congress to follow the instructions of the French with respect to any peace negotiations, American representatives entered into informal talks with British officials in Paris in April 1782, months before the formal peace negotiations began in September.

The American negotiators – Benjamin Franklin, John Adams, John Jay, and Henry Laurens – found themselves in an anomalous position. The British, with whom they had fought a bitter and bloody war, were inclined towards generosity, while their ally, France, hoped the United States would emerge from the negotiations in a weakened state. Shelburne wanted the United States to be independent of French control, and he believed that a strong United States would naturally trade with Britain. For the same reasons his French opposite number, the Comte de Vergennes, did not want Britain to make too many concessions to the Americans, whom he hoped would be dependent on France. On November 29, 1782 the British and Americans signed a provisional peace agreement. Under the terms of the agreement, the British recognized the independence of the United States, acknowledged the right of the Americans to continue to fish in the north Atlantic, and ceded to the republic all the territory south of the Great Lakes and east of the Mississippi River (with the exception of the Floridas). Thorny issues such as the status of prewar debts and compensation for loyalists were not addressed in a comprehensive manner, and were left to subsequent negotiations. The agreement was contingent on the outcome of negotiations between the British and French (and Spanish). Vergennes was dismayed by Shelburne's generosity to the Americans, and castigated the American representatives for failing to consult him over the agreement. Final agreement between all the belligerent parties ending the American War of Independence was not reached until September 23, 1783. With the exception of the significant concessions made by Britain to the United States and Britain's cession of the Floridas to Spain, the final Treaty of Paris largely restored the *status quo ante bellum* among the European powers.[14]

A civil war

The War of Independence did not only pit Americans against the British, but also Americans against each other. A large proportion of Americans did not support the rebellion or its aims. Some actively opposed the rebels and supported the continuation of British rule in America. Others, while sympathetic to the prewar movement against taxation, did not support armed resistance. Others were neutral-inclined and sought to avoid the conflict altogether. Although John Adams estimated that one-third of the population were active rebels, one-third were loyalists, and one-third were neutral, it seems likely that two-fifths of the population were active Whigs, one-fifth active Tories, and two-fifths sought neutrality. By either estimate, it seems likely that at least early in the war a majority of the population was inclined towards neutrality or loyalism. The proportions would shift as the years passed and thousands of loyalists were driven into exile. In consequence, the War of Independence was very much a civil war with all horror, pain, and suffering associated with internal conflicts. The civil war was fought alongside the larger struggle against Britain. While it was most intense in the south, violent conflicts between loyalists and rebels characterized every region where there was sustained fighting during the war. Indeed, recent research has revealed that areas around the British garrison in New York City, especially New York, Long Island, New Jersey, and Connecticut, were subject to a vicious partisan struggle between rebel and loyalist militias not unlike that in the southern backcountry described above.[15]

Loyalists were a disparate group. Many years ago, William H. Nelson demonstrated that Americans who supported the crown tended be drawn from groups who felt themselves threatened politically, economically, culturally or socially by the prospect of a rebel victory. Thus loyalists were drawn from such groups as New England merchants who depended on trans-Atlantic trade; small farmers in the southern backcountry who resented the political dominance of the tidewater Whig elite; Dutch-speaking settlers on Long Island who resented their New England-born neighbors; as well as thousands of African American slaves who believed that a rebel victory would not result in their emancipation (see Chapter 9). The varied backgrounds and motivations of the loyalists meant that they did not constitute a coherent or well-organized opposition to the Revolution. They were united only in that they feared and opposed independence. This was not enough to counter the compelling ideology of the rebels. While the rebels had a clear idea of what they fought *for*: independence and republican self-government, the loyalists only knew they stood *against* these things. Apart from that they lacked unity. Because they were often motivated by local concerns, the loyalists were unable to organize themselves on a national level; rather, they relied on the British to provide them with leadership and protection. As we have seen, in New

Jersey in 1776 and in the Carolinas in 1780–2, the British could not provide the unity, stability, or leadership which the loyalists required. Indeed, the British presence in these regions often left loyalists more exposed and vulnerable to the wrath of their vengeful Whig neighbors.

Two examples illustrate the wide range of individuals who were denominated loyalists. Samuel Curwen was a fifty-four-year-old reasonably prosperous merchant in Salem, Massachusetts when the fighting broke out between British soldiers and American militiamen at Lexington and Concord. Curwen had been opposed to the resistance movement against Britain during the previous decade, and had profited from violating the non-importation agreements. Timid by nature, Curwen had not advertised his opposition to the rebels. Nonetheless, he feared for his safety and went into exile within days of the outbreak of the war. Curwen spent the war in England and did not return to Salem until 1784. He lived in Salem on a British pension in compensation for his losses during the war until his death in 1799. In contrast to Curwen was James Moody. Moody was a thirty-one-year-old New Jersey farmer when the War of Independence had broken out. He had not been a strong supporter of the crown but neither was he strong supporter of the rebels, whose aggression he resented. In April 1777, after he was shot at by rebel partisans, he fled to the British lines in New York and enlisted in the British service. Moody, a reluctant loyalist, distinguished himself as something of a genius at the guerrilla warfare between loyalist and rebel partisans around New York during the war. He was very adept at spying on the rebels and raiding their supplies and camps. In June 1779 he captured five rebel officers and £500 worth of valuable ammunition. At war's end Moody went into exile. He traveled first to England, where he wrote a popular account of his exploits. He received a British pension and settled in Nova Scotia, where he lived as a farmer until his death in 1809. From the British standpoint, there were too many Samuel Curwens and not enough James Moodys during the war. By war's end, approximately 19,000 Americans had enlisted in the British army serving in forty-two loyalist units. Undoubtedly thousands more joined Loyalist militias during British campaigns. Nonetheless, there were never enough active loyalists to enable the restoration of British authority in the rebellious colonies.[16]

There were, however, enough loyalists to ensure that the War of Independence was a bloody internecine struggle in which atrocities against non-combatants of all political persuasions were not uncommon. For the British, the American War of Independence can be seen as one of a number of colonial wars in which they had engaged during the eighteenth century. To be sure, the nature of the conflict – a battle against rebellious colonists – was unique and its outcome was unfortunate. For those Americans who remained loyal to the crown and risked their lives to defend British authority, the war was a bloody civil war in which they were the losers.

Tens of thousands of loyalists and suspected loyalists had their civil rights violated by local committees of safety, which objected to their political views. Although military authorities, including George Washington, questioned the value of the rebel militia in waging war, it undoubtedly played an effective role in policing local communities and stifling opposition to the Revolution. Those, like James Moody, who had the temerity to oppose the Revolution might find their lives in danger. Loyalists were not only subject to threat and intimidation; the property of thousands of loyalists was confiscated and sold by the new state governments.[17] Thousands more simply had their property plundered by rebel neighbors. An untold number of loyalists, rebels, neutrals, and non-combatants were injured and killed in the fighting between rebel and loyalist militias. At the end of the war, many loyalists felt they could not remain as pariahs in the new states. As many as 100,000 loyalists left the new United States to settle in other parts of the British Empire, especially in Canada. Among those who went into exile and had their property seized were some of the wealthiest and most socially prominent families in the colonies, such as the Olivers and Hutchinsons of Massachusetts, the Penns of Pennsylvania, and the Dulanys of Maryland. For these refugees and others who suffered because of their loyalty to the old regime, the triumph of the American rebels did not represent an advance in human freedom, but an unmitigated disaster. Their displacement constitutes one of the most revolutionary steps taken during the period.

A war of conquest

Loyalists were not the only Americans who rued the triumph of the rebels. So too did Native Americans. At the same time that Americans were fighting to free themselves from British rule along the Atlantic littoral, to the west of the Appalachian mountains a bloody racial conflict between white settlers and Indians took place. The constitutional issues which characterized the war in the east had little relevance in the west, where there was a naked and brutal struggle for control. If the war in the east was concerned with protecting and extending American liberty, in the west the struggle concerned survival and the subjugation of the Native American population. The war in the west was a war of conquest.

The trans-Appalachian west had remained an area of tension and conflict in the wake of Pontiac's Rebellion. Despite the Proclamation Line of 1763, white settlers continued to cross the mountains and establish farms in western regions of Pennsylvania and Virginia as well further west in the Ohio River valley. After settlers massacred a group of Indians in 1774, the frontier region once again descended into violent racial conflict with the commencement of Lord Dunmore's War. Dunmore's War would be subsumed by the War of Independence when it began the following year, and armed conflict between whites and Indians would encompass the length of the rebellious colonies.

When the War of Independence commenced, Native Americans had to choose between supporting the British, the rebels, or attempting to maintain their neutrality. Depending on local circumstances, some Indian groups sided with the rebels. For example, the so-called Eastern Indians – the Passamaquoddy, Penobscot, and Micmac tribes of eastern Maine and Nova Scotia – lent their support to the rebels when Massachusetts authorities appropriated funds to provide the Indians with the services of a Catholic priest.[18] Ultimately, however, circumstances compelled most Indians to pursue policies of neutrality or to fight alongside the British. Native Americans recognized the threat to their livelihood posed by a rebel victory. Should the Americans win their independence then the likelihood of unfettered white expansionism and subsequent Indian displacement would increase dramatically. In consequence many Indians, armed and encouraged by the British, fought against the settlers. The British cultivated and encouraged the Indians because they had so few troops of their own at their western posts when the war began. There were several thousand Indian warriors to both the north and south of the Ohio River who could be encouraged to attack the white settlements. The British hoped, at minimum, to prevent the western settlements from lending support to the military efforts of the rebels in the east and at best to require the rebels to divert precious troops and supplies to the west.

From western New York to Georgia, the same pattern was played out along the frontier during the war. In the early stages of the conflict, Indians attacked white settlements. Generally, the Indians were unable to capture the palisades where the settlers sought refuge but they were able to terrorize, capture, or kill outlying families and destroy their farms as well as those militiamen who pursued the raiders. Although the Native Americans were usually encouraged and armed by the British, this was not always the case. In 1776 the Cherokees, for example, acted against the advice of John Stuart, Britain's Southern Indian Superintendent, and launched attacks along the frontiers of Virginia and the Carolinas. The settlers, although they suffered grievously, usually withstood the onslaughts and retaliated. Sometimes the counterattacks were conducted under the auspices of the Continental Army, such as General John Sullivan's devastating campaign against the Iroquois in western New York during the summer of 1779 in response to their raids on the Wyoming valley of Pennsylvania. Other campaigns were organized by the states, as when Virginia and the Carolinas banded together to retaliate against the Cherokees. Most commonly, settlers took matters into their own hands in conjunction with state or national authorities. The complexity and brutality of the war in the west is revealed by events in the Ohio River valley.[19]

Between 1776 and 1778 the Indians of the Ohio River region, mainly Shawnees and Delawares, attacked the American settlements in Kentucky which in recent years had seen an influx of white settlers from Virginia. This campaign was a success. As the British lieutenant-governor at Detroit, Henry Hamilton, reported in April 1778 after interviewing the Kentucky leader Daniel Boone who had been captured by the Shawnees, "the people of the frontiers have been incessantly harassed by parties of Indians. They have not been able to sow grain in Kentucky and will not have a morsel of bread by the middle of June. Cloathing is not to be had, nor do they expect any relief from Congress."[20] Despite their privation, the settlers held out. In 1778 and 1779 the settlers began to launch frequent attacks on native villages in Ohio. During the summer of 1778, twenty-five-year-old George Rogers Clark, on orders from Virginia, recruited militiamen from the frontier settlements of Pennsylvania and Kentucky and launched an ambitious campaign against the centers of British power deep in the Ohio River region. He captured the British posts at Kaskaskia and Cahokia in July. The following April Clark captured Vincennes, as well as Lieutenant-Governor Hamilton himself.

Clark's success, which did much to buoy the rebel cause, did little to alleviate the suffering in the Kentucky settlements as the war of raid and counter-raid continued unabated on both sides of the Ohio River. The struggle was marked by brutality and atrocity by both sides, and quarter was rarely given. East of the Appalachians, where the main campaigns of the war were fought, there was one war-related death for every 1,000 people. In Kentucky (which of course had a much smaller population) there was one death for every seventy inhabitants. A notorious incident which epitomized the frontier conflict was the massacre of ninety-six defenseless Christian Delaware Indians at the Moravian mission at Gnadenhütten, Ohio. The victims, who were mostly women and children, were herded into two cabins by Colonel David Williamson's Pennsylvania militia, where they were scalped and hacked to death. David Zeisberger, a Moravian missionary in the region, wrote in his diary, "the Militia themselves acknowledged that they had been good Indians. They prayed and sang until the tomahawks struck their heads."[21] In response to such atrocities, both sides were reluctant to give up in what they viewed as a struggle for survival.

After they had no use for them, the British withdrew support from their Indian allies, which left them to the mercy of the American rebels. This occurred throughout the south in 1781 and 1782. Under such circumstances, the tribes had little choice but to sue for peace or attempt to carry on resistance without outside support. In most cases Indians opted for the former. As a result, the United States concluded treaties of dubious legal and moral value at Fort Stanwix, New York and Hopewell, South Carolina in 1784, in which it won concessions of land from the Iroquois, Choctaws, Chickasaws, and Cherokees respectively. Only in the region north of the

Ohio River and south of the Great Lakes – then known as the Northwest – were the Indians able to continue their resistance.

The situation in the region was complicated. According to the 1783 Peace of Paris, the Northwest was American territory. Accordingly, Congress adopted a series of laws, the Northwest Ordinances of 1784, 1785, and 1787 which created a system for the subdivision and sale of the territory as well as the creation of local, territorial and, eventually, state governments in the region. Despite the fact that Great Britain was a signatory to the 1783 treaty, British troops still occupied posts in the region. According to the treaty, the British should have turned these posts over the United States. They failed to do so because they claimed that the United States had not honored its pledge to compensate loyalists for their losses. The Indians of the region, the Delawares, Shawnees, Miamis, Chippewas, Ottawas, and Potawatomis formed an alliance, the Western Confederacy, to resist American encroachments. Violent conflict between settlers and Indians continued unabated despite the peace of 1783. Covertly armed by the British, the Western Confederacy would prove a serious obstacle to American settlement of the region and embarrassing challenge to the sovereignty of the new nation.

The struggle to conquer the Northwest went very badly for the United States. Twice in 1790 and 1791, warriors from the Western Confederacy destroyed American armies along the present-day border between Ohio and Indiana. The first occurred in October 1790 when a combined force of United States regulars and militiamen under General Joseph Harmar was routed. A year later, General Arthur St. Clair led another American army, nearly a thousand militiamen and regulars into the Ohio country in the autumn of 1791. St. Clair, who had had an undistinguished record during the War of Independence lived down to his abilities. Despite a warning by President Washington to be on his guard, on November 4 St. Clair camped without taking the precaution of posting sentries. Warriors under the Miami war chief, Little Turtle, attacked the encampment. The militiamen broke and fled while the regulars sought to fight. The result was an overwhelming defeat for the Americans, who sustained 632 dead and 264 wounded out of a force of 920 officers and men. By contrast, sixty-six of Little Turtle's warriors were killed and nine wounded. In 1794 Washington sent a third army under General Anthony Wayne to take on the Western Confederacy. The president warned the general, "another defeat would be inexpressibly ruinous to the reputation of the government." On August 20, 1791, Wayne defeated the Western Confederacy at the Battle of Fallen Timbers. In 1794 the British finally agreed to withdraw from the western forts (see Chapter 7) and further resistance was impossible. In 1795 the western tribes agreed to the Treaty of Greenville by the terms of which they ceded their claim to most of the land in the present state of Ohio. So ended two decades of unremitting conflict over the region between American settlers and Native Americans.[22] The Battle of Fallen Timbers represents the proper end of the wars of the American Revolution. It was not until the Treaty of Greenville that the United States could legitimately lay claim to the concessions made by the British in 1783. Despite the "peace" of 1783, the conquest of the west, for conquest it undoubtedly was, did not occur in fact until 1794, and in treaty until 1795.

A revolutionary war

The War of Independence had significant consequences. Politically, the war led to the creation of the United States. The problems faced by Congress and the states in waging the war would directly influence the design of the new republican governments made necessary by independence (see Chapters 5 and 6). Diplomatically, the war not only introduced a new nation, with the potential to play a significant role in the western hemisphere, into international relations, but it re-ignited the clash over colonial interests among the European powers leading to armed confrontation in the Caribbean, Africa, the Mediterranean, and India as well as North America. From a military standpoint, the war represented a departure from past practice. The American War of Independence was one of the first of what came to be known in the twentieth century as colonial wars of liberation. It was a conflict in which the combatants (at least in its North American aspects) were motivated by ideology and a desire for national self-determination. In this respect the American Revolutionary War, anticipated the experiences of the wars of the French Revolution. The conflict over American independence, according to Stephen Conway, one of its leading historians:

> was the first appearance, on a significant scale, of a people's war, the participation of a large proportion of the free male population and the political commitment of many of those who fought for the United States certainly suggest that the Americans became a people at arms nearly two decades before the French.[23]

The impact of the War of Independence extends beyond its important political, diplomatic and military consequences. The War of Independence also transformed nearly all segments of American society. We have seen that the war generally had deleterious consequences for the Native Americans. Indeed, one of the foremost historians of the period has recently argued that the transformation of power relations between whites and Indians in the trans-Appalachian west was among the most radical changes wrought by the Revolution.[24] Chapter 9 will demonstrate that the war and its aftermath had an ambiguous impact on African Americans. Large numbers of African Americans fought on both sides during the conflict.

Unlike white Americans, who fought for "liberty" as an abstract concept, many black Americans fought for the British and rebels respectively to gain their emancipation from slavery. The freedom for which they fought was tangible. The efforts of African slaves during the conflict were of crucial military significance, and undermined slavery in the northern states leading to gradual emancipation throughout that region, yet slavery survived as an institution in the southern states. For American women, as will be shown in greater detail in Chapter 10, the War of Independence also had ambiguous consequences. The duration and brutal nature of the conflict meant that many American women, of all races, regions, and classes, endured unprecedented hardship. For some women, the war presented opportunities to exercise greater autonomy over their lives and families. The experience of the war would lead some women to call for a voice in political affairs. In the main, these calls would fall upon deaf male ears.

Poor white males, who made up the bulk of soldiers who fought for American independence, perhaps gained the most from the war. We have seen how participation in the prewar protest movement against the British led to an increase in political consciousness among Americans who were previously kept out of or marginalized within the political process. The "new military history" of the American Revolution has ably showed that the experience of war and their contributions to the rebel victory would lead humble Americans to demand, and win, a greater voice in new governments which were formed during and after the conflict.[25] Simply put, the soldiers who fought to win American independence demanded to participate in the governments which were created in the aftermath of the conflict. The War of Independence, therefore, helped to democratize the discourse of American politics. For the men who won a greater voice in their government, the war was certainly revolutionary. The debate over who should rule the United States and what form the new governments should take is the theme of the next two chapters.

5

THE CONFEDERATION ERA

Introduction

Henry Laurens was the head of one of South Carolina's most prominent families. He was an extremely wealthy planter and merchant, and an ardent supporter of the Revolution. In 1775 he served as president of South Carolina's First Provincial Congress. A year later he was elected president of the state's Council of Safety. In July 1777 he was elected to the Continental Congress. He served with distinction as the president of that body from November 1777 until 1779, when he resigned to serve on a diplomatic mission to the Netherlands. He was captured *en route* and imprisoned in the Tower of London for fifteen months before he was exchanged for General Cornwallis.

Laurens's revolutionary credentials were impeccable. Nonetheless, even before the war began he expressed concern about the unforeseen consequences of the struggle against Britain. In a letter written to his son John in January 1775, the elder Laurens expressed distaste for the politicization of "the Country people" and the notion that "no Man is now supposed to be unequal to a share in the Government." Laurens's comments highlighted the most crucial question which confronted Americans after independence: who was fit to exercise political authority? At a fundamental level, the American Revolution was a political revolution. Although it had profound intellectual, social, cultural, and diplomatic consequences, the essential issue at the center of the conflict concerned who should rule America. With the Declaration of Independence and the successful conclusion of the War of Independence, Americans had demonstrated that Britain could not govern its thirteen wayward colonies. If the British could not govern America, what type of government should the new states have? What form should the union of the states take? Who should be allowed to vote and hold office? These interrelated questions were at the heart of the political revolution which transformed America between 1776 and the ratification of the Constitution in 1788. It was these questions which, in Carl Becker's famous phrase, transformed a struggle about home rule into one about who should rule at home.[1] The purpose of the next two chapters is to examine these questions and how Americans sought to answer them.

The supporters of American independence agreed that the former colonies should have republican governments. By this, they meant that their political system would not be based on hereditary government. The new states would not be governed by a monarch nor would they have a titled aristocracy. Rather, the people would be the source of political power and authority. According to James Madison of Virginia, probably the most important American political thinker of the revolutionary era:

> we may define a republic to be, or at least may bestow that name on, a government which derives all its powers directly or indirectly from the great body of the people, and is administered by persons holding their offices during pleasure for a limited period, or during good behavior. It is *essential* to such a government that it be derived from the great body of society, not from an inconsiderable proportion or a favored class of it; otherwise a handful of tyrannical nobles, exercising their oppressions by a delegation of their powers, might aspire to the rank of republicans and claim for their government the honorable title of republic.[2]

Under a republican system, as understood by eighteenth-century Americans, the people usually exercised their sovereignty by electing representatives to govern them.

Although the revolutionaries agreed that their new governments should be republics, they disagreed widely as to what precise form these governments should have. Broadly speaking, the revolutionaries were divided into two camps – elitists and democrats – by the political questions posed by the revolution. The elitists, who frequently represented the leading figures in colonial politics, tended to draw on the traditions of British opposition ideology. They favored republican governments modeled on the British constitution and the colonial governments, with a tripartite sharing of power between a bicameral legislature and an executive. Many leading elitists had had national experience, either in Congress or the army, during the war and were acutely aware of the need for a strong national confederation. The democrats, by contrast, were frequently the "new men of the revolution," men who had been politicized by their involvement in the resistance to Britain and their participation in the War of Independence. These men, frequently from more humble backgrounds than the elitists, had been energized by their experiences. They recognized that independence could not have been achieved without their support. They were confident in their abilities and the abilities of their peers to govern. In consequence, they demanded a significant role in constructing the new republican governments. They sought to democratize the new governments, often favoring unicameral legislatures, a weak executive, a broad franchise and frequent elections.[3] The perspective of the democrats was frequently more local than that of the elitists. These two groups competed to implement their versions of republicanism during the revolution, first on the state level and then in fashioning the national confederation.[4]

Constitution-making in the states

The political transition from colony to statehood had been a gradual one. In each of the colonies, committees of safety and correspondence undertook governmental functions when British authority collapsed in the wake of the Coercive Acts. In most of the colonies, the assembly reconstituted itself as a provincial convention or congress and governed in the absence of now-discredited British institutions. With independence, the American revolutionaries had to construct governments for the new states. The *ad hoc* arrangements which had developed when British authority collapsed in 1774 had to be formalized and made more rigorous. Many saw the need to create new governments as an opportunity to remake America. Optimism was tempered by caution. History taught the Americans that republics were very fragile political entities, and needed to be designed with care. Moreover, the exigencies of war and the economic and social upheaval of the conflict distracted from the attention which Americans could devote to designing their republics. Nonetheless, Americans took the responsibility of crafting state constitutions very seriously indeed. It was a remarkable achievement that during the war in each of the new states the revolutionaries were able to draft written constitutions which embodied the principles of republican government. That these principles were contested is reflected in the different constitutional arrangements adopted by the various states.

During the spring of 1776, John Adams introduced a resolution in the Continental Congress calling on all colonies that did not have a permanent constitution based on popular sovereignty to adopt one. (Massachusetts, New Hampshire, and South Carolina had already modified their colonial governments, and Connecticut and Rhode Island, self-governing since the 1660s, amended their charters as constitutions.) On May 10, 1776, in an act tantamount to declaring independence, Congress adopted the resolution. Over the next five years the various states would adopt fifteen constitutions. In some states the provincial conventions drafted new constitutions as a matter of course. In others, special conventions were called for the task. In all the states, elitist and democratic republicans vied to control the drafting of the documents.

In general, the elitists and democrats appealed to different interests in American society. The elitists tended to be wealthier and better educated than their more democratically inclined rivals. They appealed to the residents of urban areas and commercially-oriented towns and agricultural districts. The democrats, by contrast, appealed to the small farmers who predominated in America, especially in the isolated agricultural areas removed from the coastal region.[5] These two groups made different assumptions about political behavior and had very different expectations concerning the proper form the state governments should take. The democrats believed that the common people of America were capable of self-government. They felt that the essential task of government was to preserve the liberties of the people from the greed and corruption of those who wielded political power. Consequently, they sought constitutional structures which would decentralize power and disperse decision making. As such, they tended to favor democratizing government: broadening the franchise, giving more power to the assemblies, and increasing their numbers, creating weak chief executives, and elected judiciaries. The elitists, by contrast, felt that while the revolutionary governments should maintain liberty, they must also preserve order. They felt that the democrats exaggerated the danger of centralized power and went too far in their love of liberty. They feared that democratic excesses would create unstable governments which would eventually descend into anarchy possibly giving way to tyranny. They sought to design republics in which the people would exercise their sovereignty by choosing their political betters to govern and then stand aside to let them do so. They sought to create governments along the lines of the former colonial system, whereby the franchise was limited to property-holders who exercised their right to vote infrequently, where the power of the assembly was divided between a bicameral legislature, the judiciary was free from popular interference, and the governors were strong.

It is important to note that both groups, democrats and elitists, believed broadly in republicanism. Each accepted that sovereignty derived from the people and that the people (in the form of the electorate) should exercise choice in electing their governors. Both groups accepted that there were limits both to liberty and the amount of power that the government should wield. Even the most devoted democrat, for example, would not have normally advocated extending suffrage to African Americans or women. Similarly, even the most conservative elitists accepted that the people should elect their governors, even if they favored limiting the franchise and the frequency of elections. Where they differed was over the precise details of the governments they were designing. Perhaps the best way to explore the range of republican theory and practice in revolutionary America would be to consider the most democratic and elitist constitutions produced during the period: those of Pennsylvania and Massachusetts, respectively.

In Pennsylvania the political elite was dominated by Quakers and Anglicans from the Philadelphia area, who were at best lukewarm supporters of the Revolution. The conservatives in Pennsylvania did not wish to replace the provincial government or to support independence. Reluctant to lead in the Revolution, Pennsylvania's political conservatives found themselves swept aside by it. In June 1776 the pro-independence members of the assembly withdrew from the body, denying it a quorum and rendering it impotent. A convention of county committees of inspection was called by the Philadelphia Committee of Inspection, with the support of the Philadelphia militia, to govern in lieu of the assembly. The convention met for a week in June, endorsing independence on June 24, and called elections for a special convention to meet and draft a new constitution for the state beginning on July 8. The electorate for the special election was considerably more radical than that which traditionally voted in Pennsylvania. Because of the gravity of the issue, traditional property requirements for voting were waived. Voting, however, was limited to those who supported independence. Under this formula, previously under-represented areas like the frontier counties were over-represented in the constitutional convention. Thus the convention to draft the Pennsylvania Constitution represented some of the poorest, yet most vociferous, supporters of the revolution in the state.[6]

The Pennsylvania constitutional convention consisted of ninety-six delegates, who sat from July 8 until September 28, 1776. The resulting document was the most radical experiment in republican government to emerge from the American Revolution. The Pennsylvania constitution vested legislative powers in a unicameral legislature which would be elected annually by all taxpayers over the age of twenty-one and the adult sons of taxpayers. Such a broad franchise (Pennsylvania's suffrage requirements were the most generous adopted by any state) and the creation of a large, annually elected, one-house legislature constituted a sharp break with colonial practice. Whenever possible, legislation had to be held over from one legislative session to the next so that pending legislation could be published and receive public consideration before the assembly acted. Executive power was vested not in an individual governor, but in an elected twelve-member executive council. Although the council would elect a president, his powers were largely symbolic. Crucially, the executive would have no authority to veto legislation adopted by the assembly. Judges under the system were elected to serve seven-year terms. Every seven years, a council of censors would review the actions of the government to determine whether the constitution had been violated or amendments to the constitution were necessary. Appended to the constitution was a broad declaration of rights which enumerated the freedoms guaranteed to the people of Pennsylvania.

Pennsylvania's was the most democratic of the state constitutions adopted during the era of the American Revolution. (When the rebellious north-eastern counties of New York broke away to establish Vermont in 1777, they adopted a constitution which was closely modeled on that of

Pennsylvania.) Although arrived at by means of extra-legal activity which could be criticized as undemocratic, the document called for broad-based suffrage, annual elections, and public perusal of legislative action, all of which are hallmarks of democratic government first experimented with in Pennsylvania. The constitution was not without defects. A weak plural executive meant the state frequently lacked leadership in times of crisis. Rotation in office – assemblymen could not serve more than four out of every seven years; and delegates to the Continental Congress also faced term limits – meant that able legislators were sometimes replaced by those without experience or aptitude. Conservatives opponents of the constitution, known as Republicans, agitated for its replacement or amendment. Throughout the 1780s Republicans and the supporters of the document, known as Constitutionalists, waged a bitter partisan struggle. Eventually the Republicans prevailed and Pennsylvania's experiment with what, for the period, can be termed radical democracy came to an end in 1790 when the constitution of 1776 was replaced by a more conservative model similar to that which had been adopted in Massachusetts a decade before.

Where Pennsylvania acted with relative haste to draft its constitution, deliberations in Massachusetts were much slower. In June 1775, the Massachusetts Provincial Congress (which had replaced the previous colonial assembly) adopted the colony's 1691 charter, with minor modifications, as a temporary frame of government. During the summer of 1776, while delegates in Pennsylvania and other states were drafting their constitutions, the Massachusetts assembly resolved to draft a more permanent constitution for the state. Despite the frenzy of constitutional innovation in other states, political leaders in the Bay State were still slow to act. The assembly did not create a committee to draft its new constitution until June of 1777, and that committee did not submit its plan of government until December. It was not until February 1778 that the legislature met and approved the document. In March 1778 the assembly distributed copies of the draft constitution to each town in the state, for consideration by special town meetings open to all males over the age of twenty-one. By a margin of five to one, Massachusetts voters rejected the proposed constitution. The voters had multiple reasons for rejecting the plan. Boston's voters, 968 in all, expressed the most common criticism of the plan. They unanimously noted "the Impropriety of this Matter's Originating with the General Court [the assembly]" and "all forms of government should be prefaced by a Bill of Rights," which the proposed plan lacked.[7]

The rejection of the proposed 1778 constitution by Massachusetts voters is evidence of the increased democratization caused by the resistance to Britain. When the voters were consulted about the matter, they objected because the document had been drafted by the legislature as the sitting government and not by a specially elected convention as occurred in

Pennsylvania and other states. Accordingly, on June 15, 1779 the legislature called for elections to a special constitutional convention to which delegates would be sent from every town in the state. As in Pennsylvania, the assembly waived the usual property requirements for voting to the convention. Since in republics sovereignty was derived from the people, American republicans believed popular consent was essential to the design and function of their constitutions.

The Massachusetts constitutional convention convened in Cambridge on September 1, 1779. Its nearly three hundred delegates were drawn from every town in the state. It created a subcommittee to prepare the draft constitution. The resulting document, which was largely the work of John Adams, was submitted to the convention on October 28 for discussion and amendment. The proposed Massachusetts constitution began with a declaration of rights which stated, among other things, that "All men are born free and equal." The constitution created a government which closely resembled the previous colonial system. The document called for a bicameral legislature with a Senate and a House of Representatives. The legislators would be elected by males over the age of twenty-one who earned £3 per year in freehold property or had £60 in total property. Senators were required to have £600 total property and representatives £200 of property. The governor, elected to a four-year term, had to have £1,000. The governor was a powerful executive. He could veto legislation, and he had the power to appoint all judicial officials and sheriffs. After debating the merits of the document and tinkering with aspects of it, the convention distributed hundreds of copies of the document on March 2, 1780 for consideration by special town meetings open to all males over twenty-one years of age in the state. By June the towns had responded, and the majority of voters had approved the constitution. Constitution-making in Massachusetts produced remarkable results: an elitist document – complete with property requirements, a bicameral legislature, and a strong executive – arrived at by democratic means – a special convention called for the purpose with the document submitted for the approval of all adult males in the state. Although Massachusetts was one of the slower states to act in reaching a constitutional settlement, its results proved durable. The Massachusetts constitution, which has been in effect since October 1780, is the longest continually functioning constitution in the world.[8]

The constitution-making experiences of Pennsylvania and Massachusetts reveal the diversity of republican experimentation in the various states during the revolutionary era. The procedures used also reveal the paradoxes of the constitution-making process. Pennsylvania's experiment with democratic government was undemocratically arrived at, while elitists in Massachusetts employed democratic means to win approval for an undemocratic government. In each of the new states, elitists and democrats vied to put their stamp on the structure of the government. Most of the new states adopted constitutional forms somewhat between the rapid radicalism of Pennsylvania and the slow conservatism of Massachusetts. In general terms, the state constitutions can be seen as democratic documents. They vested most power in the state legislatures, a direct legacy of the role the colonial assemblies had played in the resistance to Britain. Moreover, the authority of the new governments rested on the premise that the sovereignty of the people, the foundation of republican government, found its most appropriate expression in the states. The political and ideological struggles between elitists and democrats were not confined to the states, however. They also took place at the national level over the question of the institutional form the union of the sovereign states should take.

The Articles of Confederation

When Richard Henry Lee of Virginia introduced a resolution calling for the colonies to declare independence on June 7, 1776, he also introduced a resolution calling on Congress to frame "articles of confederation and perpetual union" for the colonies. Just as Congress created a committee to prepare a Declaration of Independence, so too on June 12 it created a committee of thirteen (with one representative from each colony) to prepare a plan to govern the former colonies after independence. John Dickinson of Pennsylvania chaired the committee to draft the articles. Dickinson, the celebrated author of *Letters from a Farmer in Pennsylvania*, had been an early supporter of American rights. By 1776 he was one of the more conservative voices in Congress. Dickinson had argued against independence, and when the crucial vote was taken in July he absented himself from Congress so that Pennsylvania could vote in the affirmative. Dickinson feared that independence would result in endless conflict between and among the newly autonomous colonies. As chair, he desired to create a confederation which would minimize the conflict between the states.[9]

Ironically, given his opposition to independence, John Dickinson was the main author of the first national constitution of the United States, the Articles of Confederation. Dickinson's draft articles were debated and discussed by the committee he chaired during the latter part of June 1776. A partially revised version of Dickinson's plan emerged from the committee and was submitted to Congress for debate on July 12. The Dickinson plan was an elitist document insofar as it was intended to create a powerful central government at the center of the American confederation. Under the proposed plan, Congress would act as the government of the United States and it would possess sole authority over war and peace, foreign relations, the resolution of intrastate conflicts and the disposition of western land. Most importantly, under the Dickinson plan, "the United States assembled shall never impose or levy any Taxes or Duties, except in managing the Post-Office, nor interfere in the internal Police of any Colony, any further than such Police may be affected by the Articles of Confederation."[10] These clauses, if adopted, would give Congress the authority to levy taxes and interfere in the internal politics of member states. Although these rights were limited to taxation in support of the post office and internal policing to uphold the articles, Americans had learned between 1765 and 1775 of the dangers posed when ambitious politicians set a seemingly minor precedent.

Over the next five weeks, in the midst of running the war, Congress debated the proposed articles. Several contentious issues, including representation, financing the war, and the disposition of western lands, emerged from the debate which revealed the differing interests of the various states. The congressmen differed over whether representation in Congress should be apportioned equally with each state casting one vote (the system used since 1774 and favored by the small states) or by population (favored by the larger states). Northern and southern states disagreed as to whether the cost of the war should be apportioned by total population, including slaves (favored by the northern delegations) or only by the free population (a system favored by the southern states.) Perhaps most crucially, all those states without claims to western lands (Rhode Island, New Jersey, Maryland, and Delaware) favored that the western lands claimed by the other states be treated as a national domain for the benefit of the whole country which could be sold to discharge the growing national debt.

The congressmen were unable to settle these thorny issues, and abandoned their debate on the articles on August 20, 1776. Congress did not turn its attention to the articles again until April 1777 when Thomas Burke, a delegate from North Carolina, proposed that "all sovereign power was in the states separately, and that particular acts of it [Congress], which should be expressly enumerated, would be exercised in conjunction, and not otherwise; but that in all things else each State would exercise all the rights and power of sovereignty, uncontrolled."[11] Along with other changes, Burke's amendment, which would eventually become the second article of the final document reading, "Each state retains its sovereignty, freedom and independence, and every Power, Jurisdiction and right, which is not by this confederation expressly delegated to the United States," transformed the proposed articles from an elitist to a democratic document. Under the revised proposal, the states would retain their political authority and their supremacy. The articles would not create a strong central government which could threaten the liberties of ordinary Americans.

Congress did not return to the Articles of Confederation in earnest until October 1777. Ultimately, the lawmakers elected to keep voting in Congress according to the one state, one vote rule which they had used since 1774; they neglected to give Congress the power to settle the western boundaries of the states, and they created a complicated formula to apportion financial responsibility for the war. On November 15, 1777 Congress endorsed the Articles of Confederation, stipulating that they would only come into force when ratified by all the states. (Subsequent amendments would also require unanimous approval by the states.) After fifteen months of on-again, off-again deliberations, Congress had watered down Dickinson's original plan. Power in the national government would be vested in a unicameral Confederation Congress. On most matters, majority voting (with each state equally represented) would prevail. On critical issues related to war, peace and finance, a two-thirds majority (nine states) was required. The Articles essentially codified what Congress had been doing since 1775. Unlike Dickinson's original plan, the articles created a relatively weak central government. Crucially, the Confederation government had no independent executive or judiciary and no power to levy taxes or raise revenue. The diplomatic authority vested in the government was limited as well. Experience would show that a central government without the power to raise revenue was a weak entity indeed.

After Congress submitted the Articles of Confederation to the states, its members acted on the assumption that they would be ratified and behaved as if the new constitution was in force. Ratification was not, however, a simple matter. The legislatures of each of the states considered the document critically. Despite concerns over specific articles, by July 1778, ten of the thirteen states had either approved of the document or pledged to do so. The three recalcitrant states were New Jersey, Delaware, and Maryland, all small states without western land interests. The assemblies in these states objected to the failure of the articles to create a national domain in the west. New Jersey and Delaware relented under protest in 1779 and ratified. Eventually, in part because the "landed" states with western claims had begun to relinquish those claims (see below), Maryland finally acquiesced and ratified in February 1781. The Articles of Confederation officially took effect on March 1, 1781.

The confederation

The United States was governed by the terms of the articles from 1781 until 1789. The confederation era saw the successful conclusion of the War of Independence. The Articles of Confederation created a relatively weak federal government. To the extent the power was decentralized under the articles, they can be seen as a victory for those who favored a democratic republican model. Under the articles, sovereignty within the union largely remained within the member states of the union. The difficulties posed in ratifying the articles revealed one of their most significant flaws, the requirement of unanimity to amend the plan. The triumph of the democrats would be short-lived. Apparent weaknesses in the Confederation were revealed during the 1780s and resulted in a movement by elitist republicans to amend and ultimately replace the articles. This movement would result in the creation of a stronger federal constitution and the triumph of an elitist republican model for the government of the United States.

The origins of the failure of the articles of Confederation lay in the difficulties which faced the United States in the aftermath of the war. The major problem which confronted the nation concerned public finance. The political implications of this issue produced social unrest which, at least in the minds of elitist politicians, undermined the viability of the Confederation.

When the Articles of Confederation took effect, the new government not only lacked the power to tax but it inherited a huge debt necessitated by the ongoing war, and a nearly worthless currency. The problems were actually interrelated. Because of the war, Congress had been forced to undertake costly expenditures in order to secure American independence. Without the power to tax, Congress issued paper money and promissory notes which, predicated as they were on the survival of the United States, proved to be a very unstable and increasingly depreciated currency. Because Congress could not tax, it relied on the states to meet requisitions in order to pay for the war. Unfortunately, the various states, which did have the authority to tax their citizens, faced similar financial problems, accumulating their own war debts while issuing their own currencies which undermined the Continental currency and contributed to the overall financial instability of the new states. Consequently, currency reform, taxation, and finance were among the most pressing issues during the Confederation era. They pitted elitists and democrats against each other, and undermined support for the Articles of Confederation.[12]

Apart from the its toll in human suffering and property loss, the War of Independence had been a costly undertaking. Between 1775 and 1780, Congress issued $241 million to pay for the cost of the war against Britain. The money was based on the assumption that the states would raise appropriate revenue by taxation to cover the value of the currency printed. Paper money was essentially a means of borrowing against the future. In so doing, Congress was relying on a tried and trusted method employed by the various colonies during previous conflicts. The revolutionary emissions of paper money, however, were far in excess of prior issuances. Because Congress lacked the power to tax, the Continental currency was very unstable and depreciated rapidly. By 1781 it required more than $167 Continental to purchase $1 worth of specie. The result of congressional emissions of paper money was runaway inflation and rapidly rising prices. Congress not only issued paper money to pay for the war, it also secured loans from friendly European governments. During the course of the conflict, Spain, the Netherlands, and especially France loaned the United States $2.2 million in specie, most of which was used to purchase supplies for the rebels. Congress also borrowed from the American people, to whom it sold $60 million in loan certificates (essentially war bonds) which it promised to repay with modest interest. Finally, Continental officers had been issued millions of dollars worth of supply certificates to American farmers and merchants during the war. These certificates were also issued to Continental soldiers in lieu of backpay and enlistment bounties. All told, these promissory notes committed Congress to finding an additional $95 million.[13]

In addition to Congressional expenses and debts, each of the states had also undertaken similar initiatives to finance their individual contributions to the war effort. Like the national government, the states had also issued paper money during the war. State monetary emissions further undermined the value of all paper money and contributed to rising prices and hyper-inflation. The states had a distinct financial advantage over Congress: they could tax their citizens. Initially, given that the Revolution had begun over disputes concerning taxation, the states were reluctant to exercise this power, but eventually the economic hardships of the war compelled the states to tax. Despite this initial reluctance, the various state governments imposed far heavier tax burdens on their citizens than even the most greedy British minister had ever envisioned. In Rhode Island, for example, the prewar government had operated on tax revenues of approximately £4,000. In 1777, the revolutionary government collected £96,000 in taxes and a further £94,000 in 1778. Similarly, Pennsylvania collected £5 million in taxes during 1778–9, whereas before the war the old proprietary govern-ment had never collected more than £34,000. The taxes were not popular and in some states there was resistance, sometimes violent, among hard-pressed taxpayers who suffered under wartime hardships. For many these hardships would continue after the peace, as the state and national governments grappled with their considerable debts.[14]

Because of rapid currency depreciation and the wide variety of currencies in circulation, it is nearly impossible to estimate accurately the level of public debt at the end of the War of Independence. In mid-1781 the value of the Continental dollar finally collapsed and Congress abandoned all hope of reviving it. Those who possessed Continental dollars were left with worthless paper. At a stroke, approximately $226 million of the inflated paper debt disappeared.[15] What remained were the debts that Congress felt had to be honored if the United States were to survive: loans (foreign and domestic), as well as the pledges issued by the army and securities issued to veterans. In 1782 Robert Morris, the congressional Superintendent of Finance, estimated the national debt to be worth $27 million in specie. Although Morris wanted Congress to assume this debt as a means of strengthening the power of the national government, according to the Articles of Confederation "all charges of war and all other expenses that shall be incurred for the common defense or general welfare," should have been "defrayed out of a common treasury, which shall be supplied by the several states." In consequence, responsibility for the war debt lay with the states of the Confederation.

Servicing their own debts was the largest financial burden which faced the states during the Confederation period. In 1786 South Carolina, for example, paid £83,184 in interest on its debt out of a total expenditure of £103,526. Accordingly, the states resorted to taxation to discharge their debts.[16] Debt and taxation raised several questions with economic, political and social significance. In North Carolina and Virginia, for example, land was taxed uniformly by the acre regardless of the value of the land or its productivity. This meant that poorer farmers on unproductive land actually bore a disproportionate tax burden. Other states resorted to poll taxes, which again placed a disproportionate share of the burden of payment on the poor. The difficulties and inequities of increased taxation were exacerbated when speculators bought up most of the debt at reduced rates. Penurious war veterans often sold their bonus and discharge certificates at a fraction of their value because they could not afford to wait for the states to make good on them. Many taxpayers felt they were being asked to bear a disproportionate tax burden to the benefit of speculators rather than the patriotic men who had risked their lives to secure American independence. Despite these difficulties some states, such as Virginia and New York, successfully discharged their debts during the 1780s.

In all states the issue of debt service, and more importantly the taxation which it required, touched off conflicts between elitists and democrats. The primary financial issue which separated elitists and democrats during the Confederation was paper money. With the collapse of the Continental currency in 1781, there was a desperate shortage of money in the states. In most states the debtors were farmers, the majority of the population, who generally lacked the specie necessary to pay their taxes and private debts. In some states, programs of tax and debt relief were adopted. In others, tax abatement measures were implemented to postpone the day of reckoning. Debtors, particularly farmers, agitated for the states to issue more paper money with which they could pay their debts. Creditors opposed such measures; they sought the prompt payment of public and private debts in specie. They contended that paper money emissions would lead to inflation and economic instability, and sought the adoption of measures to compel debtors to pay: including auctioning the assets and imprisoning of insolvent debtors.

In general, elitists tended to support hard-money policies which favored creditors. They contended that such policies, while perhaps bitter medicine, had to be taken if the states were to enjoy financial stability and prosperity. If speculators held the public debt it must still be honored, because the men who had the capital to speculate were just the men whose support, the elitists felt, was needed by the fragile new governments. In many cases the elitists were speculators and creditors themselves, and had a vested financial interest in the hard-money programs they espoused. Democrats, often from poorer rural areas, favored paper money. They felt that hard-pressed farmers, many of whom were veterans, simply could not afford to pay their taxes and debts in specie: to force them to do was impossible and unjust. They recognized that paper money would lead to inflation which would favor the debtor at the expense of the creditor, but since many of the debtors were veterans who had sold their securities at cut-rate prices to speculators, they felt there was little injustice in such an outcome. In one state, Massachusetts, disagreements over taxation and debt led to a fatal confrontation between the two groups.

Shays's Rebellion

Massachusetts had a paper debt of £11 million in 1780, most of which was due to be paid by 1785. In the spring of 1780 the outgoing provincial congress voted to postpone payment on the debt until 1788. When a new legislature, which was dominated by elitist representatives from the commercially-oriented eastern counties of the state, was elected under the constitution of 1780 and began sitting late in the year, it repealed this moratorium. It also called for the liquidation of the state's debt by declaring that the state's paper notes should be exchanged for new ones at face value. This move benefited speculators, who had accumulated the notes at a fraction of their cost. When all the notes were exchanged, the remainder of the debt consisted of promissory notes given to former soldiers and to merchants and farmers. The Massachusetts legislature levied heavy taxes to pay the balance of the debt, and mandated that the taxes should be paid in specie. Between 1780 and 1786 the state collected £1.9 million in taxes, most of which went to funding the state debt and paying congressional requisitions. As a result of this program, taxes in the state averaged $43 per person per year and nearly $200 per head of family. The tax burden was not distributed equitably. Property-less males were expected to pay more than £1 via a poll tax regardless of their ability to pay. All told, the poll tax accounted for 33 to 40 percent of the state's tax revenue, and it was especially difficult for poor farmers lacking in specie to meet.[17]

The tax burden was especially difficult to bear because of the acute lack of specie in the state. In the immediate aftermath of the war there was an increase in trans-Atlantic trade, as American merchants revived their trading relationships with their former British partners (and struck up relationships with their new European friends). The result was an influx of European goods on the American market and the flow of precious specie from America to Britain. Although American artisans opposed this trade, on the whole American consumers welcomed it. Among the latter were the small farmers of the interior who purchased imported goods retailed at country stores. In the middle years of the 1780s, the fragile American economies suffered a downturn (in part because of the instability of the American currencies and poor public finance). In consequence, European merchants called in the debts of their American partners, who in turn did the same to their customers, often small retailers, who in turn called in the debts of *their* customers, usually small farmers. Faced with mounting private debts, an increasingly heavy tax burden for their states' public debts, and a shortage of specie, many farmers and small property-holders became increasingly desperate.

By 1786, in the face of widespread rural discontent – violent protests and demonstrations had taken place in a number of states – seven states yielded to popular pressure and began to issue paper money and institute debt relief programs which included stay laws to postpone debt payments, measures to reduce court and legal fees, and valuation laws which required creditors to give debtors fair value for their property. Elitists despaired as democrats in the other states agitated for similar measures. To them, it seemed that the American experiment in republican government had given way to anarchy and the destruction of private property. In Massachusetts, the elitist-oriented administration of governor James Bowdoin refused to endorse paper money and debt relief. Consequently, in Hampshire County a third of the adult males were sued for debt between 1784 and 1786. Over 3,000 debt cases were prosecuted in the county during the same period (a 262 percent increase over prewar prosecutions for debt). When sued, debtors faced the prospect of paying their outstanding debts as well as court costs. If they could not, their property could be auctioned by the county sheriff and the debtors imprisoned. In Worcester County, located in the center of the state, 92 of the 103 men in custody in 1785 had been jailed for debt.[18]

Many of the farmers and townsmen of central and western Massachusetts, the men who had come to Boston's assistance in 1774 and had fought for American independence during the war, were frustrated and angry at the lack of support they received from their government. The Revolution had taught these men that when a government was non-responsive to the needs and rights of its citizens, they must organize to defend their liberties. In consequence, debtors in western Massachusetts held town meetings and county conventions to discuss their grievances. When their petitions fell on deaf ears, men, often veterans and members of the local militia, took up arms to close the county courts during the late summer of 1786. If the courts could not sit, they could not prosecute debtors. To the protesters, these actions were a logical means of defending their liberty and property. To the elitists in the government and their supporters, the actions of the debtors were indefensible. Massachusetts had a duly elected government and courts which were charged with enforcing the law. Stable government and private property rested on the rule of law which the citizens of the commonwealth, whether they were debtors or creditors, were obliged to respect if a republican government were to have any meaning. Democrats and elitists, with differing conceptions of the meaning of republicanism, were headed towards a confrontation.

The disturbances in Massachusetts are usually called Shays's Rebellion, after Daniel Shays, a revolutionary war veteran from Pelham, Massachusetts. Shays led some of the men who closed the courts in Springfield, Massachusetts in late September. He was among several men from localities across Massachusetts who took a leading role in the events. The elitists in Boston were not to be cowed by the supporters of Shays and his peers. The state organized and financed an army of more than four thousand men under General Benjamin Lincoln to suppress the demonstrations and reopen the courts. In so doing, it transformed what had been a series of political protests into a rebellion. On January 25, 1787 between seven and eight hundred rebel militiamen led by Daniel Shays attempted to capture the state armory at Springfield. The armory was defended by as many as 1,200 loyal militiamen, who were well-armed and possessed artillery. As the Shaysites marched towards the armory, the loyal militia fired. The Shaysites fled, leaving four dead – three rebels and one defender – in their wake. Over the next few months Lincoln's army skirmished with rebels at Petersham and the rebellion, such as it was, collapsed. Although the "Friends of Government" celebrated their victory, their joy was to be short-lived. The following year voters elected John Hancock as governor along with many new legislators. A wealthy merchant, Hancock had long been allied with those who wanted a democratic model of a republic. Working with the new legislature, Hancock ushered in a program of debt relief and most of the rebels were pardoned. Democrats saw in Shays's rebellion the specter of tyranny as the government resorted to force to impose unpopular measures on its citizens. For elitists, the uprising signaled the dangers of dema-goguery and anarchy when the rules of law and sound government were ignored.[19]

Conclusion

The denouement of Shays's Rebellion reveals the paradox of postwar American politics. The debate over what form the American republics should take divided those Americans who previously agreed on the issue of independence into those for favored a more democratic model of decentral-ized government, and those elitists who favored a more centralized model where power was vested in the hands of the wealthy and well-educated. These differences were of emphasis. Each group believed that sovereignty was derived from the governed and that the leading men in American society should play a prominent public role. John Hancock, after all, the "democrat" elected governor in the wake of Shays's Rebellion, was among the wealthiest men in Massachusetts. While he and other patricians who sympathized with a more democratic model of republic felt that the men who participated in Shays's Rebellion could and should play a greater role in government, they would not have countenanced electing such men to high political office. The Shaysites and like-minded men throughout America, however, believed that they were capable of wielding political power. They believed they had earned the right to participate fully in government during the war, and they felt it was incumbent that they defend their interests.

The militancy of the Shaysites and their peers in other states frightened elitists. They felt that democratic excesses in the states and the weaknesses of the Confederation endangered the American experiment in republicanism. In consequence, they set about first to reform and then to replace the Articles of Confederation. This movement, which ultimately succeeded, is the subject of the next chapter.

6

CREATING THE CONSTITUTION

Introduction

From the perspective of elitist republicans, Shays's Rebellion and its aftermath epitomized the failure of government as it was practiced in the states. They felt that the popular discord in Massachusetts and other states was the result of excessively democratic governments. Congress, rendered weak by the Articles of Confederation, had lost much of its popular support since the conclusion of the War of Independence, and was largely impotent in remedying the situation. From his retirement at Mount Vernon, George Washington gave his assessment of recent events in a letter to Virginia Congressman Richard Henry Lee on October 31, 1786:

> You talk, my good sir, of employing influence to appease the present tumults in Massachusetts. I know not where that influence is to be found, or, if attainable, that it would be proper remedy to the disorders. *Influence* is no *government*. Let us have one by which our lives, liberties, and properties will be secured, or let us know the worst at once. Under these impressions, my humble opinion is, that there is a call for decision. Know precisely what the insurgents aim at. If they have *real* grievances, redress them if possible; or acknowledge the justice of them, and your inability to do it in the present moment. If they have not, employ the force of government against them at once. If this is inadequate *all* will be convinced that the superstructure is bad, or wants support. To be more exposed in the eyes of the world, and more contemptible than we already are, is hardly possible.[1]

Washington's comments constitute a perceptive elitist analysis of the postwar American political situation. The general concedes that Shaysites' grievances may have been legitimate. He argues, however, that the uprising revealed a more significant problem of inadequate government. If the

111

Shaysites were correct, then the Massachusetts authorities and Congress had failed in their duty to govern properly and to protect the liberty of their citizens. If the grievances of the Shaysites were not legitimate, then the state and national governments were inadequate to the task of preserving order and justice. The problem was one of governance, and Washington felt that the Articles of Confederation had to undergo significant amendment if the revolution was to be preserved.

He was not alone. By the mid-1780s, a majority of American political leaders, both democrats and elitists, felt that reform of the national government was necessary. They differed, however, over the extent of the necessary changes. In general, democrats favored minimal reforms; they sought to tinker with the Articles of Confederation in order to strengthen the national government, while the preponderance of sovereignty remained with the states which made up the Confederation. The elitists, on the other hand, favored more substantial changes. Many of the elitists, men such as Robert Morris of Pennsylvania, who served as Superintendent of Finance under the Confederation from 1781 to 1784, Alexander Hamilton, who represented New York in Congress in 1782 and 1783, and James Madison of Virginia, who had served in Congress from 1780 to 1783, had experience in national politics during the years when the national government was in apparent decline and political authority was mainly exercised at the state level. They saw in the political upheavals of the 1780s an opportunity to recapture the political momentum and to create a strong national government which would have the power to curb the democratic excesses of the states at home while defending and promoting American interests abroad.[2] The elitists seized the reform initiative and ultimately overturned the Articles of Confederation, replacing them with a more durable Constitution.

The movement for reform

The impetus for political reform had two sources: the apparent democratic excesses of the states discussed in the previous chapter, and the perceived weakness of the national government under the Confederation. With respect to the former, the elitists had little choice but to fight at the local level where they found themselves at a disadvantage. As British policy-makers had learned a generation before, American assemblies jealously protected their rights and prerogatives. In the more democratic atmosphere in the wake of the War of Independence, this was even more true than in the decade before the war. Under the best of circumstances, it was unlikely that popularly elected state governments would willingly agree to curbs on their authority or to surrender a significant measure of their sovereignty. As events in Massachusetts revealed, when state governments undertook unpopular measures they faced the specter of rebellion or defeat at the polls. Given that those Americans who favored the implementation of more elitist-oriented governments sought to limit popular political control, they were unlikely to meet with much success in the states where that control was strongest. Rather, they looked to the central government, the Confederation Congress, to seek remedies for the country's political ills.

The Continental, later Confederation, Congress had had a schizophrenic existence. Beginning in May 1775 when the Second Continental Congress began sitting at Philadelphia, it acted as the *de facto* national government of the rebellious colonies. Congress assumed this role out of the necessity of war. In the main, the men who sat in Congress acquitted themselves well during the rebellion. They took the decision to declare the colonies independent, assuming responsibility for diplomacy as well as financing and managing the war against Britain. Despite obvious handicaps, notably the inability to tax, unstable finances, diplomatic uncertainty, the presence of large numbers of Americans who denied and resisted its authority, and a foe which was better equipped and trained than its own force, the congressional effort was successful. The United States won its independence and Congress, along with its creation the Continental Army, was the only national institution with which Americans could identify. Despite its achievements, however, the authority of Congress steadily diminished after 1783. With the arrival of peace the states no longer felt the necessity of cooperating with each other or with Congress. In consequence, a once-respected institution became increasingly weak and moribund. By the mid-1780s, American finances were in disarray, and by 1786 the United States had suspended the repayment of its loans from France, Spain, and the Netherlands. The crisis in national government revealed by financial difficulties was also reflected in the nation's diplomatic relations. The British made a mockery of the Peace of Paris and the Northwest Ordinances by continuing to occupy their forts in the Northwest. The Spanish, meanwhile, refused to allow American settlers the right to navigate the Mississippi in order to market their crops. In the face of these difficulties, Congress could not protect and promote American interests. An institution which had acted as midwife at the birth of the United States had been rendered powerless by the indifference and contempt of its creation.[3]

The Articles of Confederation limited the options of those who sought to reform the national government from within. The Articles could only be amended with the unanimous agreement of all thirteen states. For example, when Superintendent of Finance Robert Morris proposed that Congress secure its own revenue by collecting a duty on imports, the states dithered for nearly four years before the proposal died for lack of unanimous support. Members of Congress recognized the need for reform. In May 1786, Charles Cotesworth Pinckney of South Carolina proposed that Congress create a committee to review national affairs and propose amendments to the Articles of Confederation. The committee labored throughout the summer, and in August it proposed new articles which would create a federal court to oversee the actions of the states, give Congress a limited authority to tax and regulate trade, and diminish the number of states required to approve new articles from thirteen to eleven. Congress never acted on the proposals. Had it done so, it is unlikely that all thirteen states would have agreed to such changes. Under the articles, Congress was unable to take steps which its members felt were in the best interests of the country.

Had they been approved, the amendments to the articles proposed by Congress would have been met with skepticism for a number of reasons. Not only did the states jealously defend their rights, but many Americans of the revolutionary era questioned whether governments and office-holders should initiate constitutional reform. At the state level, a model of constitution-making had evolved whereby new frames of government were drafted by special conventions and submitted to the people, often a broader spectrum than those traditionally allowed to vote, for popular ratification. There was no reason that the same process could not be tried at the national level. The Constitutional Convention should be seen, therefore, not as an illegal conclave but the culmination of the series of extralegal meetings which began with the Stamp Act Congress of 1765.

The immediate origins of the Constitutional Convention lay in a dispute between Virginia and Maryland over the navigation of the Potomac River. Such intramural disagreements were not uncommon during the 1780s, and the national government was largely powerless to act as an arbitrator in them. In March 1784 James Madison, then a member of the Virginia assembly, proposed that commissioners from the two states meet to negotiate a solution. Representatives from the two states were hosted by George Washington at his estate at Mount Vernon on March 25, 1785. The delegates agreed on questions of jurisdiction and navigation of the Potomac. They then went beyond their brief and suggested that their states should cooperate on financial and customs policy, and they recommended that an appeal should be made to Pennsylvania to join in future deliberations on such matters of common interest. Madison, who had previously served in Congress and witnessed its ineffectiveness at first hand, saw an opportunity for interstate cooperation for constitutional reform in the meeting. In the wake of the events at Mount Vernon, he proposed a resolution to the Virginia assembly for a national convention to meet at Annapolis, Maryland in 1786 to discuss commercial regulations.

The Annapolis Convention, which met from September 11–14, 1786, was a mixed success. Although eight states expressed interest in the meeting, in the end delegates from only five attended. In practical terms, a meeting of such an unrepresentative body could not propose reforms, commercial or otherwise, to the nation with any credibility. But the meeting at Annapolis did bring together elitist republicans from across the country, who agreed on the urgent need for constitutional change. They resolved to build on their meeting by calling for an additional meeting to be held at Philadelphia the following spring. The purpose of the Philadelphia meeting was made clear in a public address adopted by the Annapolis Convention. The address stated that the delegates to the convention at Philadelphia should "devise such provisions as shall appear to them necessary to render the Constitution of the Federal Government adequate to the exigencies of the Union." The Annapolis Address was the handiwork of Alexander Hamilton of New York, a successful lawyer and leading elitist. The delegates at Annapolis intended that the Philadelphia meeting should initiate wholesale constitutional change. Congress acquiesced to this purpose on February 21, 1787 when it endorsed the meeting at Philadelphia, "for the sole and express purpose of revising the Articles of Confederation." During the summer of 1787, the Constitutional Convention would produce a constitutional plan which would supersede and overturn the articles.

Anti-democratic revolutionaries

Because of the endurance of the constitutional settlement which emerged from its deliberations, admirers of the Constitution have largely endorsed the view of Thomas Jefferson, who described the Constitutional Convention as "an assembly of demigods." According to this view, the "Founding Fathers" intervened at the crucial moment to save the American Revolution. They thus re-launched the American republic and laid the foundation its expansion and democratization during the nineteenth and twentieth centuries. Critics of the Constitution see the convention that produced the document as a conclave of self-interested elitists who sought undermine the democratic principles of the Declaration of Independence in order to safeguard the interests of the wealthy. For some, the Constitution represents a counter-revolutionary subversion of American liberty. In truth (and apparent contradiction), the convention and Constitution it produced were anti-democratic *and* revolutionary.[5]

There is no question that most of the men who gathered in Philadelphia were anti-democratic. Before the meeting, former Continental Army general Henry Knox declared "mad democracy sweeps away every moral trait from the human character," and that the Convention "should clip the wings of mad democracy." Within the convention, Elbridge Gerry of Massachusetts declared, "the evils we experience flow from the excess of democracy." Virginia's Edmund Randolph clearly stated the purpose of the convention when he "observed that the general object was to provide a cure for the evils under which the U.S. labored; that in tracing these evils to their origin every man had found it in the turbulence and follies of democracy."[6] Although anti-democratic, the movement for constitutional reform was not counter-revolutionary, as some historians have suggested. Indeed, if George Washington, who was to lead the new elitist republic, is to be believed then the elitists sought to prevent a counter-revolution. He wrote in August of 1786:

> I am told that even respectable characters speak of a monarchical form of government without horror. From thinking proceeds speaking; thence to acting is often but a single step. But how irrevocable and tremendous! What a triumph for our enemies to verify their predictions! What a triumph for the advocates of despotism to find that we are incapable of governing ourselves, and that systems founded on the basis of equal liberty are merely ideal and fallacious! Would to God that wise measures may be taken in time to avert the consequences we have but too much reason to apprehend.[7]

Most delegates at the convention, like elitist republicans across the United States, believed that the nation's problems sprung from the democratic excesses of the states, and that the antidote to these difficulties would be to erect a national government powerful enough to counter the force of popular will. This is what they set out to accomplish at Philadelphia.

The anti-democratic tendencies of the framers of the Constitution need to be placed in the context of eighteenth-century republicanism. According to the political ideas which circulated in the Anglo-American political world, the most stable governments were those which mixed and balanced the interests of society. The unwritten British constitution achieved this (when it functioned properly) by balancing the elements of monarchical (in the person of the king), aristocratic (in the House of Lords), and democratic (in the House of Commons) government. Whenever one or the other element predominated, it was believed, liberty was under threat. Having eliminated the monarchical element from their society, Americans faced the difficulty of constructing enduring republics. At stake was the outcome of the Revolution and the survival of liberty. In 1787, Benjamin Rush of Pennsylvania reflected back on the constitutional experiments since 1776 and observed, "Although we understood perfectly the principles of Liberty yet most of us were ignorant of the forms and combinations of power in republics." The crucial distinction, therefore, was between a properly designed republic which protected liberty and democracy which would eventually endanger it. Excessive democracy was as dangerous as the monarchical tyranny from which Americans had just freed themselves. Writing in 1807, John Adams tried to explain the difference: "I was always for a free republic, not a democracy, which is as arbitrary, tyrannical, bloody, cruel, and intolerable a government as that of Phalaris with his bull is represented to have been." The purpose of the Philadelphia convention was to perfect those forms so as to safeguard liberty and consolidate the achievements of the Revolution.[8]

There was, of course, an alternative view. There were American republicans who felt that the chief danger to liberty lay in the creation of a strong, centralized government which vested power in the hands of a few. These were republicans, whom we have described as democrats, not because they favored the type of excessive democracy described by Adams, but because they felt the American republics must have a high degree of popular input if liberty were to be preserved. The elitists, conversely, accepted that some degree of popular participation was necessary in a republic. As James Wilson, the Scots-born delegate to the Constitutional Convention from Pennsylvania, explained, "No government could long subsist without the confidence of the people. In a republican Government this confidence was peculiarly essential." Nonetheless, elitists felt that popular participation should be limited. Elitists lacked faith in the ability of the common people to exercise careful judgment. Elbridge Gerry explained, "The people do not want virtue, but are the dupes of pretended patriots."[9] The difference between the elite- and democratically-inclined republicans was not over whether America should be a republic, but over how much popular influence there should be in the republic. In a crucial miscalculation, the democrats largely abstained from participating in the Constitutional Convention, believing that because the Articles of Confederation could not be amended except by unanimous decision, they could block any proposals they found distasteful. In consequence, they left it to the elitists to set the agenda on political reform.

The Constitutional Convention

The Constitutional Convention – or Federal Convention, as it was known at the time – was scheduled to begin its deliberations on May 17, 1787. When the appointed day arrived, the delegations of only two states – Pennsylvania, the hosts, and Virginia, which had taken the lead in proposing the convention – were present. Poor weather and poorer roads delayed the arrival of the other delegates. The Virginia delegation contained two of the most important delegates to the conclave, George Washington and James Madison. Washington was probably the most famous and respected man in America. His success commanding the rebel forces during the recent War of Independence had won him nearly universal acclaim. He rose still further in the public's esteem at the end of the war when, like a modern-day Cincinnatus, he relinquished his command, submitted to civilian authority and retired from public life. To many Americans, Washington embodied the selfless virtue which they believed was essential to a successful republic. Although his political ideas were unknown to most Americans, the general's presence lent immediate credibility to the convention and its work.

Thirty-six-year-old James Madison was not well known to most of his countrymen, or at least not to those who were not Virginians. Nonetheless he, more than any other man, would have the greatest impact on the events which were about to unfold. Intellectually gifted, Madison was educated at Princeton. Although frail health prevented him from undertaking military service during the war, Madison had assisted the rebel effort in his native Virginia through extensive public service. He served in the Virginia Convention which severed the state's ties with Britain and created one of the earliest state constitutions. While representing the state in Congress during the early 1780s, Madison became acutely aware of the limitations of the Articles of Confederation, which convinced him of the urgent need to strengthen the national government. Madison spent the winter of 1786–7 intently studying the history and theory of republican government. He came to the convention not only with a clear idea of what was wrong with America but also of how to fix it. In April 1787 he wrote a lengthy memorandum entitled "The Vices of the Political System of the United States," in which he outlined the defects in the present government and his proposed remedy for those defects: the creation of a powerful national republic with a centralized government. In anticipation of the meeting, he circulated his memo among prospective delegates. As such, he set the agenda for the convention. William Pierce, who represented Georgia at the convention, aptly summarized the role played by the Virginian: "In the management of every great question he evidently took the lead in the Convention." The Georgian continued, "he always comes forward the best informed Man of any point in debate."[10] While waiting for the delegates from the other states, Madison met in caucus with Virginia's representatives – Washington, George Wythe, John Blair, John McClurg, Edmund Randolph, and George Mason – in order to outline and sell his plan for a stronger federal union. By the time the other delegates arrived the Virginians were ready to dominate the opening stages of the convention.

By Friday, May 25, 1787, twenty-nine delegates from seven states had arrived giving the convention a quorum. Over the next few weeks a further twenty-six delegates straggled in. Each of the thirteen states which had declared independence in 1776, with the exception of Rhode Island, was represented in convention. All told, fifty-five delegates attended the gathering. Most had been selected by their states' legislatures. The delegates brought a broad range of experience in public service to the meeting. All fifty-five had held public office: forty-two had served in the Continental or Confederation Congresses, seven were sitting or former governors, and eight were judges in their home states. Twenty of the delegates had helped to draft their state's constitution. The delegates, therefore, had practical experience of the strengths and limitations of republican government in America as it had been experimented with at the state and national levels. They also brought a high level of energy and commitment to their deliberations. Although there were several older delegates at the meeting such as the eighty-one-year-old Benjamin Franklin and Connecticut's Roger Sherman, who was sixty-six, most of the delegates who took a leading role in the deliberations were in the their thirties and early forties.[11]

Whether or not the delegates to the Constitutional Convention were Jefferson's "assembly of demigods," they were certainly a remarkable group. There were notable omissions from the convention's ranks, including Jefferson (who was representing the United States in France) and John Adams (who was representing the United States in Britain). Leading "democratic" politicians such as Patrick Henry of Virginia eschewed the convention because they did not agree with its purpose. More significant were those who were not represented at all at the convention. The delegates to the Constitutional Convention were assuredly not a cross-section of the four million Americans in 1787. There were of course no women delegates to the convention. The six hundred thousand African Americans (most of whom were still enslaved) had no representatives: rather, they had to rely on the good will of the thirty-six delegates who had no slaves and the willingness to compromise of the nineteen delegates who owned black bondsmen and women. Native Americans too were unrepresented at the convention. Despite the fact that tens of thousands of Indians lived within the borders of United States, the framers of the Constitution never seriously considered including Native Americans in the revolutionary political settlement. In so doing, they closely followed colonial precedents. As Gregory Evans Dowd has recently noted, "if in the 1780s American citizens failed to see Indians as potential citizens, so British subjects in the 1760s generally refused to see Indians as British subjects." During the colonial period, Indians had been excluded from public life and marginalized as dangerous outsiders. The framers of the Constitution continued this regrettable tradition and denied the right of citizenship to Indians under the Constitution produced by the convention.[12]

The exclusion of women, African Americans and Indians from the Constitutional Convention is not particularly remarkable. By tradition, law and custom, all of these groups were outside the recognized polity – be it imperial or republican – in eighteenth-century America. Common white men – the small farmers, artisans, sailors, traders, and laborers – had, however, won an increased voice in American politics since the Stamp Act. It was primarily by their efforts that independence had been won. As a result of their contributions, the average white male head of household had won a greater voice in his own government. There were no common men at the Constitutional Convention. Twenty-six of the delegates were college graduates, thirty-four were lawyers, three were physicians, and the balance were large planters and merchants. Although there were self-made men like Benjamin Franklin among the delegates, all enjoyed economic success above the norm. The delegates were as elite as the political outlook which most of them shared.

During its first days the Constitutional Convention took two important procedural decisions. On May 25, George Washington was elected the president of the convention which would certainly help win public support for outcome of the meeting. Three days later, the convention decided that its deliberations would be kept secret. There would be no public account of the convention during the meeting (or for years afterwards). This decision encouraged frank discussion and prevented those who were politically opposed to the meeting from marshaling their opposition. It also meant that the public would be kept in the dark until the convention had a formal proposal to lay before it. Since one objective of the meeting was to limit democracy within the United States, such an approach had clear advantages. Also on May 28, it was decided that the voting in the convention would be conducted as it had been in Congress: that is, each state delegation would have one vote.

Having dealt with procedural matters, the convention got down to its work in earnest on Tuesday, May 29. That day, Governor Edmund Randolph of Virginia rose and delivered a lengthy speech in which he reviewed the troubles which had plagued the country in recent years including the proliferation of paper money, the rebellion in Massachusetts, and the commercial discord among the states. He noted that many of these problems stemmed from the "the democratic parts of our [state] constitutions." He further noted that the Confederation government was largely powerless to remedy these difficulties. In consequence, Randolph submitted a series of fifteen resolutions which would create a new, stronger, federal government. The content of Randolph's resolutions, known as the Virginia Plan, were largely the handiwork of James Madison. Madison's plan, if adopted, would radically alter the government of the United States by replacing the Confederation government with one modeled after the elitist state constitutions like that of Massachusetts. Under the Virginia Plan, the new government would be divided into three branches: legislative, judicial, and executive. The legislature would have two houses, both to be elected according to population. The first house of the legislature would be directly elected by the voters in the states. The members of the second house would be elected from among those of the first. The legislature would have the authority to adopt national laws, to negate laws adopted by the individual states, and to tax. The judiciary would be elected by the legislature and would arbitrate disputes between the states and oversee the collection of federal revenue. The government would have a plural executive elected from among the legislature, which would be charged with executing the laws adopted by the legislature. Madison's plan also had a provision which called for the creation of a Council of Revision, elected from among the members of executive and judiciary. The council would review all legislative acts whether adopted by the national legislature or the states, and it could exercise a veto over these acts.[13]

Madison's thinking, as reflected in the Virginia Plan, combined elements of the traditional and the new. The tripartite separation of power in the plan, derived from the British constitution and tested at the state level, had become common by 1787. The size and scope of Madison's proposed republic government, however, flew in the face of the theory and practice. It was a commonplace of eighteenth-century republican thinking, derived from Montesquieu's *Spirit of the Laws*, that a successful republic must be confined to a relatively small geographic area. Republics large in geographical extent were felt to be unstable and ungovernable. This is one reason why in their first attempt at national government the revolutionaries opted for a confederation of fairly autonomous republics. Under Madison's plan, the federal government with its veto over state action, would have clear superiority in its dealing with the states. The Virginia Plan lacked much in the way of specific details. Nonetheless it was a bold proposal, one which went far beyond the convention's brief to recommend revisions to the Articles of Confederation. Most importantly, because it was the first proposal put before the convention, the Virginia Plan set the agenda for the gathering. For the remainder of the summer the delegates would debate and amend Madison's proposal. Although the convention would make significant changes to the plan, it would remain at the center of its deliberations.

Beginning on May 30, the convention agreed with Madison's intention to create a government "national and supreme," and proceeded to debate the specific details of the plan. The delegates rejected Madison's proposed plural executive and Council of Revision as unworkable and replaced them with a single executive, the president, who would have the authority to veto legislation. One of the first difficult issues which the Convention confronted concerned whether slaves should be counted for the purposes of representation in the national legislature. Northerners feared that southerners would reap undue political benefit (and influence) if their slaves were fully counted for the purposes of representation. The convention took a crucial decision on June 6 when it revived a formula first proposed by James Madison in 1783, and voted that representation in the national legislature and the apportionment of taxation would be calculated according to a proportion of the free population plus three-fifths of the slave population. This so-called three-fifths clause represented a compromise between the interests of the southern and northern states. It was the first of several crucial compromises made during the summer which sought to reconcile competing interests.[14]

The most significant conflict of interests at the convention was not between the North and the South but between the large and the small states. In the Virginia Plan, Madison proposed to create a super-republic with the states reduced to the status of administrative units not unlike English counties in relation to Parliament. The implementation of such a scheme would naturally result in a significant diminution of authority of states. This would affect the small states especially. In the Continental and Confederation Congresses (as well within the Constitutional Convention), all the states were equally represented. If representatives to the proposed national legislature were selected according to population, then the authority of the states would be undermined in two significant ways. First, if legislators were directly elected by the voters, as proposed by Madison, then the state legislatures would no longer be able to delegate their representatives as they had traditionally done. More significantly, if representation were based on population, then the representatives of the small states might easily be outvoted by the representatives of the large states. In consequence, delegates from a collection of states with small populations – New Jersey, New York, Connecticut, Maryland – prepared a proposal to counter the Virginia Plan and safeguard the interests of the small states.

On June 14 and 15, William Paterson of New Jersey presented the small states' alternative, which came to be known as the New Jersey Plan. Paterson outlined a proposal in which the government would retain a unicameral legislature, with each state delegation having one vote. This system had the force of recent history behind it, as it had been used at every major representative gathering of the revolutionary era since the Stamp Act Congress. Because the legislature would be organized by state, the states would continue to play a crucial role within the national government. Under the New Jersey Plan, the Congress would be vested with the power to tax, regulate commerce, and coerce recalcitrant states. Additionally, the nation would be administered by a plural executive and a national judiciary would oversee the implementation of national law which would be superior to state legislation. This plan was much closer to the convention's brief of suggesting revisions to the Articles of Confederation. The authors of the New Jersey Plan recognized the importance of strengthening the national government. Proponents of the plan contended that it would create more vigorous central government which would still safeguard the interests of the individual states, particularly the smaller ones. Its critics felt that the small states would exercise undue and unfair influence within the government, and that the changes proposed did not go far enough to create a national government potent enough to address the nation's ills. On June 19, the plan was defeated decisively when seven states voted against and three in favor of it. That two small state delegations – Connecticut and Maryland – voted against the design they had helped draft, indicates that the plan may have been as much a protestation by the small states that their interests must be considered as a real alternative to the Virginia Plan. [15]

Although the convention rejected the New Jersey Plan, the issue of representation in the national legislature went unresolved. For the next two weeks, the issue was thoroughly debated with increasing acrimony yet without a successful conclusion. The convention was deadlocked and facing collapse. On July 2, Roger Sherman of Connecticut declared, "We are now at a full stop, and nobody he supposed meant that we should break up without doing something."[16] Facing failure, the convention agreed to Sherman's proposal that the question of representation be referred to a committee chaired by Elbridge Gerry. Three days later, on July 5, the committee proposed a compromise to the convention: representation in the lower house of the legislature would be apportioned according to population and in the upper house each state would have an equal vote. Equal representation in the upper house had been suggested by small state delegates earlier in the Convention. It took the specter of failure to convince the large states to accede to the proposal. On July 16, the convention narrowly voted in favor of proposal – which came to be known as the Great Compromise – by five votes to four.

From July 17 to 26, the convention dealt with miscellaneous details regarding the form of the constitution before adjourning to allow a committee of detail to attempt to make sense of the various recommendations and amendments to the Virginia Plan which had been agreed and suggested over the previous two months. Crucially, during this period the convention agreed to drop Madison's cherished federal veto over state actions. Although national law would be superior to state law, this was a blow to Madison's vision of total federal supremacy. The committee of detail was charged with producing a draft Constitution. In so doing, it fleshed out many of the features of the Constitution and lived up to its name by taking important decisions regarding specific aspects of the structure and powers of the proposed government. In its draft Constitution, the committee specified that the national government would have the power to tax, regulate commerce, engage in war and peace, establish courts, and adopt any laws "necessary and proper" to achieve these ends. The states were forbidden from waging war, engaging in diplomacy, coining money, or laying duties on imports. The committee named the lower house of the legislature as the House of Representatives and the upper house as the Senate: the whole legislature would continue to be called the Congress. As in the states with bicameral legislatures, the approval of both houses was required for a bill to become law. Under the committee's draft Constitution, the president was to be elected by Congress and the powers of the executive had yet to be fully elaborated.

In the weeks after the committee of detail made its report, a new clash of interests emerged in the convention. In August, slavery again emerged as an issue at the meeting as the delegates from the southern states, particularly those of the lower south, sought protection for their labor practice in the Constitution. They had already secured limited recognition for their peculiar institution in the three-fifths clause. Article VII, section 4 of the proposed Constitution submitted by the committee of detail prohibited Congress from taxing or banning the slave trade. The Convention began debating the article on August 21. Cantankerous Luther Martin, the Attorney General of Maryland, criticized the clause as being "inconsistent with the principles of the revolution and dishonorable to the American character." The issue was hotly debated on August 22. The debate did not simply pit northern against southern delegates: indeed, some northern delegates like Connecticut's Oliver Ellsworth and Roger Sherman argued that Congress should not interfere with the slave trade. There was also division among southerners. Delegates from the upper south, which had a surfeit of slaves, wanted to abolish the slave trade so that they could increase the value of their excess chattel. Thus George Mason, the largest slaveholder at the convention, had the audacity to declaim the slave trade as an "infernal trafic," the blame for which he ascribed to "the avarice of British Merchants." Delegates from the lower south, especially the Carolinians Charles Cotesworth Pinckney and John Rutledge, threatened that their states would leave the union rather than allow Congress to interfere with slavery. As with other divisive issues, the convention decided to refer the question of the slave trade to a committee which would seek a compromise solution.[17]

Although some delegates found the slave trade objectionable, it did not present the same obstacle to a settlement that the question of representation had. The opponents of the slave trade were more concerned with securing a constitutional settlement and creating a strong federal government than they were with the inhumanity of the slave trade. In the face of threats to leave the union by delegates from the lower south, the opponents of the slave trade expressed a willingness to be flexible over the issue. In late August a compromise was reached whereby Congress would not have the authority to abolish the slave trade until 1808 at the earliest, and the federal government would compel states to assist in returning runaway slaves to their masters. The elitists who framed the Constitution were more concerned about creating a strong, stable national government than they were about addressing any inconsistencies posed by the ownership of slaves and the principles of the Revolution.

In late August and early September the convention turned its attention to the presidency. Several major questions had to be addressed: the manner by which the executive would be elected, how long he would serve, and what particular powers and responsibilities he would have. Eventually the convention rejected a proposed seven-year term in favor of a four-year span with unlimited re-election. The election of the president was removed from Congress and vested in an electoral college. Each state legislature would select electors for the electoral college, which would be apportioned according to population. Each elector would cast two votes, and the leader in the polling would become president and the runner-up would become vice-president. In the event of a deadlock in the electoral college, the House of Representatives would determine the outcome of an election. The president would have considerable powers. His signature was required make acts of Congress law. He would have the authority to veto acts of Congress. He would serve as commander-in-chief of the armed forces. Further, he was authorized to direct the nation's diplomacy (the Senate was required to ratify treaties), and to appoint judges and diplomats (again with Senate approval). If the Constitution were adopted, then the American president would have more authority to influence the lives of American citizens than George III had ever exercised over his American subjects. Crucially, the voters would be the master of the president. For all his power, the president had to be elected and could be removed by the voters.

On September 17, thirty-nine of the remaining forty-two delegates at the Constitutional Convention signed their handiwork and adjourned. The convention had gone far beyond simply recommending simple modifications to the Articles of Confederation. The delegates had audaciously proposed the creation of a powerful federal government in which power was separated between the three branches of the government: the Congress, the President, and the judiciary. Laws originated with Congress, which also had to approve the federal budget. The president had to give his assent to congressional acts (and he could exercise his veto of such acts), and the Supreme Court was empowered to oversee and uphold the Constitution. Most significantly, the power of the federal government under the proposal would be superior to that of the states. Here was an elitist solution to the problems facing the nation, but would it become law?

Ratification

When the Constitutional Convention finished its work, it immediately transmitted a copy of the proposed Constitution to the Congress, which was sitting in New York. Article VII of the proposed frame of government stipulated the means by which the convention felt the Constitution should be ratified: "The Ratification of the Conventions of nine States, shall be sufficient for the Establishment of this Constitution." In a covering letter which accompanied the Constitution, the convention provided specific advice as to how the process should work. After Congress received the document, "it should afterwards be submitted to a Convention of Delegates, chosen in each State by the People thereof, under the recommendation of its Legislature, for their Assent and Ratification." The

Constitution was read before the Congress on September 20. On September 28, Congress unanimously voted to submit the document to the states for ratification according to the method outlined by the convention. Thus the American people – at least those with political rights – would have two opportunities to express their views on the proposed Constitution: when they voted for delegates to their state ratifying conventions, and when those delegates debated and voted on the proposed frame of government.[18]

By 1787 it had become a common procedure to submit state constitutions to special ratifying conventions, so it is not surprising that the same procedure was recommended at the national level. Such a process had a strong ideological basis. The American revolutionaries were committed to republican government. Although its proponents intended that the Constitution should curb the democratic excesses of the Confederation governments, they also intended that the American electorate should give its consent to its new system of government. As James Madison put it somewhat awkwardly, if the Constitution "be found to depart from the republican character, its advocates must abandon it as no longer defensible." Given the commitment of even elitists to republican government, it was crucial that the proposed frame of government be submitted to the public for some form of approval; otherwise the government which it created would lack legitimacy. Although drafted in secret by elitist-inclined opponents of democracy, the Constitution was not the engine of counter-revolution because it was submitted before the American polity for (in theory) careful consideration and discussion.[19]

There were pragmatic as well as ideological reasons why the Constitutional Convention suggested the ratification process it did. The assent of all thirteen states was required to amend the articles of Confederation. The proposed Constitution was far more than an amendment of the articles. As such, the framers of the Constitution recognized that it would be impossible to achieve such unanimity for a radical overhaul of the political system. Faced with an impossible set of rules, they proposed to change them. Moreover, because the supporters of the Constitution recognized that opposition to the plan would coalesce in the state governments, they proposed to bypass the state legislatures with special ratifying conventions. Such conventions gave the impression – often legitimate – of appealing directly to the people. At the same time, they excluded many opponents of the proposed plan while allowing its supporters to exercise great influence within the conventions. This mix of the idealistic with the pragmatic characterized the struggle over ratification. The result was a contest of supreme importance – each side believed the very outcome of the Revolution was at stake – marked by discourse of the very highest order concerning the meaning of the American experiment with republicanism and by hard-nosed politicking which frequently reduced the contest to the political equivalent of bare-knuckles boxing.

The supporters of the Constitution won an important first trick in the struggle for ratification when they appropriated the term "Federalists" to describe themselves and designated their opponents as "Antifederalists." (These are the first of several labels adopted by the groups we have thus far denoted as elitists and democrats.) Jackson Turner Main has noted that these terms are not really accurate: "Originally the 'federal' meant anyone who supported the Confederation." Since the Antifederalists actually sought to defend the Confederation against the innovative and (from the standpoint of the Confederation) destructive plan advocated by the Federalists, it would be more appropriate to swap the labels. Nonetheless the men who would destroy the Confederation called themselves Federalists and their opponents Antifederalists. In so doing, they scored an important propaganda victory for they not only cast themselves as defenders of the Confederation but, more importantly, they cast their opponents in the negative role as opponents of reform. Main writes, "The victors took what name they chose, and fastened on the losers one which condemned them. Since the victory was a lasting one, the name and the stigma have endured."[20]

At the conclusion of the Constitutional Convention Alexander Hamilton, one of the leading Federalists, speculated about the prospects of the Constitution during the forthcoming ratification process. According to Hamilton, the "very great weight of influence of the persons who framed, particularly the universal popularity of General Washington," augured well for the Constitution. He felt especially that "the commercial interest" as well as men of property and creditors would welcome the stable, powerful government promised by the Constitution and support it at their state ratifying conventions. When coupled with the "strong belief in the people at large of the insufficiency of the present confederation," he was fairly confident that the proposed frame of government would be ratified. Hamilton recognized that there would be opposition to the Constitution. He expected the ranks of the Antifedederalists to be drawn from local office-holders — both competent and incompetent — who would fear a diminution of their authority, ambitious trouble-makers who would profit from continued political and economic instability, debtors, and "the democratical jealousy of the people which may be alarmed at the appearance of institutions that may seem calculated to place the power of the community in the hands of a few individuals to stations of great preeminence." Recognizing the bias of his comments, Hamilton's analysis proved remarkably accurate.[21]

John Jay, a leading advocate of the Constitution in New York, succinctly summed up Federalism when he declared "those who own the country ought to govern it." This view has been corroborated by the leading student of Antifederalism. According to the most important study of Antifederalism, the crucial socioeconomic factor in distinguishing between supporters and opponents of the Constitution was their level of engagement in commercial trading. "In all parts of the country," writes Jackson Turner Main, "the commercial interest with its ramifications, including those who depended primarily and directly upon commerce were Federal, and the 'non-navigating' folk were Antifederal." Federalism drew its main support from among the men engaged in commerce and those dependent upon them. As a rule, men of wealth were usually Federalists. So too were creditors, those who held both public and private debts. This has led some commentators and historians to conclude that the struggle over the Constitution was class-based. Although this interpretation has some merit, it does not account for the wide support for Federalism among all classes in towns where class divisions where most acute. Every major town and city in the United States had a Federalist majority. Thus urban artisans, laborers, and seamen often supported the Constitution because they, like their wealthy employers, depended on the commercial stability they believed the new government would provide. Antifederalism, by contrast, drew its strength from among the small farmers of rural America, including the backcountry and more isolated parts of settled regions. Small farmers, debtors and proponents of debt relief, as well as local office-holders, opposed the Constitution.[22]

Antifederalists made a number of criticisms of the proposed Constitution. They felt that the Constitutional Convention had exceeded its mandate in proposing a system to replace the Articles of the Confederation. They further objected to the proposed ratification process, which was at odds with the articles. Their greatest fear was that the powerful, centralized government to be created by the proposed Constitution would destroy the sovereignty of the individual states and undermine republicanism. They contended, along with Montesquieu, that it was impossible to maintain republican government over an extended land area and that the government must inevitably threaten the liberty of its citizens. Samuel Bryan, a Pennsylvania Antifederalist, described the Constitution in October 1787 as "the most daring attempt to establish a despotic aristocracy among freemen that the world has ever witnessed." The chief defect of the plan was that those in power would not really be accountable to the governed. Thus republican principles would be permanently undermined. The Constitution, Bryan continued, "is devoid of all responsibility or accountability to the great body of the people, and that so far from being a regular balanced government, it would be in practice a *permanent* ARISTOCRACY." Many Antifederalists were especially concerned that the proposed document lacked a Bill of Rights – a list of enumerated and legally protected liberties – such as were appended to many of the state constitutions. All in all, the Antifederalists objected to the means by which the Constitution was drafted, how it would be ratified, and its provisions for a strong national government at the expense of the states and its failure to protect individual liberty. The Antifederalists conceded that something had to be done to reform the national government. They also realized they had made a crucial error in failing to attend to the Constitutional Convention. Many proposed that a second convention be held to redraft the Constitution.[23]

Federalists addressed the criticisms of the Antifederalists in hundreds of pamphlets and newspaper articles. Of these, the most famous are a series of eighty-five *Federalist* essays which appeared in New York newspapers in 1787 and 1788. Written under the pseudonym "Publius," the Federalist essays were the handiwork of Alexander Hamilton, James Madison, and John Jay. Taken together, they constitute the most coherent explication of Federalist principles with respect to the Constitution. Although they addressed a multiplicity of issues with respect to the Constitution, perhaps the most significant argument made in the series was that of James Madison in the tenth *Federalist*. In that essay, Madison addressed the Antifederalist tenet, derived from Montesquieu, that a large republic was impossible to sustain. On the contrary, Madison argued, republics were suited to large nations because the large number of competing interest groups in a large republic would ensure that no one faction or group could predominate and oppress the others. In other essays the authors, especially Madison and Hamilton, argued that the separation of powers and checks and balances within the Constitution would guarantee civil liberty and that Antifederalist concerns about governmental abuse were unfounded. Only time would tell whether the Federalist or Antifederalist interpretation of the Constitution was correct.

The debate over the merits of the Constitution constitutes the most significant public discourse in American political history. It was also a political battle played out across the thirteen states. Although it is difficult to be precise, it seems likely that a majority of American voters were probably opposed to the Constitution. The Federalists, however, enjoyed several considerable advantages during the ratification contest. Perhaps most importantly, the Federalists were offering a specific set of solutions to the pressing political problems which faced the nation. Most Antifederalists conceded that some reform was necessary. When set against their suggestion that another convention be called, the Constitution seemed a surer solution. Even those who were displeased with parts of the proposed plan felt it was better than inaction. People felt it was necessary to accept the proposed Constitution, even with its flaws, in order to create a more vigorous national government, rather than endure the weakness of the Articles of Confederation any longer. Such feelings prevailed in the towns and cities of the United States which, as previously noted, were overwhelmingly Federalist. Most of the ratifying conventions were held in such towns, and local people gave delegates the impression that the majority of Americans favored the Constitution. The Antifederalists' support, by contrast was scattered across the small farms of the hinterland. It was widely dispersed and difficult to organize. In the main, rural Antifederalism did not directly influence the ratifying conventions, especially when the Federalists could champion a concrete plan which they could argue was the antidote for the country's ills.

Federalists also enjoyed social advantages over their rivals which gave them an edge in the ratification struggle. The leading Federalists were well-educated, wealthy men with inter-state political and economic connections, and many had had experience of leadership during the War of Independence and its aftermath. Most importantly, they had a strong national outlook. In consequence, they were much better placed to conduct a national campaign for ratification than the Antifederalists. The Antifederalists were, in the main, locally oriented. Although there were certainly wealthy and prominent Antifederalists, the majority were small farmers. The Antifeder-alists often felt ill at ease with their wealthier, more polished rivals. According to Amos Singletary, a miller from Sutton, Massachusetts who opposed the Constitution, the Federalists would derive direct benefits from their apparent social advantages:

> These lawyers, and men of learning, and moneyed men, that talk so finely and gloss over matters so smoothly, to make us poor il-literate people swallow down the pill, expect to get into Congress themselves, they expect to be the managers of this Constitution and get all the power and all the money into their own hands, and then they will swallow up all us little folks, like the great Leviathan ...[24]

The Federalists undoubtedly did use their social, economic, and political advantages to good effect. They were better organized and better able to produce and disseminate propaganda in support of the Constitution. The overwhelming majority of newspapers in the country, for example, were Federalist owned and inclined. Indeed, only five major newspapers (out of approximately one hundred) consistently opposed the Constitution. The newspapers did much to promote the view that the Federalists were in the majority. They did not always allow the truth to stand in the way of their cause, as when the *Pennsylvania Gazette* informed its readers that Patrick Henry, the leading Virginia Antifederalist, was working hard for the ratification of the Constitution.[25]

The Federalists, who had outmaneuvered their opponents in drafting the Constitution, used their advantages to good effect during ratification. Where their support was strong they moved rapidly to secure approval, and where it was weak they prevaricated to allow themselves time to campaign effectively. Because of poor weather and the haste of the elections, perhaps only a third of qualified voters participated in the elections for the state ratifying conventions. Those most likely to stay away were Antifederalists in isolated communities. Thus even from the outset, the Federalists seemed likely to have a significant advantage when the conventions began to meet. Delaware was the first state to act. A small state used to living in close economic and political harmony with its large neighbor, Pennsylvania, the Delaware convention voted unanimously in favor of the Constitution on December 7, 1787. Pennsylvania was the first real test of the Constitution. The assembly there had been bitterly divided over the Constitution, and resisted calling elections for the ratifying convention. The Federalists resorted to political strong-arm tactics (a crowd prevented Antifederalist representatives from leaving the chamber and denying the assembly a quorum) to secure the call for a convention. On December 12, the Pennsylvania convention ratified the Constitution by a vote of 46 to 23. Less than a week after Pennsylvania approved the Constitution, New Jersey, another small state which depended on harmonious commercial relations with its neighbors, gave its verdict on the document. On December 18 the New Jersey ratifying convention voted 38 to 0 in favor of the Constitution. On January 2, 1788 Georgia, which hoped for Federal protection for its frontiers from the Spanish and Indians, voted 26 to 0 for the Constitution. One week later the Connecticut ratifying convention added its assent by a margin of 128 to 40. Thus within the first month of the ratification campaign the Federalists had secured the support of five states and enjoyed significant momentum before the Antifederalists had hardly begun to organize their opposition.

While happy with their results thus far the Federalists recognized that they needed four more states, and a union without Massachusetts, Virginia, New York, and South Carolina in particular would be a weak entity. The Massachusetts ratifying convention began its deliberations on January 9, 1788. Although forty-six towns, the majority of which were probably Antifederalist, failed to send delegates to the conclave, the Federalists reckoned at the start of the meeting that the Antifederalists would prevail. Defeat in Massachusetts, one of the largest states and a leader in the Revolution, would be a severe blow to the Federalist campaign. Moreover, in Massachusetts the Antifederalists had competent leadership in the revolutionary stalwarts Samuel Adams and John Hancock. The Federalists in the Massachusetts convention sought to delay a vote on the Constitution in order to sway the leading Antifederalists. They did so by debating the proposed Constitution clause by clause. Behind the scenes appeals were made, especially to Adams and Hancock. When Boston artisans demonstrated in favor of the document, Adams was swayed. The Federalists suggested to Hancock that he might be vice-president if the Constitution were ratified, which appealed to the one-time

President of the Continental Congress. Eventually moderate Antifedederalists were won over by a Federalist pledge to consider appending a Bill of Rights to the Constitution. On February 9, Hancock recommended nine proposed amendments to the Constitution (which were non-binding) to guarantee civil liberties, and he endorsed the document. That day the Federalists narrowly triumphed by a margin of 187 to 168. In other states a similar formula was followed whereby Antifederalists came to support the Constitution on the condition that it be amended to protect civil liberty.

After Massachusetts, there was a delay in the pace of ratification. Maryland became the seventh state to endorse the Constitution when its convention voted in favor by 63 to 11 on April 21. The Federalists triumphed in South Carolina by 149 to 73 on May 23. On June 21, after a bitter contest within its convention, New Hampshire narrowly ratified by 57 to 47. In so doing, New Hampshire became the ninth state to approve the Constitution and it became the law of the land. Four states – Virginia, New York, North Carolina, and Rhode Island – remained outside the federal fold. The first two were crucial to the success of the union, and the ratification campaigns continued. In Virginia the Antifederalists had the able leadership of Patrick Henry (newspaper reports notwithstanding). As in Massachusetts, the promise of a Bill of Rights swayed moderate Antifederalists and on June 26, 1788 the Virginia convention approved by 89 to 79. In New York the struggle was even closer. Under the aggressive leadership of Alexander Hamilton and John Jay and with threats by the commercial leadership of New York City, the convention narrowly ratified by 30 to 27 on July 26. With the agreement of eleven of the thirteen states – including the largest and wealthiest states – the Federalists had affected their own revolution.[26]

Finishing touches: The Judiciary Act and the Bill of Rights

After ratification, there were two significant additions to the constitutional structure of the United States which should be viewed as part of the political settlement to emerge from the Revolution. These were the Judiciary Act and the Bill of Rights, adopted in 1789.

The Constitution had created a federal judiciary for the United States but left the detail as to how it should be structured, what its precise responsibilities should be, and what its relationship with the state courts should be for settlement at another time. In 1789, the first Congress under the new Constitution adopted the Judiciary Act to address many of these issues. This act gave form and breathed life into the judicial system of the United States, thereby completing the tripartite structure of the federal government. According to the act, the Supreme Court created by the Constitution would have six members. The Supreme Court would be at the apex of a federal system of three circuit and thirteen district courts. Under this system, the federal courts were to uphold the Constitution and adjudicate federal laws. Although federal law would be superior to that of the states if the two came into conflict, state courts were still responsible for upholding laws in their own jurisdictions. The Judiciary Act, therefore, divided judicial authority between the federal government and the states. The act did provide that when a state court denied a claim of federal right the case could be appealed to the Supreme Court, thereby establishing the principle of judicial review. The Supreme Court would not, however, begin to exercise that right in a meaningful way until the nineteenth century.

One of the chief Antifederalist criticisms of the Constitution had been that it lacked a Bill of Rights. Some Federalists were opposed to adding such a list because they felt that the Constitution provided sufficient safeguards for personal liberty. Nonetheless, after the Massachusetts ratifying convention agreed to recommend proposed amendments to the new Congress as a condition of ratification, every subsequent state to ratify (except Maryland) resorted to the same mechanism. In essence, Antifederalists had secured a Federalist commitment to a Bill of Rights during the ratification contest. Given the significance the Bill of Rights has come to have in American life (many Americans identify "the Constitution" as the Bill of Rights), the Antifederalist contribution was crucial. That the opponents of the Constitution helped ensure what has become the most prominent feature of the Constitution is ironic indeed.

More than two hundred suggested amendments were submitted by the state ratifying conventions. As a leading member of the first Congress, James Madison, who had argued that a Bill of Rights was unnecessary, made drafting the Bill of Rights a high priority. Madison was swayed by the amendments recommended by his home state of Virginia. The Virginia ratifying convention submitted forty proposed amendments, many drawn from the Virginia constitution of 1776. From these Madison pared the list down. On September 24–5, 1789, the House of Representatives and Senate approved twelve proposed amendments to protect civil liberty and limit federal power, and submitted them to the states for ratification. Of these, the states approved ten, including those guaranteeing freedom of religion and of speech, the right to bear arms, protection from unlawful searches, the right to due process of law, and the right to a speedy trial by jury. Other amendments prohibited quartering soldiers with civilians in time of peace, excessive fines and cruel and unusual punishments. The final amendments stipulated that the enumeration of these rights did not "deny or disparage" the other unspecified rights which the American people retained and that all powers not expressly delegated to the United States by the Constitution were reserved to the states and the people. The amendments took effect in December 1791 when Virginia, appropriately, became the last state to ratify them. The adoption of the Bill of Rights helped to convince Antifederalists in North Carolina and Rhode Island to drop their opposition to the Constitution and allowed those states to enter the new union.[27]

Conclusion

The adoption of the Bill of Rights ended a generation of constitutional experimentation on the part of Americans. The fundamental question raised by American protests to British taxation had been that of the constitutional relationship between the colonies and Parliament. The Americans had resolved that question by declaring independence. In so doing, they raised a host of new constitutional questions: what form should their new governments take, who was entitled to participate in those governments, what should the relationship between the states be, what rights did citizens have. At the state and national level, Americans experimented with a range of governmental structures in their search for the answers to these questions, from the democratic egalitarianism of Pennsylvania and Vermont to the elitism of Massachusetts and New York and the Federalist solution of James Madison. The revolutionaries never wavered in their commitment to republican government: that is government where sovereignty was derived from the people. Thus the Constitution of 1787, while antidemocratic and adopted, in part, to limit popular participation in government, was not counter-revolutionary. Drafted in secret, it was subject to popular scrutiny by a public ratification process. Although the Federalists enjoyed decided advantages in that process, both sides accepted its outcome as legitimate and binding.

Having agreed on the structure of the national government for the second time in a decade, the key question was whether the new Constitution would last longer than the Articles of Confederation. Over the coming decade the new government would endure several severe challenges, including the rise of political partisanship. The most important challenges arose from how the new republic reacted to events thousands of miles from the United States. As Americans launched their new republic in 1789, their French allies began a process leading them to overthrow their monarchy and add another nation to the world's short roster of republics. The French Revolution and the political, diplomatic, and ideological questions it raised would be at the heart of American life for the next decade and beyond.

7

THE FEDERALIST ERA

Introduction

George Washington was inaugurated as the first president of the United States on April 30, 1789. To the surprise of no one, the general came out of retirement to stand for the office. As the most famous and popular man in the country, he was a consensus choice to be the first executive under the new Constitution and he stood unopposed. The first presidential election had been held in January 1789, when the electors selected by the states gathered as the Electoral College, as mandated by the Constitution, to cast their votes for the presidency. The Constitution allowed each state to decide how to choose its own presidential electors. In the first presidential election, only Pennsylvania and Maryland held elections for this purpose; elsewhere, the state legislatures chose electors. Washington received 69 votes in the Electoral College. John Adams of Massachusetts was elected vice-president with 34 electoral college votes.

When Washington was inaugurated, there was widespread public support for the new government and the Constitution. Given the passion which had characterized the ratification debate, the Antifederalists were notably gracious in defeat. They accepted a popular verdict, as expressed in the ratifying conventions, and agreed to participate in the new political system in good faith. Given their democratic inclinations, it would have been very difficult for the Antifederalists to reject the judgment of the people. This was especially true since massive public demonstrations had been held in the major American cities to celebrate the constitution. These demonstrations certainly fostered an impression that the decision of the ratifying conventions was in keeping with the views of the majority of Americans.[1] The speed with which the Antifederalists reconciled themselves to the new order is remarkable. According to historian Lance Banning, who has paid particular attention to this issue, "As early as the spring of 1791 the Constitution was accepted on all sides as the starting point for further debates." The process of political reconciliation began with the conclusion of the ratification process. Indeed when the first Congress began sitting on March 4 a large number of former opponents of the Constitution were among its members, particularly in the House of Representatives.[2]

Although they rapidly came to embrace the Constitution, many of its former opponents were still concerned about the danger posed to liberty by federalism. The former Antifederalists were determined to preserve American liberty from Federalist encroachments. Indeed, it is telling that the first controversy which divided the new Congress concerned not financial or foreign policy but the question of what the proper title of the president should be. In early May the Senate, under the direction of Vice-President John Adams, debated the proper title with which President Washington should be addressed. Adams, who had been a radical proponent of independence in 1776, believed that the president needed a suitable title to confer legitimacy upon the new government. A Senate committee recommended that the president be known as "His Highness the President of the United States of America, and Protector of their Liberties." The proposal was rejected by the popularly elected House of Representatives, which advocated the republican simplicity of "Mr. President."[3] The debate over the appropriate titles for the president and other government officers was of more than symbolic importance: it presaged the breakdown of the political consensus over the Constitution in ensuing years. The 1790s witnessed the emergence of fierce political partisanship in the United States. The development of competing political parties was an important step in the development of American democracy. This partisan division began within the Washington administration and spread throughout American society. The catalyst for its emergence was a series of important questions which faced the United States during the 1790s, concerning political economy and foreign policy. The appearance of partisanship profoundly transformed American politics and was probably the most notable development in American public life during the 1790s. Nonetheless, the advent of partisanship was deeply distressing to many Americans.

Washington was not only the obvious choice as first president, he was an inspired choice. His wartime experience taught the Virginian the import-ance of vesting the central government with significant powers to address the nation's problems. Nonetheless, as commander-in-chief during the War of Independence, Washington had demonstrated respect for civilian control over the military under very trying circumstances. As president, Washing-ton scrupulously followed his mandate as outlined in the Constitution. Since he had presided over the convention which created the presidency – and the delegates to the Constitutional Convention assumed that Washington would be the first president – the former general was acutely aware of the demands, potential, and limits of the presidency. As the first executive under the new system Washington set important precedents. It fell to him as the most powerful and public figure in the new government to breathe life into the Constitution. Washington would be, as far as the public was concerned, the public face of the new government – the very personification of the Constitution. One of Washington's most important tasks would be to win respect for the infant federal government. As a Virginia planter, Washington was well aware of the importance of public displays of power. For example, on a visit to Boston in 1789 the Massachusetts governor John Hancock refused to pay a first social call on the president in the vain belief that as governor he should take precedence over Washington in his own state. Hancock expected Washington to call upon him first. A social stand-off ensued and Washington refused a dinner invitation from the governor. Hancock gave in and called upon the president, protesting that he had been incapacitated by gout. With the ratification of the Constitution, Americans found themselves in largely uncharted political territory. As the dispute over the president's title revealed, such matters of protocol were of crucial importance in establishing the legitimacy of the new constitutional arrangements.[4]

Washington did not anticipate the acrimonious divisions that would emerge within his administration when he put his cabinet together. The president selected his cabinet on the basis of three criteria: merit, service, and geography. In consequence, Thomas Jefferson was named Secretary of State, Henry Knox Secretary of War, Edmund Randolph Attorney-General and Alexander Hamilton Secretary of the Treasury. When Washington selected the six members of the Supreme Court, he chose three jurists from the north and three from the south. John Jay of New York was named the first Chief Justice of the nation's highest court. Washington believed that he had appointed men who shared his commitment to the Constitution and would set aside any personal or ideological differences in the interests of the public good. Such hopes proved overly optimistic, as sharp divisions developed within the president's cabinet.

Hamiltonianism

Of all Washington's appointments, Alexander Hamilton was the most important. Hamilton was born in the West Indies in 1755, and migrated to New York in 1772. Although he lacked social connections, Hamilton was admitted to King's College (presently Columbia University) in 1773 based on his intelligence. In 1776 he joined the rebel army, serving as an artillery captain at the Battle of Long Island. In 1777 the young Hamilton, only twenty-two, was named as a member of Washington's staff and served as the general's secretary and aide-de-camp until 1781. He then served in Congress during 1782–3. Hamilton had seen at first hand how bickering within Congress and among the states had undermined the war effort. As Washington's aide, Hamilton gained valuable administrative experience and came to embrace the general's national outlook. His experience at the center of the army and in Congress made Hamilton an early and fervent proponent of the creation of a strong central government.

Hamilton established a lucrative legal practice in New York during the 1780s (in 1780 he had married the wealthy Elizabeth Schuyler, securing his entrée into New York's elite) but he kept a hand in political affairs. He had taken a leading role at the Annapolis Convention. At the Constitutional Convention, he gave a lengthy address praising the virtues of the British constitution and extolling monarchical rule. During the ratification contest he worked closely with James Madison to campaign for the Constitution. He took a leading role in drafting the *Federalist*, and helped deliver New York's approval of the Constitution. Hamilton was a very clever and ambitious proponent of Federalism. He had given a great deal of thought to the financial and economic difficulties confronting the United States, and seemed a natural choice as Washington's Secretary of the Treasury. Hamilton's appointment was crucial for two reasons: first, finance was the most important problem facing the United States; and second, Hamilton came to the Treasury with an activist agenda determined to transform the government and the United States.

Putting the nation on a sound financial footing was the preeminent problem confronting the new government. In 1789 the debt stood at over $50 million – $11.7 million was owed to Spain, France, and the Netherlands, and approximately $40 million was owed as securities to citizens of the United States. As we saw in the previous chapter, the inability to retire the public debt had led to the downfall of the Confederation government. In October 1789, Washington instructed Hamilton to prepare a report demonstrating how the finances of the United States could be placed on a sound footing. On January 9, 1790 the Treasury Secretary submitted his *Report on Public Credit* to Congress. The *Report on Public Credit* was a statement of Hamilton's political and financial philosophy and his vision of the future political and economic development of the United States.

Hamilton's position was that the only way the federal government could establish credit was to deal honestly with its creditors, both foreign and domestic. Although everyone agreed that the portion of the debt owed to foreign governments had to be paid if the United States was to maintain its honor and credibility, there was a strong feeling in Congress that it might not be necessary to pay the debt on the public securities issued to revolutionary war veterans. Most of these securities had been purchased at a reduced rate by speculators, and there was a clamor in Congress that the government could and should repudiate these debts while making some provision to compensate the veterans. Hamilton was opposed to such proposals. He wanted to pay the whole debt, he proposed in his report to convert the arrears of interest (approximately $13 million) into principal, and to fund the entire debt with federal funds derived from taxes and loans from a new national bank (see below). Although many in Congress criticized the speculators who had purchased public securities, Hamilton felt that it was crucial to win the loyalty of such men to the new government and thereby to guarantee the financial security of the United States. Hamilton had little faith in the common people of America. At the Constitutional Convention, he had given a lengthy speech in which he called for the president to be elected for a life term in order to protect him from the ignorant prejudices of the electorate. He felt that Americans were too wed to their states and localities and did not think of the good of the nation or of its future development. On the other hand, Hamilton believed, the merchants, lawyers, and manufacturers who possessed capital and had speculated in public securities were crucial to the success of the new government. He felt it was imperative that the government honor its obligations to these men because it would need to borrow from them in the future and that if their economic interests and those of the federal government were merged the country would eventually prosper.

A key element of the *Report on Public Credit* was a proposal that the federal government should not only pay its own debts but that it should assume the outstanding war debts of the various states. This marked a reversal of previous practice. During the Confederation, many states had undertaken to retire their portion of the national debt. Hamilton's proposal was controversial because, if the federal government assumed the state debts, those states which had retired their debts would be asked to pay additional taxes to retire the unpaid debts of other states. The assumption of state debts was a crucial component of Hamilton's program because the Treasury Secretary believed it would strengthen the bonds of union by striking at the roots of state sovereignty. If the debt was truly *national*, then retiring the debt would become a national responsibility. In the *Report on Public Credit*, Hamilton laid the cornerstone of a financial program which would transform the nation by undermining state sovereignty and marrying the wealthy to the interests of the federal government. In so doing, he intended that the federal government should take a leading role in directing the economic development of the United States.[5]

Hamilton's proposals in the *Report on Public Credit* met with opposition in the House of Representatives. The opposition was strongest among southern congressmen. The New Yorker's proposals had a double benefit for his fellow northerners. In the first place, most of those financiers who had speculated in public securities lived in northern towns. Second, most of the southern states had paid their war debts, while the several northern states – including Pennsylvania, New York, and Massachusetts – had considerable outstanding debts. South Carolina was alone among the southern states with a large outstanding debt. In consequence southerners, would be required to subsidize the debts of their northern counterparts if the features of Hamilton's report were enacted. To Hamilton's surprise, James Madison led the opposition to his program in Congress. Madison opposed the plan because he felt it rewarded speculators at the expense of revolutionary veterans, and that it would be disadvantageous to his home state of Virginia. Under Madison's leadership, Hamilton's proposals were defeated four times in the House by June 1790. As leader of the House of Representatives, Madison's opposition to the *Report on Public Credit* marked the beginning of his transformation from being the architect of American federalism to becoming one of the leading opponents of the Federalists in power. In mid-July the Secretary of State, Thomas Jefferson, brokered a deal between Madison and Hamilton. Under the terms of the agreement, southern congressmen would withdraw their opposition to Hamilton's funding proposals and the federal assumption of state debts if the nation's capital was moved from New York to the south. The capital would temporarily shift from New York to Philadelphia before a permanent move in 1800 to a new capital city on the banks of the Potomac River between Virginia and Maryland. By August 1790, Congress had enacted the essential elements of the *Report on Public Credit*.[6]

The implementation of the provisions of the *Report on Public Credit* marked the first step in Hamilton's plan to marry the federal government and the commercial and manufacturing interests of the United States. The objective of this plan was to unite the wealth and political power in the hands of those men who could wield them to best effect. In Hamilton's view, the government required the assistance and support of the men who controlled the nation's capital and commerce. The government in turn should take positive steps to promote commerce and economic development. Restoring the nation's credit was but the first step in realizing Hamilton's objective. In January of 1791, Hamilton revealed the next element of his program. In another report to Congress, he proposed that Congress create a national bank, the Bank of the United States. As in so many of his economic policies, Hamilton's thinking on the bank was influenced by British examples. He believed that the Bank of England had been a crucial factor in Britain's economic growth and prosperity during the eighteenth century. He proposed that the Bank of the United States should be a public institution founded on public and private investment that would hold government funds, exercise control over state banks, and issue bank notes which would effectively serve as a national currency. While he took his cue from British, especially English, economic development, Hamilton intended that the federal government should take a more active role in the economic life of the nation than occurred in Britain. The government would not only deposit its funds in the bank, it would also borrow from the bank, thereby further binding the wealthy who would invest in the bank to the interests of the government.[7]

Hamilton's bank proposal raised a significant question with respect to constitution. As with the *Report on Public Credit*, James Madison led the opposition to the proposed bank in Congress. Madison argued that the Constitution did not provide Congress with the authority to charter a bank. Such an interpretation was based on what has come to be known as *strict construction* of the Constitution. Proponents of strict construction, including Madison, argued that the government could only undertake measures and actions which were specifically enumerated in the Constitution. Proponents of the bank argued that the "necessary and proper" clause empowered Congress to take steps which were not specifically allowed for in the Constitution. They advocated a *broad construction* of the document. After the House of Representatives passed the Bank Bill by a vote of 39 to 20, Washington polled his cabinet on the proposal. Although Secretary of State Jefferson and Attorney General Edmund Randolph opposed the measure, Hamilton made a case for the bank based on broad construction of the Constitution. The president agreed, on the military logic of backing the man responsible for the policies of his own department, and a significant precedent was set. Hamilton and Washington had demonstrated that broad interpretation of the Constitution could allow a vigorous government to pursue an activist agenda.[8]

The *Report on Public Credit* and the Bank Bill laid the foundation for Alexander Hamilton's main objective, the centralization of political power and the manufacturing development of the United States. The capstone to his program was the *Report on Manufactures* which he submitted to Congress in December, 1791. In the report, Hamilton argued that the United States should promote manufacturing by providing protected markets for American products and capital and assistance to infant American industries. Manufacturing should be further promoted via protective tariffs, bounties for new industries, premiums for improvement of quality, and the encouragement of inventions. Again, according to Hamilton, the United States should follow the British example by promoting industry and protecting markets. The *Report on Manufactures* also outlined Hamilton's views on political economy. The United States should not rely on agricultural exports, which were unreliable, especially in a world of warring empires, but should make itself economically independent through promoting its own manufacturing and industrial development. Taken together with the *Report on Public Credit* and the Bank Bill, the *Report on Manufactures* can be seen as Alexander's Hamilton economic addendum to the Constitution. By his policies and proposals as Secretary of the Treasury, Hamilton attempted to create a union of centralized economic and political power in the United States. In his view, a powerful central government must intervene to promote the interests of American commerce and industry. Hamilton intended to put wealth into the hands of those best qualified to use it for constructive national purposes: financiers, manufacturers, and professionals. The Hamiltonian program reflected the social beliefs of the Federalists who were, of course, no friends of democracy. The

Federalists claimed that they served the best interests of all the people by creating and leading a stable society which was immune from anarchy and tyranny. Hamilton's vision did not go unchallenged.[9]

Jeffersonianism

The opponents to the Hamiltonian program coalesced around Thomas Jefferson and James Madison. Although Madison had played a leading role in the creation of the United States Constitution and would continue to make a crucial contribution to American politics in leading the congressional opposition to the Federalists during the 1790s, it was Jefferson who emerged as the leader of the political party which would challenge, and eventually supplant, the Federalists. Although there was no small amount of personal animus and political rivalry between Hamilton and Jefferson – Hamilton claimed that Jefferson delivered his opinion on the Bank Bill "in a manner which I felt was partaking of asperity and ill humor towards me" – the root of their differences was ideological.[10] They differed profoundly over a number of issues, most especially with respect to the future economic development of the United States. The wealthy, slaveholding Jefferson had more faith in the ability of the common man than the common-born Hamilton, who routinely expressed disdain for the body of the American people. Jefferson feared the consequences of the manufacturing economy which Hamilton extolled. Jefferson was not opposed to commercial activity; rather, he feared for the social and political consequences of certain types of economic activity. Manufacturing, Jefferson had observed during his lengthy European travels, depended on a large class of property-less laborers who were normally mired in poverty and ignorance. Such men and women were not the stuff upon which to base a republic. On the contrary, Jefferson believed that the United States should forestall such economic developments as long as possible. The American republic, if liberty were to be preserved, should be based on commercial agriculture. He was optimistic that so long as the majority of American citizens (white males, of course) held their own property, then the republic would be on sound footing. The United States would prosper and its citizens enjoy their freedom so long as the majority of its citizens tilled the land and exported their surpluses for the consumption of hungry Europeans. Some small-scale manufacturing, of course, would be essential to service the agricultural economy, but Americans could purchase most manufactured goods they needed or desired from Europe.

In his most important published work, *Notes on the State of Virginia*, Jefferson contrasted the circumstances in Europe and America. In the work, first published in French in 1784 and then in English in 1785, Jefferson outlined the vision of an agricultural republic:

> In Europe the lands are either cultivated, or locked up against the cultivator. Manufacture must therefore be resorted to of necessity not of choice, to support the surplus of their people. But we have an immensity of land courting the industry of the husbandman. Is it best then that all our citizens should be employed in its improvement, or that one half should be called off from that to exercise manufactures and handicraft arts for the other? Those who labor in the earth are the Chosen people of God, if ever He had a chosen people, whose breast He has made His peculiar deposit for substantial and genuine virtue. It is the focus in which he keeps alive that sacred fire which might otherwise escape from the face of the earth. Corruption of morals in the mass of cultivators is a phenomenon of which no age nor nation has furnished an example. ... While we have land to labor then, let us never wish to see our citizens occupied at a workbench, or twirling a distaff. Carpenters, masons, smiths, are wanting in husbandry; but, for the general operations of manufacture, let our workshops remain in Europe.

Although Jefferson felt that Americans should eschew manufacturing, he was not opposed to prosperity. Rather, he felt such prosperity should rest on the export of American agricultural surpluses. He explained:

> It is better to carry provisions and materials, and with them their manners and principles. The loss by the transportation of commodities across the Atlantic will be made up in happiness and permanence of government. The mobs of great cities add just so much to the support of pure government, as sores do to the strength of the human body. It is the manners and spirit of a people which preserve a republic in vigor. A degeneracy in these is a canker which soon eats at the heart of its laws and constitution.

According to Jefferson, the United States had the perfect ingredients for both prosperity and a healthy republican body politic. The best way to achieve this was for Americans to reject the British model and exploit their natural resources as a nation composed primarily of small farmers.[11]

Jefferson's economic vision had political ramifications. Unlike Hamilton, Jefferson believed that the government should not interfere in the economy and promote manufacturing. Taking a cue from Adam Smith's *The Wealth of Nations*, which he greatly admired, Jefferson advocated free trade and felt that tariffs erected to protect industry would harm American farmers who sought to export their surpluses. In consequence, he opposed the Hamiltonian program of government aggrandizement of power and economic intervention to promote manufacturing. He believed such a program would result in increased inequality and a diminution of liberty. Moreover, the concentration of political and economic power in the hands of the government and its friends would be a direct threat to personal liberty. Despite his membership in Washington's cabinet, Jefferson came to see Congress, especially the House of Representatives, as the guarantor of freedom against the encroachments of the executive, especially the Secretary of the Treasury who he described as "a man whose history ... is a tissue of machinations against the liberty of the country." Jefferson and Hamilton therefore advocated two distinct political and economic visions. The latter promoted a strong central government which would use its power to promote the economic interests of its friends by encouraging manufacturing. Jefferson's philosophy stressed the importance of agrarianism. The United States should, in his mind, remain a country of small property-holders who produced for their own needs and sold their surpluses. He believed the federal government should not interfere with the economy or with the people's liberties. Their differences would be the catalyst for the emergence of political parties in the United States.[12]

The rise of partisanship

It was a tenet of republican thinking during the revolutionary era that political parties were a sign of sickness in the body politic. President Washington wrote in 1790, "If we mean to support the Liberty and Independence which it has cost us so much blood and treasure to establish, we must drive far away the dæmon of party spirit and local reproach." The *Providence Gazette* declared in 1786: "Parties are the dangerous diseases of civil freedom; they are only the first stage of anarchy, cloathed in mild language." Such protestations, which were common among American political leaders, did not conform with reality. We have seen that local partisan divisions characterized American politics during the Revolution. It is not surprising, therefore, that partisanship should emerge at the national level once a competent national government was created. Indeed, during the ratification debate James Madison had argued in the *Federalist* that competing interests could actually have a beneficial political impact by undermining the centralizing tendencies of the national government. Madison assumed that there would be a plethora of local interests which would counterbalance each other at the national level. One of the chief consequences of the development of political parties in the United States during the 1790s was an increased democratization of American life. Ironically, given such a result, the genesis of party system lay at the top of the American political system – in Congress and in the Washington administration – and spread downwards. In reality, the parties would not emerge out of local political interests, but at the very center of the government.[13]

Although the party in power in 1792 retained the name "Federalists," they were not necessarily the same men who embraced that denomination in 1787–8. The Federalists of the 1790s were the men who coalesced around the Washington administration and its programs. Their opponents, in the main, had been Federalists themselves (that is, supporters of the Constitution) in 1788 but had come to oppose the Washington administration's policies, particularly the Hamiltonian program of government-assisted economic development. Thus Madison and Jefferson, who had supported the Constitution, could be described as Federalists in 1788 but not by 1792. Before the elections of 1792, the consensus which had characterized the national political scene in the immediate aftermath of ratification had broken down and two embryonic political parties – the Federalists and their opponents, who came to be known as Republicans – vied for power in Congress.[14] As we have seen, James Madison led the opposition in Congress to the program of economic and political centralization promulgated by his one-time political ally. Within the Washington administration, Thomas Jefferson assumed the role of Hamilton's opponent. It was their dispute which first brought the differences between Federalists and Republicans to the attention of the public.

In order to promote his economic program, Hamilton called upon the services of John Fenno, publisher of the *Gazette of the United States*. Fenno established the *Gazette* at Philadelphia in 1789. With the largest readership of any newspaper in the country and printed in the nation's capital, the *Gazette* was the paper of record during Washington's first term. It was also the public mouthpiece of Hamiltonian Federalism. The Secretary of the Treasury not only supplied Fenno with copy for his columns but, more importantly, lucrative printing contracts from the Treasury. In consequence, the *Gazette* consistently heaped praise on the administration, especially Hamilton, while championing the Treasury Secretary's economic program. The arch-Federalist Fisher Ames of Massachusetts said of Fenno, "No printer was ever so *correct* in his politics." Fenno was too correct in his politics as far as Thomas Jefferson was concerned. On February 28, 1791, three days after Washington had signed the Bank Bill, Jefferson wrote to Philip Freneau of the New York *Daily Advertiser* offering him a clerkship as a translator in the State Department. The *Daily Advertiser* had been one of the few newspapers to endorse Antifederalism. As editor, beginning in 1790, Freneau had been critical of Hamilton's funding proposals and the speculators who would benefit from them. When Jefferson offered Freneau a post as a translator, he was more interested that the journalist should translate his antipathy towards Hamilton into popular invective than he was about foreign dispatches. Born to a well-to-do Huguenot family in New York in 1752, Freneau was raised in New Jersey and attended Princeton with James Madison. He worked as a schoolteacher, newspaperman, poet, and mariner. As a journalist, he was noted for his use of abusive and effective calumny against political rivals. When Jefferson offered Freneau a clerkship (in consultation with James Madison), he intended that the newspaperman should establish a periodical to rival Fenno's pro-Hamilton organ. At the end of October 1791, Freneau took his $250 salary as a State Department translator and began publishing the *National Gazette*, which became the public voice of the opposition to Federalism and Hamilton's policies.[15]

Although Freneau began publishing the *National Gazette* in the autumn of 1791, it was not until the spring of 1792 that a full-fledged newspaper war between the mouthpieces of Hamilton and Jefferson broke out. In mid-March Freneau launched a systematic *ad hominem* attack on Hamilton and his policies, especially the newly-released *Report on Manufactures*. The major thrust of Freneau's attack was the assertion that Hamilton sought to impose tyranny on the American people by allowing speculators and financiers to rob them and by vesting absolute power in the hands of a few at the center of government. John Fenno sought to defend his patron, and Hamilton himself joined the fray, personally attacking Jefferson in a series of pseudonymous essays in the *Gazette of the United States*. For the remainder of the decade, extreme partisanship characterized American journalism. Federalist and Republican editors delighted in excoriating and impugning the motives of their political rivals. According to a judge in a 1798 libel case:

> Our satire has been nothing but ribaldry and billingsgate: the contest has been who could call names in the greatest variety of phrases: who could mangle the greatest number of characters, or who could excel in the magnitude of their lies: hence the honor of families has been stained, the highest posts rendered cheap and vile in the sight of the people and the greatest services and virtue blasted.

This trend in American journalism began in earnest with the Philadelphia newspaper war of 1792. While many — including Jefferson and Hamilton — condemned such practices even as they encouraged them, such partisan journalism played a crucial role in raising party awareness among voters and thereby contributed to the development not only of partisanship but democratic political practices in America.[16]

The partisan rhetoric that issued forth from the presses of Fenno and Freneau was all the more impassioned because 1792 was an election year. Having successfully launched the federalist experiment, Washington had planned to retire after his first term. The growth of political factionalism within his own cabinet dismayed the president, who had largely remained outside and above the partisan squabbling of Hamilton and Jefferson. When Washington solicited the advice of Madison, Jefferson, and

Hamilton – arguably the men most responsible for the partisan divisions – each enjoined the president to stand for another term. Washington, they argued, was the only one who could unite the country. With genuine reluctance Washington, who had answered the call of king, colony, Congress, and country for more than four decades, agreed to serve another term. The elections of 1792 witnessed the first expression of partisan bias at the ballot box. To be sure the Federalists and Republicans were not yet full-fledged parties with the appropriate party machinery and discipline, but at the state level, especially in New York, they engaged in direct competition for office. The national elections were also a partisan contest. Although George Washington was again a unanimous choice, winning 132 electoral votes, the battle for the vice-presidency was not so clear. The incumbent, John Adams, had as *president pro tem* of the Senate been clearly identified with the Federalist interest. Republicans mounted a campaign to displace Adams and replace him with George Clinton, the Republican governor of New York. The plan failed when Adams received 77 electoral votes to Clinton's 55, but the election presaged that future elections were likely to be contested by the competing parties.

Political parties require a firmer foundation than the personality differences of their leaders. What then did the embryonic Federalist and Republicans stand for, and to whom did their leaders look for support? The Federalists had a clearer political lineage than the Republicans. In the main, they had been men who supported the Constitution back in 1788 and, they claimed, had been resolute in supporting it, and federal authority, ever since. Leading Federalists were men of commerce and business, merchants, lawyers, and commercial farmers. The Federalists sought a strong national government which would preserve order and promote commerce and manufacturing. Geographically, the Federalists predominated in the coastal towns and river valleys where commerce thrived. Their stronghold was in the northeast of the country. They also drew considerable support in South Carolina, especially in Charleston and its environs. They adopted a paternalistic attitude toward the common people of America, for whom they had contempt mixed with a measure of fear. As an earlier historian of the party noted, "Surely the frankest politicians who ever graced the American scene, the Federalists made no pretense of being any other than what they were: upper-class Americans who had a natural-born right to rule their inferiors in the social and economic scale." Such attitudes in a republican system placed them at an electoral disadvantage which would ultimately prove fatal to the party. Nonetheless, they did draw support from urban artisans who would profit from the economic policies advocated by the Federalists, especially protectionist legislation which would promote manufacturing.[17]

Perhaps the apotheosis of Federalism was the Washington administration's response to a tax insurrection in western Pennsylvania. In March of

1791, as part of the legislative program necessitated by the assumption of state debts by the federal government, Congress adopted an excise tax on whiskey. This tax was very unpopular in the frontier settlements of the Appalachian region, where the production of whiskey was a crucial economic activity. In that region, which had very poor roads, distillation proved to be one of the most profitable means of preserving and marketing grain. During the summer of 1794 there were violent altercations between government tax collectors and local farmers, which led to two deaths. Just as in 1774 and 1786, protesters closed the courts and harassed government agents to prevent the collection of an unpopular tax. The Washington administration's reaction to the "Whiskey Rebellion," as these events came to be known, was quite revealing of Federalist attitudes. After appealing unsuccessfully for the rebels to desist, President Washington called upon the states to furnish him with more than twelve thousand men to suppress to the insurrection. Alexander Hamilton, whose tax policies had caused the uprising, led the troops to western Pennsylvania in September and October. By the time the army had arrived the rebellion had collapsed. Nonetheless, Hamilton felt the "campaign" against the rebels had been a success because the government had asserted its authority. Ideologically, the Federalists valued order more than liberty. The Whiskey Rebellion marked a deliberate challenge to law and order. Taxation with representation must be accepted, Federalists contended, if the government were to have any credibility. Although the decision to suppress the rebellion had had strong bipartisan support, it would be very difficult for the Federalists to sustain such highhanded methods for long. As the perceptive Massachusetts Federalist Fisher Ames noted in the wake of the rebellion, "elective rulers can scarcely ever employ the physical force of a democracy without turning the moral force, or power of public opinion, against the government."[18]

In contrast to their Federalist counterparts, Republicans valued liberty more than order. As their leader, Thomas Jefferson, famously remarked to James Madison in the wake of Shays's Rebellion, "a little rebellion, now and then, is a good thing, and as necessary in the political world as storms in the physical." While the Republicans professed to uphold and defend the Constitution, they favored limits on the power of the federal government. They saw Congress – especially the House of Representatives – and the states as crucial bulwarks against the encroachments of a Federalist tyranny. While the Federalists were the party of urban-based commerce and manufacturing, the Republican appealed to farmers, large and small. As Jefferson wrote with some overstatement in 1796, "the whole landed interest is republican." In consequence, the Republicans were a party led by large southern, particularly Virginian, planters and whose rank and file was drawn from the vast number of small farmers across the country. The paradox that the party devoted to liberty in early America was led by men whose fortunes were derived from the labor of African slaves did not trouble many Republicans. (The Federalists, by contrast, despite their contempt for common people had more opponents of slavery in their ranks than did the Republicans.) The Republicans had a more optimistic view of their supporters than did the Federalists. The Republicans believed that so long as most American voters were small farmers who lived independently and exported their small surpluses, the country would prosper and liberty would flourish in a genuinely republican system where the mass of small freeholders, not a clique of stockjobbers, speculators, bankers, manufacturers, and the benighted laborers who were dependent upon them, held sway.[19]

The Federalists and Republicans, therefore, stood in marked contrast to each other. Indeed, they arguably presented American voters in the 1790s with a greater ideological choice than the subsequent two-party system has. Whereas the Federalists were elitist in their outlook, believing the government must preserve law and order and favoring government intervention in the economy and the promotion and protection of American manufacturing, the Republicans favored a more democratic model and held that the government should not interfere in the economy or in people's lives. These differences are perhaps clearer in historical hindsight than they were to contemporaries. In the early 1790s, many if not most political leaders, including those who were proponents of Federalism and Republicanism, still professed to abhor political parties. The parties described here were at that time embryonic: they had little popular support, and would not fully mature until the end of the decade. The catalyst for their development, and that which separated Federalists and Republicans more than any other issue, was the French Revolution.

The French Revolution in America

Soon after George Washington took office in 1789 the French Estates-General began meeting at Versailles, setting in motion the French Revolution. In general, Americans of all political persuasions welcomed the news from France, including the meeting of the Estates-General, the formation of the National Assembly in June 1789, the storming of the Bastille in July, and the adoption of the Declaration of the Rights of Man in August. These events were congruent with the American revolutionary tradition and seemed to validate that tradition just as Americans were launching their experiment with federal republicanism. American enthusiasm for the French Revolution continued over the next several years. When news reached America in December 1792 that the revolutionary French armies had turned back Prussian and Austrian forces at Valmy on September 20, and that the monarchy was abolished two days later, Americans turned out in the streets for massive public celebrations. Soon thereafter American opinion began to change. The execution of Louis XVI on January 21, 1793 and the onset of the Reign of Terror as well as the French declaration of war on Britain on February 1 alienated many Federalists. The arrival of a new French ambassador to the United States – Citizen Edmond Charles Genêt – prompted a partisan division over the French Revolution which would dominate American politics and diplomacy for the rest of the decade.

Citizen Genêt was thirty years old when he arrived in the United States in the spring of 1793. Though born of noble parentage and a beneficiary of royal patronage as young man, expediency and enthusiasm had made him an ardent revolutionary of the Girondist variety by the time he was dispatched to the United States in January 1793. Genêt's mission was not only to represent the revolutionary French government in the United States, but also to assist France in its struggles with its enemies. To that end, he planned to commission privateers in American ports to prey upon British shipping in the West Indies (as Benjamin Franklin did in France during the American War of Independence). He also planned to intrigue among the American and French settlers of the frontier region in an effort to attack the colonial holdings of France's enemies, especially Spanish Florida and Louisiana and British Canada. Diplomatically, Genêt hoped to remind the American people of their treaty obligations to France under their 1778 agreement and, if possible, to negotiate a closer alliance between the two republics. Such an agenda would have challenged the most experienced and skilled diplomat. Events were to reveal that Genêt, though dashing and charismatic, was certainly not an able diplomat.

Genêt arrived in Charleston, South Carolina on April 8, 1793. He was met at the pier by a large and enthusiastic crowd of well-wishers. He spent ten days in Charleston conferring with local officials and commissioning four privateers whom he authorized, without consulting the United States government, to attack British shipping and to dispose of their prizes in the South Carolina port. On April 18 the French envoy left Charleston to travel by land to Philadelphia. Genêt's journey, which lasted four weeks, took on all the attributes of a triumphal procession. Everywhere the ambassador went he was greeted by cheering crowds and enthusiastic local officials. His overland trip convinced Genêt that he and the revolution which he represented enjoyed wide popular support in the United States. While Genêt traveled to Philadelphia, Washington met with his cabinet to decide upon the policy of the United States with respect to the war between Britain and France. The cabinet was unanimous that the United States should stay out of the European war. After consulting the cabinet, Washington decided that although he would receive Genêt as the representative of the new French republic, he would keep the United States out of the European conflict. On April 22, President Washington issued a proclamation which asserted America's neutrality in the European war.[20]

With public accolades still ringing in his ears, Citizen Genêt was unwilling to accept Washington's decision. He continued to commission privateers to operate from American ports while demanding that the United States do more to protect French property on American vessels from seizure by the British. Additionally he schemed with western settlers, encouraging them to attack Spanish and British territory in North America. When the Washington administration took steps to enforce the Neutrality Proclamation by prohibiting American citizens from equipping French privateers or from participating in expeditions against Spanish and British territory, Genêt attempted to test his strength against that of George Washington. In August, the French minister demanded that Washington call Congress into session to review American policy toward France. Citizen Genêt threatened to go above the president's head and appeal directly to the American people. Washington refused to capitulate to Genêt's demands, and requested that the French government recall their representative in Philadelphia.[21]

The Genêt imbroglio revealed a sharp partisan division had developed in America with respect to the French Revolution. Opposing attitudes toward the events in France did as much as Hamilton's fiscal policies to encourage the development of formal political parties. The Federalists, as admirers of Britain and proponents of social stability, opposed the French Revolution and sympathized with their British trading partners in their struggle against the forces of mob rule and anarchy. Fisher Ames expressed the sentiments of most Federalists: "Behold France an open Hell, still ringing with agonies and blasphemies, still smoking with sufferings and crimes in which we see ... perhaps our future state." According to the Federalists, although the Jacobins in France had little in common with the American republicans of 1776, they did however have everything in common with the American Republicans of the 1790s, who would like nothing better than to overturn American society and submit to the rule of the mob and law of the guillotine. Federalists came to see the British struggle against revolutionary France as an international manifestation of their own domestic struggle against the forces of disorder and social leveling. For the remainder of the decade and beyond, the favored Federalist epithet for their political rivals was "Jacobin," and for the remainder of their years in power the Federalists advocated a pro-British and anti-French policy.[22]

The Republicans, by contrast, were warm supporters of revolutionary France, which they considered America's true mother country. Republicans reminded Americans that France had stood by them in their hour of need and that they had a moral (as well as a treaty) obligation to do the same for the French. Moreover, since France and the United States shared membership in the relatively exclusive club of the world's republics, Americans also shared an ideological bond with the French. If some moderate Republicans were concerned about the executions of Louis XVI and Marie Antoinette as well as the bloodshed associated with the Terror, not so their leader. On the eve of the Terror, Thomas Jefferson attempted to explain away the excesses of the Jacobins:

> In the struggle which was necessary, many guilty persons fell with-out the forms of trial, and with them some innocent. These I de-plore as much as any body, & shall deplore some of them to the day of my death. But I deplore them as I should have done had they fallen in battle.... The liberty of the whole earth was depending on the issue of the contest and was ever such a prize won with so little innocent blood? My own affections have been deeply wounded by some of the martyrs to this cause, but rather than it should have failed, I would have seen half the earth desolated. Were there but an Adam & an Eve left in every country, & left free, it would be better than it now is.[23]

To most Republicans, the cause of France was the cause of liberty. Like the Jacobins, American Republicans were locked in a struggle with the forces of reaction and monarchical tyranny with their Federalist adversaries. Events in France, seen through the lens of American politics, encouraged thousands of Americans to join Democratic-Republican Societies, modeled after the French Jacobin clubs. These societies became not only vehicles for Americans to express support for republican France but also for the Republican party in the United States. They served as centers for the organization of Republican supporters at the grassroots level. Washington believed that the societies represented a threat to the United States, blaming them for fomenting war on behalf of France and even accusing them of causing the Whiskey Rebellion. The misgivings of the President notwith-standing, Republican support for the French Revolution enhanced the popular appeal of the party which would, in time, allow it to displace the Federalists at the ballot box. The French Revolution became the touchstone for determining political allegiances in American politics during the 1790s.[24]

The Jay Treaty

One reason that the French Revolution took on such significance in domestic American politics was because the issues and difficulties raised by that upheaval seemed always to be intruding into American life. Neither the British nor the French were pleased by Washington's declaration of American neutrality. The British in particular were unhappy at the American assertion of freedom of the seas on behalf of neutrals, which manifested itself in American vessels trading with and supplying the beleaguered French colonies in the West Indies. As a consequence, on November 6, 1793 the British government adopted an order in council directly aimed at disrupting the American trade with the French West Indies. The edict authorized British vessels to seize any neutral vessels carrying supplies to the French islands. In addition to seizing American vessels and impressing American sailors into the Royal Navy, the British continued to occupy forts on American territory in the Northwest and to encourage the Indians in that region to resist American expansion. All of these circumstances combined to bring Anglo-American relations to the point of crisis in late 1793.

The British government may have taken heart that British–American tensions would subside when the Anglophobic Thomas Jefferson retired as Secretary of State in early December 1793. If so, the hope was short-lived. In January 1794, James Madison introduced a series of proposals to the Congress calling for commercial retaliation against Britain. The measures, which included duties to protect and promote American manufactures (Hamilton must have been amused by the measures if not their intent), were defeated in a sectional vote: southern Republicans favored the measures while northern Federalists, who profited from trade with Britain, opposed them. Despite the signs of hostility from Congress, British aggression against American shipping continued unabated. Under the recent order-in-council, British privateers and naval vessels seized over two hundred and fifty American merchantmen on the grounds that they were carrying contraband. In February, Congress authorized the building of six new frigates for the United States Navy, and in March Jonathan Dayton, a Republican congressman from New Jersey, proposed that the United States should sequester the debts owing to British merchants as security against the American property seized by the British. By the spring of 1794, war between Britain and the United States seemed inevitable for the second time in a generation.

In a last-ditch effort to avoid an open breach with Britain, a group of Federalist senators appealed to Washington to send a minister plenipoten–tiary to Britain to attempt to negotiate a peaceful resolution to the crisis. Washington dispatched Chief Justice John Jay to London in May with orders to seek a settlement, under the terms of which the British would agree to vacate the western forts, repay the losses suffered by American shippers, and compensate Americans for slaves taken away by the British at the conclusion of the peace of 1783. If possible, Jay was to seek a commer-cial agreement with the British. Jay was eager to reach an agreement with the British, and he confided to Hamilton, "I will endeavour to accommodate rather than dispute." He reached an agreement which would avert war in November 1794. Under the terms of the agreement, which came to be known as Jay's Treaty, the British agreed to evacuate the western posts by

June 1796 and made concessions to open India and the British West Indies (with restrictions) to American trade. In exchange, Jay surrendered America's right as a neutral carrier by agreeing to the British "Rule of 1756," which stated that neutral countries could not trade in times of war with nations and places where they were forbidden in peacetime. (This effectively closed American trade with the French West Indies.) Moreover, Jay guaranteed that American ports would not be used by French privateers to sell their prizes, and that Britain would receive most favored nation trading status; that is, the United States would not impose discriminatory duties against British goods. Essentially, Jay averted an Anglo-American war by committing the United States to a close trading and economic relationship with Britain.[25]

Copies of the agreement did not reach Philadelphia until early March 1795. When they did, President Washington and the leader of the Senate, Edmund Randolph, agreed that the terms of the treaty should be kept secret while the Senate deliberated over its ratification. After lengthy debate, the Senate eventually gave its approval to the treaty in June by a margin of twenty to ten, thereby barely gaining the two-thirds majority required by the Constitution. Leading Republicans in the House of Representatives, working closely with Citizen Pierre Auguste Adet (the latest French minister in Philadelphia), unsuccessfully tried to block ratification of the treaty by asserting that it required the approval of the House as well as the Senate. When this tactic failed, Republicans, with Adet's assistance and encouragement, leaked the text of the treaty to Benjamin Franklin Bache's Philadelphia *Aurora*. The text duly appeared in the newspaper and set off a fierce public reaction against the agreement, which was seen as a humiliating submission to the British. Despite the outcry, Washington signed the treaty at the end of July.

The Jay Treaty did much to crystallize the partisan divisions which had been developing over the previous four years. The agreement was unpopular with Republicans and with the public. From an economic standpoint, the Federalists were vindicated by the agreement. Thanks to the treaty, American trade with the British Empire boomed over the next few years. Although the treaty placed limits on the size of American vessels which could trade in the British West Indies, the limits were routinely ignored. As they had been before the Revolution, the British West Indies were once again dependent upon the United States for flour, meal, salted meat, dried fish and lumber, very much to profit of American farmers and shippers. The treaty also gave American shippers and traders an entrée into the British Empire in India. Despite these economic benefits, however, the treaty remained unpopular with many Americans. Politically, the agreement was very costly to the Federalists. It gave the Republicans a solid platform from which to challenge the ruling party. In the election of 1796, the Republicans could charge the Federalists with abandoning the neutral rights espoused by Washington in 1794.

The election of 1796 and the quasi-war with France

By 1796, George Washington had tired of public life. He had only reluctantly agreed to serve a second term in 1792 in the hope that he could forestall the development of partisanship. In the aftermath of the Jay Treaty it was clear that such an objective was impossible; indeed, after the ratification of the treaty Washington himself was, for the first time, subject to partisan attacks. Before he signed the treaty a Republican newspaper opposed to the agreement declared, "thanks to heaven we have yet a WASHINGTON to check the growth of British influence." After he signed the agreement, another paper expressed views that became increasingly common in the Republican press and to a much lesser extent in the nation at large:

> does the President fancy himself the grand Lama of this country that we are to approach him with superstitious reverence or relig-ious regard? ... He has disdained to look down with an eye of com-placency from the eminence on which they [Federalists] have placed him. We have been guilty of idolatry for too long.[26]

Weary of the incessant party bickering and personal attacks, Washington decided in the summer of 1796 not to run for re-election in the upcoming elections. His was not to be one of the frequent political retirements which occurred during the period whereby the individual concerned remained publicly active. Indeed Jefferson had "retired" from public life in December 1793, as had Hamilton in January of 1795, yet both remained leading figures in their respective parties. With the assistance of Hamilton and John Jay, Washington prepared a valedictory message to the nation. Washington's "Farewell Address" appeared in newspapers throughout the country in September 1796. In the message, the president warned his countrymen against the evils of partisanship. He counseled them to promote harmonious relations and commerce abroad but to avoid entan-gling alliances or involvement in European conflicts. Though Washington remained a highly respected figure in American life well beyond his death in 1799, many Americans ignored the admonitions of his final address.[27]

With Washington headed for retirement at Mount Vernon, the election of 1796 would be the first presidential election which would be an open contest between the Federalists and Republicans. A caucus of Federalist congressmen nominated John Adams of Massachusetts and Thomas Pinckney of South Carolina as their candidates. Adams had served two terms as Washington's vice-president and had been active in public life since his defense in Boston Massacre trial in 1770. Pinckney was attractive because he came from South Carolina, the only Federalist stronghold in the south, and because he had successfully negotiated a treaty with Spain. Under the terms of the Pinckney Treaty of 1795, Spain settled its border with the United States at the thirty-first parallel and acknowledged an American right to use the Mississippi River and to store goods at New Orleans. Unlike the Jay Treaty, the Pinckney Treaty was hailed as a success, especially in the traditionally Republican west. Federalist strategists hoped that nominating Pinckney might win their party some support among southern and western voters. The Republicans nominated Thomas Jefferson, who remained in "retirement" at his Monticello plantation in Virginia, and the New York lawyer and politician Aaron Burr. Alexander Hamilton played a major role in the 1796 election. Hamilton had never liked Adams, and he rightly feared that if Adams were elected, he himself would not have the same influence with the executive that he had enjoyed with Washington. In consequence, Hamilton tried to get some Federalist electors to give their votes to Pinckney and not Adams in the hope that the Carolinian would be elected president and Adams would again be relegated to the vice-presidency. Hamilton's plan did not work and his interference nearly cost the Federalists the election as Adams eked out a narrow victory over Jefferson, who became vice-president. Adams received 71 electoral votes to Jefferson's 68. Pinckney only received 59 votes. The election revealed the sectional nature of the partisan division in American politics, as Adams only received two votes from south of the Potomac and Jefferson only eighteen from north of it.

The post-Jacobin government of France, the Directory, took a keen interest in outcome of the 1796 election. The Directory viewed the Jay Treaty as a declaration of hostility. There was a feeling in Paris, however, that the American public was generally sympathetic to the French cause and that the Federalist administration was out of step with the voters. The Directory decided to await the election result before taking action against the United States. Like Genêt, the new French ambassador Citizen Adet had few reservations about interfering in American domestic politics. Adet consulted with Republican congressmen and newspaper editors, and in November 1796 he published a series of proclamations in American newspapers threatening a hostile French reaction to a Federalist victory, including a suspension of diplomatic relations and a tougher attitude toward American vessels trading with Britain. For the Directory, the election of John Adams signaled a turning point in the deterioration of Franco-American relations. Just as the British had attacked and seized American vessels trading with France and its colonies in 1793, in 1797 the French undertook a similar program. Although the bulk of the French navy had its hands full with the British, hundreds of French privateers preyed on American shipping in the West Indies, the Atlantic and even in American territorial waters. In response to French aggression, the Adams administration took steps to strengthen the army and navy in anticipation of the apparently inevitable war with France.

As in 1794, the government appealed to diplomacy before war. President Adams dispatched a three-man negotiating team – Charles Cotesworth Pinckney, John Marshall, and Elbridge Gerry – to seek a negotiated settlement with France. The American ministers arrived in Paris in October 1797. They were rebuffed by the French foreign minister, Charles Maurice Talleyrand. The American diplomats were preparing to give up their mission and return home when three agents representing Talleyrand – designated X, Y, Z, by the Americans – approached the Americans demanding that the United States loan France $12 million and pay Talleyrand a $250,000 bribe before they could discuss a new Franco-American treaty. In April 1798 the dispatches of the American mission were published, and public opinion shifted dramatically. Thanks to the "XYZ Affair," public support for the Federalists and an immediate declaration of war rose immediately. Congress appropriated money to enlarge the army and navy and declared the treaties of 1778 in abeyance. Despite his newfound popularity, John Adams refused to take the next step and ask Congress for a declaration of war. Adams preferred to temporize in the hope that a peaceful solution could be found and that an all-out war could be avoided. In consequence, the United States and France engaged in an undeclared "quasi-war" at sea.[28]

As the nation prepared for the anticipated war with France, Federalists in Congress declared war against their domestic enemies. In June and July of 1798, at the behest of leading Federalists, Congress adopted a series of laws intended to stifle internal dissent. These acts (there were four, only two of which were enforced) were collectively known as the Alien and Sedition Acts. The first of the laws to be adopted was the Naturalization Act. This act, adopted by Congress on June 18, 1798, lengthened the amount of time immigrants had to be resident in the country before they could be naturalized from five to fourteen years. The intention of the act was to prevent foreign-born voters from having an undue influence in American elections. This was a patently partisan action, since the majority of immigrants voted for the Republicans. On July 14, Congress adopted the Sedition Act by a narrow partisan vote of 44 to 41. This act called for fines and imprisonment for writing, speaking, or publishing anything deemed, "false, scandalous, and malicious" about the government or its officers. This act was directed at the Republican newspaper editors – many of whom had cooperated with Citizen Adet's efforts to interfere with the 1796 election – who were deemed a threat to the war effort. Fifteen men, mostly newspaper editors, were indicted under the Sedition Act, of whom ten were convicted, fined, and imprisoned for various lengths of time.[29]

The Alien and Sedition Acts were unpopular with Republicans, especially when open war with France never occurred. Thomas Jefferson and James Madison played the leading role in the most prominent protest against the acts. On November 13 and December 24, 1798 the respective legislatures of Kentucky and Virginia adopted sets of resolutions condemning the acts. Jefferson was the author of the Kentucky resolves and Madison those of Virginia. Taken together, the resolutions endorsed a strict construction interpretation of the Constitution, asserting that the government had no authority to adopt such restrictive measures. The resolves took as their point of departure that the Constitution was a compact of sovereign states, and that it was up to the states themselves to judge whether the actions of the federal government were constitutional or not. The most radical implication of this reasoning was that states could nullify unjust federal laws. Although none of the other fourteen state legislatures – now including Vermont and Tennessee as well as Kentucky – endorsed the resolves (ten actually rejected them), they were significant for ideological and political reasons. Ideologically, the resolutions provided the foundation for the states' rights interpretation of the Constitution. That this view originated, in part, with James Madison is an interesting comment on the evolution of the Constitution in its first decade. In 1787 James Madison had been the driving force behind the creation of a strong federal government, which he hoped would have a veto over state actions. A decade later, Madison had come to believe that the federal government had become too strong and contended that the states must intervene on behalf of their citizens to protect them from its encroachments.[30]

The Virginia and Kentucky resolutions were of more immediate political than ideological import. The resolves were very much the opening salvo of the 1800 election campaign. The burst of popularity and enthusiasm for the Federalists in the wake of the XYZ Affair had largely dissipated by 1799. The Alien and Sedition Acts and the taxes which the preparation for war necessitated had proved unpopular. In January and February 1799, German settlers in eastern Pennsylvania took up arms in protest of an unpopular property tax levied by the Federalists to pay for the expansion of the army. In March, a party of armed men led by one John Fries compelled the federal marshal of Bethlehem to release eighteen tax protesters whom he had arrested. President Adams sent troops to suppress "Fries's Rebellion," an action which proved unpopular and reinforced the Republican view that Federalist were high-handed and willing to trample on civil liberties. Both Federalists and Republicans believed the election of 1800 would be a referendum on the crucial issues – foreign policy, political economy, and the power of the Federal government – which divided the two parties.

There were sixteen states in the United States by 1800. In ten of the states, presidential electors were chosen by the state legislatures. In the remaining six, electors would be chosen in state-wide or district elections.

In May 1800, a caucus of Federalist Congressmen and Senators again nominated John Adams and Charles Cotesworth Pinckney of South Carolina as its candidates. The Republican caucus nominated Jefferson and Aaron Burr. The campaign of 1800 was a bitter one. Jefferson was portrayed by Federalists as an atheistic Jacobin, whereas Adams was, according to the Republicans, a monarchical tyrant. Adams was ultimately undone not by Republican propaganda but by members of his own party. Alexander Hamilton had never liked Adams and, as in 1796, intrigued during the campaign against the New Englander. In an effort to influence the Federalist voting in the hope of condemning Adams to the vice-presidency, Hamilton produced a pamphlet for circulation among Federalists which was highly critical of Adams's presidency and questioned the president's judgment and sanity. Aaron Burr procured a copy of Hamilton's attack and gave it to the newspapers. Whether Hamilton's attack swayed many voters is doubtful, but it certainly opened a wide rift at the top of the Federalist party. When the votes were finally tallied, Adams and Pinckney had secured 65 and 64 electoral votes respectively, which was not enough to defeat Jefferson and Burr.

The Republican victory in 1800 was not clear-cut. Both Jefferson and Burr tallied 73 votes in the Electoral College. According to the Constitution, in such cases the House of Representatives should decide the outcome of the contest. As if the defeat of their party at the elections was not enough, the outgoing Federalist-dominated Congress would have to choose Adams's successor. After thirty-five ballots, Jefferson was elected on February 16, 1801. The Federalists would never win the presidency again.

Conclusion

The election of 1800 was significant in that it represented the first peaceful transfer of power in the history of the American republic. Such an outcome was not inevitable, as the political instability in France had demonstrated. The Federalist era witnessed several notable successes. Despite being caught between France and Britain, the United States managed to avoid war with both powers. Three new states were added to the union, and the British and Indians were neutralized as obstacles to American settlement in the Northwest. From a commercial standpoint, Hamilton's controversial economic policies had proved successful as American trade and commerce flourished. Most significantly, despite significant internal and external pressures, the constitutional settlement of 1788 endured a turbulent first decade. To some extent, much of the credit for the initial success of the Constitution belongs to the Federalists. In their arrogance, the Federalists asserted that they were better able to govern the country than their rivals or the common people. In the short term they may have been right. The Federalists gave life to the federal republic, but in so doing they made themselves redundant. For all their contempt of the American public, the Federalists ultimately bowed to popular will, which was the essence of republicanism as understood by Americans. The Federalist era therefore witnessed a profound political transformation of the United States. Though condemned by contemporaries, the rise of political partisanship helped to democratize American politics. The important questions which faced the United States during the 1790s, concerning economic development, the French Revolution, and internal security, provided a clear focus and distinction between the emerging political parties. American voters were faced with as much of an ideological choice during the 1790s as they would be at any other time in their history. The decade witnessed a steady increase in political participation. This was not only represented at the ballot box – only two states held elections for the 1789 presidential election compared to six in 1800 – but also in popular culture. Party differences manifested themselves on the streets as common people made their voices heard. Faced with a steady increase in popular political participation, the Federalists with their elitist paternalistic attitudes were unlikely to retain power for long. With the election of 1800, the democratically inclined Republicans came to power. They, especially Thomas Jefferson, would come to find that the demands of administration were considerably different from those of opposition. Jefferson and his successor, James Madison, would face a grave threat to the young republic as the sovereignty and independence of the new nation were threatened by France and Britain.

8

AN EMPIRE OF LIBERTY:
1801–1815

Introduction

On November 18, 1805, Captain William Clark of the United States Army and eleven men, including Clark's slave York, explored the mouth of Columbia River and beheld the Pacific Ocean for the first time. Clark, along with Captain Meriwether Lewis, had led an exploratory expedition from St. Louis to the Pacific which had set out in May of 1804. They were the first citizens of the United States to make an overland journey to the Pacific. Clark noted that the "men appear much Satisfied with their trip beholding with estonishment the high waves dashing against the rocks & this emence Ocian." Clark carved his name on a tree overlooking the ocean with the wonderfully understated caption, "By Land from the U. States in 1804 & 1805."[1] The Lewis and Clark expedition was one of the remarkable achievements of Thomas Jefferson's two-term presidency. The expedition was the apotheosis of the ideological vision of the third president, who conceived of the expedition as a commercial, scientific, and diplomatic exercise. As such, it was the capstone of Jefferson's vision of an expansive American republic.

Under the guidance of Jefferson and his successor James Madison, the United States would experience dramatic geographic and economic development between 1801 and 1815. While in power, the Republicans pursued a policy of geographic and commercial expansionism which had its roots in the party's agrarian philosophy. The growth and vibrancy of the young republic would bring it into conflict once again with the premier European powers, Britain and France, which, although they valued American trade, were dismissive of American military and diplomatic claims. The result was a desultory war with Britain which, although it had little impact on the geopolitical situation, had profound consequences for American national identity. The War of 1812 not only marked the close of active American concern with European political events for the first time since British settlement, but also the culmination of the nation-building process begun in 1776. The geographic and commercial expansion of the years between 1801 and 1815 constitute the last act of the drama which began in 1763.

An empire of liberty

When Jefferson entered office in 1801, he was both lauded and derided for his alleged democratic tendencies. Jefferson has been celebrated ever since, by historians and laypeople alike, as the apostle of liberty among the "Founding Fathers." Jefferson's reputation owes much to his pre-presidential career as the author of the Declaration of Independence and a leader of Republican opposition to Federalism, especially the Alien and Sedition Acts. As president, Jefferson was the architect of a massive territorial and commercial expansion of the United States. During the age of Napoleon, Jefferson proved himself an adept empire-builder; he more than doubled the land area of the United States and asserted an American claim, realized by his successors, to the Pacific coast during his presidency. By comparison Napoleon's empire-building, while it bathed Europe in blood, was not nearly as durable. Arguably the most successful imperialist of the age was not the Corsican, but the Virginian best remembered for declaring that all men were created equal. That Jefferson committed himself to a program of territorial aggrandizement is perfectly consistent with his previous actions and his views on political economy.

The agrarian philosophy of the early Republican party as espoused by Jefferson and Madison was predicated on a belief that republics, like all states, experienced a life cycle not unlike that of individuals. Jefferson and Madison contended that an agrarian republic would keep the United States youthful, vigorous, and healthy. To pursue a program of intensive manufacturing along the lines which Alexander Hamilton had advocated, while it might increase prosperity for a few, would lead to an increase in luxury and corruption which would eventually undermine America's republican institutions. Just as Hamilton looked to Britain as a forerunner for American economic development and prosperity, to be eclipsed in due course by the United States, Republicans, especially Jefferson, looked to Britain as an awful warning of the social and political consequences of such development. They saw not prosperity, but the extremes of wealth and the moral and political corruption which they believed were the concomitants of manufacturing. Rather than embrace and encourage such an eventuality, Jefferson felt it should be forestalled as long as possible. The realization of such a vision relied on two factors: American farmers must be able to produce and market their crops for international consumption, and the United States must have enough land to guarantee the future expansion of American agriculture.

Historians have long debated over the nature of the agriculture practiced by early American farmers. Some have suggested that most American farmers before the late eighteenth century produced for their own subsistence and traded locally whatever surplus they might have had. According to this view, at some time in the late eighteenth or early nineteenth centuries American farmers became more deeply involved in producing commodities for sale in what is usually termed a "market revolution." Other historians have suggested that American farmers were more deeply engaged in the market, seeking to produce and sell surpluses, at a much earlier date. These analyses rest on an assumption that American farmers made a transition from subsistence to market farming. They differ over when, but not whether, such a transition occurred.

Recently, Richard L. Bushman has suggested an alternative model. Bushman argues that most American farms were "composite farms" which, depending upon their location, combined subsistence and market farming. According to Bushman, the composite farm may have characterized American agriculture for several centuries. Bushman's model certainly provides an accurate description of American agricultural practice during the early nineteenth century, where even the rudest frontier farm household sought to produce enough to survive and to market its surplus, and the largest plantation produced not only for export across the Atlantic but also to feed its unfree laborers and free residents. The crucial components for American agricultural health – and, Republicans contended, American political and economic health – were access to land and markets. Without the former, subsistence was impossible. Without the latter, so too was prosperity. Consequently, the most pressing issues of the presidencies of Thomas Jefferson and James Madison would be the promotion and protection of American trade and the geographic expansion of the nation.[2]

Jefferson had long been an advocate of American western expansion. He was the author of the 1784 Land Ordinance (the predecessor of the 1787 Northwest Ordinance) which established a system for the settlement of the west and the admission of new states from the national domain. The ordinance, with its provisions that western territory should be divided into new states which would enjoy parity with the older original states when admitted to the union, was testimony to Jefferson's strong belief that the future of the republic lay in western expansion and settlement. Jefferson's belief that the settlement of the west was the key to the future of the United States led to the major achievement of his presidency: the acquisition of the Louisiana Territory from France.

The Louisiana Purchase and the Lewis and Clark Expedition

As the nineteenth century dawned, Napoleon Bonaparte seized power in France. In late 1798 Napoleon overthrew the Directory; in 1799 he orchestrated his own elevation as First Consul of France and assumed dictatorial powers over a country which remained a republic in name only. Although his main ambitions were in Europe, Napoleon's imperial interests extended to the New World as well. France had ceded Louisiana to Spain in 1762 so as to involve her in the Seven Years' War. By the second Treaty of San Ildefonso, in October 1800 Talleyrand, Napoleon's foreign minister, compelled Spain to "retrocede" Louisiana to France in exchange for an enlargement of Spanish interests in Italy. Napoleon acquired Louisiana as a prelude to reviving French interests in the Caribbean and in North America. To that end, in January 1802 Napoleon dispatched a 30,000 man expeditionary force to Saint-Domingue to suppress a slave revolt against French control over the rebellious colony (see Chapter 9). The French prepared a second force to be sent to New Orleans.

In Washington, the Jefferson administration viewed the French acquisition of Louisiana with foreboding. American settlers in the west depended on access to the Mississippi River and New Orleans to market their produce. Without access to the port at New Orleans American farmers would have to transport their crops overland, which was both expensive and extremely difficult. In 1801, President Jefferson instructed his new minister to France, Robert Livingston, to open discussions with the French government regarding American access to the Mississippi. The president authorized Livingston to discuss the possibility of an American purchase of sufficient area at the mouth of the river to guarantee free navigation and trade for American citizens. The urgency of the situation was made clear in October 1802 when the Spanish Intendant at New Orleans (Spain had not yet returned Louisiana to France) denied American citizens the right to deposit their goods at the port for trans-shipment and export. In consequence, Jefferson dispatched James Monroe to France to assist Livingston with his negotiations, authorizing them, as a wild hope, to purchase New Orleans with $2 million appropriated by Congress.

Meanwhile, Napoleon's desire for imperial glory in the Americas had begun to wane. The French expeditionary force in Saint-Domingue was defeated by the intractable resistance of the Haitian rebels and ravaged by yellow fever. Although France and Britain had been nominally at peace since early 1802, both nations recognized that the "peace" was actually a truce and war was likely to begin again in 1803. Having lost one army in the New World and anticipating renewed warfare in Europe in March 1803, Napoleon decided not to send a second force to Louisiana. Cognizant of the Congressional appropriation for the purchase of New Orleans, Napoleon instructed his ministers to enter into serious negotiations with the American representatives for the purchase of the entire territory. After two years of frustration Robert Livingston found the French much more amenable to striking a deal. On April 12, 1803, just days after Monroe's arrival in Paris, Livingston agreed to purchase not just New Orleans but the whole of the Louisiana Territory from the French. At a total cost of approximately 80 million francs (approximately $16 million), the United States would acquire not only total control of the Mississippi but also 828,000 square miles of territory extending from the Mississippi to the Rocky Mountains as well as New Orleans. Living in the territory were approximately 50,000 French, Spanish and creole settlers who would become American citizens and 150,000 Native Americans who, though denied citizenship, would be compelled to treat with the United States government. Livingston and Monroe reached a formal accord on the terms of the agreement on April 30.[3]

The Louisiana Purchase transformed the United States. It confirmed and encouraged the westward growth of the nation which, along with the dispute over slavery, would be the dominant theme in the history of the country during the nineteenth century. Ultimately, the purchase would allow the United States to turn away from a direct involvement in the affairs of Europe. Between 1763 and 1815, American development was closely entwined with and determined by European events. However, between 1815 and 1914 the United States would largely be unconcerned with and untouched by events in Europe, save with their effect on immigration to the United States. For most of the nineteenth century the United States would be concerned with questions of its internal economic and political development, particularly slavery, industrialization, and westward expansion. The purchase more than doubled the geographic area of the United States. Just forty years after the British government had attempted to restrict American settlement to the east of the Appalachians, the United States now extended as far west as the Rockies. Eventually, thirteen new states would be carved out of the territory acquired in 1803 from France. While Napoleon would squander the money generated by the sale of Louisiana in spreading hardship and death across Europe, the territory sold would become a permanent part of the United States.

The acquisition of the Louisiana Territory would have deleterious consequences for Native Americans both to the east and west of the Mississippi River. With the spread of slave-based cotton agriculture during the early decades of the nineteenth century the pressure on eastern Indians, especially those in the southeast, increased considerably as white settlers coveted their land. Louisiana provided the federal government with the territory to which these Indians would be forcibly removed during the 1820s and 1830s. For the Native Americans of the Great Plains, the Louisiana Purchase brought them into contact and eventual conflict with the United States government and its citizens who, in their prior dealings with Indians, had demonstrated a marked aggressiveness and acquisitiveness which did not augur well for the future. Indeed, relations between the Plains Indians and the federal government were characterized by conflict throughout the nineteenth century. In short, the acquisition of Louisiana facilitated the displacement of Native Americans.[4]

Most significantly from the perspective of the president and his party, the purchase of Louisiana seemed to guarantee that the United States would have enough land to ensure that the nation remained a republic of small farmers. Given Jefferson's strict construction of the Constitution during the Federalist period – his opposition to the Hamiltonian fiscal program and the Alien and Sedition Acts was based on the assertion that the Constitution did not provide for such actions – the Louisiana Purchase can be construed as an ideological departure for the president. There is no provision in the Constitution, after all, for the president to initiate the purchase of hundreds of thousands of square miles of foreign territory. Such a view is too narrow. Jefferson was committed to the idea that the United States should be an agrarian republic, for only in such a republic could individual liberty be maintained. His opposition to the Hamiltonian program which sought to promote American manufacturing was grounded in the belief that the political and social consequences of such development would have a deleterious impact on the American republic and its citizens. It was with the objective of promoting the agriculture and commerce upon which he felt the republic must be based that Jefferson sent Livingston and Monroe to France to negotiate for New Orleans. When they returned with an agreement for the whole of Louisiana Jefferson, whose outlook and ambitions for the American republic were continental in scale, was thrilled. He had no qualms with respect to the Constitution because he believed the purchase would safeguard the future of the republic. The public and the Republican party agreed. So too did the Senate, which approved the purchase by a wide margin on October 20, 1803.

Land without commerce was useless. The Republican vision of success and prosperity depended on agriculture, which required increasing amounts of land *and* access to markets so that America's farmers could sell what they grew and profit from their labor. The significance of commerce to the Jeffersonian conception of Republicanism is epitomized by the Lewis and Clark expedition. Jefferson had an abiding interest in exploiting the commercial potential of the west which long antedated the Louisiana Purchase. In 1792, encouraged by the seaborne explorations of the Columbia River and the Pacific coast by Captain George Vancouver of the Royal Navy and the American captain Robert Gray, Jefferson proposed that the American Philosophical Society undertake a subscription to sponsor an overland journey to the Pacific. The Society raised £1,000 and Jefferson selected a French botanist, André Michaux, to lead the expedition in 1793. Michaux, who proved to be a French spy, never traveled further west than Kentucky. Undeterred, in January 1803 President Jefferson secured a secret appropriation from Congress of $2,500 to sponsor an exploratory mission to the headwaters of the Missouri River and across to the Pacific for the purpose of extending "the external commerce of the United States."

The planning for the Lewis and Clark expedition long preceded the Louisiana Purchase. Jefferson, who took an avid and personal interest in the mission, believed the expedition would serve multiple functions. Not only would Lewis and Clark gain invaluable geographic and scientific information about the land, flora, and fauna of the west – objectives to which the president, who saw himself as an Enlightenment *philosophe*, was committed – but they should advance the commercial and diplomatic interests of the United States. Jefferson hoped that Lewis and Clark would discover a route to the Pacific which was largely by water. He hoped that the headwaters of the Missouri River and those of the Columbia River would not be that far apart, and would allow for a relatively easy transport across the continent. If Lewis and Clark could discover such a passage while securing the fealty of the Native Americans they encountered, then the United States might wrest control of the fur trade from the British in Canada. More importantly, such a water route would make the far-flung American republic economically viable as even the most remote parts of the continent would be open to commercial exploitation. Lewis and Clark would not be exploring solely for the sake of the advance of scientific knowledge but also to advance the commercial interests of the United States. That Jefferson conceived of such a venture long before the purchase of Louisiana indicates that, in his own way, his imperial ambitions matched those of his counterpart and contemporary Napoleon. Unlike the Napoleonic empire, that of Jefferson would be an empire of liberty: liberty, that is for white men who owned land, not for the slaves who might work that land or the Native Americans whose displacement was necessary if the agrarian republic were to grow and prosper.[5]

The acquisition of Louisiana gave added urgency to the Lewis and Clark expedition, which departed from St. Louis in May of 1804. Approximately fifty men, mostly hand-picked members of the United States army, comprised the members of the "Corps of Discovery" which the two captains led. Between May 1804 and September 1806 the corps traveled thousands of miles up the Missouri River, across the Rockies, and to the Pacific Coast and back in one of history's remarkable feats of exploration. Along the way, the corps established generally positive relations with the Native American tribes of the Plains, Rockies, and Pacific Coast.

On August 18, 1805 Meriwether Lewis wrote one of the more remarkable diary entries in the history of American letters:

> This day I completed my thirty first year, and conceived that I had
> in all probability now existed about half the period which I am to

remain in this Sublunary world. I reflected that I had as yet done but little, very little, indeed, to further the hapiness of the human race or to advance the information of the succeeding generation. I viewed with regret the many hours I have spent in indolence, and now soarly feel the want of that information which those hours would have given me had they been judiciously expended. [B]ut since they are past and cannot be recalled, I dash from me the gloomy thought, and resolved in future, to redouble my exertions and at least indeavour to promote those two primary objects of human existence, by giving them the aid of that portion of talents which nature and fortune have bestoed on me; or in future, to live for *mankind*, as I have heretofore lived *for myself*.

Lewis wrote these words as he and the Corps of Discovery were about to become the first Americans to traverse the Continental Divide. His concern that he had failed to add to human knowledge is ironic since he expressed it in the journals of the expedition which have come to be recognized as its greatest legacy. Lewis and Clark were not only explorers but careful observers, who kept a detailed daily record of all they saw and did on their transcontinental journey. They were not the first men to traverse the continent, but they were certainly the first who did so with the intent not only to discover but record all they could about the flora, fauna, and people of vast and unknown (at least to most American citizens) interior of North America. Of the tens of thousands of documents concerned with aspects of early American history, none are more remarkable than the journals of Lewis and Clark.

There is an air of tragic irony about this passage as well. Meriwether Lewis did not have another thirty-one years to live: on October 11, 1809, aged thirty-five, he shot himself at a Tennessee inn. In part, the pressure to edit the journals for publication, his contribution to human knowledge, had caused him to take his own life.[6]

To the disappointment of the president, the corps demonstrated that there was indeed no easy water route to the Pacific. Nonetheless the expedition did demonstrate that the continent could be traversed, and it advanced an American claim beyond the Rockies. Moreover, the reports of the expedition gave testimony to the commercial potential of the trans-Mississippi west. The Louisiana Purchase and the Lewis and Clark expedition seemed to guarantee the future development of the United States according to the Jeffersonian ideal as an agrarian republic. But while the long-term health of the republic seemed assured, the country Lewis and Clark returned to in 1806 faced a host of very serious diplomatic and economic concerns which seemed to threaten its very existence.

American diplomacy in a world at war

On May 16, 1803, just over two weeks after the United States agreed to purchase Louisiana, France and Britain resumed their war. For most of the next twelve years the British and French waged war on each other, until Napoleon's final defeat at Waterloo on June 18, 1815. As a nation which was actively involved in maritime trade and the primary neutral carrier in a world at war, Americans profited from trading with the belligerents. Although profitable wartime trade was also risky, particularly when one of the warring nations was the world's foremost naval power. In consequence, the United States sought to steer a perilous diplomatic course between Britain and France while trading with both. The course proved impossible to follow, and in 1812 the United States went to war with Great Britain for the second time since 1776.

Commerce was a crucial component of the vision of agrarian republicanism which characterized Jeffersonian America. If the United States was to remain a nation of prosperous farmers, then those farmers needed not only land but markets. It was access to markets which had made the Mississippi question so crucial. International trade would not only provide Americans with revenue, but also with access to manufactured goods without inviting the baneful influence of manufacturing on the United States. Commerce would, therefore, allow the United States to prosper without undergoing the transition to a manufacturing economy which many Jeffersonians believed was antithetical to republican government.

Just as the United States experienced a spectacular geographic expansion at the turn of the nineteenth century, American commerce similarly increased at the same time. Thanks to the conflict in Europe and the intrepidity of American merchants and seamen, the United States became the most important merchant carrier in the Atlantic world between 1790 and 1810. American vessels carried nearly three times the tonnage in 1810 that they had in 1790. Political independence freed Americans from British navigation restrictions and allowed American vessels to travel the world from China to the Mediterranean and Africa. The most common branch of the commerce was the re-export trade between the United States, the West Indies, and Europe. American vessels, often from New England and New York, carried American produce such as wheat or flour to the French, British, and Spanish West Indies, where they traded for tropical produce such as sugar which they brought back to the United States. The sugar could then be re-exported on neutral American vessels to European markets. This trade contravened the spirit and often the letter of the mercantile regulations of the various European empires, but although risky, American trade was also very lucrative. Between 1795, when the Jay Treaty was ratified, and 1807, the value of the American re-export trade increased from $8 million to $60 million. The overall value of American exports during the same period increased from $48 to $108 million. During the same period the amount of sugar imported by Americans from the West Indies, much of which was re-exported, increased from 64 million pounds to 221 million pounds.[7]

Despite the growing importance of the carrying trade during the early nineteenth century, the United States did not have commensurate diplomatic and military strength to protect its commercial interests. The Republicans were frugal when it came to investing in the military, in large part because they inherited an ideological belief from the Revolution and from the Glorious Revolution of 1688 that standing armies were tools of state oppression. Jefferson was especially reluctant to invest in a costly naval buildup, particularly when the United States could never hope to compete with Britain's naval supremacy. The vulnerability of American commerce was revealed during Jefferson's first term as president when the Barbary states of North Africa harassed American shipping with relative impunity. The leaders of Tripoli, Tunis, Algiers, and Morocco had traditionally extorted cash from maritime nations by kidnapping, and threatening to kidnap, the crews of their vessels. Before independence, American vessels in the Mediterranean had enjoyed the protection of the Royal Navy. After independence, American vessels were subject to capture by these potentates, often with the encouragement of the British. During the 1790s the United States concluded treaties with each of the kingdoms in question, committing itself to paying the leaders approximately $100,000 per year to protect its seamen from capture. In 1801, with payment in arrears, the Barbary corsairs began seizing American vessels again. The United States responded by dispatching most of its deep-water navy to the Mediterranean to blockade Tripoli between 1801 and 1805. The situation became critical in 1803 when one of the blockading ships, the U.S.S. *Philadelphia*, ran aground and its crew of more than three hundred was captured by the Pasha of Tripoli, Yusuf Qaramanli. After some small-scale heroic, but largely ineffective, actions by the Navy and marines in attacking Tripoli, the United States agreed to pay the Pasha $60,000 for the release of the prisoners and the resumption of diplomatic relations in 1805.[8]

The "Tripolitan War" probably saved the United States Navy from total dissolution by President Jefferson and his Treasury Secretary Albert Gallatin. Events in North Africa revealed that if the United States were to profit from overseas trade, it must have some naval presence to protect its interests. Nonetheless, by 1807 Jefferson's program for the defense of American commerce consisted of coastal fortifications and the construction of more than 250 gunboats intended for coastal protection and service on the nation's inland waters. As a result, the nation's seaborne naval presence was minuscule. Coupled with European contempt and hostility for the fledgling American republic, the nation's weak naval presence meant that it could do little to protect its commercial interests in the event of a foreign threat more serious than that posed by the Pasha of Tripoli. The French and British would soon present such a challenge to American commerce.[9]

During the years between 1803 and 1812, both France and Britain sought to enjoy the benefits of the American carrying trade while denying those benefits to their enemies. In consequence, while individual American carriers – especially those who were daring and lucky – profited from the lucrative wartime trade, American commerce and diplomacy in general was caught in a bewildering tangle of ship seizures, impressments, and blockades which wrought havoc and posed a grave danger to the American economy and the republic itself. Unlike the situation in North Africa, the United States could not buy its way out of its troubles with France and Britain. The diplomatic morass wrought by the maritime upheaval of the period at various times seemed likely to draw the United States into war with either Britain or France. Although both powers interfered with American shipping and abused the rights of American citizens – thereby challenging American independence and credibility – British naval supremacy guaranteed that relations between the new nation and its former colonial master would be especially difficult.

In the immediate aftermath of the Jay Treaty, the United States and Britain had enjoyed a period of harmonious trade relations. Although the Jay Treaty was anathema to most Republicans and its terms obnoxious to American pride, under its terms the United States enjoyed a favorable trading relationship with Britain. By 1805 American carriers exported $15 million worth of goods and merchandise to Britain, which was more than one-quarter of American trade with Europe and one-sixth of the overall foreign trade of the United States. With advent of war between Britain and France in 1803, however, American trade with France steadily increased. In 1803 United States exports to France were valued at a mere $4 million. This figure increased to $9 million in 1804 and $13 million in 1805. The British victory at Trafalgar in October 1805, effectively destroyed French naval power thereby rendering the American carrying trade more important to the French. Important as the American trade was to Britain, it seemed likely that Franco–American trade would continue to increase in coming years.[10]

As the world's most important neutral carrier, the United States championed freedom of the seas, asserting that neutral countries could trade with belligerents. As the world's foremost naval power and one of the chief European belligerents, Britain sought to smother the trade between the United States and France on the grounds that such commerce by benefiting France must be harmful to British interests. In opposition to the American assertion of freedom of the seas, Britain revived its unilateral Rule of 1756, which stipulated that trade which was closed in time of peace could not be opened during war. Under the terms of this rule, the Royal Navy began seizing American vessels bound to and from France searching for contraband. In 1805, a British admiralty court took steps to tighten the unilateral British restrictions by declaring the American re-export trade to be a violation of the Rule of 1756. This ruling opened the way for further seizures of American vessels. In the wake of Trafalgar the British enjoyed undisputed control of the seas around Europe, and in May 1806 the British declared the continent under blockade except for an area open to neutrals provided they were not bound to an enemy (French-controlled) port. In response, Napoleon issued the Berlin Decree in November which declared a European blockade of Britain. Napoleon's was a "paper blockade," largely unenforceable, but it did encourage French privateers to attack American shipping to and from Britain as well as in the West Indies. The British responded to Napoleon's paper blockade with a series of orders-in-council in 1807 which prohibited all neutral trade with French-controlled Europe. Napoleon responded with yet another declaration, the Milan Decree (December 1807), which declared that ships lost their neutral character if they obeyed the British orders-in-council or if they submitted to search by the British.

French and British efforts to interfere with each other's trade, while directed at all neutral shippers, mainly affected the United States. The chief beneficiaries of the trade imbroglio were the British and New England merchants. Because the British were better able to enforce their blockade than the French, American trade with Britain increased in value from $15 million in 1805 to $23 million in 1807, which was nearly one-quarter of the total value of American exports. American exports to France, by contrast, were worth $13 million in 1805. In 1806 they dropped in value to $11 million, before returning to $13 million in 1807. American, particularly New England, shipowners and merchants benefited because, although the risks posed to their vessels (and their insurance rates) increased, so too did prices and their profits. In consequence, the total value of American exports increased steadily from $78 million in 1804 to $108 million in 1807. American shipping employed 65,000 seamen, and the growth of trade meant that more than 4,000 new sailors were added to the seagoing workforce each year. New York and New England alone had nearly half the ship tonnage of the entire United Kingdom, and 70,000 tons of new American shipping was launched annually. Wartime trading, while risky, was also very lucrative. Given the rewards, American merchants were willing to risk the dangers of the blockades.[11]

Despite the benefits of wartime commerce for merchants, British efforts to stifle the trade posed a serious diplomatic problem for the Jefferson administration. Trade was not the only area of maritime contention between the two nations. Since the conclusion of the War of Independence, British-born seamen had found work in the American merchant marine as well as in the small United States Navy. By the first decade of the nineteenth century, perhaps one-quarter of the seamen on American vessels were British-born. Some of the Britons were American citizens, others were deserters from British warships, attracted by the better wages and conditions offered by American merchantmen by comparison with the Royal Navy. In order to complete their crews, British vessels persisted in the practice, antedating American independence, of stopping American merchant vessels and impressing suspected deserters into the Royal Navy. Often the impressed seamen were not even British-born, but American-born seamen alleged to have deserted. The practice was common, and nearly 10,000 seamen were impressed from American vessels between 1793 and 1811. With the resumption of war in 1803, British impressments increased; the British impressed 6,000 sailors from American vessels in the years between 1803 and the outbreak of war with the United States in 1812. Although many shippers – comfortably ensconced at home in New York, Salem, or Boston counting their profits – viewed impressment as one of the risks inherent to their trade, the issue was a constant feature of the deteriorating relationship between the British and Americans during the years from 1803–12.[12]

Impressment was at best a nuisance to be endured in the merchant trade and at worst a direct challenge to the sovereignty of the United States, as thousands of American citizens were kidnapped against their will into the service of another nation. Perhaps the most galling aspect of impressment was that British vessels stopped and searched merchant vessels – British and American – in American territorial waters in disregard of the political and diplomatic independence of the United States. Occasionally there was more a stake than national honor. In the spring of 1806 the crew of the H.M.S. Leander accidentally killed an American civilian when they attempted to stop a merchantman off New York by firing across its bow. The greatest affront to American sovereignty occurred in 1807 in international waters just off the Virginia coast. On June 22, the U.S.S. Chesapeake, a United States Navy frigate, was hailed by H.M.S. Leopard and ordered to stand to while the British searched the American vessel's crew for deserters. Occasionally in the past British vessels had stopped American warships, but in the main impressment had been confined to merchant vessels. When the captain of the Chesapeake hesitated, the Leopard opened fire, causing extensive damage to the Chesapeake and wounding twenty-one American seamen, three of whom died. Four alleged deserters were removed from the American vessel. Many American newspapers and their readers clamored for war in the aftermath of the incident. Jefferson demurred, and the British eventually disavowed the action and offered to pay reparations.[13]

The French too harassed American shipping. French privateers seized more than 200 American merchant vessels in the Caribbean between 1800 and 1807.[14] The British, however, were in a much stronger position to interfere with American commerce and, owing to the popular outrage in the wake of the Chesapeake–Leopard affair, the primary diplomatic problem facing the United States by 1807 was relations with Great Britain. Due to his philosophical and financial objections to the use of force and to a large naval establishment, Jefferson instead sought to rectify matters by a combination of negotiation and economic coercion. In 1806, the president dispatched James Monroe and William Pinckney in a vain attempt to negotiate an agreement with the British which would satisfy the commercial interests of the United States and resolve the impressment problem. As the Barbary potentates had demonstrated, American diplomacy did not count for much and the British did not take American grievances or threats seriously. Although American commerce was vital to both the British and French, both nations felt that the Americans could do little to protect and promote their interests. In their eagerness to defeat each other, both Britain and France disregarded the sovereignty of the seemingly impotent United States.

Faced with British and French blockades, the seizure of American merchantmen, and the impressment of American seamen, Jefferson felt compelled to act in late 1807. The president sponsored an Embargo Act, which was adopted by Congress on December 22. In essence the United States refused to trade until its rights as a neutral carrier were respected and Britain and France withdrew all obnoxious trade restrictions. Drawing on their experience during the Stamp Act and Townshend Duties crises, Americans had faith in the efficacy of economic coercion as a means of achieving political objectives. The Embargo Act forbade the departure of ships for foreign ports, excepting foreign vessels in port at the time the act was passed. While coasting vessels were still permitted to sail, they were required to provide a bond that they would only land their cargoes at American ports. Eventually the embargo was extended to inland waters in an effort to prevent trade with Spanish Florida and British Canada.

When measured by official statistics, it would seem that the embargo was effective. American exports to Britain and France plummeted by $20 million and $10 million respectively between 1807 and 1808. Perhaps more strikingly, the overall value of American exports declined from $108 million in 1807 to a mere $22 million in 1808. These figures belie the degree to which Americans evaded the embargo. Just as they disregarded British and French trade restrictions, Americans disregarded the prohibitions of their own government as well. This was especially true of New Englanders. The embargo, intended to harm British and French trade, was potentially very harmful to the New Englanders who were so active in the carrying trade. In consequence, they evaded the embargo and flouted the provisions allowing for the coasting trade. Coastal smuggling was common as was an illicit overland trade between the United States and Canada and Florida. In an unsuccessful attempt to enforce the embargo, Jefferson sponsored a series of "Enforcement Acts" in 1808 and 1809 which gave extensive police powers to federal customs agents and the military to enforce the embargo.[15]

Despite widespread smuggling, the embargo undoubtedly had a deleterious effect on the American economy. Indeed, the embargo ushered in the worst crisis to threaten the American economy since the 1780s. The disruption in trade led to a decline in agricultural prices. Nationally, the wholesale price of agricultural products declined by 21 percent between 1807 and 1808. For example, the price for a bushel of wheat declined from $1.30 to $1.00. Evidence suggests that the impact of the embargo was not evenly felt. While commodity prices in Philadelphia only declined by 0.6 percent between 1807 and 1808, other regions suffered much more: commodity prices in Charleston, by contrast, declined by 20 percent, and the price of South Carolina's staple exports declined by 30 percent. Similarly, the price of commodities in New Orleans declined by 15 percent during the same period. Although the disruption in trade threatened those directly involved in the carrying trade, it was the farmers of the south and west – the core of the Republican party – who suffered most because of the embargo.[16]

One unintended consequence of the embargo was the revival of the moribund Federalist party. After the defeat of the Federalists in 1800, the party had been in steady decline. Its last stronghold was New England. The embargo inspired a revival of Federalism in the region as well as attempts to reestablish the party in the south and west.[17] Despite its unpopularity, the embargo was not enough to revive the fortunes of the Federalists outside of New England and James Madison was elected to succeed Jefferson as president in 1808. The election of Madison was not, however, a vindication of the embargo; in the dying days of the Jefferson administration, Congress took steps to repeal the embargo. On March 15, 1809, just eleven days after Madison took office, the repeal of the Embargo Act took effect. The embargo had not compelled Britain and France to come to terms with the United States but had undermined American shipping, depressed the agricultural sector, and revived the Federalists. However, the Republicans had not wholly renounced economic suasion. In May 1809, Congress passed a Non-Intercourse Act which prohibited trade with Britain and France but permitted it with all other nations. Since it was impossible for the United States to prevent ships from visiting Britain or France when they left port, the act was unenforceable.

Madison still had to contend with the fundamental diplomatic problem facing the United States, the lack of respect which the United States commanded from the European powers. Despite the decline in trade as measured by official figures, the embargo had failed and American commerce was still subject to interference from France and Britain. Indeed, between 1807 and 1812 Britain and France seized approximately 900 American vessels.[18] In the main, Britain benefited from the Non-Intercourse Act since the Royal Navy could intercept American vessels bound for France and the French could not retaliate in kind. In 1809 and 1810, Madison and the Congress sought a legislative solution to the diplomatic impasse. On May 1, 1810 Congress adopted Macon's Bill, Number 2 which stipulated the repeal of all American restrictions on trade and provided that if either Britain or France should remove their restrictions on American trade, the president should renew non-intercourse with the other country. Napoleon cannily exploited the opportunity by announcing the revocation of the Berlin and Milan decrees, effective November 1. Napoleon's declaration was not sincere, and the French continued to seize American vessels when the opportunity presented itself. Nonetheless, Madison accepted the French offer as genuine and on November 2 proclaimed the American renewal of non-intercourse with Britain to commence in ninety days.

British–American relations did not improve in 1811. Impressment remained an unresolved problem. In the hope of deterring the Royal Navy from stopping American vessels, the government ordered the heavy frigate U.S.S. *President* to cruise the Atlantic coast. On the evening of May 16 the *President* fell in with the H.M.S. *Little Belt*. The two vessels exchanged shots and the smaller British ship emerged worse for the encounter. In a reverse image of the *Chesapeake–Leopard* affair, the *President* killed nine of the *Little Belt*'s crew and wounded twenty-three others. While Americans smugly viewed the encounter as just revenge for the attack on the *Chesapeake*, this time it was the turn of the British press and public to beat the tocsin of revenge and war.

Meanwhile, far from the coast, 1811 saw ominous tidings in the west as well. In a sequence of events remarkably similar to those which had seen the rise of Neolin and Pontiac two generations previously, a message of cultural revival and resistance once again flourished among the Native Americans of the Old Northwest. Beginning in 1805, two Shawnee brothers, Tecumseh and Tenskwatawa (known to whites as the Prophet), sought to revive the dream of a pan-Indian confederacy in order to resist American encroachments. Tenskwatawa was one of several Native American prophets who preached a message of cultural renewal, resistance, and revival. Simultaneously, Tecumseh sought to forge a military alliance among the remaining eastern tribes. The resistance movement was centered on the Shawnee settlement, Prophet's Town, at the confluence of the Wabash and Tippecanoe rivers in Indiana Territory. Violent clashes between American settlers and Indians prompted the governor of the Indiana Territory, William Henry Harrison, to launch an attack on Prophet's Town in November 1811. Harrison's forces destroyed Prophet's Town – but not Indian resistance – at the battle of Tippecanoe. Since the Native Americans of the Northwest had been traditional allies of the British, westerners incorrectly suspected that the British were behind the growing movement for Indian unity. As the *Reporter* of Lexington, Kentucky declared, "the War on the Wabash is purely BRITISH. [T]he SCALPING KNIFE and TOMAHAWK of *British savages, is now, again devastating our frontiers*." Western disaffection, primarily laid at the feet of the British for disrupting trade and fostering Indian resistance, led to calls for aggressive action with some westerners advocating war with Britain and the conquest of Canada.[19]

Western disaffection contributed, in part, to the emergence of a more militant attitude within Congress towards Britain. The elections of 1810 returned a group of representatives from western and southern states – dubbed War Hawks – who felt that the United States should pursue a more vigorous policy in defense of its interests. The rise of the War Hawks represented a generational shift in American politics. The revolutionary generation, men such as Jefferson and Madison, would soon give way to younger politicians whose formative years did not encompass the founding of the republic but its travails as a new nation. Notable among the War Hawks were Henry Clay of Kentucky and John C. Calhoun of the South Carolina, men who would play leading roles in antebellum politics. This generation, perhaps best epitomized by Andrew Jackson of Tennessee, were more aggressively nationalistic than their predecessors. Theirs was a vision of an aggressive, expansionist, republic which must take its rightful place and defend its interests in the world of nations. The War Hawks' vigorous rhetoric contributed to rising tensions between Britain and the United States. Nevertheless, it was the persistent difficulties over maritime and commercial issues which finally brought the nations to war.[20]

War

Sometime in late 1811 or early 1812, President Madison resolved that war with Britain would be necessary unless there was a dramatic change in British treatment of the United States and its commerce. Early in 1812, Madison and the Congress began to prepare for war. In January the government adopted a bill to enlarge the regular army to 25,000 men. The navy was to be refitted and rearmed. In March, Congress adopted a finance bill which authorized the government to borrow $11 million and to raise tariffs to pay for the anticipated conflict. In April, Madison proposed a ninety-day embargo to allow American ships to safely return to port before war was declared. On June 1, 1812 James Madison delivered a war message to Congress which stipulated that impressment, violation of the three-mile international limit, blockades, orders-in-council which interfered with American trade, and incitement of the western Indians by the British meant that Britain was in "a state of war with the United States." Based on Madison's message, the House of Representative voted to declare war on Britain by a margin of 79 to 49 on June 4. The Senate concurred by a more narrow margin of 19 to 13 on June 17.

Support for the American declaration of war was not universal. As in the War of Independence, the War of 1812 would be fought in the face of significant internal dissent. There was very strong opposition to the war in the northeast, especially New England. The declaration helped the Federalists consolidate their position in the region after their embargo-inspired revival. Despite the fact that interference with American shipping and commerce was the *causus belli*, those most directly engaged in the maritime trade were largely opposed to the conflict. Support for the war was fairly strong in other regions, especially – but not only – in the south and west. Despite the flurry of last-minute preparations, that United States entered the conflict with Britain woefully unprepared for a war by land and sea with a major European power whose forces were battle-hardened by a generation of conflict with France.

Ironically, as the Americans prepared for war the British government softened its attitude towards the United States. By 1812, with British forces actively involved in Iberia fighting the Peninsular War, Britain experienced severe economic reverses brought on by poor harvests and the wartime disruption of trade. Pressure to withdraw restrictions on American commerce increased both within and without Parliament. On June 23 the government relented and the foreign minister, Viscount Castlereagh, announced the suspension of the orders-in-council restricting American trade. Unbeknownst to Castlereagh and everyone else in London that day, the United States had declared war on Britain six days earlier. Americans would not learn of the revocation of the orders-in-council until August. The war that was so long in coming could have been averted at the last minute with slightly more fortunate timing and better communication.[21]

The major theater of the war would be the border between the United States and British Canada. The conquest of Canada, many Americans believed, would not only be a blow to the British but would constitute a welcome addition to the expansive American republic. American strategy called for the invasion of Canada on three fronts: along the Champlain corridor to Montreal, across the Niagara frontier, and from Detroit. The American campaigns undertaken in the summer and fall of 1812 all ended in disaster. The British captured Detroit in August. The Niagara invasion force was defeated in October at the Battle of Queenstown Heights and the Champlain invasion force never really got underway. Events in 1813 went little better for the United States. Despite winning the naval Battle of Lake Erie on that inland water and Battle of the Thames in Canada, the Americans were unable to make serious inroads in Canada. Surprisingly, the greatest American successes in the early years of the war occurred at sea, where the vessels of the fledgling, long-abused United States Navy won a series of dramatic victories in single-ship actions against the British. In August 1812 the U.S.S. *Constitution* defeated the *Guerriere* in a

178

bloody fight. Later in the year the *United States* captured the British frigate *Macedonian*. In 1813 the *Constitution* defeated the *Java* off the coast of Brazil. These victories did nothing to tip the balance of power at sea, and the Royal Navy effectively blockaded the American coast during the war.

In 1814, as the European war began to wind down, the British were able to undertake offensive actions against the United States. In July the British attempted to invade the United States along the Niagara frontier, encountering stiff resistance from the Americans. In August, however, British forces captured and burned Washington. The latter part of the year saw a revival of American fortunes. The British force that occupied Washington was unable to capture Baltimore, and in September the Americans won another naval battle on inland waters at the Battle of Plattsburg Bay on Lake Champlain, stopping another British invasion force. Meanwhile, American and British negotiators had been holding talks in Belgium since August 1814. With the European war ending and the defeat at Plattsburg Bay, the British did not have a strong interest in pursuing the conflict further. The two sides reached final agreement on the Treaty of Ghent on December 24, 1814. The treaty provided for the return of captured territory and a return to the *status quo ante bellum*. Since peace had been restored in Europe, the issue of neutral rights and commerce ceased to be significant and the reason for the war evaporated. News of the peace of Ghent did not reach America in time to forestall a final British invasion force which sought to capture New Orleans. This force was decisively defeated by an American army commanded by Andrew Jackson on January 15, 1815, a battle which the treaty rendered an exercise in deadly futility but which launched Jackson's political career. News of the victory in Louisiana and the peace circulated simultaneously, and left many Americans with the impression that the conflict which in military and diplomatic terms was little short of a bloody waste of life and treasure was in fact an American success.

Conclusion

Despite its relatively small scale and less than impressive results, the War of 1812 had profound consequences for the United States. In political terms, it drove the final nail into the coffin of the Federalists. Many leading Federalist politicians like John Quincy Adams backed Madison's policies and went over to the administration. Rank and file Federalism, such as it was by 1812, did not follow suit. During the war, New England Federalists continued to trade with the British in Canada and even supplied British vessels blockading the American coast. A conclave of disgruntled New England Federalists met in Hartford in December 1814 and January 1815 and mooted among other threats the possibility of secession. The Hartford Convention coincided with the victory at New Orleans and the Treaty of Ghent, thereby tainting the Federalists with a whiff of treason and disloyalty, and rendering them a spent force in American politics.

The most profound consequence of the war was its impact on American character and nationalism. It is appropriate in this context that the most lasting legacy of the War of 1812 was "The Star Spangled Banner," written as a poem by Francis Scott Key during the bombardment of Fort McHenry in Baltimore and destined to become the national anthem of the United States. The tension and Anglophobia in Key's poem are impressive. It realized the fear which animated the United States since 1783; the fear that Britain would conquer the United States and effect a counter-revolution. This fear underlay the desire to create a stronger federal government in the 1780s, and concern over British interference with American trade and intrigue among western Indians after that. Had Baltimore fallen to the British in 1814, it is plausible that the republic might have collapsed and with it the Revolution. Key's poem captures a moment when the American experiment in republican government faced its greatest peril since 1776. As such, it is an appropriate national anthem insofar as it commemorates the ultimate survival of the revolutionary legacy of 1776. The War of 1812 was properly seen as a second War of Independence. Although the grandiose visions of those ardent Republicans who sought to add Canada to the national domain were not realized, Americans felt that their nation was vindicated in the conflict. For the second time in as many generations, Americans had withstood British aggression. Apparent American success in the war seemed to epitomize and endorse the burgeoning expansion – economic and geographic – and optimism which had characterized the United States since the inauguration of Thomas Jefferson. The war validated the results of the Revolution. Americans had won their independence and created a national republic with a thriving economy. In 1815 they could take pride and satisfaction in their successful defense of these achievements.[22]

In 1815, the United States was the most democratic nation in the world. Thomas Jefferson's republican vision, however, while democratic by comparison with the elitism of the Federalists, was limited in significant ways. In 1815 the majority of Americans, though affected by the actions of their leaders, were excluded from participating in American public life. Political participation was largely confined to white men who owned property. Although the early years of the nineteenth century saw a relaxation of property requirements and a concomitant expansion of the franchise, the benefits of such reforms were confined to white males. The major groups which were largely excluded from public life, women and African Americans, made vital contributions to the creation of the republic. In consequence, their lives and experiences were transformed during the age of the American Revolution as well. Despite attempts to limit its impact, the American Revolution transformed the whole of American society. The next two chapters examine the unintended consequences of the revolution for these groups.

9

AFRICAN AMERICANS IN THE AGE OF REVOLUTION

Introduction

During the spring of 1800, a group of Virginia slaves under the leadership of a Richmond blacksmith named Gabriel, the slave of Thomas Prosser, hatched a complex plot to win their freedom. The slaves agreed that groups of bondsmen would converge on Richmond under a banner emblazoned with the slogan "death or liberty," seize the state capitol and the governor, James Monroe, and undertake to negotiate for their freedom while slaves from surrounding areas descended on Richmond to swell their ranks. The rising would not be bloodless, as large planters and prominent slaveholders would be put to death. The killing, however, would not be indiscriminate. Gabriel insisted that "Quakers, Methodists, and French people" were to be spared. He believed that these groups were opposed to slavery, and he intended to cultivate their support in the aftermath of the rebellion. The day chosen for the rising was August 30. The appointed day was accompanied by torrential rains and flooding which made it impossible for the conspirators to gather. In the meantime, several slaves who had heard of the plot informed their masters of the plan. The conspiracy collapsed as Governor Monroe called out the militia and the suspected rebels were arrested. Over the next several months, special courts sat to hear the cases of the accused rebels. Justice was swift and harsh in Jefferson's Virginia. Twenty-five slaves were put to death for their roles, actual and alleged, in the plot.[1]

Gabriel's Rebellion, as the abortive plot came to be known, was a direct consequence of the age of revolution. The American Revolution represented a fundamental challenge to the institution of slavery as practiced by eighteenth-century Americans. At the heart of the Revolution were two ideas which came into conflict in the institution of slavery: the belief in human liberty and the sanctity of property. The problem of reconciling these beliefs when *people* were *property* was the most vexing of the era of the American Revolution. Revolutionaries north and south took steps to address this contradiction, which fundamentally altered and undermined slavery in America. The most radical revolutionaries in America were not the Jeffersonians with their belief in a democracy limited to white males, but the enslaved men and women of America who recognized in the Declaration of Independence's promise that "all men are created equal" the key to their own freedom. Just as Gabriel's followers were to appropriate the revolutionary slogan "death or liberty" to apply to their own circumstances, so too did tens of thousands of their fellow slaves who secured their freedom by means of force of arms, flight, lawsuits, and political pressure during the years from 1775 to 1815. Slavery survived the Revolution and indeed thrived in the years after 1800, but it no longer went unchallenged or unquestioned. In 1763 slavery was accepted throughout America. By 1800 it was a regional institution under threat from without and, as Gabriel demonstrated, from within. The effect of the Revolution on slavery was very much determined by region. The institution was abolished in the north but survived, with fundamental changes, in the south.

African Americans and the American Revolution: the North

On the eve of the outbreak of the War of Independence, the English lexicographer Samuel Johnson posed a difficult question to the rebellious colonists in America: "How is it we hear the loudest yelps for liberty among the drivers of Negroes?" Prior to the American Revolution, almost all white colonists had taken slavery for granted as part of the natural order of society, perhaps unfortunate but immutable. Few bothered to defend slavery because few European-Americans questioned it. However, once some Americans began to justify their struggle against Britain in the name of human equality and natural rights and proclaimed that they rebelled to save themselves from what they termed as slavery, they confronted the fact that nearly one-fifth of their fellow colonists were actual slaves because of their skin color and ancestry. Johnson was not alone in pointing out this disparity. On the eve of the Revolution, an anonymous loyalist asked readers of *The Pennsylvania Packet* whether they could "reconcile the *exercise of* SLAVERY with our *professions of freedom.*" Some Whigs were sensitive to such criticism, and in the years immediately before the outbreak of war slavery's foundation in the northern colonies began to erode.[2]

Not all white Americans had accepted slavery uncritically during the eighteenth century. Quakers in the mid-Atlantic region were among the early critics of chattel slavery in America. Beginning in 1759, Pennsylvania Quaker Anthony Benezet published a series of pamphlets exposing the horrors of the trans-Atlantic slave trade. Slavery's opponents drew inspiration from the protest movement against Britain, as an anonymous writer in the *Pennsylvania Chronicle* made the connection between the two movements during the furor over the Townshend Duties in 1768: "you who spurn at the thoughts of paying a poor pittance of a glass, a paper, a paint tax, and cry aloud on *freedom and virtue*, how can you lift up your heads in the noble contest for Liberty, and be at home the greatest tyrants on earth!" Some in the Whig camp made the same connection. In one of the earliest pamphlets in favor of American rights, James Otis of Massachusetts declared, "the colonists, black and white, born here, are free born British subjects, and entitled to all the essential civil rights of such." A decade later Abigail Adams wrote to her husband John, who was representing Massachusetts at the First Continental Congress, "I wish most sincerely there was not a Slave in the province. It allways appeard a most iniquitous Scheme to me – fight ourselfs for what we are daily robbing and plundering from those who have as good a right to freedom as we have." The same year the Pennsylvania radical Benjamin Rush published a pamphlet attacking slavery.[3]

The growing unease over slavery among some northerners manifested itself in more than a few pamphlets and newspaper contributions. At the same time that the colonial assemblies took steps to resist British taxation, some also adopted measures to interfere with slavery. In 1767 the Massachusetts assembly, the Great and General Court, debated a proposal to ban the slave trade, and eventually adopted a bill to that effect in 1771. In 1773 the Pennsylvania assembly adopted a measure to increase the duty on imported slaves from £10 to £20, an action which would have effectively banned the trade. Later in the same year the lower house of the New York assembly adopted similar measure. At the same time New Jersey Quakers inundated their assembly with petitions calling for the prohibition of the slave trade and an easing of restrictions on manumission. While these measures are significant in that they reveal the concomitant growth of opposition to slavery and Britain in the northern colonies, it is revealing that little came of them. Governor Thomas Hutchinson refused to give his consent to the Massachusetts bill banning the slave trade. The Board of Trade overturned Pennsylvania's increased duty on slave imports, and in New York the upper house of the assembly and the governor likewise opposed the increased duty. Only in the corporate colonies of Rhode Island and Connecticut was substantive action taken against slavery before the War of Independence. In both of those colonies the slave trade was prohibited in 1774. The preamble of Rhode Island's act banning the slave trade reflected the egalitarian impulse of the times: "those who are desirous of enjoying all the advantages of liberty themselves should be willing to extend personal liberty to others." These measures reflect an attempt to answer criticisms like Samuel Johnson's, and recognize that the defense of American liberty should not coexist with slavery.

The results of pre-revolutionary movement against slavery are paltry. It took the coming of the War of Independence and, more importantly, the efforts of bondsmen and women themselves to destroy slavery in the north. African Americans in the north, slave and free, were mainly American-born, English-speaking, and disproportionately urban. As such, they were more openly engaged in the prewar protest movement than their southern counterparts. In Massachusetts, where the revolutionary ferment was strongest, African American slaves and freemen were very active in campaigning against slavery. In the years immediately before the outbreak of the war, Massachusetts slaves bombarded the assembly, the governor, and the newspapers with petitions for their freedom. One such petition, issued as a public letter to the representatives of the General Court on April 20, 1773 by Peter Bestes, Sambo Freeman, Felix Holbrook, and Chester Joie, is typical. The slaves made a connection between the protest movement against Britain and their own plight:

> The efforts made by the legislature of this province their last sessions to free themselves from slavery, gave us, who are in that deplorable state, a high degree of satisfaction. We expect great things from men who have made such a noble stand against the designs of their *fellow-men* to enslave them. We cannot but with hope Sir, that you will have the same grand object, we mean civil and religious liberty, in view in your next session. The divine spirit of *freedom* seems to fire every human breast on this continent except such as are bribed to assist in executing the execreble plan. ... We acknowledge our obligations to you for what you have already done, but as the people of this province seem to be actuated by the principles of equity and justice, we cannot but expect your house will again take our deplorable case into serious consideration, and give us that ample relief which, *as men*, we have a natural right to.

This petition, one of five issued by Massachusetts slaves during 1773 and 1774 demonstrates that the slaves were not only conversant in the ideology of the colonial protest movement, they recognized the truly revolutionary implications of that ideology: an appeal to natural rights must, of necessity, include slaves. For, as a group of New Hampshire slaves reportedly declared, "the *God* of nature gave them life and freedom, upon the terms of the most perfect equality with other men."[4]

Northern slaves resorted to tactics other than petitions. Massachusetts slaves brought a series of lawsuits in the 1760s and 1770s arguing that the colony's charter, which declared that all men were free, prohibited slavery. Although the suits only pertained to individuals and were frequently unsuccessful, they served to undermine slavery as an institution. Slaves took more direct action by participating in crowd disturbances and demonstrations against British rule. Before the War of Independence these efforts politicized and empowered many African Americans, further undermining slavery's hold, at least in the northern port cities where both slavery and the resistance movement were centered. Slaves were willing to do more than petition, sue, and rely on the goodwill and idealism of their masters. In the autumn of 1774 a group of Boston slaves approached General Thomas Gage, the British governor of the province, and offered their services in assisting the British to suppress the imminent American rebellion in exchange for their freedom. Nothing came of the approach, but it reveals that some African Americans saw in the dispute between white Americans and their British rulers an opportunity to secure their freedom. In pursuing that objective, slaves might be willing to side with either the British or the Whigs, depending upon which group offered them the best chance for success.[5]

If the efforts of northern slaves and a small number of white abolitionists and revolutionaries undermined the foundation of slavery in the decade before 1775, it was the onset of the War of Independence which brought the edifice of northern slavery crashing down. The war was a catalyst for profound social change as thousands of African Americans, north and south, took advantage of and contributed to the upheaval in order to secure their liberty. The war constituted, in the words of a leading scholar, "a black Declaration of Independence." By tradition Americans, especially New Englanders, had allowed their slaves to serve in the militia in times of crisis. Indeed, when the first shots of the war were fired at Lexington, Prince Eastabrook, a local minuteman and slave, was among the wounded. African Americans, free and slave, were among the thousands of New Englanders who besieged Boston during the spring of 1775. Indeed, when the Virginia slaveholder, George Washington, took command of the army before Boston one of his first acts was to ban all African Americans from the Continental Army. In November 1775 the Continental Congress endorsed this action by banning all African Americans, slave and free, from Continental service. Nonetheless, northern slaves continued to serve in the militias of northern states, usually in exchange for promises that they would be freed by their masters at the conclusion of the war. By 1777 Washington and the Continental Congress bowed to chronic manpower shortages and accepted African American soldiers in the ranks of the Continental Army. This action met with resistance among delegates from the southern states, but eventually every state north of and including Maryland accepted African American soldiers. These soldiers fought for a much more tangible concept of liberty than their white counterparts. Slaves who enlisted in the ranks of the Continental Army or the state militias received their freedom in exchange for their service. By the end of 1777, free blacks and slaves served in mixed regiments in most northern states. Some northern slaves also eschewed service in the rebel cause to lend their efforts to the British forces. African Americans, in the wake of Lord Dunmore's proclamation in November 1775 which promised freedom to any Virginia slave who fled a

186

rebel master to serve the British, were among the most fervent loyalists the British found in America. Regardless of which side they opted for, slaves who took up arms did so with the intention of securing their freedom. Still others sought to achieve their freedom by taking advantage of the confusion wrought by the war to flee their masters and the fighting.[6]

African Americans and their white allies took advantage of the exigencies of war and the requirements of constitution-making necessitated by the political revolution to destroy slavery in much of the north. Newly independent Vermont prohibited the practice of slavery in its 1777 constitution. In 1780, the radical government of Pennsylvania adopted a law requiring gradual emancipation of slaves when they became adults. In the immediate aftermath of the war Connecticut and Rhode Island also adopted gradual emancipation laws in January and March 1784, respectively. In the rest of New England, slavery was destroyed not by abolitionist lawmakers but by slaves who continued to bring suits for their freedom in court. Between 1781 and 1783 Massachusetts courts ended slavery in the state by a series of decisions in response to suits brought by slaves who sought their freedom based on the state's 1780 constitution, which declared all men free. New Hampshire courts followed the example of their southern neighbors. By the spring of 1784, only New Jersey and New York among the northern states had failed to either abolish slavery or adopt a gradual emancipation law. Both states, particularly New York, had sizeable slave populations. Only after a prolonged campaign by black and white abolitionists did these states reluctantly act. Not until 1799 did the New York legislature adopted a gradual emancipation law. New Jersey was even tardier; its government did not embrace emancipation until 1804. Its law was so gradual that there were still seventy-five slaves in Monmouth County, New Jersey as late as 1850.[7]

It has been argued that the revolutionary generation was remarkable for its failure to take substantive action against slavery.[8] The evidence in favor of such an interpretation is compelling. The overwhelming majority of American slaves, after all, were not directly affected by the abolition of slavery in the north because they lived in the south. Abolition in parts of the north was so gradual as to allow slaveholders to sell their chattel in the south if they so chose. Moreover, the emancipation laws usually did not free enslaved adults but promised to free their children when they became adults. Perhaps most significantly, the framers of the Constitution were unwilling to take any meaningful action against slavery for fear of destroying the union before it got started. Such a view does not take account of the significant changes which the Revolution wrought with respect to slavery. After the Revolution, slavery was a regional institution which divided the new United States. During the conflict, thousands of northern slaves won their freedom. Their example would inspire and tempt their southern counterparts. Perhaps most significantly, the Revolution forced southerners, black and white, to attempt to reconcile slavery and freedom. Although slavery survived the Revolution in the South, it did so as a changed and much more defensive institution. Slavery would either be abolished or become an irrational badge of regional identity as a consequence of the Revolution: it could no longer exist casually without particular remark.

African Americans and the American Revolution: the South

It was relatively easy for northern slaves to win their freedom by comparison with their southern counterparts. On the eve of the Revolution African Americans, slave and free, composed 3 percent of the New England population and 6 percent of that of the Middle Colonies. By the late eighteenth century northern slaves, because of their relative isolation, were more easily assimilated into the dominant Anglo-American culture. This meant that they had access to the skills, particularly literacy, which allowed them to participate in the American resistance movement and to appropriate its ideology to secure their own freedom. By comparison, African slaves comprised 40 percent of the population south of Pennsylvania. Their labor was vital to the prosperity of the plantation economy. Although their greater numbers afforded southern slaves the opportunity to build an independent African American cultural life to a degree impossible for their northern counterparts, southern slaves faced particular constraints. In law and often in practice, limits were placed on their education, literacy, freedom of movement, and legal status. Unlike northern slaves, southern slaves were not able to sue in the courts for their freedom, nor could they petition southern governments. If southern planters were embarrassed by the contradiction between their professed devotion to liberty and their reliance on an economic system which rested on the violent coercion of unfree labor, they were reluctant to admit it, and far less willing than their northern colleagues to do anything about it.

Although they may not have been as well versed in the ideological aspects of the dispute between their masters and the British as their northern counterparts, southern slaves were well aware of the dispute and its potential to change their circumstances. Like their African American neighbors, many southern whites were illiterate. The prewar resistance was, by necessity, an oral movement as well as a written one. As such, slaves were exposed, usually indirectly, to the dispute. Whether they recognized in the appeal to natural rights the potential for their own liberation, they undoubtedly saw in the controversy an opportunity to improve their conditions and undermine slavery. Just as Charleston slaves appropriated the language and forms of the Stamp Act protests to demonstrate for liberty in January 1766 (see Chapter 2), other black southerners asserted claims to their independence in years before the war. Unlike northern slaves, southerners were not able by law or customs to write petitions or initiate lawsuits. Rather, they relied on covert resistance to secure their freedom and in the years before the war the incidence of southern slave resistance increased. In November 1774, for example, a group of Virginia slaves met to elect a leader, "who was to conduct them when the English troops should arrive – which," James Madison wrote, "they foolishly thought would be very soon and that by revolting they should be rewarded with their freedom." In December ten slaves in Georgia killed four and wounded three whites – including their overseer and owner – before they were captured. In the years before independence there was also an increase in the number of slaves who ran away. The upsurge in conspiracy, violent resistance, and running away indicates that southern slaves saw in the turmoil generated by the dispute between the colonists and the British, if not in its ideology as well, an opportunity to secure their freedom. The advent of the war presented southern slaves with unprecedented dangers and opportunities.[9]

For many northerners, black and white, the War of Independence was a catalyst for change with respect to slavery. In the south the advent of war had a different impact on slavery. Many southern whites were divided by politics, ethnicity, class, and religion. They were united, however, in their support for the slave system. In the wake of Dunmore's proclamation, many southerners feared that the British might promote wholesale emancipation as a means of defeating the rebellion. This fear drove many southern whites into the rebel camp. Thus when North Carolina's provincial assembly became the first body to call for independence in April of 1776, it did so in part because, "[British] Governors in different Colonies have declared protection to slaves, who would imbrue their hands in the blood of their masters." For many of North Carolina's revolutionaries, as well as those across the slaveholding south, the Revolution was very much about the protection of their "right" to hold persons as property.[10]

When the British shifted the emphasis in the war from the north to the south in 1779, the slave system of region confronted a dramatic challenge. As a brutal war, which pitted not only the British against the rebels but also irregular partisan bands against each other, raged across the region from 1779 to 1782, slaves faced unprecedented dangers and opportunities to obtain their freedom. The decisions they made were often matters of life and death. A very small proportion of slaves opted to lend their support to the rebels. In the main southern rebels opposed arming slaves, except on a temporary basis and only when they faced imminent defeat. Given the adherence of southern rebels to the slave system this option, not surprisingly, attracted few takers. Most slaves eschewed serving a cause which promised them little hope of attaining their liberty.

Like many of their white neighbors, many black southerners sought to avoid the conflict and keep themselves and their families out of harm's way. The decision to do so was not entirely up to slaves, as many slaveholders took their slaves with them when they fled the fighting. The slaves of those who did not do so often remained on their plantations and farms. These men and women, often elderly or with young children, may have hoped that if their masters failed to return that they would secure their freedom by default. Moreover, the myriad dangers which confronted slaves at large in the war zone may have convinced them to remain at home and await the outcome of the conflict. Such a course was not without dangers. During the southern phase of the war, society deteriorated into anarchy as law and order gave way not only to the dangers of combat but also rapine and plunder as soldiers from the contending armies, the militias, and irregular gangs of armed men who were little more than bandits roamed the countryside. Slaves, especially female slaves, were particularly at risk in such circumstances because they were often treated like livestock, as moveable property to be seized. Those who endured such a fate might be pressed into service by the competing military forces, or simply sold for profit. Slaves living alone on plantations and farms without masters were particularly susceptible to such treatment. In December 1781, Lewis Morris, a young New Yorker serving as an aide to Nathanael Greene, wrote with respect to the situation in the south, "I envy everything I see, except the poor unhappy blacks who, to the disgrace of human nature, are subject to every species of oppression while we are contending for the rights and liberties of mankind."[11]

There were two other options available to southern slaves during the war, apart from serving the rebels or trying to avoid the conflict: they could take flight or seek to serve the British. It is very difficult to estimate how many southern slaves fled during the war. After the war a Charleston merchant estimated that more than twenty thousand slaves – as many as 25 percent of the state's bondsmen and women – took flight during the conflict. Between eighty and one hundred thousand black southerners, approximately one in five slaves, fled during the war. In the Virginia counties nearest to Cornwallis's base at Yorktown alone, there were 12,000 fewer African Americans after the war than there were before it. Many, perhaps most, of these did not achieve their liberty.[12] Many refugees fled urban areas and went to the north where they might pass themselves off as free. Others sought to locate relatives and loved ones from whom they had been separated by sale. Still others sought a haven in Florida which, under both the Spaniards and British, had been a haven for runaways from the lower south. Additional slaves congregated in remote areas and established maroon communities.[13]

Perhaps the majority of those who fled sought succor and service with the British. Since Dunmore's proclamation, southern slaves had come to see the British and loyalists as potential liberators. Military necessity compelled the British to attack slavery in the south. As the mainstay of the southern economy, slave labor was essential: by seizing slaves or encouraging them to flee, the British struck not only at the ability of southern rebels to make war but also at their wealth. Moreover, eighteenth-century military campaigns were laborious affairs requiring thousands of hands to help an army to move and feed itself. During a siege such as that of Charleston in 1780, a great deal of hard physical labor was required to construct siege works and invest the city. Southern slaves, like the region's other resources, seemed a natural pool of labor for the British to exploit. Before undertaking the southern campaign in 1779 the British commander-in-chief, General Sir Henry Clinton, issued a proclamation from his headquarters in Philipsburg, New York, aimed at the bondsmen and women of the south in which he declared that any slaves captured in service to the rebels would be sold but those who deserted the rebels and served the British would receive, "full security to follow within these Lines, any Occupation which [they] shall think proper."[14] Unlike Dunmore's proclamation of 1775, the Philipsburg proclamation offered enslaved women as well as men the opportunity to serve the British.

Although not an explicit promise of freedom, southern slaves interpreted Clinton's Philipsburg proclamation as such. Slaves, men, women, and children, fled in their thousands to the British lines across the South. In the main the runaways were relegated to ancillary and support roles. Black southerners were employed as menial laborers, servants, guides and pioneers by the British. A Hessian soldier, Johann von Ewald, serving with Cornwallis in Virginia near the end of the war, noted, "every soldier had his Negro, who carried his provisions and bundles. ... Every officer had four to six horses and three or four Negroes, as well as one or two Negresses for a cook and maid. Every soldier's woman was mounted and also had a Negro and Negresses on horseback for her servants. Each squad had one or two Negroes, and every noncommissioned officer had two horses and one Negro." The British were almost as reluctant to arm slaves as were the rebels. In times of crisis, such as during the siege of Savannah or when the British campaign in the south failed in 1781 and 1782, slaves were armed to fight the rebels. Similarly a few African American combat units, like Dunmore's Ethiopian Regiment, were created by the British. By far the largest number of slaves who took arms in the south during the war probably did so as members of the irregular partisan bands which proliferated in the region.[15]

Although they welcomed and relied upon the assistance of runaway slaves to conduct the war in the south, the British did not seek to overturn slavery in the region. Indeed, since the British objective was to suppress the rebellion and restore the colonies to the empire and the profitability of the southern colonies relied upon slave labor, it could be argued that the British intended, in the long run, to uphold the region's system of unfree labor just as sincerely as did their rebel adversaries. In the short run, however, they needed the slaves to pursue their war in the south.

While military necessity compelled them to offer freedom to slaves who aided them in fighting the rebels, the British never intended to overturn slavery as a labor system. British ambivalence toward their African American allies is revealed in the fates of those who were evacuated by the British at the conclusion of the war. In a particularly ignominious act, when supplies ran low during the siege of Yorktown, General Cornwallis ordered hundreds of slaves who had served the British driven from their lines and into certain enslavement by the besieging rebel force. Ewald noted bitterly, "We had used them to good advantage and set them free, and now, with fear and trembling, they had to face the reward of their cruel masters." At the end of the American war the British transported approximately one hundred thousand loyalists from the United States. Approximately twenty thousand of the refugees were black. Despite removal the majority of these remained slaves, and in some cases faced a more wretched future than if they had remained in the United States. Thousands of these were the slaves of white loyalists who resettled in different parts of the British Atlantic world – especially in Jamaica and the Bahamas – taking their slaves with them. Some of the slaves were kept as war booty by British officers and resold, usually in Jamaica. Perhaps several thousand slaves who had taken up arms were absorbed into the British army either as free men or as military slaves. Among these were the Black Carolina Corps formed in 1779. At the end of the war the corps was distributed throughout the British West Indies. Its members fought for the British in the Caribbean during the wars of the French Revolution. Eventually its members, as well as the slave soldiers of other West Indian units, were rewarded with their freedom by Parliament in 1807.

In a minority of cases the African American loyalists won their freedom. After the war, nearly three thousand African American men, women and children who had served the British were given manumission certificates and removed to Nova Scotia. A decade later many of these, frustrated by racial intolerance, poor land and an inhospitable climate, were among the first settlers in Britain's west African colony, Sierra Leone. The fate of the African American loyalists reveals that choosing to side with the British was a risky option for southern slaves. To opt for the British in no way guaranteed freedom. Nonetheless, the majority of southern slaves felt that the British represented the best of a set of dangerous options.[16]

The War of Independence was the gravest threat to slavery in America before the Civil War. By their actions during the war, slaves transformed the conflict into a true war of liberation. The actions of the tens of thousands of slaves who risked their lives in flight and combat to secure their freedom was far more eloquent testimony to the powerful implications of the revolutionary ideology than Jefferson's words in the Declaration of Independence. For many, capture, resale, or death through disease or war awaited them after their escapes. Some, however, won their freedom through military service or escape. Regardless of the outcome for individuals, such mass flight represented a direct and forceful challenge to slavery as a labor system. When coupled with the challenge posed by the ideology of Revolution, slavery in the south was under threat at the end of the war. While northerners resolved the revolutionary dilemma of slavery by embracing gradual emancipation, southern slaveholders took contrary actions. On one hand they took steps which weakened slavery slightly and resulted in the creation of a significant free African American community in the south. At the same time they adopted measures and took actions to strengthen and expand slavery. They pursued these actions against the backdrop of a republican challenge to slavery which came not from the north but from the south, as the French Revolution swept the West Indies.

African Americans in the age of the French Revolution

In 1820, Thomas Jefferson famously wrote of slavery, "we have a wolf by the ears, and we can neither hold him, nor safely let him go." Jefferson, like many leading revolutionaries who were also slaveholders, had expressed hopes that slavery in the south would wither and die in the wake of the Revolution. Although the War of Independence provided a shock to southern slavery, the institution survived and indeed thrived in subsequent years. In large part this was because leading southerners who disapproved of slavery failed to take decisive action in favor of emancipation. Nonetheless, in the face of the pressure brought to bear by rebellious slaves during the war and the force of the natural rights ideology which lay at the heart of the revolutionary movement, southern whites modified slavery in significant ways.[17]

The most significant change to the southern slave system in the wake of the Revolution was a liberalization of the manumission laws in the south. Prior to the Revolution, there had been strict legal limits on the ability of masters to set their slaves free. For example, under a law adopted in 1723, Virginians could only set their slaves free with the consent of the colony's governor and his council. In 1782 the Virginia Assembly adopted a law which allowed slaveowners to free their chattel in their wills. Other slave states adopted similar statutes. A significant number of planters took advantage of these laws. Many were motivated by the late Revolution. Richard Randolph, a Virginia planter, explained in his will that he desired to manumit his slaves:

> To make retribution, as far as I am able, to an unfortunate race of bondsmen, over whom my ancestors have usurped and exercised the

most lawless and monstrous tyranny, and in whom my countrymen (by their iniquitous laws, in contradiction of their own declaration of rights, and in violation of the every sacred law of nature; of the inherent, inalienable, and imprescritable rights of man, and of every principle of moral and political honesty) have vested me with absolute property.

As a result, there was a dramatic increase in the number of free African Americans in the south. The free black population in the south numbered between three and five thousand in 1780, but increased steadily over the next generation. There were 60,000 free African Americans in the south in 1790, and more than 180,000 in the United States by 1810. Despite the gradual emancipation of northern slaves during the same period, which contributed to this total, more liberal manumission laws allowed the south to have the largest free African American population in the country. The practice was most common in the Chesapeake states. One-third of all free blacks in the United States resided in Virginia and Maryland in 1810. The change was most dramatic in Maryland. Although only 4 percent of Maryland blacks were free in 1755, the proportion increased steadily after the Revolution. In 1810 20 percent of Maryland blacks were free, and by the outbreak of the Civil War nearly half of the state's African Americans were free.[18]

The prospects of free African Americans in the United States, north or south, during the early republic were not enviable. The growth of the free African American community was accompanied by an increase in racist feeling among whites. In consequence, many free African Americans congregated in cities such as Boston, New York, Philadelphia, Baltimore, and Charleston, where their numbers afforded them a degree of safety from white hostility as well as opportunities to forge an autonomous cultural life. Economically, most free African Americans were relegated to menial and low-paying jobs. Females frequently labored as domestics, while males often found work in the maritime community of the port cities. In the face of white intolerance, and in an exercise of their newly won freedom, former slaves worked assiduously to construct their own independent cultural life by forming families, churches, and voluntary organizations such as Masonic lodges free from the interference of their former masters. Although urban blacks faced considerable barriers of white intolerance and economic privation, rural freedmen and women were often in a more parlous position. They faced the same snares of racism and poverty, yet they often did so in relative isolation. They were forced to hire themselves as laborers under conditions which were often little different than those they had endured as slaves. Despite having to contend with very real obstacles to their success, the emergence of the free African American community, especially in the south, was one of the notable legacies of the American Revolution. After the

Revolution, race could no longer be automatically equated with unfree servitude. The free African American community, by its very presence, was a challenge to the slave system. Former slaves offered an example and personified the aspirations of their enslaved brothers and sisters. The presence of African Americans who were free and the cultural institutions they created gave testimony to the liberating potential of the Revolution.

In addition to liberalizing restrictions on manumission, several southern states also prohibited participation in the trans-Atlantic slave trade in the aftermath of the Revolution. The trade had been temporarily prohibited by the Continental Association and disrupted by the war. Virginia prohibited the trade in 1778 and Maryland in 1783. Georgia followed suit in 1798, and North Carolina levied a prohibitive import duty to discourage human imports. These actions were motivated more by local conditions than a concern over the inhumanity of the trade or a revolutionary concern for liberty. Notwithstanding the substantial loss of slaves as a result of the war, the slave population, especially in the upper south, grew rapidly in the years after the conflict. Virginia's slave population expanded from 165,000 in 1776 to more than 290,000 in 1790. Likewise in Maryland the slave population increased from around 80,000 in 1776 to 103,000 in 1790. This population boom occurred as tobacco declined in profitability and many Chesapeake planters made the transition to raising cereals. In the upper south, at least, there was little need to import additional slaves. By closing the slave trade, planters could help maintain the value of their slaves as they sought to sell them in the internal market for slaves which flourished in the early republic.[19]

Increased manumission and restrictions on the slave trade were the biggest concessions made by white southerners in the wake of the Revolution. In contrast to these steps efforts were made to strengthen slavery during the same period. Despite more liberal manumission laws, the overwhelming majority of African Americans in the south remained enslaved and most whites remained committed to the slave system. Outside of the tidewater areas of the Chesapeake, especially in Maryland, manumission was relatively rare. Indeed, fewer than three hundred slaves were manumitted in South Carolina between 1770 and 1790. More significantly, the postwar years witnessed the expansion of southern slavery. Before the Revolution the southern slave population was concentrated along the coast, especially in the Chesapeake and in lowland South Carolina. During the war, many slaveholders fled to the backcountry with their slaves. Their flight initiated a westward shift in the slave population, which continued during the early republic and antebellum years as the introduction of cotton as a staple crop encouraged the rapid spread of the plantation regime across the southwest to the Mississippi. Rather than simply fade away in the wake of the Revolution, as Jefferson and some slaveholders hoped, the institution spread and flourished. The growth of slavery after the war can be measured by the willingness of South Carolinians to import new slaves. In 1783–4 alone, South Carolina planters imported more than 6,500 new slaves. In the decade between 1790 and 1800 they imported approximately 14,000 slaves, and in the years between 1800 and the final abolition of slave imports in 1808, Carolina planters purchased nearly 40,000 more Africans. Thus more than 60,000 Africans paid with their freedom and that of their posterity for the "compromises" which secured the Constitution and kept the slave trade open for another twenty years.[20]

Black resistance to slavery intensified during the years of the early republic. Although African American opposition to slavery, both overt and covert, long antedated the American colonial struggle for independence, the Revolution transformed African American resistance. In the first place, the chaotic wartime conditions had made flight, while fraught with danger, a realistic option for many slaves. Wartime service moreover gave many male slaves military experience upon which they could draw if they sought to pursue violent resistance to slavery. As Sylvia Frey, the leading student of southern slavery during the Revolution, has written, "African Americans had emerged from the Revolution with a heightened self-awareness, which manifested itself in economic assertiveness and intensified rebelliousness. The wartime experience had also spawned a small nucleus of African American leaders, 'new men' who believed in violent rebellion for the sake of the abstract principle of freedom. In the postwar period, they undertook the organization of resistance." During the final decades of the eighteenth century southern slaves became more restive as the incidence of violent assaults on whites, maroon activities, plots and insurrections all increased. The most notable example of slave resistance during the postwar period was Gabriel's Rebellion. Clearly, southern blacks were not satisfied by the rather timid steps taken by white slaveholders – more liberal manumission laws and limits on the slave trade – to reconcile slavery with the ideology of the Revolution. They sought to acquire the independence and autonomy denied them by their white neighbors.[21]

The ideology of the Revolution, with its emphasis on natural rights, equality, and liberty, undoubtedly encouraged militancy among slaves during the immediate postwar years. Revolutionary fervor among slaves intensified during the 1790s when slaves in the French West Indies successfully revolted and created a black republic. The most radical revolution during the "Age of Revolution" was not American or French, but that which resulted in the creation of the Haitian Republic. Events in the French colony of Saint-Domingue, as Haiti was known before independence, were to have a direct impact on the American republic, particularly its slaves.

In 1789, when Washington took office and French crowds stormed the Bastille, Saint-Domingue had a population of nearly 600,000, five-sixths of whom were black slaves. The free population was divided between a sizable group of mixed race planters and approximately 50,000 French planters and colonial administrators who controlled the colony. In the wake of the outbreak of the revolution and France, the free mulatto population pressed a claim for greater political liberty. The division among the free population encouraged the enslaved African majority to seize their freedom in 1791. The rebels were initially led by a slave named Boukman; when he died, he was succeeded by another slave, Toussaint L'Ouverture. By 1793 the rebels had seized control of most of the colony. For the next decade violence and confusion reigned in Saint-Domingue. Both the Spanish and British unsuccessfully tried to seize the French colony at great cost. In an effort to keep the rebels loyal, the French Convention abolished slavery in 1794 and named Toussaint general-in-chief of the island in 1797. In 1802, Napoleon sent an expeditionary force of twenty-five thousand troops to reconquer the colony. Although the French managed to capture and imprison Toussaint, who died in custody, their army was destroyed by the Saint-Dominguan forces and yellow fever. On January 1, 1804, Toussaint's successor, Jean-Jacques Dessalines, proclaimed himself the ruler of the independent black republic of Haiti. In a little more than a decade the slaves of Saint-Domingue had effected a political revolution more far-reaching in its implications than those of their counterparts in the French and American republics.

From the beginning of the upheavals on Saint-Domingue, Americans, black and white, took an active interest in the events on the island. There were direct links between the American and Haitian revolutions. A number of men who played a leading role in the Dominguan rebellion had served with the French forces in America during the War of Independence. Similarly, African American veterans served with the British forces which sought to conquer Saint-Domingue. Saint-Domingue was, after Britain, the most important trading partner of the United States in 1791. Yankee shippers and distillers valued the colony's sugar and molasses, while American manufactures sold manufactured goods and supplies to the French planters. With the French Revolution lapping the very shores of America via the Caribbean, the Haitian Revolution posed a complex challenge to American politicians. Despite their professed love of liberty and admiration for the French Revolution, the Republicans were no friends of the Haitian Revolution. As a party whose leadership was drawn from the ranks of southern slaveholders, the Republican leadership could not countenance the events in Saint-Domingue which they interpreted as a perversion of republicanism. As president, Thomas Jefferson would advocate a policy of economically and politically isolating the Haitian Republic, a policy which fostered widespread poverty in America's sister republic. Ironically, the elitist-oriented Federalists were more amenable to a Haitian Republic than the Republicans. During the Quasi-War with France, John

Adams pursued a policy of accommodation with Toussaint L'Ouverture and even recommended that he declare Haiti independent.[22]

The Haitian Revolution had its greatest American impact on relations between slaves and their masters. Southern slaveholders were horrified by the news from Saint-Domingue, which represented a direct threat to their way of life. The events in Saint-Domingue were widely covered in the southern press and must have been a major topic of conversation among slaveholders. In such circumstances, slaves could not but have been aware of the rising. African American mariners brought news of the tumult in the Caribbean as well. Soon southerners, black and white, would have a more direct source of information on events in the rebellious colony. During the summer of 1793, thousands of white Dominguan planters arrived in American ports fleeing from the victorious rebels. Southern slaveholders initially welcomed the refugees, whose plight was a manifestation of their worst nightmares. The refugees brought their slaves with them. The West Indian servants communicated news of the Dominguan situation to their American counterparts. When combined with their own revolutionary heritage, the events in Saint-Domingue inspired American slaves to further resist their bondage. In August 1793, a letter was discovered detailing the plans for a massive slave rising in South Carolina and Virginia, prompted by the Dominguan uprising. The final years of the eighteenth century witnessed an upsurge of similar conspiratorial activity among southern slaves. Ultimately the southern states took steps to ban the importation of slaves from French West Indies in an effort to stem revolutionary activity among their own slaves. It is only in the context of events in Saint-Domingue that the persistent militancy of American slaves during the period can be fully appreciated. The slaves of Saint-Domingue and the United States sought freedom in the political disputes which divided their masters. In so doing, they wrought a truly revolutionary movement for black freedom which threatened slavery in the New World. Governor James Monroe of Virginia explained the connection in the wake of Gabriel's Rebellion: "The scenes which are acted in St. Domingo must produce an effect on all the people of color in this and the States south of us, more especially our slaves, and it our duty to be on guard to prevent any mischief arising from it." In the Dominguan case, the black revolutionary movement was successful. In the American context, where African American slaves were a minority of the population, bondsmen and women failed to overturn slavery. Nonetheless, the tradition of militant resistance of the revolutionary era continued until slavery in America was ultimately destroyed by the Civil War.[23]

Conclusion

The story of slavery in the era of the American Revolution is a complex and frustrating one. It reveals that the majority of white Americans were unwilling or unable to recognize the consequence of their independence. In 1776 the Continental Congress declared, in words penned by a slaveholder, "that all men are created equal and endowed by their creator with certain inalienable rights and among these are life, liberty, and the pursuit of happiness." Such a declaration was antithetical to the practice of slavery. Although whites might have refused to recognize such a conclusion, it was not lost on the slaves themselves. As one of the insurgents in Gabriel's Rebellion declared at his trial, "I have nothing more to offer than what General Washington would have had to offer, had he been taken by the British and put to trial. I have adventured my life endeavoring to obtain the liberty of my countrymen, and am a willing sacrifice to their cause."[24] In the north, slaves won their freedom by their actions and the pressure they brought to bear on the slave system. In the south, slaves strove to bring the slave system down but met with failure. At the heart of the Revolution lay a promise of freedom. The revolutionary generation failed to keep that promise. In so doing, they postponed the day of reckoning and condemned the United States and millions of slaves to another four generations of injustice and suffering.

10

AMERICAN WOMEN IN THE AGE OF REVOLUTION

Introduction

If, from the perspective of America's slaves, the Revolution had an ambiguous impact, what, then of American women? Historians disagree as to the consequences of the Revolution for American women. In an important anthology published to coincide with the bicentenary of the Declaration of Independence, a leading historian of American women declared in an essay entitled "The Illusion of Change" that "the American Revolution produced no significant benefits for American women." In subsequent years, a significant body of scholarly literature has appeared which has recovered the experiences of women during the revolutionary era and which undermines this bold declaration. This literature has revealed the complexity of women's experiences during the Revolution and demonstrates that while some women gained from the upheaval, they did so in the face of significant opposition from American males, be they rebels or loyalists. Moreover, the scholarship has revealed that class, race, and region were important determinants as to how the revolution affected American women. In 1989, in the introduction to a collection of essays based on this new scholarship, another leading women's historian called for the writing of a new narrative history of the Revolution which took account of the Revolution from the perspective of women. According to such a narrative, wrote Linda Kerber, the Revolution

> will be understood to be more deeply radical than we have heretofore perceived it because its shock reached into the deepest and most private human relations, jarring not only the hierarchical relationships between ruler and ruled, between elite and yeoman, between slave and free, but also between men and women, husbands and wives, mothers and children.[1]

Radical change or the illusion of change? Undoubtedly the period was one of trauma and change in women's lives as women took an active role in revolutionary events. But the crucial questions raised by the revolution – those concerning the meaning of the changes it wrought in women's lives, and the nature of the relationship between men and women and women and the state – continue to be debated. To some extent, the answers depend on whether one takes a short-term or a long-term view. Viewed in the short term, the revolutionary era witnessed upheaval and minimal legal, economic, and social changes for American women. From the longer term perspective, the revolutionary experience gave women, like other Americans, a language and legacy to draw upon in demanding and winning greater freedom and equality.

The American Revolution was, fundamentally, a political event. Political questions – should the colonies declare themselves independent, what type of government should the new states have, what should be the relationship between and among the new states – were at the heart of the Revolution. Although the whole of American society – white and black, slave and free, male and female, rich and poor – was drawn, often involuntarily, into the dispute and attendant war caused by these crucial questions, the power to answer them remained largely the purview of white males. We have seen, however, that the political and social upheaval which was a concomitant of the Revolution allowed disenfranchised groups in American society – notably African American slaves – to press for greater political and personal freedom. Their campaign would meet with mixed results. In some respects, the difficulties facing black and white American women were more formidable than those facing African American men in their quest for freedom.[2] American women had no explicit political rights during the era of the American Revolution. They were largely prevented by custom and practice from exercising a voice in political affairs. As such, they were at a distinct disadvantage in exploiting what was primarily a political dispute to ameliorate their condition. The purpose of this chapter is to examine the contributions of American women to the Revolution and to assess the impact the Revolution had on their lives. We shall do so by examining the increased politicization of American women during the prewar resistance; their experiences during the war; and the changing political role of women in the wake of the conflict.

Resistance

American women were excluded from political life by custom and practice which confined their activities to the "domestic sphere" of home-making, child-rearing, and feeding and clothing their families. During the decade before the outbreak of war between the colonies and Britain, domestic concerns assumed a political significance. Although they would not be its primary beneficiaries, the Revolution made profound demands upon women. It is unlikely that the prewar colonial boycott movement would have been successful without the support of women as both consumers and domestic producers. Moreover, women participated in many of the crowd actions which were such important vehicles of protest against parliamentary measures. Alfred F. Young, in a study of Boston women, has revealed that female support was crucial to the resistance movement in a variety of ways. Notably, women gave aid to the resistance as spectators to male demonstrations; as supporters of colonial boycotts; by increasing domestic manufacturing in response to the boycotts; as participants in crowd actions and popular protests; as mourners at political funerals; and by exhorting males to resist British encroachments, eventually by force of arms. As residents of a center of revolutionary resistance, the contributions of Boston women were crucial. Anecdotal evidence suggests women lent such support to the resistance movement in other regions and towns.[3]

Perhaps the most important prewar contribution made by American women was the support that they gave to boycotts against British imports. The boycotts required the aid of women as both consumers and domestic manufacturers. For the boycotts to succeed, it was crucial that urban women agree to forgo imported goods. Appeals were made to women to protest unjust taxes by refusing to consume the items enumerated in the Townshend Duties in 1767. As a female patriot appealed to her fellow women in 1768:

> Let the Daughters of Liberty, nobly arise,
> And tho we've no Voice, but a negative here,
> The use of Taxables, let us forbear.

The poet recognized that women, although denied a formal political voice, could play a key role in registering their disapproval of the taxes. In so doing they could take the lead, for, "Thus acting – we point out their Duty to men." Female adherence to the boycotts was widespread. In late 1767 Boston women pledged not to consume taxed items. In early 1770, several hundred Boston women declared that they would abstain from tea in protest of the Tea Act. Failing to appreciate the significance of such widespread commitment, the Boston loyalist Peter Oliver sarcastically noted that, "it was highly diverting to see the names & marks to the Subscription, of Porters & Washing Women," who pledged not to purchase luxury items such as imported "silks, Velvets, Clocks, Watches, Coaches & Chariots." Perhaps nothing sums up the revolutionary nature of the changes wrought during the period than Oliver's contempt for the washing women's endorsement of the boycott movement. For it was only with the support of "the Porters & Washing Women" that men like Oliver could be swept from power. Oliver's disdainful observation is vivid testimony to power of the protest movement to transcend the boundaries of class, gender, and race. It was in the crossing of such boundaries that the colonial American protest movement became truly revolutionary. In perhaps the most famous of the prewar women's protests, fifty-one North Carolina women proclaimed their support for the colony's provincial congress in the so-called Edenton Tea Party of October 1774.[4]

When protesting colonists boycotted imports, they not only had to forgo luxury items like tea but also important everyday consumer goods such as clothing. As the primary domestic manufacturers, it fell to women to increase their production in order to meet the increased demand produced by the boycotts. A verse in the *Boston Post-Boy* offered the following counsel:

> Young ladies in town and those that live round,
> Let a friend at this season advise you:
> Since money's so scarce, and time's growing worse
> Strange things may soon hap and surprize you:
> First then, throw aside your high top knots of pride
> Wear none but your own country linnen;
> Of Œconomy boast, lest your pride be the most
> To show cloaths of your own make and spinning.

Although spinning for domestic consumption was widespread in rural areas, urban women often had to learn it as a new skill and an additional responsibility. Peter Oliver noted, "the Women & Children, both within Doors & without, set their Spinning Wheels a whirling in Defiance of *Great Britain*. The female Spinners kept on spinning for 6 Days of the Week." Though a domestic task adopted to meet domestic demand, the rise in home manufacture was necessitated by political protest. The very domestic acts of spinning and weaving therefore had political implications. The political nature of domestic manufacturing was epitomized by the spinning bees held by gatherings, often termed Daughters of Liberty, which were widely reported in American newspapers.[5]

Male patriots were often dismissive, or failed to recognize the significance, of female contributions to the prewar resistance movement. Women's actions in support of the protest movement were, after all, largely confined to the domestic sphere, where they acted as consumers and manufacturers. The significant development, however, was that female domestic activity was now invested with political significance. As Linda Kerber has written, "women who had thought themselves excused from making political choices, now found that they had to align themselves politically, even behind the walls of their own homes." With the advent of the War of Independence in 1775, women would be called upon to make even greater sacrifices and contributions. Their actions during the conflict, while still largely "domestic" would have even greater political implications. Women's domestic actions during the War of Independence would be of such significance that it could be said that American women acted as midwives to the birth of the American Republic.[6]

American women at war

The War of Independence made unprecedented demands upon American women. Although war had been a feature of colonial life, the War of Independence was longer and spread over a wider geographic area than any previous conflict in the region. Unlike previous conflicts, which were usually inspired by competing imperial claims to North American territory, or by Indian resistance to Euro-American settlement and expansion, the War of Independence was a military struggle caused by a political question: what should be the appropriate relationship between the American colonies and the British Empire? When the rebels declared themselves independent and determined to establish governments based on popular sovereignty, their war became a popular political struggle. As such, the whole of the American population was drawn into the conflict. As we saw with respect to African American slaves, the political struggle over independence had unforeseen social consequences. The military conflict would have a similar impact on American women. By their participation, both willing and unwilling, in the war they wrought a transformation of their place and role in American society.

As a prolonged, internecine, and bloody struggle, the War of Independence affected nearly all American women. Those traditonally most immune to the disruptions of war, the upper classes, were frequently made exiles. Thousands of women and their families were made refugees by the fighting. For example, in the aftermath of outbreak of fighting at Lexington and Concord, between twelve and thirteen thousand men, women, and children fled from British-occupied Boston. The day after the fighting an observer noted that the roads around Boston were "fill'd with frightened women and children, some in carts with their tattered furniture, others on foot fleeing into the woods." The same scenes were repeated up and down the country with each new campaign. In some cases families were only briefly displaced by fighting, but in others the war meant a more permanent dislocation. For women, whose traditional roles included childcare and home-making, flight presented difficult challenges. Maintaining and caring for a family was a laborious task in the eighteenth century; to do so in a war zone was a remarkable feat indeed.[7]

Whether women took flight or not, the war held myriad dangers for them and their families. Chief among these were epidemic disease and the threat posed by marauding armies. Camp diseases, especially smallpox and dysentery, did not distinguish between soldiers and civilians. Wherever the armies went, disease and death accompanied them. During the siege of Boston in the autumn of 1775, a dysentery epidemic swept through eastern

Massachusetts which probably had its origins in the camps of the contending armies. On October 1, Abigail Adams wrote of the situation on the day that her mother succumbed to the illness: "Tis a dreadful time with this whole province. Sickness and death are in almost every family. I have no more shocking and terible Idea of any Distemper except the Plague than this." Eight days later she reported that four corpses, including that of her niece, were buried in the town of Braintree on one day and that "in six weeks I count 5 of my near connections laid in the grave." Such epidemic conditions recurred throughout America wherever large numbers of soldiers camped for a prolonged period of time. Disease, not combat, took the lives of the overwhelming majority of soldiers and civilians, male and female, who died during the War of Independence.[8]

American women were threatened by the armies themselves as well as by the diseases which they spread. Families might have their homes and farms plundered or soldiers billeted with them. Such unforeseen demands upon their resources might threaten impoverishment and starvation. An untold number of American women lived with the consequences of wartime rape. The best-documented of such atrocities occurred in New Jersey during late 1776, when the British pursued a policy of what a leading historian has termed "systematic and especially brutal" rape. In the wake of the British depredations, the Continental Congress collected depositions which reveal horrific cases, including sixteen girls kidnapped in Hopewell, New Jersey and repeatedly raped in a British camp, and thirteen-year-old Abigail Palmer, who was repeatedly raped by British soldiers at her grandfather's home in Hunterdon County. The New Jersey atrocities may have been the worst of the war perpetrated against women. They are remarkable for their systematic nature. It is probable that the British, frustrated by their inability to capture and defeat Washington's army, may have been trying (unsuccessfully) to break rebel morale by granting license to their soldiers to abuse American civilians. Nonetheless, the fear of rape and instances of rape during the war were not unique to New Jersey. Certainly women faced the same danger in the anarchic conditions which characterized the southern states between 1778 and 1783.[9]

American women were not simply the victims of the war; without their active support it would have impossible for either side, particularly the rebels, to have waged the conflict as long as they did. Women contributed to the war effort in two ways: by replacing absent husbands as temporary heads of households, and by serving with the military forces in an ancillary capacity. Eighteenth-century American wives (at least white women) were recognized as having responsibility for the domestic sphere, which included the preparation of food and clothing as well as nurturing children. Men, in contrast, were responsible for leading their families in public sphere which included overseeing the economic and political interests of the family. The notion of separate spheres could be blurred considerably by circumstances.

Urban women, for example, frequently operated in "public" sphere of the market place. During the war, thousands of American women assumed responsibility for their families during the often prolonged absences of their husbands during military, political, or diplomatic service. Necessity compelled women to manage farms or businesses and to take decisions on behalf of their families without consulting their husbands. Some women fared better than others, but without such efforts it is unlikely that the struggle for independence would have been sustained as long as it was.

Throughout the war, many women made a more direct contribution to the war effort by serving the armies as camp followers. One historian estimates that around 20,000 served the rebel forces in an ancillary capacity. A return of the British forces in America in 1777 reveals more than 23,000 soldiers as well as 2,776 women and 1,901 children. On both sides, women provided crucial labor as cooks, cleaners, laundresses, and nurses. Most of the women who followed their husbands into the army were poor and had no means to support themselves. To some extent they fulfilled their traditional domestic roles in a different, military context. In a few exceptional cases, a small number of women exceeded their traditional roles and served in combat. Without the ancillary support of the women and children who followed the army, it would not have been possible for an eighteenth-century army to stay in the field for long.[10]

The war years were years of hardship for many women. This is perhaps illustrated by examining the travails of one woman by way of example. Mary Richardson was born into a large family in Cambridge, Massachusetts in 1753. Mary's father, Moses, was a carpenter of moderate success. In the early 1770s William Russell, a teacher from Boston, began to court Mary Richardson, and in 1772, at the age of nineteen, she gave birth to an illegitimate son by Russell. Several months later Mary and William were married. William Russell was active in the radical politics of Boston. A member of the Sons of Liberty, he participated in the Boston Tea Party in 1773. The outbreak of war had a direct impact on Mary Richardson Russell. Her father, Moses, was killed in the fighting on the first day of the conflict. Her husband's political activism rendered him suspect to the British. Soon after the fighting broke out the family, which now included three children, was forced to flee their Boston home. For the next year the Russells lived as refugees, relying on the sympathy and charity of friends and relatives. After the evacuation of Boston in March 1776, William Russell returned to discover that the British had plundered and destroyed the family home. Facing poverty, the family moved in with their Richardson kin in Cambridge. During the period when the family were refugees, Mary Richardson Russell gave birth to two children, a daughter and a son, both of whom died in infancy. Facing poverty, William Russell joined the crew of a rebel privateer in late 1778. When William went to sea, Mary Richardson Russell was left to cope with four young children. She lived with her widowed mother. The family relied on the magnanimity of friends and neighbors and the money Mary raised by washing and sewing. What could have been a temporary situation became permanent due to the misfortunes of war. William Russell was largely unsuccessful as a privateersman: he was twice captured and spent most of the period from 1779 to 1783 in British custody in England and in New York. In the latter he was confined on the notorious prison hulk, H.M.S. *Jersey*. While on the *Jersey* William contracted tuberculosis, which killed him in 1784. The war had cost Mary Richardson Russell both her father and her husband and possibly two children. It reduced the remainder of her family to the brink of poverty. In the postwar years, Mary would continue to struggle to make ends meet and to provide for her remaining children. American independence was purchased with the sacrifices of women like Mary Richardson Russell. Unlike soldiers whose service ended with the conclusion of the war, many women like Mary Richardson Russell paid for American freedom for the rest of their lives.[11]

"An Illusion of Change"?

American independence could not have been won without the support of American women. Partly in consequence of women's contributions to independence, Americans, female and male, sought to redefine the political role of women. The major impetus for the redefinition of the political role of women was the republican ideology which was at the heart of the political system created in the wake of independence. Before independence, all Americans were British subjects who owed their allegiance to the crown. The system was patriarchal and premised on an unequal relationship between those who wielded power and those whom they governed. Under this system, women, who were subordinate to male heads of household – fathers in the case of unmarried minors, and husbands in the case of married women – exercised no political rights. Indeed, according to colonial law, a wife who killed her husband was guilty not of murder but *petit treason* and thus was subject to harsher penalties than those reserved for murderers. The reasoning behind these laws was the assumption that upon marriage a husband and wife enjoyed the same unequal relationship as the king to his subjects. For a wife to kill her husband was to challenge the very order of society and the authority of the crown itself, and she would be punished accordingly. By contrast, if a husband killed his wife he would be charged with the lesser crime of murder. Although the law of *petit treason* was rarely applied in pre-revolutionary America, it well illustrates the subordinate role of women before independence.

The political and legal subordination of early American women extended to economic relations. Before the Revolution, married women were bound by the terms of coverture, another common law concept. Under its terms, a married woman could not own nor control property in her own name. All her legal and economic independence and autonomy was forfeited to her husband. Thus married women could not sue or be sued, draft wills, or enter into legally binding agreements. In a society where all adult women were expected to be married, these constraints limited the legal and public status of the majority of women. In theory and in practice, the political and economic autonomy of American women were severely circumscribed in the years before independence.

The advent of republicanism offered American women the prospect of change. After all, Americans had overturned the patriarchal authority of the British state and replaced it with a confederation of self-governing republics. Having successfully challenged and overturned a patriarchal political system, would Americans be willing to overturn their patriarchal system of gender relations? Would it be possible for American women to enjoy greater political freedom in the new republic which their efforts had helped to create? The answers to these questions lay in the larger debate over the meaning of republicanism which occurred during the generation after the conclusion of the war. When they overthrew monarchical authority, Americans transformed themselves from subjects into citizens. Whereas subjects had obligations, citizens had rights and responsibilities. If Americans were to base their political culture on citizenship and popular sovereignty, then they must define who could exercise political rights and enjoy the full responsibilities of citizenship. This debate offered women the promise of improved social and political conditions.

The debate over who should exercise rights in a republican polity was largely conducted by the propertied white males who provided leadership to the independence movement. During the years of the early republic these men, by their words and actions, would attempt to define the limits of the freedoms won in the revolutionary movement. We have already seen that they sought to exclude American Indians from participation in the American Republic by attempting to keep them out of its bounds and by denying them citizenship. In the case of African Americans, the revolutionary generation was of course divided on the issue of slavery. Although slavery was abolished in the north, it was retained and ultimately strengthened and deepened in the south. While the Revolution created a substantial free black population in both regions, in the main African Americans were excluded by law and custom from exercising their political rights. Unlike American Indians, free African Americans were taxed by a republic in whose government they had no representation. The years of the early republic did see an improvement in the political rights of poor white males. The rise of partisanship resulted in the amendment and liberalization of electoral laws which resulted in a broader franchise. Eventually property requirements were lessened and removed, and by the 1830s white males in the United States would enjoy nearly universal suffrage. Although the elite which led the Revolution sought to delineate the limits of freedom in the new republic, their efforts did not go unchallenged. By their contributions before independence and during the war disenfranchised groups, such as poor whites and African Americans, sought to stretch the rather conservative limits of freedom as conceived by the leaders of the new republic. They demanded and, to a limited extent, won a greater voice in American society and politics. What about American women?

Perhaps the most famous discourse on the place of women in the new republic took place between John and Abigail Adams on the eve of the Declaration of Independence. On March 31, 1776, Abigail Adams wrote to her husband, who was serving in the Continental Congress;

> I long to hear that you have declared an independancy – and by the way in the new Code of Laws which I suppose it will be necessary for you to make I desire you would Remember the Ladies, and be more generous and favourable to them than your ancestors. Do not put such unlimited power into the hands of Husbands. Remember all Men would be tyrants if they could. If perticular care and attention is not paid to the Laidies were are determined to foment a Rebelion and will not hold ourselves bound by any Laws in which we have no voice, or Representation.

Abigail Adams recognized the connection between overthrowing a patriarchal political system and a system of patriarchal gender relations. She was aware that a colonial declaration of independence would necessitate a fundamental reordering of American political life, and she hoped that such a change would lead to more equitable treatment of women by the law. Her quip that women would rebel rather than be subject to laws to which they had not given their consent, while intended as a joke, indicates that some women were applying the lessons of the Revolution in unforeseen ways.[12]

John Adams's response to his wife's letter reveals the depth of opposition women would meet in seeking to improve their status under the new republican order. He wrote a flippant response to his wife on April 14:

> As to your extraordinary Code of Laws, I cannot but laugh. We have been told that our Struggle has loosened the bands of Government every where. That Children and Apprentices were disobedient – that schools and Colledges were grown turbulent – that Indians slighted their Guardians and Negroes grew insolent to the Masters. But your Letter was the first Intimation that another Tribe more numerous and powerfull than all the rest were grown discontented. – This is rather too coarse a Compliment but you are so Saucy, I wont blot it out.[13]

Although John Adams adopted a jocular, dismissive tone, his comments reveal an awareness that the ideology and logic of the Revolution would lead to marginal groups like the poor and African Americans to demand greater control over their lives. Adams was clearly reluctant to see revolutionary changes in the status of women. In late May 1776 Adams, possibly with Abigail's letter in mind, wrote to a friend who advocated that voting requirements be examined: "Depend upon it sir, it is dangerous to open So fruitfull a Source of Controversy and Altercation, as would be opened by attempting to alter the Qualifications of Voters. There will be no end to it. New claims will arise. Women will demand a Vote."[14] At the time he wrote this letter, Adams was on the radical edge of the revolutionary movement. With respect to gender relations, he spoke for most of his colleagues. The male leaders of the Revolution would prove to be very conservative indeed when the issues of gender relations and women's rights were raised.

Nearly twenty years later, at a Fourth of July oration delivered at Elizabeth, New Jersey in 1793, the revolutionary leader Elias Boudinot declared "The Rights of Women are no longer strange sounds to an American ear. They are now heard as familiar terms in every part of the United States."[15] If one considers the legal, social, economic or political status of women from a relatively narrow perspective, then Boudinot's words seem ill-chosen. Indeed, the postwar legal, economic, and political status of women would seem to substantiate Joan Hoff Wilson's assertion that the legacy of the Revolution for women was an "illusion of change." The middle- and upper-class white males, like John Adams, who wielded power were unwilling to radically alter gender relations in American society. Although some changes were instituted which improved the legal and economic status of women – the abolition of *petit treason*, the liberalization of divorce laws, and the abolition of primogeniture – the main legal constraints on women remained in place. Coverture, for example, did not face any significant challenge during the revolutionary era or the early republic. American courts during the period consistently took decisions which upheld the patriarchal system of gender relations. In political terms, women were excluded from exercising the franchise (with one exception) or holding office. The record of the revolutionary generation with respect to the rights of women seems paltry indeed.

There is one instance where American women were given a direct voice in political matters. It illustrates the potential for greater liberty offered to women by the Revolution and the considerable obstacles placed in their way by male revolutionaries. The New Jersey constitution of 1776 defined voters not by gender but as "all free inhabitants" who could meet property and residence requirements. This wording could be interpreted as enfranchising widows and unmarried women with property as well as African Americans. (Whether the law was intended to enfranchise these groups is unclear.) During the 1780s, some New Jersey women who could meet the state's property requirements voted. It is possible that the wartime struggles and suffering of New Jersey women reinforced the notion that they had won a political voice in the new republic. Soon the practice was commonplace and widely accepted, as evidenced by a 1790 law which unambiguously referred to voters as "he or she." In 1796 the state legislature took steps to disenfranchise African American men and women but affirmed the right of white women to vote. With the rise of intensive partisanship during the 1790s, women played an important electoral role. In the 1797 legislative election in Elizabeth, for example, seventy-five women cast votes for the Federalists who were narrowly defeated by the Republicans. Fierce party competition in the state led to electoral fraud, which resulted in women who could not meet property requirements – such as married women and daughters who lived at home – (as well as unqualified males) casting votes. By 1800 women were active and open participants in the political life of New Jersey.[16]

There was male opposition to women's voting in New Jersey. Most critics agreed the voting was incompatible with femininity. In the wake of the 1797 election, the following verse appeared in Newark's *Centinel of Freedom*:

To Congress, Lo! widows shall go,
like metamorphosed witches!
Cloath'd in the dignity of state,
and eke! in coat and breeches!

Critics believed that women were unsuited to voting because they were incapable of exercising independent judgment on political matters. In consequence they were liable to be influenced unduly by men. In the wake of widespread voter fraud during the first decade of the nineteenth century, the Republican-controlled legislature disenfranchised African Americans and all women voters in order to restore "the safety, quiet, good order and dignity of the state."[17] Although males made up the majority of the fraudulent voters, the Republicans, a party dedicated to promoting liberty, sought as scapegoats those on the margins of political life. In so doing they brought New Jersey into line with rest of the country.

Republican Motherhood

Viewed in legal, economic, and political terms, American women in the generation after the Revolution remained in a subordinate position within a patriarchal social order. This pattern of gender relations did not solve the inherent tension between republican citizenship and patriarchy. Women could not remain subjects in a nation of citizens. If the males who dominated the revolutionary generation denied the same political rights and liberties they enjoyed to their wives, sisters, mothers, and daughters, it was still necessary for that generation – both male and female – to define the place of the female citizen in a republican polity. In the aftermath of the Revolution, therefore, a new role for women emerged from newspaper accounts, magazine articles, pamphlets, fiction, and public orations. In these varied sources, republican theorists, usually men, sought to redefine the role of women in republican society in a manner which acknowledged their contribution to the success of the republic without undermining patriarchal control. Although the literature on the subject is large and the solutions posed diverse – indicating the significance of the issue – certain common themes emerge.

At the theoretical level, Americans developed a new role for women which drew on their traditional responsibilities but invested them with political significance. In so doing, Americans were attempting to reconcile patriarchal gender relations to a republican political culture. They created a new role for women which, at least on the cultural and ideological level, was vital to the success of the republic and thus was revolutionary. This new female role has been called Republican Motherhood. It was a central tenet of the republican ideology, as understood and embraced by eighteenth-century Americans, that only a morally vigorous republic could survive. History taught Americans of the revolutionary generation that societies that were characterized by moral and political degeneracy could not long survive as republics. For a republic to endure, its citizens must be virtuous. According to the new women's role articulated by republican theorists, women as mothers played the crucial role in promoting virtue and hence defending the republic from the greatest danger it faced, corruption. The Republican Mother inculcated the values of civic and personal virtue into her children – raising her sons to be good republican citizens and her daughters to become republican mothers themselves – while making sure that her husband stayed on a morally sound path as well by gently correcting his moral lapses. According to this view, women participated indirectly in the political life of the nation. The proponents of Republican Motherhood invested the traditional female roles of nurturing mother and homemaker with political implications. Women might not be able (or capable, republican writers implied) to exercise full political rights, but their activities would have a direct impact on the survival of the American experiment in republican government. As one speaker told America's women, "While you thus keep our country virtuous, you maintain its independence."[18]

Republican Motherhood could be limiting or liberating for American women. In an age which witnessed widespread discussion, debate and changes concerning rights and liberty Republican Motherhood seems a rather limited advance for women. While American men, at least those of European descent, were invited to enjoy the rights articulated in the

Declaration of Independence and codified in the Bill of Rights, Republican Motherhood seemed to limit women to their traditional roles as nurturing mothers and supportive wives. Viewed in this way, Republican Motherhood is little more than a patronizing sop from male republican thinkers who sought to pacify American women rather than invite them to partake of the fruits of American independence to which their contributions over the previous generation entitled them. By investing traditional women's activities with political importance through the doctrine of Republican Motherhood, men sought to prevent women from making greater political demands which might disrupt American society and gender relations. Republican Motherhood, in short, did not reconcile republicanism with patriarchy; it sought to keep the two separate, maintaining the latter by paying lip service to the former.

While it is tempting to stress the constraints that the concept of Republican Motherhood may have imposed on American women, such an interpretation has limitations. Republican Motherhood was not a political policy. Unlike, for example, the decision by an individual state or its government to abolish or retain slavery, Republican Motherhood was not a political program. Nor was it the product of a small group of political leaders. Rather, it was expressed in a myriad of newspaper columns, periodicals, pamphlets, short stories, and novels by many different writers, male and female. In defining the Republican Mother as a type, Linda Kerber and the scholars who have followed her lead have identified an important shift in cultural attitudes toward women and their place in republican society. Undoubtedly some writers recognized and valued that the new doctrine might constrain women in an age of revolutionary political and social change. To suppose this was a predominant view is, however, unrealistic. Such a conclusion assumes a coherence among the proponents of Republican Motherhood which did not exist, and it ignores the positive consequences of the doctrine for American women.

If American women were to be Republican Mothers, then they would have to be properly prepared for the task of inculcating republican values and civic virtue in their children and protecting their husbands from political and personal vice. If Republican Motherhood invested traditional female roles with political significance, it also changed the requirements of those roles. Mothers would now need to understand the rudiments of republicanism. This could only be achieved through improved education for girls. In the wake of the Revolution, a number of academies for young women were established to educate properly American females for their new role as Republican Mothers. While such academies were relatively few in number and accommodated a small fraction of middle- and upper-class women, they are symptomatic of a broader culture recognition that a sound virtuous republic rested on a properly educated citizenry. In consequence, education for boys and girls improved in the years following the Revolution.

213

Among women, improved education resulted in improved rates of literacy; literacy among Boston women, for example, rose from 60 percent before the Revolution to 78 percent by 1795 to over 80 percent during the early decades of the nineteenth century.[19] Increased literacy and better education were accompanied by a rise in women's reading and authorship. The years of the early republic witnessed the advent of publishing for and often by women. Periodicals and books were now aimed at women readers and frequently addressed their concerns. (It was in this literature that Republican Motherhood found expression.) Improved education and the rise of women as readers and writers was a direct and beneficial consequence of Republican Motherhood and the Revolution.[20]

Conclusion

Republican Motherhood and its attendant benefits – improved education and literacy – was largely the concern of middle- and upper-class women. For poor white and nearly all African American women, the immediate impact of the Revolution was, at first glance, negligible. Although the war made great demands upon them, they did not reap immediate benefits from independence. Nonetheless, the changes wrought by the Revolution would have a long-term impact on all American women. The upheaval of the War of Independence and the crucial role played by women in the conflict necessitated a change in the relationship between men and women. As Linda Kerber has eloquently written:

> Wars that are not fought by professional armies almost always force a renegotiation of sex roles, if only because when one sex changes its patterns of behavior the other sex cannot help but respond. In this the American Revolution was not distinctive. The Revolution does seem to have been distinctive, however, in the permanence of the newly negotiated roles, which took on lives of their own, infusing themselves into Americans' understanding of appropriate behavior for men and for women deep into the nineteenth and even twentieth centuries.[21]

In this view, the rather limited and ambiguous advances for women – more liberal divorce laws, improved education for elite women, Republican Motherhood – need to be viewed in the context of a longer struggle for equality and women's rights. The Revolution initiated but did not complete the movement for political and economic equality for American women. As with African Americans, the years which gave birth to the United States were an important step on the path to freedom for American women, but they would not reach their objective during the early years of republic. The importance of the revolutionary legacy to American women was expressed by the women's rights activists who gathered in Seneca Falls, New York in 1848 and adopted a "Declaration of Sentiments," modeled on Jefferson's Declaration of Independence, which declared, "We hold these truths to be self-evident: that all men and women are created equal." As with other Americans, the Revolution provided American women with the language to demand their freedom.

CONCLUSION

We the People

Perhaps the most passionate debate in the vast historiography of the American Revolution concerns the nature of the event itself. Neither contemporaries nor subsequent students of the subject have been able to agree over just how revolutionary the American Revolution was. Indeed, some critics argue that the events which led to creation of the United States were not revolutionary at all but merely the culmination of political, economic, and social trends at work in British North America long before independence. According to this view, since the same class of property-holding white men were in power in the United States as had dominated the old colonial societies, political independence alone was not enough to claim a revolutionary heritage for the United States. Proponents of the view that the American Revolution was indeed revolutionary point to the creation of republican governments in the United States as well as the substantial social disorder which accompanied their creation – including the displacement of thousands of loyalists – as evidence for a radical revolutionary tradition in the United States.[1]

It is the premise of this book that the American Revolution can only be properly appreciated when placed in a broad chronological context. Only by considering the changes between the creation of the United States in 1776 and the successful defense of its independence in 1815 can one fully appreciate the significance of the American Revolution.

The nation which celebrated the American victory at New Orleans in January 1815 was fundamentally different from the group of colonies that celebrated the British triumph over France two generations before. Fewer than two million people lived in Britain's North American colonies in 1763. The overwhelming majority of them were clustered in towns and villages along the Atlantic littoral. By 1815, the United States had a population of 8.4 million which was scattered throughout the region east of the Mississippi River. Moreover, the United States claimed, at the expense of Native Americans, sovereignty over all of the territory south of Canada and north of Mexico from the Atlantic to the Rocky Mountains.

Arguably, the demographic and geographic growth of British North America would have happened regardless of whether the colonies achieved political independence. The Revolution, however, influenced both of these developments. Chapter 8 demonstrates that there was a direct correlation between the republican ideology which prevailed in the United States and the geographic expansion of the new republic. It is likely that Americans, had they remained colonists, would have continued to settle in the west just as they had during the seventeenth and eighteenth centuries. The Proclamation Act of 1763, however, indicates that they would have done so without the support of London. By contrast, the new United States positively encouraged and promoted westward expansion when it used its resources to displace Native Americans and acquire more territory while making that land available to European-American settlers.

Given the steady increase in the American population during the colonial period, there is no reason to suppose that the colonies would not have been as populous by the early nineteenth century had they not achieved independence. There is evidence, however, that the Revolution affected the nature of American population growth. Aaron S. Fogleman has recently argued, for example, that political independence led to a shift in the pattern of immigration to America. Before independence, most migrants to British North America were unfree slaves, indentured servants, and convicts. After independence, however, free immigrants outnumbered unfree migrants to the United States. Among these were radical European emigrés who contributed to the increasingly strident political culture of the early republic.[2]

Perhaps the greatest legacy of the Revolution was that the majority of male Americans in 1815 were citizens of a republic rather than subjects of a monarch. American men seized control of their political lives when they rebelled against Britain. When they created republics, be they elitist or democratic in nature, Americans erected governments whose sovereignty was derived from the people. The creation of enduring republics by eighteenth-century Americans was an unprecedented success which can only be described as revolutionary.[3]

American republicans did not agree on the form their republics should take. The years immediately following independence witnessed the adoption of constitutional structures, such as those of Pennsylvania and Vermont, which were democratic in spirit and form. These constitutions reflected the confidence that common men had in their ability to govern themselves and their country. The resistance movement against Britain and the subsequent War of Independence made unprecedented demands upon the common people of America. These men earned and demanded a voice in the new political order which their efforts made possible. They would not yet dominate American politics, which remained the purview of the wealthy and well-educated, but they would exercise a far greater voice in affairs of state than they had previously been the case.

From the outset, the elite gentlemen who led the resistance to British rule were troubled by the "new men" brought to the fore by the Revolution. They sought to curb their influence in state and national government. When the fledgling republic faced external threats and internal stresses during the 1780s, these elitist republicans sought to diminish the democratic excesses they saw in the states. They believed excessive democracy endangered the American experiment in republican government. In 1787 they seized the political initiative and drafted a new Constitution to replace the Articles of Confederation. The new Constitution created a strong federal government at the expense of the more democratic states.

The federal Constitution, while intended to curb democratic excess, was not counter-revolutionary. The Federalists of 1788, like James Madison and Alexander Hamilton, unquestionably believed in the Revolution and in republican government. The first words in the preamble of the Constitution – "We the people" – are crucial testimony to this. The Federalists recognized that the new Constitution had to be based on some form of popular consent. It would have been impossible in 1788 to swindle the American people, at least those white males who could claim political rights, out of what they had won over the previous generation. The Federalists acted, they believed, to preserve the Revolution from external and internal threats. In so doing, they curbed the powers of the states with the approval (after the fact) of their fellow citizens. It could not have happened any other way.

The leaders of the revolutionary generation possessed the greatest sense of history of any group of politicians in the history of the United States. They knew that history, ancient and modern, provided no examples of enduring republics. They, like no other generation of Americans, felt the burden of history and sought to defy it by designing republics that would stand the test of time. The very fragility of republican government made every political controversy of the early republic, whether the Jay Treaty, or the Hamiltonian fiscal program, assume cosmic proportions. For in every political dispute lay, they believed, the seeds of the destruction of the republic and the failure of the Revolution. While in hindsight the early republic seems a stable polity with extensive natural resources, a growing population, and generally healthy institutions, contemporaries did not enjoy such perspective. Indeed, until 1815 many Americans felt that the republic was in mortal peril. Only in this context can the passion and vitriol which characterized the first party system (c.1790–1815) be appreciated. Federalists and Republicans believed they battled not simply for the spoils of office but the soul of the republic.

There were limits to the American Revolution. The expansive new republic acquired its land, often by force, from Native Americans who were largely excluded from the rights and privileges of citizenship.[4] A crucial concomitant to the expansionist impulse at the heart of the revolutionary ideology was the extension of race-based chattel slavery. While some revolutionaries, both black and white, argued that racial slavery was incompatible with republicanism and successfully campaigned for abolition in the northern states, slavery as an institution survived the Revolution. Slavery was perfectly compatible with the vision of agrarian republicanism espoused by the Jeffersonian republicans. If, as the Continental Congress declared on July 4, 1776, all men were created equal, then the only way to reconcile slavery and republicanism would be to deny the humanity of African Americans. Consequently the first years of the republic witnessed not only the abolition of slavery in the north and the creation of a free black population in the south, but also an upsurge in virulent anti-black racism among white Americans. In its early days, the United States was one of the world's only republics, but it was a republic of white men who used African American slaves to work land from which Native Americans had been displaced.

American women of all races were also denied their rights in the new republic. Unlike Native Americans, who had been deemed enemies, and African Americans, whose loyalties were considered suspect by white Americans during the war, American women played a crucial role in winning independence. With the coming of independence and the creation of republican governments, some (often middle-class) women demanded a role within the new polity. The result was Republican Motherhood which, while investing women's responsibilities with political significance, did not allow women to transcend traditional boundaries.

When the history of the early years of United States is approached from the perspectives of Native Americans, African Americans, and women, the limited contours of the Revolution become apparent. The ideology of the Revolution, however, proved impossible to contain. In the immediate aftermath of independence there is evidence that African Americans and women became more restive and willing to challenge the authority of white males. More significantly, the Revolution provided those on the political margins in the United States with a language with which they could demand their rights. It is not a coincidence that during the nineteenth century, reformers who promoted the interests of white working men, women, African Americans and Native Americans embraced the rhetoric and logic of the Revolution to advance their demands for political rights. In so doing, they laid claim to legacy of the Revolution. They applied the lessons of the Revolution in ways which most male revolutionaries had been unwilling or unable to do.

To approach the history of the American Revolution from the perspectives of Native Americans, African Americans and women, while essential to an understanding of the event, does not tell the whole story. Such an approach, albeit revealing the limits of the Revolution, ignores much of its detail. One can only speak of the limits of the American Revolution if one accepts that there was, indeed, a revolution. To celebrate the achievements of the revolutionaries while ignoring their limitations would be ahistorical. Conversely, to dwell on the failures of the revolutionaries while ignoring their very real accomplishments would be to commit a similar historical injustice. The revolutionaries of 1776 did not leave a perfect world to their heirs. If subsequent generations have failed to live up to the ideals of 1776, however, no blame can be ascribed to the men and women who first gave voice to those ideals and attempted, in a limited way, to put them into practice.

NOTES

INTRODUCTION

1 Robert Middlekauff, *The Glorious Cause: The American Revolution, 1763–1789* (New York: Oxford University Press, 1982); Edward Countryman, *The American Revolution* (New York: Hill and Wang, 1985); and Colin Bonwick, *The American Revolution* (London: Macmillan, 1991).

2 Countryman, *The American Revolution*, 274.

3 See George Otto Trevelyan, *The American Revolution*, 14 vols. (London: Longman, 1880–1914); Marcus Cunliffe, *The Nation Takes Shape, 1789–1837* (Chicago: University of Chicago Press, 1959); Esmond Wright, *Fabric of Freedom, 1763–1800* (New York: Hill and Wang, 1961, revised 1978); and Michael J. Heale, *The American Revolution* (London: Methuen (Lancaster Pamphlets), 1986) for excellent examples of this tradition.

4 I have been influenced in adopting this approach by R.R. Palmer's classic work, *The Age of Democratic Revolution: A Political History of Europe and America, 1760–1800*, 2 vols. (Princeton: Princeton University Press, 1959–64).

5 Linda K. Kerber has called for a narrative of the Revolution written from the perspective of women. Linda K. Kerber, " 'History Can Do it No Justice': Women and the Reinterpreation of the American Revolution," in Ronald Hoffman and Peter J. Albert, eds., *Women in the Age of the American Revolution* (Charlottesville: University Press of Virginia, 1989), 63–99. Kerber, among others, has devoted a large part of her professional life writing just such a narrative. The same can also be done for African Americans and Native Americans. See Sylvia Frey, *Water from the Rock: Black Resistance in a Revolutionary Age* (Princeton: Princeton University Press, 1991) and Colin G. Calloway, *The American Revolution in Indian Country* (Cambridge: Cambridge University Press, 1995).

6 In political terms, Native Americans were excluded from the revolutionary settlement. Their experiences are discussed in Chapter 4.

1 THE THIRTEEN COLONIES IN 1763

1 The classic account of this conflict – to which Pontiac owes his enduring, if inaccurate, historical reputation – is Francis Parkman, *The Conspiracy of Pontiac and the Indian War after the Conquest of Canada*, 2 vols. (Boston, 1851, repr. New York: Library of America, 1991). For more recent, and balanced, accounts see Howard H. Peckham, *Pontiac and the Indian Uprising* (Princeton: Princeton University Press, 1947, repr. 1994), and Francis Jennings, *Empire of Fortune:*

Crowns, Colonies & Tribes in the Seven Years' War in America (New York: Norton, 1988).

2 Gregory Evans Dowd, *A Spirited Resistance: The North American Struggle for Unity, 1745–1815* (Baltimore: Johns Hopkins University Press, 1992), especially Chapter 2. Also see Peter Mancall, *Deadly Medicine: Indians and Alcohol in Early America* (Ithaca: Cornell University Press, 1995).

3 For the Proclamation Act, see Peter Marshall, "The West and the Indians, 1756–1776," in *The Blackwell Encyclopedia of the American Revolution*, Jack P. Greene and J. R. Pole, eds. (Oxford: Blackwell, 1991), 153–60. Also see Bernhard Knollenberg, *Origin of the American Revolution, 1759–1766* (New York: Macmillan, 1960), Chapter 7.

4 James Kirby Martin, "The Return of the Paxton Boys and the Historical State of the Pennsylvania Frontier, 1764–1774," *Pennsylvania History*, 38 (1971), 117–33; Brooke Hindle, "The March of the Paxton Boys," *WMQ*, 3 (1946), 461–86; John R. Dunbar, ed., *The Paxton Papers* (The Hague: Nijhoff, 1957).

5 In addition to the thirteen colonies that rebelled in 1775 – New Hampshire, Massachusetts, Rhode Island, Connecticut, New York, New Jersey, Pennsylvania, Delaware, Maryland, Virginia, North Carolina, South Carolina, and Georgia – there were Nova Scotia, Quebec, East Florida, and West Florida.

6 For an interesting discussion of the political implications of eighteenth-century American population growth, see Theodore Draper, *A Struggle for Power: The American Revolution* (Boston: Little Brown, 1996), Chapter 6. For a discussion of the nature and causes of American population growth, see Robert V. Wells, "Population and Family in Early America," in *The Blackwell Encyclopedia of the American Revolution*, 39–52 and Jim Potter, "Demographic Development and Family Structure," in *Colonial British America: Essays in the New History of the Early Modern Era*, Jack P. Greene and J.R. Pole, eds. (Baltimore: Johns Hopkins University Press, 1984), 123–56.

7 U.S. Bureau of the Census, *Historical Statistics of the United States, Colonial Times to 1970*, 2 vols., (Washington: U.S. Bureau of the Census, 1975) 2: 1168. Wells, "Population and Family in Early America," 42.

8 Wells, "Population and Family in Early America," 48. For the role of women in eighteenth-century America, see Mary Beth Norton, *Liberty's Daughters: The Revolutionary Experience of American Women, 1750–1800* (Boston: Little Brown, 1980), Chapter 1. On childbirth, see Laurel Thatcher Ulrich, *Goodwives: Image and Reality in the Lives of Women in Northern New England, 1650–1750* (New York: Knopf, 1980), Chapter 8, and Laurel Thatcher Ulrich, *A Midwife's Tale: The Life of Martha Ballard Based on Her Diary, 1785–1812* (New York: Knopf, 1990).

9 The figures for eighteenth-century immigration are not precise. Bernard Bailyn estimates that between 401,500 and 573,500 persons migrated to America. See Bernard Bailyn, *Voyagers to the West: A Passage in the Peopling of America on the Eve of the Revolution*, with the assistance of Barbara DeWolfe (New York: Knopf, 1987), 25–6. Aaron S. Fogleman estimates that 585,800 immigrants arrived; Aaron S. Fogleman, "Migration to the Thirteen British North American Colonies, 1700–1775: New Estimates," *Journal of Interdisciplinary History*, 22 (1992), 691–709. Also see Aaron S. Fogleman, "From Slaves, Convicts, and Servants to Free Passengers: The Transformation of Immigration in the Era of the American Revolution," *JAH*, 85 (1998), 43–77.

10 Bailyn, *Voyagers to the West*, 26.

11 Fogleman, "Migration to the Thirteen British North American Colonies," 698.

12 See Aaron Spencer Fogleman, *Hopeful Journeys: German Immigration, Settlement, and Political Culture in Colonial America, 1717–1775* (Philadelphia: University of Pennsylvania Press, 1996); also see A.G. Roeber, " 'The Origin of Whatever is not English among Us': The Dutch-speaking and the German-speaking Peoples of Colonial British America," in Bernard Bailyn and Philip D. Morgan, eds., *Strangers within the Realm: Cultural Margins of the First British Empire* (Chapel Hill: University of North Carolina Press, 1991), 220–83, and Marianne Wokeck, "Harnessing the Lure of the 'Best Poor Man's Country': The Dynamics of German-Speaking Immigration to British North America, 1683–1783," in Ida Altman and James Horn, eds., *"To Make America": European Emigration in the Early Modern Period* (Berkeley: University of California Press, 1991), 204–43.

13 Fogleman, "Migration to the Thirteen British North American Colonies," estimates only 66,100. Most other sources put the figure of Scots-Irish emigrants much higher. Bailyn, *Voyagers to the West*, 26, puts the figure between 155,000 and 225,000, whereas James G. Leyburn, *The Scots-Irish: A Social History* (Chapel Hill: University of North Carolina Press, 1962), 180, estimates 200,000 emigrants, and Wayland Dunaway, *The Scotch Irish in Colonial Pennsylvania* (Chapel Hill: University of North Carolina Press, 1944), 20, puts the figure at 250,000.

14 Wells, "Population and Family in Early America," 46. Forrest McDonald and Ellen Shapiro McDonald, "The Ethnic Origins of the American People, 1790," *WMQ*, 37 (1980), 179–99, figures from table V, p. 198.

15 *Historical Statistics of the United States, Colonial Times to 1970*.

16 For the racial, social and legal constraints faced by African Americans, see William M. Wiecek, "The Statutory Law of Slavery and Race in the Thirteen Mainland Colonies of British America," *WMQ*, 34 (1977), 258–280 and Winthrop Jordan, *White Over Black: American Attitudes toward the Negro, 1550–1812* (Chapel Hill: University of North Carolina Press, 1968). For other unfree emigrants, see Richard S. Dunn, "Servants and Slaves: The Recruitment and Employment of Labor," in *Colonial British America*, 157–194 and Roger Ekirch, *Bound for America: The Transportation of British Convicts to the Colonies, 1718–1775* (Oxford: Clarendon, 1987).

17 For a description of the American elite and its attributes, see Gordon S. Wood, *The Radicalism of the American Revolution* (New York: Knopf, 1992), chaps 1–3. For an excellent discussion of the literature on the social structure of pre-Revolutionary America, see James A. Henretta, "Wealth and Social Structure," in *Colonial British America*, 262–89. Also see Jackson Turner Main, *The Social Structure of Revolutionary America* (Princeton: Princeton University Press, 1965). Recently, Michael Zuckerman has contested the notion that eighteenth-century American society was characterized by hierarchy and deference; see Michael Zuckerman, "Tocqueville, Turner, and Turds: Four Stories of Manners in Early America," *JAH*, 85 (1998), 13–43. For critiques of Zuckerman's argument, see John M. Murrin, "In the Land of the Free and the Home of the Slave, Maybe there was Room even for Deference," *JAH*, 85 (1998), 86–91; and Robert A. Gross, "The Impudent Historian: Challenging Deference in Early America," *JAH*, 85 (1998), 92–7.

18 Henretta, "Wealth and Social Structure," 281. For the breakdown in occupations, see Edwin J. Perkins, "Socio-Economic Development of the Colonies," in *The Blackwell Encyclopedia of the American Revolution*, 52–63, esp. 58–9.

19 For social development in the towns, see Gary Nash, *The Urban Crucible: Social Change, Political Consciousness and the Origins of the American Revolution* (Cambridge, Mass.: Harvard University Press, 1979); Sharon V. Salinger, *"To Serve Well and Faithfully": Labor and Indentured Servants in Pennsylvania, 1680–*

1800 (Cambridge: Cambridge University Press, 1987), and Ronald Schultz, *The Republic of Labor: Philadelphia Artisans and the Politics of Class, 1720–1830* (Oxford: Oxford University Press, 1993). Figures on wealth are from Nash, *The Urban Crucible*, 396. For the overall distribution of wealth in eighteenth-century America, see Henretta, "Wealth and Social Structure," 275–9. For the size of the urban population, see Wells, "Population and Family in Early America," 46. Also see Billy G. Smith, *The "Lower Sort": Philadelphia's Laboring People, 1750–1800* (Ithaca: Cornell University Press, 1990).

20 For a discussion of the growth rate of the American economy, see Henretta, "Wealth and Social Structure," 269–75. Also see Perkins, "Socio-Economic Development of the Colonies," 53, and see John J. McCusker, "Measuring Colonial Gross Domestic Product: An Introduction," *WMQ*, 56 (1999), 3–9.

21 Perkins, "Socio-Economic Development of the Colonies," 55; Richard B. Sheridan, "The Domestic Economy," in *Colonial British America*, 43–85; John J. McCusker and Russell R. Menard, *The Economy of British America, 1607–1789* (Chapel Hill: University of North Carolina Press, 1985).

22 For the trans-Atlantic trade, see McCusker and Menard, *Economy of British America*; Marc Egnal, "The Economic Development of the Thirteen Continental Colonies, 1720–1775," *WMQ*, 32 (1975), 191–222; John J. McCusker, "The Current Value of English Exports," *WMQ*, 28 (1971), 607–28; Jacob M. Price, "New Time Series for Scotland's and Britain's Trade with the Thirteen Colonies, 1740 to 1791," *WMQ*, 32 (1975), 307–25; Jacob M. Price, "The Trans-Atlantic Economy," in *Colonial British America*, 18–42; Kenneth Morgan, "The Organization of the Colonial American Rice Trade," *WMQ*, 52 (1995), 433–52.

23 *Historical Statistics of the United States, Colonial Times to 1970*, 2: 1183–84.

24 For the trans-Atlantic trade and its political and cultural consequences, see James D. Tracy, ed., *The Rise of Merchant Empires: Long Distance Trade in the Early Modern World, 1350–1750* (Cambridge: Cambridge University Press, 1990); David Hancock, *Citizens of the World: London Merchants and the Integration of the British Atlantic Community, 1735–1785* (Cambridge: Cambridge University Press, 1995); T.H. Breen, "Narrative of Commercial Life: Consumption, Ideology, and Community on the Eve of the American Revolution," *WMQ*, 50 (1993), 471–501; Draper, *A Struggle for Power*, Chapter 6.

25 See for example, Daniel B. Thorp, "Doing Business in the Backcountry: Retail Trade in Colonial Rowan County, North Carolina," *WMQ*, 48 (1991), 387–408.

26 Figures from Alice Hanson Jones, *Wealth of a Nation to Be: The American Colonies on the Eve of the Revolution* (New York: Columbia University Press, 1980), Table 9.3. Quotation from James Henretta, "Wealth and Social Structure," 274.

27 Norton, *Liberty's Daughters*, Chapter 1; Ulrich, *Goodwives*, Chapters 1–2; Barry J. Levy, *Quakers and the American Family* (New York: Oxford University Press, 1988); Daniel Blake Smith, *Inside the Great House: Planter Family Life in Eighteenth-Century Chesapeake Society* (Ithaca: Cornell University Press, 1980).

28 Carole Shammas, "Anglo-American Household Government in Comparative Perspective," *WMQ*, 52 (1995), 104–44.

29 Robert E. Brown in *Middle Class Democracy and Revolution in Massachusetts* (Ithaca: Cornell University Press, 1955) argued that New England's pre-Revolutionary politics were democratic. Also see Robert J. Dinkin, *Voting in Provincial America: A Study of Elections in the Thirteen Colonies, 1689–1776* (Westport, Conn.: Greenwood, 1977).

30 Bernard Bailyn, *The Ideological Origins of the American Revolution* (Cambridge, Mass.: Harvard University Press, 1967, repr. 1992).

31 For an excellent and concise summary of the immense literature on the intellectual origins of the Revolution, see Isaac Kramnick, "Ideological Background," in *The Blackwell Encyclopedia of the American Revolution*, 84–91.

32 For the number of congregations in America by denomination, see Edwin S. Gaustad, "Religion before the Revolution," in *The Blackwell Encyclopedia of the American Revolution*, 64–70, especially 69. For church attendance, see Patricia Bonomi and Peter Eisenstadt, "Church Adherence in the Eighteenth Century," *WMQ*, 34 (1982), 245–86. Rhys Isaac, *The Transformation of Virginia, 1740–1790* (Chapel Hill: University of North Carolina Press, 1982) provides a superb examination of the social implications of the Great Awakening. For works which argue that there was a direct link between American religion and the Revolution, the classic study is Alan Heimert, *Religion and the American Mind from the Great Awakening to the Revolution* (Cambridge, Mass.: Harvard University Press, 1966). Also see Nathan O. Hatch, *The Sacred Cause of Liberty: Republican Thought and the Millennium in Revolutionary New England* (New Haven: Yale University Press, 1977); Harry S. Stout, "Religion, Communications, and the Ideological Origins of the American Revolution," *WMQ*, 24 (1997), 519–41; and Francis D. Cogliano, *No King, No Popery: Anti-Catholicism in Revolutionary New England* (Westport, Conn.: Greenwood, 1995). Jon Butler, by contrast, argues that religion was not an especially important causal factor in the Revolution. See Jon Butler, *Awash in a Sea of Faith: Christianizing the American People* (Cambridge, Mass.: Harvard University Press, 1990), Chapter 7.

2 THE IMPERIAL CRISIS

1 The figures in these paragraphs are from Allen Johnson, "The Passage of the Sugar Act," *WMQ*, 16 (1959), 507–14; and Peter D.G. Thomas, "The Grenville Program, 1763–1765," in *The Blackwell Encyclopedia of the American Revolution*, Jack P. Greene and J.R. Pole, eds., (Oxford: Blackwell, 1991), 107–12, as well as Bernhard Knollenberg, *The Origin of the American Revolution* (New York: Macmillan, 1960), Chapter 11.

2 Peter D.G. Thomas, "The Stamp Act Crisis and its Repercussions, including the Quartering Act Controversy," in *The Blackwell Encyclopedia of the American Revolution*, 113–25; figures on distilleries, 113. For colonial objections to admiralty courts see, David S. Lovejoy, "Rights Imply Equality: The Case Against Admiralty Jurisdiction in America, 1764–1776," *WMQ*, 16 (1959), 459–84, and Carl Ubbelode, *The Vice-Admiralty Courts and the American Revolution* (Chapel Hill: University of North Carolina Press, 1960) For the significance of rum, see W.J. Rorabaugh, *The Alcoholic Republic: An American Tradition* (New York: Oxford University Press, 1979); Mark E. Lender and James Kirby Martin, *Drinking in America: A History* (New York: Free Press, 1987), and Peter Mancall, *Deadly Medicine: Indians and Alcohol in Early America* (Ithaca: Cornell University Press, 1995).

3 James Otis, *The Rights of the British Colonies Asserted and Proved* (Boston, 1764), reprinted in Bernard Bailyn, *Pamphlets of the American Revolution, 1750–1776* (Cambridge, Mass.: Harvard University Press, 1965), 419–82, quotations 461, 448.

4 For the adoption of the Stamp Act, see Peter D.G. Thomas, *British Politics and the Stamp Act Crisis; The First Phase of the American Revolution, 1763–1767* (Oxford: Clarendon, 1975), and John Bullion, *A Great and Necessary Measure: George Grenville and the Genesis of the Stamp Act, 1763–1765* (Columbia: University of Missouri Press, 1982). Also see Thomas, "The Grenville Program, 1763–1765"; and Edmund S. Morgan and Helen M. Morgan, *The Stamp Act Crisis:*

Prologue to Revolution (Chapel Hill: University of South Carolina Press, 1953, repr. 1995), Chapter 5; and Philip Lawson, *George Grenville: A Political Life* (Oxford, 1984).

5 Douglass Adair and John A. Schutz, eds., *Peter Oliver's Origin & Progress of the American Rebellion: A Tory View* (Stanford: Stanford University Press, 1961), 53–4.

6 For American resistance to the Stamp Act, see Morgan and Morgan, *The Stamp Act Crisis*, Chapters 8–11, and Pauline Maier, *From Resistance to Revolution: Colonial Radicals and the Development of American Opposition to Britain, 1765–1776* (New York: Vintage, 1972), Chapters 3–4. For the ideological implications of the non-importation movement, see T.H. Breen, "Narrative of Commercial Life: Consumption, Ideology, and Community on the Eve of the American Revolution," *WMQ*, 50 (1993), 471–501.

7 For the repeal of the Stamp Act, see Thomas, *British Politics and the Stamp Act Crisis*, Chapters 11–12, and John L. Bullion, "British Ministers and American Resistance to the Stamp Act, October–December 1765," *WMQ*, 49 (1992), 89–107.

8 The figures in this paragraph are from Thomas, "The Stamp Act Crisis and its Repercussions," 122. Most of the revenue generated by the Stamp Act was collected in the West Indies. For the Stamp Act in areas outside of the thirteen colonies, see Andrew J. O'Shaughnessy, "The Stamp Act Crisis in the British Caribbean," *WMQ*, 51 (1994), 203–26; W.B. Kerr, "The Stamp Act Crisis in Quebec," *English Historical Review*, 47 (1932), 648–51; and W.B. Kerr, "The Stamp Act Crisis in Nova Scotia," *New England Quarterly*, 6 (1933), 552–66.

9 *Peter Oliver's Origin & Progress of the American Rebellion*, 55–6.

10 For the adoption of Townshend's program, see Thomas, *British Politics and the Stamp Act Crisis*, Chapters 15–16; Peter D.G. Thomas, *The Townshend Duties Crisis: The Second Phase of the American Revolution* (Oxford: Clarendon, 1987), Chapter 2; and Robert J. Chaffin, "The Townshend Acts of 1767," *WMQ*, 27 (1970), 90–121.

11 John Dickinson, *Letters from a Farmer in Pennsylvania* (Philadelphia, 1768); see also Milton E. Flower, *John Dickinson: Conservative Revolutionary* (Charlottesville: University Press of Virginia, 1983).

12 "The Virginia Association," in Julian Boyd *et al.* eds., *The Papers of Thomas Jefferson*, 24 vols. to date (Princeton: Princeton University Press, 1950–), 1: 29, italics added.

13 See Peter H. Wood, " 'Liberty is Sweet': African American Freedom Struggles in the Years before White Independence," in Alfred F. Young, ed., *Beyond the American Revolution: Exploration in the History of American Radicalism* (DeKalb: Northern Illinois University Press, 1993), 149–84, especially 157–9.

14 Mary Beth Norton, *Liberty's Daughters: The Revolutionary Experience of American Women, 1750–1800* (Boston: Little Brown, 1980), 156–70. Quotation, *Boston Evening Post*, February 12, 1770.

15 The definitive work on these events remains Hiller B. Zobel's *The Boston Massacre* (New York: Vintage, 1971).

16 For the committees of correspondence, see Richard D. Brown, *Revolutionary Politics in Massachusetts: The Boston Committee of Correspondence and the Towns, 1772–1774* (Cambridge, Mass.: Harvard University Press, 1970). Also see Maier, *From Resistance to Revolution*, Chapter 7.

17 For the Tea Act, see P.D.G. Thomas, *Tea Party to Independence: The Third Phase of the American Revolution, 1773–1776* (Oxford: Clarendon, 1991), and Philip Lawson, *The East India Company: A History* (London: Longman, 1993). For the Boston Tea Party the standard work remains Benjamin Woods Labaree, *The Boston Tea Party* (New York: Oxford University Press, 1964).

18 As quoted in Henry Steele Commager and Richard B. Morris, eds., *The Spirit of Seventy-Six: The Story of the American Revolution as Told by Participants* (New York: Harper and Row, 1958, repr. New York: Da Capo, 1995), 12.

19 *The Papers of Thomas Jefferson*, 1: 108. For colonial support for Boston, see "Correspondence between a committee of the town of Boston and contributors of donations for the relief of the sufferers of the Boston Port Bill," Massachusetts Historical Society *Collections*, 4th series, 4: 4–6, 38–40, 50–2, 75–6, 81–3, 144–5, 251.

20 Gaillard Hunt and Worthington C. Ford, eds., *Journals of the Continental Congress, 1774–1789*, 34 vols. (Washington: Government Printing Office, 1904–1937), 1: 67.

3 REVOLUTION, 1775–1776

1 Bonamy Dobrée, ed., *The Letters of King George III* (London: Cassell, 1935, repr. New York: Funk and Wagnalls, 1968), 105–6.

2 For the activities of Gage's spies, see *General Gage's Instructions of 22d February 1775 ... with a Curious Narrative of Occurrences during their Mission, wrote by the Ensign ... also an Account of the Transactions of the British Troops from the Time they Marched out of Boston* (Boston, 1779).

3 *Letters of King George III*, 106.

4 Sylvanus Wood account in Henry Steele Commager and Richard B. Morris, eds., *The Spirit of Seventy-Six: The Story of the American Revolution as Told by Participants* (New York: Harper and Row, 1958, repr. New York: Da Capo, 1995), 82–3; Barker quotation in R.H. Dana, ed., "Diary of a British Officer," *Atlantic Monthly*, 39 (1877), 399.

5 G.D. Scull, ed., *Memoir and Letters of Captain W. Glanville Evelyn of the 4th Regiment (King's Own) from North America, 1774–1776* (Oxford, 1879), 53. For another British account see Charles K. Bolton, ed., *Letters of Hugh, Earl Percy from Boston and New York, 1774–1776* (Boston: Charles Goodspeed, 1902), 49–55. The most recent and thorough account of Lexington and Concord is David Hackett Fischer, *Paul Revere's Ride* (New York: Oxford University Press, 1994).

6 For rebel views of the battle see Amos Farnsworth, "Diary," Massachusetts Historical Society *Proceedings*, 2nd Series, 12 (1899), 74–107, especially 83–4. For British accounts, see *Report on the Manuscripts of the Late Reginald Rawdon Hastings*, 4 vols. (London: Great Britain Historical Manuscripts Commission, 1930–47), 3: 154–5; and *Letters of Hugh, Earl Percy*, 56–8.

7 Clarence Edwin Carter, *The Correspondence of General Thomas Gage with the Secretaries of State, and with the War Office and the Treasury, 1763–1775*, 2 vols. (New Haven: Yale University Press, 1933, repr. 1969), 2: 686.

8 Gaillard Hunt and Worthington C. Ford, eds., *Journals of the Continental Congress*, 34 vols. (Washington: Government Printing Office, 1904–1937), 2: 67, 75, 109–10. On the Canadian situation, see Reginald C. Stuart, *United States Expansionism and British North America, 1775–1871* (Chapel Hill: University of North Carolina Press, 1988), Chapter 1; Gustave Lanctot, *Canada and the American Revolution*, Margaret Cameron, trans. (Cambridge, Mass.: Harvard University Press, 1967), Chapters 5–10; Robert McConnell Hatch, *Thrust for Canada: The American Attempt on Quebec in 1775–1776* (Boston: Houghton Mifflin, 1979); George M. Wrong, *Canada and the American Revolution: The Disruption of the First British Empire* (New York: Macmillan, 1935, repr. 1968); Charles P. Hanson, *Necessary Virtue: The Pragmatic Origins of Religious Liberty in New England* (Charlottesville: University Press of Virginia, 1998), Chapters 2–3;

Francis D. Cogliano, *No King, No Popery: Anti-Catholicism in Revolutionary New England* (Westport, Conn.: Greenwood, 1995), Chapters 3–4.

9 *Journals of the Continental Congress*, 2: 153, 155–6; for the Olive Branch Petition, see *Journals of the Continental Congress* 2: 156–62.

10 R.C. Simmons and Peter D.G. Thomas, eds., *Proceedings and Debates in Parliament Respecting North America, 1754–1783*, 6 vols. to date (Millwood, New York: Krauss International, 1982–) 6: 69–70.

11 For Paine, see Eric Foner, *Tom Paine and Revolutionary America* (New York: Oxford University Press, 1976); David Freeman Hawke, *Paine* (New York: Harper and Row, 1974, repr. 1989); John Keane, *Tom Paine: A Political Life* (London: Bloomsbury, 1995). For Benjamin Rush's role in encouraging Paine to write *Common Sense*, see George W. Corner ed., *The Autobiography of Benjamin Rush* (Princeton: Princeton University Press, 1948), 113–14.

12 Quotations from Thomas Paine, *Common Sense*, Isaac Kramnick, ed. (Harmondsworth: Penguin Books, 1976), 65, 72, 76, 78, 81, 83, 87. For the influence of *Common Sense* see Foner, *Tom Paine and Revolutionary America*, Chapter 3. Pauline Maier has recently suggested that Paine may not have been as influential as most historians contend because support for independence was widespread by 1776. See Pauline Maier, *American Scripture: Making the Declaration of Independence* (New York: Knopf, 1997), 91.

13 Although most of these "declarations" have been in print since the nineteenth century, they have only recently been subjected to systematic analysis. See Maier, *American Scripture*, Chapter 2.

14 Peter Force, ed., *American Archives*, 4th Series, 6 vols. (Washington: St. Clair and Force, 1837–46), 6: 420. For the timing and content of the various local actions concerning independence, see Maier, *American Scripture*, appendices A and B.

15 Julian Boyd *et al.* eds., *The Papers of Thomas Jefferson*, 24 vols. to date (Princeton: Princeton University Press, 1950–), 1: 290–1.

16 For the debate over independence, see *Papers of Thomas Jefferson*, 1: 309–13, quotation, 309.

17 L.H. Butterfield, ed., *Diary and Autobiography of John Adams*, 4 vols. (Cambridge, Mass.: Harvard University Press, 1962), 3: 398. For a fascinating account of the role played by Adams in drafting the Declaration of Independence, see Robert E. McGlone, "Deciphering Memory: John Adams and the Authorship of the Declaration of Independence," *JAH*, 85 (1998), 411–38.

18 Robert J. Taylor *et al.* eds., *The Papers of John Adams*, 10 volumes to date (Cambridge, Mass.: Harvard University Press, 1977–), 4: 245.

4 WINNING INDEPENDENCE: THE WARS OF THE AMERICAN REVOLUTION

1 My thinking on this approach has been influenced by Professor E. Wayne Carp's essay, "The Wars of the American Revolution," which was published at the web site "The American Revolution: National Discussions of our Revolutionary Origins," located at http://revolution.h-net.msu.edu.

2 Margaret Wheeler Willard, ed., *Letters on the American Revolution, 1774–1776* (Boston: Houghton Mifflin, 1925), 119–20.

3 As quoted in Stephen Conway, *The War of American Independence, 1775–1783* (London: Edward Arnold, 1995), 55.

4 As quoted in Allen French, *The First Year of the American Revolution* (Boston: Houghton Mifflin, 1934), 300–1.

5 Rodney Atwood, *The Hessians: Mercenaries from Hesse-Kassel in the American Revolution* (Cambridge: Cambridge University Press, 1980). A number of useful

diaries by German soldiers have been translated and published. For examples see, Carl Leopold Baurmeister, *Revolution in America: Confidential Letters and Journals. 1776–1784, of Adjutant General Major Baurmeister of the Hessian Forces*, Bernhard A. Uhlendorf, trans. and ed. (New Brunswick: Rutgers University Press, 1957); Johann Ewald, *Diary of the American War*, Joseph P. Tustin, trans. and ed. (New Haven: Yale University Press, 1979); Johann Conrad Döhla, *A Hessian Diary of the American Revolution*, Bruce E. Burgoyne, trans. and ed. (Norman: University of Oklahoma Press, 1990); Robert A. Selig, "A German Soldier in America: The Journal of Georg Daniel Flohr," *WMQ*, 50 (1993), 575–90.

6 Quoted in Conway, *War of American Independence*, 84.

7 John C. Fitzpatrick, ed., *Writings of George Washington*, 39 vols. (Washington: Government Printing Office, 1931–44), 6: 398.

8 Quotations from Henry Steele Commager and Richard B. Morris, eds., *The Spirit of Seventy-Six: The Story of the American Revolution as Told by Participants* (New York: Harper and Row, 1958, repr. New York: Da Capo, 1995), 527, 424. On the behavior of British troops during the war, see Stephen Conway, " 'The Great Mischief Complain'd Of': Reflections on the Misconduct of British Soldiers in the Revolutionary War," *WMQ*, 47 (1990), 370–90.

9 For the Burgoyne campaign, see Richard Ketchum, *Saratoga: Turning Point of America's Revolutionary War* (New York: Henry Holt, 1997); and James Kirby Martin, *Benedict Arnold: Revolutionary Hero* (New York: New York University Press, 1997), Chapters 15–16.

10 The best concise account of the global aspects of the American War of Independence is found in Conway, *American War of Independence*, Chapter 6. Figures are from 157–8.

11 As quoted in Ronald Hoffman, "The 'Disaffected' in the Revolutionary South," in Alfred F. Young, ed., *The American Revolution: Explorations in the History of American Radicalism* (DeKalb: Northern Illinois University Press, 1976), 273–316, 295.

12 As quoted in *The Spirit of Seventy-Six*, 1112.

13 As quoted in Hoffman, "The 'Disaffected' in the Revolutionary South," 309.

14 The definitive study of the peace negotiations remains Richard B. Morris, *The Peacemakers: The Great Powers and American Independence* (New York: Harper and Row, 1965, repr. Boston: Northeastern University Press, 1983).

15 See Mark V. Kwasny, *Washington's Partisan War, 1775–1783* (Kent, Ohio: Kent State University Press, 1996). Also see Joseph S. Tiedman, "Patriots by Default: Queen's Country, New York and the British Army, 1776–1783," *WMQ*, 43 (1986). 35–63.

16 For loyalists serving in the British army, see Paul H. Smith, "The American Loyalists: Notes on Their Organization and Numerical Strength," *WMQ*, 25 (1968), 267–9. The material on Samuel Curwen is from Frank Cogliano, "Was Samuel Curwen a Loyalist?" unpublished paper presented at the Peabody Essex Museum, Salem, Massachusetts, July 22, 1993. For James Moody, see James Moody, *Lieut. James Moody's Narrative of his Exertions and Sufferings in the Cause of Government since the Year 1776* (London, 1783, repr. New York: New York Times, 1968).

17 For example, see Richard D. Brown, "The Confiscation and Disposition of Loyalists' Estates in Suffolk County, Massachusetts," *WMQ*, 21 (1964), 534–50; and Robert S. Lambert, "The Confiscation of Loyalist Property in Georgia, 1782–1786," *WMQ*, 20 (1963), 80–94.

18 Francis D. Cogliano, " 'To Obey Jesus Christ and General Washington': Massachusetts, Catholicism and the Eastern Indians during the American Revolution," *Maine Historical Society Quarterly*, 32 (1992), 108–33.

19 See John Mack Faragher, *Daniel Boone: The Life and Legend of an American Pioneer* (New York: Henry Holt, 1992); Eric Hinderaker, *Elusive Empires: Constructing Colonialism in the Ohio River Valley, 1673–1800* (New York: Cambridge University Press, 1997); Elizabeth A. Perkins, *Border Life: Experience and Memory in the Revolutionary Ohio Valley* (Chapel Hill: University of North Carolina Press, 1998).

20 As quoted in Faragher, *Daniel Boone*, 168.

21 Quotation from *The Spirit of Seventy-Six*, 1057. Casualty figures from Faragher, *Daniel Boone*, 144.

22 The best account of these events is Wiley Sword, *President Washington's Indian War: The Struggle for the Old Northwest, 1790–1795* (Norman: University of Oklahoma Press, 1993).

23 Conway, *War of American Independence*, 247. See Chapter 2 for a full discussion of the war as the first "modern" conflict. Also see John Shy, "The American Revolution: The Military Conflict Considered as a Revolutionary War," in Stephen G. Kurtz and James H. Hutson, eds., *Essays on the American Revolution* (Chapel Hill: University of North Carolina Press, 1973), 121–56.

24 Edward Countryman, "Indians, the Colonial Order, and the Social Significance of the American Revolution," *WMQ*, 53 (1996), 342–62.

25 See Conway, *War of American Independence*, Chapter 7, especially 172–5. Also see Royster, *Revolutionary People at War*; Neimeyer, *America Goes to War*; Holly A. Mayer, *Belonging to the Army: Camp Followers and Community during the American Revolution* (Columbia: University of South Carolina Press, 1996); Steven Rosswurm, "The Philadelphia Militia, 1775–1783: Active Duty and Active Radicalism," in Ronald Hoffman and Peter J. Albert, eds., *Arms and Independence: The Military Character of the American Revolution* (Charlottesville: University Press of Virginia, 1984), 75–118; Steven Rosswurm *Arms, Country and Class: The Philadelphia Militia and "Lower Sort" during the American Revolution, 1775–1783* (New Brunswick: Rutgers University Press, 1987); and James Kirby Martin, "A 'Most Undisciplined and Profligate Crew': Protest and Defiance in the Continental Ranks, 1776–1783," in Hoffman and Albert, eds., *Arms and Independence*, 119–40.

5 THE CONFEDERATION ERA

1 Philip M. Hamer *et al.* eds., *The Papers of Henry Laurens*, 14 vols. to date (Columbia: University of South Carolina Press, 1968–), 10: 18; Carl Lotus Becker, *The History of Political Parties in the Province of New York, 1760–1776* (Madison: University of Wisconsin Press, 1909), 22.

2 Quotation from Isaac Kramnick, ed., *The Federalist Papers* (London: Penguin Books, 1987), 255.

3 For the democratization of American politics during the Revolution and its limits, see Jackson Turner Main, "Government by the People: The American Revolution and the Democratization of the Legislatures," *WMQ*, 23 (1966), 391–406; Jerome J. Nadelhaft, " 'The Snarls of Invidious Animals': The Democratization of Revolutionary South Carolina," in Ronald Hoffman and Peter J. Albert, eds., *Sovereign States in an Age of Uncertainty* (Charlottesville: University Press of Virginia, 1981), 62–94. Also see Gary J. Kornblith and John M. Murrin, "The Making and Unmaking of an American Ruling Class," in Alfred F. Young, ed., *Beyond the American Revolution: Explorations in the History of*

American Radicalism (DeKalb: Northern Illinois University Press, 1993), 28–79; Michael A. McDonnell, "Popular Mobilization and Political Culture in Revolutionary Virginia: The Failure of the Minutemen and the Revolution from Below," *JAH*, 85 (1998), 946–81; and Edward Countryman, *A People in Revolution: The American Revolution and Political Society in New York, 1760–1790* (Baltimore: Johns Hopkins University Press, 1981), Chapter 8.

4 My thinking with respect to this division has been influenced by the work of Merrill Jensen. In *The Articles of Confederation: An Interpretation of the Socio-Constitutional History of the American Revolution, 1774–1781* (Madison: University of Wisconsin Press, 1940), Jensen classified the political supporters of the Revolution as radicals and conservatives. In *The New Nation: A History of the United States during the Confederation, 1781–1789* (New York: Knopf, 1950), he divided them into "true federalists" and "nationalists". Other historians have used a variety of categories to classify the political behavior of Americans before the ratification of the Constitution. For example, Jackson Turner Main in *Political Parties before the Constitution* (Chapel Hill: University of North Carolina Press, 1973) categorizes American politicians as "localists" and "cosmopolitans"; see Chapters 12 and 13 for a thorough discussion of these categories and their attributes. Van Beck Hall has placed Massachusetts voters on a commercial–cosmopolitan continuum; See Van Beck Hall, *Politics without Parties: Massachusetts, 1780–1791* (London: University of Pittsburgh Press, 1972), especially Chapter 1. My use of democrats and elitists as labels does not preclude the analysis of Jensen, Main and others. Rather, it reflects the political and ideological interests of the competing groups. In all the states there was competition between those who sought to create a more democratic political system and those who sought to limit (but not eliminate) popular participation in government. Democrats and elitists should be seen as a shorthand for these two groups. In general, the former favored broader political participation and the latter sought to concentrate political authority among the social and political elite. Although this division anticipated the split between Antifederalists and Federalists over the Constitution, nonetheless it is crucial to emphasize that these were *not* yet political parties. Nor, despite my own generalizations, were all democrats local-oriented men of humble origins nor all elitists wealthy, conservative, avatars of the *status quo*. These are broad groupings, not prescriptive categories.

5 My typology here closely follows Jackson Turner Main's distinction between localists and cosmopolitans. See *Political Parties before the Constitution*, Chapter 13.

6 For the situation in Pennsylvania, see Richard Alan Ryerson, *The Revolution is Now Begun: The Radical Committees of Philadelphia, 1765–1776* (Philadelphia: University of Pennsylvania Press, 1978); Steven Rosswurm, *Arms, Country, and Class: The Philadelphia Militia and the "Lower Sort" during the American Revolution* (New Brunswick: Rutgers University Press, 1987); Ronald Schultz, *The Republic of Labor: Philadelphia Artisans and the Politics of Class, 1720–1830* (New York: Oxford University Press, 1993); Main, *Political Parties before the Constitution*, Chapter 7; Eric Foner, *Tom Paine and Revolutionary America* (New York: Oxford University Press, 1976), Chapter 4. For the Pennsylvania Constitution, see J. Paul Selsam, *The Pennsylvania Constitution of 1776: A Study in Revolutionary Democracy* (Philadelphia: University of Pennsylvania Press, 1936); Willi Paul Adams, *First American Constitutions: Republican Ideology and the Making of the State Constitutions in the Revolutionary Era* (Chapel Hill: University of North Carolina Press, 1980), and Richard Alan Ryerson, "Republican Theory and Partisan Reality in Revolutionary Pennsylvania: Toward a New View of the Constitu-

tionalist Party," in Hoffman and Albert, eds., *Sovereign States in an Age of Uncertainty*, 95–133.

7 "Boston Town Meeting, June 1, 1778," Boston Record Commissioners, *Report of the Record Commissioners*, 38 vols. (Boston, 1876–1908), 26: 22–4.

8 For the Massachusetts constitution see Ronald M. Peters, *The Massachusetts Constitution of 1780: A Social Compact* (Amherst: University of Massachusetts Press, 1978); Samuel Eliot Morison, *A History of the Constitution of Massachusetts* (Boston, 1917); Robert J. Taylor, "Construction of the Massachusetts Constitution," American Antiquarian Society, *Proceedings*, 2nd Series, 90 (1980), 317–46. The returns from the individual town meetings held to consider the document have been published in Oscar Handlin and Mary Handlin, eds., *The Popular Sources of Political Authority: Documents on the Massachusetts Constitution of 1780* (Cambridge Mass.: Harvard University Press, 1966). Also see Owen Dudley Edwards, "John Adams and Constitutions," in Thomas J. Barron, Owen Dudley Edwards, and Patricia J. Storey, *Constitutions and National Identity* (Edinburgh: Quadriga, 1993), 62–100.

9 The definitive work on the Articles of Confederation remains Jensen, *The Articles of Confederation*. See Chapters 5–8 for the drafting of the Articles; Chapter 9 for ratification, and Chapters 10–11 concerning the issue of western lands. The appendix reprints both the Dickinson draft and the final version of the Articles of Confederation.

10 Article XVIII of the Dickinson draft, Jensen, *Articles of Confederation*, 260.

11 Gaillard Hunt and Worthington C. Ford, eds., *Journals of the Continental Congress, 1774–1789*, 34 vols. (Washington: Government Printing Office, 1904–37), 9: 908.

12 For financial and currency issues see Jensen, *The New Nation*, Chapters 15, 16, and 19; William G. Anderson, *The Price of Liberty: The Public Debt of the Revolution* (Charlottesville: University Press of Virginia, 1983); and E. James Ferguson, *The Power of the Purse: A History of American Public Finance, 1776–1790* (Chapel Hill: University of North Carolina Press, 1961). For the political implications of these questions, see Cathy D. Matson and Peter S. Onuf, *A Union of Interests: Political and Economic Thought in Revolutionary America* (Lawrence: University Press of Kansas, 1990).

13 The figures in this paragraph are from Ferguson, *Power of the Purse*, 32–63.

14 Taxation figures are from Robert A. Becker, "Currency, Taxation and Finance, 1775–1787," in Jack P. Greene and J. R. Pole, eds., *The Blackwell Encyclopedia of the American Revolution* (Oxford: Blackwell, 1991), 367. For a useful study of the complexity of wartime finance at the state level, see Edward C. Papenfuse, "The Legislative Response to a Costly War: Fiscal Policy and Factional Politics in Maryland, 1777–1789," in Hoffman and Albert eds., *Sovereign States in an Age of Uncertainty*, 134–156. On the broader implications of taxation during the period, see Roger H. Brown, *Redeeming the Republic: Federalists, Taxation, and the Origins of the Constitution* (Baltimore: Johns Hopkins University Press, 1993).

15 Ferguson, *Power of the Purse*, 67.

16 Jensen, *The New Nation*, 304.

17 Jensen, *The New Nation*, 307–8, and Jonathan Smith, "The Depression of 1785 and Daniel Shays' Rebellion," *WMQ*, 5 (1948), 77–94.

18 Smith, "The Depression of 1785 and Daniel Shays' Rebellion."

19 There is an extensive literature on Shays's Rebellion. The best place to start in approaching the rebellion is Robert A. Gross's excellent review of that literature, "White Hats and Hemlocks: Daniel Shays and the Legacy of the Revolution," in Ronald Hoffman and Peter J. Albert, eds., *The Transforming Hand of*

Revolution: Reconsidering the American Revolution as a Social Movement (Charlottesville: University Press of Virginia, 1995), 286–345.

6 CREATING THE CONSTITUTION

1 John C. Fitzpatrick, ed., *Writings of George Washington*, 39 vols. (Washington: Government Printing Office, 1931–44), 29: 34.

2 Because they favored the creation of a strong national government, these men are often termed nationalists. See Merrill Jensen, *The New Nation: A History of the United States during the Confederation, 1781–1789* (New York: Knopf, 1950), conclusion. While they were, indeed, nationalists, I prefer the term "elitist" to describe them because it indicates the type of republican government they sought to create at *both* the state and national levels. Although the major struggle between elitists and democrats was at the national level, this was, in part, because of the widespread perception among elitists that the democrats had won the battle at the state level.

3 For a useful history of the Continental Congress see Jack N. Rakove, *The Beginnings of National Politics: An Interpretive History of the Continental Congress* (New York: Knopf, 1979).

4 Boston Record Commissioners, *Report of the Record Commissioners*, 38 vols. (Boston, 1876–1908), 26: 22.

5 Jefferson quotation from Lester J. Cappon, ed., *The Adams–Jefferson Letters: The Complete Correspondence between Thomas Jefferson and Abigail and John Adams* (Chapel Hill: University of North Carolina Press, 1959), 196.

6 Knox quoted in Jensen, *The New Nation*, 426; Gerry and Randolph quotations from James Madison, *Notes of Debates in the Federal Convention of 1787* (New York: Norton, 1987), 39 and 42. Madison's *Notes* remains an indispensable primary source on the Constitutional Convention. Also see Max Farrand, ed., *The Records of the Federal Convention of 1787*, 4 vols. (New Haven: Yale University Press, 1911–37).

7 *Writings of George Washington*, 28: 503.

8 Rush quotation from Dagobert Runes, ed. *The Selected Writings of Benjamin Rush* (New York: Philosophical Library, 1947) 26. Adams quotation in "Letters of John Adams to Mercy Warren, 1807," Massachusetts Historical Society, *Collections*, 5th Series, 4: 394. There is a vast literature on republicanism; see Chapter 1. For democracy, see Gordon S. Wood, *The Creation of the American Republic, 1776–1787* (Chapel Hill: University of North Carolina Press, 1969), especially 222–6; and Bernard Bailyn, *The Ideological Origins of the American Revolution* (Cambridge, Mass.: Harvard University Press, 1967, repr. 1992), 272–301.

9 Wilson and Gerry quotes in Madison, *Notes*, 40, 39.

10 *The Records of the Federal Convention*, 3: 87. For Madison's contribution to the convention, see Jack N. Rakove, *Original Meanings: Politics and Ideas in the Making of the Constitution* (New York: Knopf, 1996), Chapter 3; Irving Brant, *James Madison*, 6 vols. (Indianapolis: Bobbs-Merrill, 1941–61), vols. 2–3; Lance Banning, *Sacred Fire of Liberty: James Madison and the Founding of the Federal Republic* (Ithaca: Cornell University Press, 1995); Thornton Anderson, *Creating the Constitution: The Convention of 1787 and the First Congress* (University Park: Pennsylvania State University Press, 1993); and William Lee Miller, *The Business of May Next: James Madison and the Founding* (Charlottesville: University Press of Virginia, 1992).

11 At the time of the convention Madison was 36; Gouverneur Morris, 35; James Wilson, 35; Rufus King, 32; George Mason, 32; Edmund Randolph 34; Charles C. Pinckney, 30; Elbridge Gerry, 43. For the backgrounds of the delegates, see

Rossiter, *1787: The Grand Convention*, Chapters 5–8. Also see Forrest McDonald, *We the People: The Economic Origins of the Constitution* (Chicago: University of Chicago Press, 1958).

12 Gregory Evans Dowd, review of Eric Hinderaker, *Elusive Empires: Constructing Colonialism in the Ohio River Valley, 1673–1800*, in *WMQ* 56 (1999), 208. For a study of Indians in settled areas after the Revolution, see Donna Keith Barron, J. Edward Hood, and Holly V. Izard, "They Were Here All Along: Native American Presence in Lower-Central New England in the Eighteenth and Nineteenth Centuries," *WMQ*, 53 (1996), 561–86. Donald A. Grinde, Jr. and Bruce E. Johansen have argued that Native Americans had a profound impact on the deliberations of the Constitutional Convention. They argue that Iroquois practices had a direct influence on the deliberations of the Convention and the ideas about sovereignty and representative government which emerged from it. They assert, "there is an abundance of inferential and direct evidence to support the thesis that American government was influenced by Native American political concepts." Douglas A. Grinde, Jr., and Bruce E. Johansen, *Exemplar of Liberty: Native America and the Evolution of American Democracy* (Los Angeles: American Indian Studies Center, 1991), xxiv. If so, then the exclusion of Indians from the constitutional settlement after independence is all the more remarkable. This thesis has been extremely controversial. See Philip A. Levy *et al.*, "The 'Iroquois Influence' Thesis – Con and Pro," *WMQ*, 53 (1996), 587–636. While there is some circumstantial evidence to support the arguments of Grinde and Johansen their analysis, while intriguing, is not especially convincing.

13 For Randolph's speech and an outline of the Virginia Plan, see Madison, *Notes*, 28–33.

14 Howard Ohline, "Republicanism and Slavery: Origins of the Three-fifths Clause in the United States Constitution," *WMQ*, 28 (1971), 563–84.

15 For the New Jersey Plan, see Madison, *Notes*, 117–54.

16 Madison, *Notes*, 232.

17 Madison, *Notes*, 502–10, Martin quotation 502, Mason quotation 503. Also see Paul Finkelman, "Slavery and the Constitutional Convention: Making a Covenant with Death," in Richard Beeman, Stephen Botein, and Edward C. Carter, eds., *Beyond Confederation: Origins of the Constitution and American National Identity* (Chapel Hill: University of North Carolina Press, 1987), 188–225; John Kaminski, ed., *A Necessary Evil? Slavery and the Debate over the Constitution* (Madison: Madison House, 1995); Mark E. Brandon, *Free in the World: American Slavery and Constitutional Failure* (Princeton: Princeton University Press, 1998).

18 Bernard Bailyn, ed., *The Debate on the Constitution: Federalist and Antifederalist Speeches, Articles, and Letters during the Struggle over Ratification*, 2 vols. (New York: Library of America, 1993), 1: 967. The most complete record of the ratification process is Merrill Jensen, John P. Kaminski, and Gaspare J. Saladino, eds., *The Documentary History of the Ratification of the Constitution*, 18 vols. to date (Madison: State Historical Society of Wisconsin, 1976–). Also see John P. Kaminski and Richard J. Leffler, eds., *Federalists and Antifederalists: The Debate over the Ratification of the Constitution*, 2nd edn (Madison: Madison House, 1998).

19 Publius [James Madison], *The Federalist*, Number 39, *Independent Journal*, January 16, 1788, in *Debate on the Constitution*, 2: 26–32. Also see Rakove, *Original Meanings*, Chapter 5.

20 Jackson Turner Main, *The Antifederalists: Critics of the Constitution, 1781–1787* (Chapel Hill: University of North Carolina Press, 1961; repr. New York: Norton, 1974), xi.

21 *Debate on the Constitution*, 1: 9–11.

22 Main, *The Antifederalists*, Chapter 11, is especially valuable on the contrasting profiles of Federalists and Antifederalists. Quotation is from 274.

23 [Samuel Bryan] *Centinel*, Number 1, *Independent Gazetteer*, October 5, 1787, published in Bailyn, *Debate on the Constitution*, 1: 52–62, quotations 57, 61. For Antifederalist criticisms of the Constitution, see Main, *The Antifederalists*, Chapters 6–7; Cecelia M. Kenyon, "Men of Little Faith: The Anti-Federalists on the Nature of Representative Government," *WMQ*, 12 (1955), 3–43; Christopher M. Duncan, *The Anti-Federalists and Early American Political Thought* (DeKalb: Northern Illinois University Press, 1995); Saul Cornell, "Aristocracy Assailed: The Ideology of Backcountry Anti-Federalism," *JAH*, 76 (1990), 1148–72; and Saul Cornell, *The Other Founders: Anti-Federalism and the Dissenting Tradition in America* (Chapel Hill: University of North Carolina Press, 1999).

24 *Debate on the Constitution*, 1: 906.

25 *Pennsylvania Gazette*, October 17, 1787. See Main, *The Antifederalists*, Chapter 11 for the relative advantages of the Federalists.

26 North Carolina rejected the Constitution 184 to 84 on August 1, 1788, and a second convention ratified by 194 to 77 on November 21, 1789. Cantankerous Rhode Island – which had failed to send any delegates to the Constitutional Convention – finally capitulated and narrowly ratified by 34 to 32 on May 29, 1790.

27 See Ronald Hoffman and Peter J. Albert, eds., *The Bill of Rights: Government Proscribed* (Charlottesville: University Press of Virginia, 1998); Irving Brant, *The Bill of Rights: Its Origin and Meaning* (Indianapolis: Bobbs-Merrill, 1965); Leonard W. Levy, *Constitutional Opinions: Aspects of the Bill of Rights* (New York: Oxford University Press, 1986); Robert A. Rutland, *The Birth of the Bill of Rights, 1776–1791* (Chapel Hill: University of North Carolina Press, 1955), and Stuart Leiberger, "Parchment Barriers: James Madison and the Amendments to the Constitution, 1787–1789," *Journal of Southern History*, 59 (1993), 441–68.

7 THE FEDERALIST ERA

1 For popular celebrations of the Constitution, see Len Travers, *Celebrating the Fourth: Independence Day and the Rites of Nationalism in the Early Republic* (Amherst: University of Massachusetts Press, 1997); Simon P. Newman, *Parades and the Politics of the Street: Festive Culture in the Early American Republic* (Philadelphia: University of Pennsylvania Press, 1997); David Waldstreicher, *In the Midst of Perpetual Fetes: The Making of American Nationalism, 1776–1820* (Chapel Hill: University of North Carolina Press, 1997); and Garry Wills, "Enacting the Constitution: Philadelphia's Grand Procession," in Thomas J. Barron, Owen Dudley Edwards, and Patricia J. Storey, eds., *Constitutions and National Identity* (Edinburgh: Quadriga, 1993), 34–44.

2 Lance Banning, "Republican Ideology and the Triumph of the Constitution, 1789 to 1793," *WMQ*, 31 (1974), 167–88, quotation 167. Observing that revolutionary France experimented with six constitutions in fifteen years, Banning notes, "The quick apotheosis of the American Constitution was a phenomenon without parallel in the western world. Nowhere has a fundamental constitutional change been accepted with such ease" (168). This view has recently been endorsed by Gordon S. Wood, who notes that the immediate aftermath of ratification was a period of popular consensus not seen since the heady days of 1776 when Independence was declared. Gordon S. Wood, "Launching the 'Extended Republic': The Federalist Era," in Ronald Hoffman and Peter J. Albert, eds., *Launching the Extended Republic: The Federalist Era* (Charlottesville: University Press of Virginia, 1996), 1–24.

3 The debate over titles is discussed in Stanley Elkins and Eric McKitrick, *The Age of Federalism: The Early American Republic, 1788–1800* (New York: Oxford, 1993), 46–50. Also see James H. Hutson, "John Adams' Title Campaign," *New England Quarterly*, 41 (1968), 30–9.

4 For the dispute between Washington and Hancock, see John C. Miller, *The Federalist Era, 1789–1801* (New York: Harper, 1960), 12. For Washington's importance in conferring legitimacy on the new government, see Elkins and McKitrick, *The Age of Federalism*, 34–46. For the symbolic and cultural significance of Washington as President, see Newman, *Parades and the Politics of the Street*, Chapter 2, and Waldstreicher, *In the Midst of Perpetual Fetes*, Chapter 3.

5 For the *Report on Public Credit*, see Harold C. Syrett *et al.* eds., *The Papers of Alexander Hamilton*, 27 vols. (New York: Columbia University Press, 1961–87), 6: 51–168.

6 For Madison's opposition to Hamilton's program, see Elkins and McKitrick, *The Age of Federalism*, Chapter 3. For the compromise over the assumption of state debts and the location of the capital, see Jacob E. Cooke, "The Compromise of 1790," *WMQ*, 27 (1970), 523–45; Kenneth R. Bowling, "Dinner at Jefferson's: A Note on Jacob E. Cooke's 'The Compromise of 1790," *WMQ*, 28 (1971), 629–48; and Norman K. Risjord, "The Compromise of 1790: New Evidence on the Dinner Table Bargain," *WMQ*, 33 (1976), 309–14. Also see Whitney K. Bates, "Northern Speculators and Southern State Debts, 1790," *WMQ*, 19 (1962), 30–48.

7 *Report on the National Bank*, in *The Papers of Alexander Hamilton*, 7: 236–342. Carl Lane argues that Hamilton's bank proposal made sound economic sense for the government. See Carl Lane, " 'For a Positive Profit': The Federal Investment in the First Bank of the United States, 1792–1802," *WMQ*, 54 (1997), 601–12.

8 For the debate over the bank see, Elkins and McKitrick, *The Age of Federalism*, 223–44; and Benjamin B. Klubes, "The First Federal Congress and the First National Bank: A Case Study in Constitutional Interpretation," *Journal of the Early Republic*, 10 (1990), 19–41.

9 *Report on Manufactures*, in *The Papers of Alexander Hamilton*, 10: 1–340.

10 Quotation from Miller, *The Federalist Era*, 88.

11 Thomas Jefferson, *Notes on the State of Virginia* (London, 1785 and multiple modern editions). Quotation from Merrill D. Peterson, ed., *Thomas Jefferson: Writings* (New York: Library of America, 1984), 290–1. The best discussion of these ideas is Drew R. McCoy, *The Elusive Republic: Political Economy in Jeffersonian America* (Chapel Hill: University of North Carolina Press, 1980). Also see Joyce Appleby, *Capitalism and the New Social Order: The Republican Vision of the 1790s* (New York: New York University Press, 1984).

12 Quotation from Miller, *The Federalist Era*, 77.

13 Washington quotation from John C. Fitzpatrick, ed., *The Writings of George Washington*, 39 vols. (Washington: Government Printing Office, 1931–44), 31: 48; *Providence Gazette* quotation in Gordon S. Wood, *The Creation of the American Republic, 1776–1787* (Chapel Hill: University of North Carolina Press, 1969), 403. Also see Jackson Turner Main, *Political Parties before the Constitution* (Chapel Hill: University of North Carolina Press, 1973).

14 For the emergence of partisan divisions, in Congress see David P. Currie, *The Constitution in Congress: The Federalist Period, 1789–1801* (Chicago: University of Chicago Press, 1997). The Federalists' opponents are sometimes called Democratic Republicans and sometimes Republicans. In the interests of simplicity I shall call them Republicans.

15 Fisher Ames, *Works of Fisher Ames: As published by Seth Ames*, 2 vols. (Boston, 1854), 1: 240. For Freneau, see Mary W. Bowden, *Philip Freneau* (Boston:

Twayne, 1976); Philip M. Marsh, *Philip Freneau: Poet and Journalist* (Minneapolis: Dillon Press, 1968); and Lewis Leary, *That Rascal Freneau: A Study in Literary Failure* (New Brunswick: Rutgers University Press, 1941).

16 Quotation from James Melvin Lee, *History of American Journalism* (Boston: Houghton Mifflin, 1917), 101. For the 1792 newspaper war, see Elkins and McKitrick, *The Age of Federalism*, 282–93.

17 Quotation from Miller, *The Federalist Era*, 109.

18 Quotation from, *Works of Fisher Ames*, 2: 362. For another Federalist view of the Whiskey Rebellion, see *Papers of Alexander Hamilton*, 17: 24–58.

19 Quotations *Papers of Thomas Jefferson*, 24 vols. to date (Princeton: Princeton University Press) 11: 93; *Thomas Jefferson: Writings* 1036–7. Also see Lance Banning, *The Jeffersonian Persuasion: Evolution of a Party Ideology* (Ithaca: Cornell University Press, 1978); Noble E. Cunningham, Jr., *The Jeffersonian Republicans: The Formation of Party Organization, 1789–1801* (Chapel Hill: University of North Carolina Press, 1957); Paul Goodman, *The Democratic Republicans in Massachusetts: Politics in a Young Republic* (Cambridge, Mass.: Harvard University Press, 1964); Alfred F. Young, *The Democratic Republicans of New York: The Origins, 1763–1797* (Chapel Hill: University of North Carolina Press, 1967).

20 For Genêt's reception see Newman, *Parades and the Politics of the Street*, 139–40, and Waldstreicher, *In the Midst of Perpetual Fetes*, 133–6. For the Neutrality Proclamation of 1793, see *The Writings of George Washington*, 32: 430–1; Alexander DeConde, *Entangling Alliance: Diplomacy and Politics under George Washington* (Durham: Duke University Press, 1958) and Charles M. Thomas, *American Neutrality in 1793: A Study in Cabinet Government* (New York: AMS Press, 1967).

21 In the meantime Genêt's Girondists had been replaced by the Jacobins, who accused their man in Philadelphia with crimes against the republic. Facing the guillotine, Genêt was given sanctuary in the United States. He settled in New York and married the daughter of Governor George Clinton. He did not die until 1836.

22 *Works of Fisher Ames*, 2: 112. Also see Elkins and McKitrick, *The Age of Federalism*, Chapter 8.

23 *Thomas Jefferson: Writings*, 1004. This passage was written, it should be noted, *before* the worst excesses of the Terror. For a critical view of Jefferson's attitudes toward the French Revolution, see Conor Cruise O'Brien, *The Long Affair: Thomas Jefferson and the French Revolution, 1785–1800* (London: Sinclair-Stevenson, 1996).

24 On popular attitudes toward the French Revolution, see Newman, *Parades and the Politics of the Street*, Chapter 4. On Washington's attitudes toward the Democratic-Republican societies, see *Writings of George Washington*, 33: 133, 321–2, 464, 476, 506, and 523.

25 Quotation in Henry Johnston, ed., *The Correspondence and Public Papers of John Jay*, 4 vols. (New York: Putnam, 1890–3), 4: 30.

26 Quotations from *New Hampshire Gazette*, July 21, 1795; *American Mercury*, August 31, 1795.

27 Victor Hugo Paltsits, *Washington's Farewell Address: In Facsimile, with Transliterations of all the Drafts of Washington, Madison, & Hamilton, Together with their Correspondence and Other Supporting Documents* (New York: New York Public Library, 1935); Matthew Spalding and Patrick J. Garrity, *A Sacred Union of Citizens: George Washington's Farewell Address and the American Character* (New York: Rowman and Littlefield, 1995).

28 Alexander DeConde, *The Quasi-War: The Politics and Diplomacy of the Undeclared War with France 1797–1801* (New York: Scribners, 1966); William Stinch-

combe, *The XYZ Affair* (Westport: Greenwood, 1980). For Adams's actions during the crisis, see Stephen G. Kurtz, *The Presidency of John Adams and the Collapse of Federalism* (Philadelphia: University of Pennsylvania Press, 1957); John E. Ferling, *John Adams: A Life* (Knoxville: University of Tennessee Press, 1992), Chapter 17. Also see William G. Anderson, "John Adams, the Navy, and the Quasi-War with France," *American Neptune*, 30 (1970), 117–32.

29 James Morton Smith, *Freedom's Fetters: The Alien and Sedition Laws and American Civil Liberties* (Ithaca: Cornell University Press, 1956); John C. Miller, *Crisis in Freedom: The Alien and Sedition Acts* (Boston: Little Brown, 1951). The charge that immigrants tended to oppose the government was not without foundation. See Michael Durey, *Trans-Atlantic Radicals and the Early American Republic* (Lawrence: University Press of Kansas, 1997); Michael Durey, "Thomas Paine's Apostles: Radical Emigrés and the Triumph of Jeffersonian Republicanism," *WMQ*, 44 (1987), 661–88; Edward C. Carter II, "A 'Wild Irishman' Under Every Federalist's Bed: Naturalization in Philadelphia, 1789–1806," *Pennsylvania Magazine of History and Biography*, 94 (1970), 331–46. For post-revolutionary immigration, see Aaron S. Fogleman, "From Slaves, Convicts, and Servants to Free Passengers: The Transformation of Immigration in the Era of the American Revolution," *JAH*, 85 (1998), 43–76.

30 Adrienne Koch and Harry Ammon, "The Virginia and Kentucky Resolutions: An Episode in Jefferson's and Madison's Defense of Civil Liberties," *WMQ*, 5 (1948). 145–76; Elkins and McKitrick, *The Age of Federalism*, 719–26.

8 AN EMPIRE OF LIBERTY: 1801–1815

1 Journal quotation from Bernard DeVoto, ed., *The Journals of Lewis and Clark* (Boston: Houghton Mifflin, 1953, repr. 1997), 287. Tree carving quoted in Stephen E. Ambrose, *Undaunted Courage: Meriwether Lewis, Thomas Jefferson, and the Opening of the American West* (New York: Simon and Schuster, 1996), 309.

2 See Richard L. Bushman, "Markets and Composite Farms in Early America," *WMQ*, 55 (1998), 351–74.

3 The most complete treatment of the Louisiana Purchase is Alexander DeConde, *This Affair of Louisiana* (New York: Scribner, 1976). For a concise summary of events, see Bernard DeVoto's introduction to *The Journals of Lewis and Clark*. Also see Dumas Malone, *Jefferson the President: The First Term, 1801–1805* (Boston: Little Brown, 1970), Chapters 14–19.

4 See Francis Paul Prucha, *American Indian Policy in the Formative Years: The Indian Trade and Intercourse Acts* (Cambridge: Harvard University Press, 1962); Francis Paul Prucha, "Andrew Jackson's Indian Policy: A Reassessment," *JAH*, 56 (1969), 527–39; Daniel H. Usner, Jr., "American Indians on the Cotton Frontier," *JAH*, 73 (1985), 297–313; Mary Young, "Indian Removal and Allotment: The Civilized Tribes and Jacksonian Justice," *AHR*, 64 (1958), 31–45; Ralph K. Andrist, *The Long Death: The Last Days of the Plains Indians* (New York: Macmillan, 1964); Jeffrey Ostler, "Conquest and the State: Why the United States Employed Massive Military Force to Suppress the Lakota Ghost Dance," *Pacific Historical Review*, 65 (1996), 217–49.

5 The best statement concerning the aims and objectives of the expedition is Jefferson's instructions to Lewis dated June 20, 1803, which are published in DeVoto, *The Journals of Lewis and Clark*, 481–7.

6 Quotation from DeVoto, *The Journals of Lewis and Clark*, 206. A complete modern edition of the journals fills eight volumes; Gary E. Moulton, ed., *The Journals of the Lewis and Clark Expedition*, 8 vols. (Lincoln: University of Nebraska Press, 1986–93). At present Moulton is preparing five additional vol-

umes of supplementary materials for publication by the University of Nebraska Press.

7 The dollar value of the re-export trade during the first decade of the nineteenth century would not be equaled again until 1916, when the American carriers again profited from their relations with a Europe at war. For trade figures, see the U.S. Bureau of the Census, *Historical Statistics of the United States, Colonial Times to 1957* (Washington: Bureau of the Census, 1960), 538, 549. Also see John H. Coatsworth, "American Trade with European Colonies in the Caribbean and South America, 1790–1812," *WMQ*, 24 (1967), 243–66; Alice B. Keith, "Relaxation in the British Restrictions on the American Trade with the British West Indies, 1783–1802," *Journal of Modern History*, 20 (1948), 1–18; Bradford Perkins, *The First Rapprochement: England and the United States, 1795–1805* (Berkeley: University of California Press, 1955, repr. 1967).

8 For a lively retelling of these events see Robert J. Allison, "Sailing to Algiers: American Sailors Encounter the Muslim World," *American Neptune*, 57 (1997), 5–17. Also see Robert J. Allison, *The Crescent Observed: The United States and the Muslim World, 1776–1815* (New York: Oxford University Press, 1995); Jamil Abun-Nasr, *A History of the Maghrib of the Corsairs* (Norman: University of Oklahoma Press, 1976); and William Spencer, *Algiers in the Age of the Corsairs* (Norman: University of Oklahoma Press, 1975).

9 Howard I. Chappelle, *The History of the American Sailing Navy* (New York: Norton, 1949), 179–241.

10 *Historical Statistics of the United States, Colonial Times to 1957*, 551.

11 *Historical Statistics of the United States, Colonial Times to 1957*, 551. Also see Marshall Smelser, *The Democratic Republic, 1801–1815* (New York: Harper Row, 1968), 162.

12 James Fulton Zimmerman, *Impressment of American Seamen* (New York: Columbia University Press, 1925); Clement Cleveland Sawtell, "Impressment of American Seamen by the British," *Essex Institute Historical Collections*, 76 (1940), 314–44. On the question of national identity among seamen during the period, see Francis D. Cogliano "We all Hoisted the American Flag: National Identity Among American Prisoners in Britain During the American Revolution," *Journal of American Studies*, 32 (1998), 19–37. Also see Donald R. Hickey, *The War of 1812: A Forgotten Conflict* (Urbana: University of Illinois Press, 1989), 11.

13 The best account of these events is Spencer C. Tucker and Frank T. Reuter, *Injured Honor: The Chesapeake-Leopard Affair, June 22, 1807* (Annapolis: Naval Institute Press, 1996).

14 Smelser, *Democratic Republic*, 147.

15 *Historical Statistics of the United States, Colonial Times to 1957*, 551.

16 *Historical Statistics of the United States, Colonial Times to 1957*, 116, 124, 119, 121, 120, 122.

17 See Linda K. Kerber, *Federalists in Dissent: Imagery and Ideology in Jeffersonian America* (Ithaca, N.Y.: Cornell University Press, 1970); David Hackett Fischer, *The Revolution in American Conservatism: The Federalist Party in the Era of Jeffersonian Democracy* (New York: Harper & Row, 1965).

18 Hickey, *The War of 1812*, 19.

19 As quoted in Hickey, *The War of 1812*, 26. Also see Gregory Evans Dowd, *A Spirited Resistance: The North American Indian Struggle for Unity: 1745–1815* (Baltimore: Johns Hopkins University Press, 1992), Chapters 7–9; R. David Edmunds, *The Shawnee Prophet* (Lincoln: University of Nebraska Press, 1983); R. David Edmunds, *Tecumseh and the Quest for Indian Leadership* (Boston: Little

Brown, 1984); Reginald Horsman, "American Indian Policy in the Old North-west, 1783–1812," *WMQ*, 18 (1961), 35–53.

20 Harry W. Fritz, "The War Hawks of 1812," *Capitol Studies*, 5 (1977), 25–42; Ronald L. Hatzenbuehler, "The War Hawks and the Question of Congressional Behavior," *Pacific Historical Review*, 65 (1976), 1–22; Reginald Horsman, "Who were the War Hawks?" *Indiana Magazine of History*, 60 (1964), 121–36; Norman K. Risjord, "1812: Conservatives, Warhawks, and the Nation's Honor," *WMQ*, 18 (1961), 196–210.

21 See Hickey, *The War of 1812*, Chapter 2. Also see J.C.A. Stagg, "Enlisted Men in the United States Army, 1812–1815: A Preliminary Survey," *WMQ*, 43 (1986), 615–45.

22 For the emotional and intellectual impact of the war on the Americans, see Steven Watts, *The Republic Reborn: War and the Making of Liberal America, 1790–1820* (Baltimore: Johns Hopkins University Press, 1987).

9 AFRICAN AMERICANS IN THE AGE OF REVOLUTION

1 Douglas Egerton, *Gabriel's Rebellion: The Virginia Slave Conspiracies of 1800 and 1802* (Chapel Hill: University of North Carolina Press, 1993), quotation from p. 51. Also see James Sidbury, *Ploughshares into Swords: Race, Rebellion, and Identity in Gabriel's Virginia, 1730–1810* (Cambridge: Cambridge University Press, 1997), Chapters 2–4.

2 Donald J. Greene, *Samuel Johnson: Political Writings* (New Haven: Yale University Press, 1977), 454; *Pennsylvania Packet*, January 8, 1774.

3 *Pennsylvania Chronicle* quotation in Arthur Zilversmit, *The First Emancipation: The Abolition of Slavery in the North* (Chicago: University of Chicago Press, 1967), 94; James Otis, *The Rights of the Colonies Asserted and Proved* (Boston, 1765), 37; L.H. Butterfield *et al.* eds., *Adams Family Correspondence*, 6 vols. to date (Cambridge, Mass.: Harvard University Press, 1963–), 1: 162. Also see Benjamin Rush, *An Address to the Inhabitants of the British Settlements in America, Upon the Slave Keeping* (Philadelphia, 1773). For early criticism of slavery see [Anthony Benezet], *Observations on the Inslaving, Importing and Purchasing of Negroes* (Germantown, Penn., 1759); [Anthony Benezet], *A Short Account of that Part of Africa, Inhabited by the Negroes* (Philadelphia, 1762); Anthony Benezet, *Some Historical Account of Guinea* (Philadelphia, 1771). On the role of Quakers in the early movement against slavery, see Jean R. Soderlund, *Quakers and Slavery: A Divided Spirit* (Princeton: Princeton University Press, 1985).

4 The petition is reproduced in Sidney Kaplan and Emma Nogrady Kaplan, *The Black Presence in the Era of the American Revolution*, revised edn. (Amherst: University of Massachusetts Press, 1989), 14. The quotation by New Hampshire slaves is in Winthrop D. Jordan, *White over Black: American Attitudes Toward the Negro, 1550–1812* (Chapel Hill: University of North Carolina Press, 1968), 291. For an analysis of the petitions see Thomas J. Davis, "Emancipation Rhetoric, Natural Rights and Revolutionary New England," *New England Quarterly*, 57 (1989), 246–64. Also see Zilversmit, *The First Emancipation*, Chapter 4; Charles W. Akers, "'Our Modern Egyptians': Phillis Wheatley and the Whig Campaign against Slavery in Revolutionary Boston," *Journal of Negro History*, 60 (1975), 397–410; and Ruth Bogin, "'Liberty Further Extended': A 1776 Antislavery Manuscript by Lemuel Haynes," *WMQ*, 40 (1983), 85–105.

5 For the pre-Revolutionary legal challenges to slavery, see L. Kinvin Wroth and Hiller B. Zobel, eds., *Legal Papers of John Adams*, 3 vols. (Cambridge, Mass.: Harvard University Press, 1965), 2: 48–67; L.H. Butterfield *et al.* eds., *Diary*

and Autobiography of John Adams, 4 vols. (Cambridge, Mass.: Harvard University Press, 1961), 1: 321, 3: 289. For the contribution of African Americans to the prewar resistance movement, see Gary Nash, *Forging Freedom: The Formation of Philadelphia's Black Community, 1720–1840* (Cambridge, Mass.: Harvard University Press, 1988), 45–65. For the approach to Gage, see *Adams Family Correspondence*, 1: 162.

6 See Benjamin Quarles, "The Revolutionary War as a Black Declaration of Independence," in Ira Berlin and Ronald Hoffman, eds., *Slavery and Freedom in the Age of the American Revolution* (Charlottesville: University Press of Virginia, 1983), 283–301; Kaplan and Kaplan, *The Black Presence in the Era of the American Revolution*, Chapter 3. For slaves who enlisted in the Continental Army, see Charles P. Neimeyer, *America Goes to War: A Social History of the Continental Army* (New York: New York University Press, 1996) and Sylvia R. Frey, *Water From the Rock: Black Resistance in a Revolutionary Age* (Princeton: Princeton University Press, 1991), 77–9. For slaves who ran away, see Billy G. Smith, "Runaway Slaves in the Mid-Atlantic Region during the Revolutionary Era," in Ronald Hoffman and Peter J. Albert, eds., *The Transforming Hand of Revolution: Reconsidering the American Revolution as a Social Movement* (Charlottesville: University Press of Virginia, 1995), 199–230. For an excellent local case study on the impact of the war on northern slavery, see Graham Russell Hodges, *Slavery and Freedom in the Rural North: African Americans in Monmouth County, New Jersey, 1665–1865* (Madison: Madison House, 1997), Chapter 3.

7 Hodges, *Slavery and Freedom in the Rural North*, Chapter 4 (figure for Monmouth County, 120).

8 For an eloquent presentation of this view see Nash, *Race and Revolution*, Chapter 2. Also see John P. Kaminski, ed., *A Necessary Evil? Slavery and the Debate over the Constitution* (Madison: Madison House, 1995).

9 William T. Hutchinson and William M.E. Rachal, eds., *The Papers of James Madison*, 17 vols. to date (Chicago: University of Chicago Press, 1962–), 1: 129. For prewar slave resistance see Frey, *Water From the Rock*, Chapter 2, especially 53–4; Peter H. Wood, " 'Liberty is Sweet': African American Freedom Struggles in the Years before White Independence," in Alfred F. Young, ed., *Beyond the American Revolution: Explorations in the History of American Radicalism* (DeKalb: Northern Illinois University Press, 1993), 149–84; Sidney Kaplan, "The Domestic Insurrections of the Declaration of Independence," *Journal of Negro History*, 61 (1976).

10 Quotation from Frey, *Water From the Rock*, 61. For an excellent discussion of the role played by slavery in diminishing the differences between and among southern whites, see Edmund S. Morgan, *American Slavery, American Freedom: The Ordeal of Colonial Virginia* (New York: Norton, 1975).

11 Quotation from Frey, *Water From the Rock*, 133.

12 Richard S. Dunn, "Black Society in the Chesapeake, 1776–1810," in Berlin and Hoffman, *Slavery and Freedom*, 49–82.

13 Estimate of South Carolina slaves who fled in Julian P. Boyd *et al.* eds., *The Papers of Thomas Jefferson*, 24 vols. to date (Princeton, 1950–), 8: 199. Sylvia Frey estimates the total loss of slaves in South Carolina during the Revolution at approximately 25,000; Frey, *Water From the Rock*, 174.

14 Quotation from Frey, *Water From the Rock*, 113–14.

15 Johann von Ewald, *Diary of the American War: A Hessian Journal*, Joseph P. Tustin, trans. and ed. (New Haven: Yale University Press, 1979), 305–6.

16 Ewald, *Diary of the American War*, 335. The estimate of the number of slaves removed by the British is from Frey, *Water From the Rock*, 182. For an excellent summary of the experience of the black loyalists, see Frey, *Water from the Rock*,

Chapter 6. Also see James W. St. George Walker, *The Black Loyalists: The Search for the Promised Land in Sierra Leone and Nova Scotia, 1783–1870* (London, 1976, repr. Toronto: University of Toronto Press, 1992); Ella Gibson Wilson, *The Loyal Blacks* (New York: Capricorn, 1976); Phyllis R. Blakeley, "Boston King: A Negro Loyalist who Sought Refuge in Nova Scotia," *Dalhousie Review*, 48 (1968), 347–56; Mary Beth Norton, "The Fate of Some Black Loyalists of the American Revolution," *Journal of Negro History*, 58 (1973), 402–26; John N. Grant, "Black Immigrants into Nova Scotia, 1776–1815," *Journal of Negro History*, 58 (1973), 253–70; Gary B. Nash, "Thomas Peters: Millwright and Deliverer," http://revolution.h-net.msu.edu/

17 The most complete treatment of Jefferson's views with respect to slavery is John C. Miller, *The Wolf by the Ears: Thomas Jefferson and Slavery* (New York: Free Press, 1977, repr. Charlottesville: University of North Carolina Press, 1992). Also see Annette Gordon-Reed, *Thomas Jefferson and Sally Hemings: An American Controversy* (Charlottesville: University Press of Virginia, 1997). Gary Nash has argued that the Founding Fathers could have taken steps to eliminate slavery during the revolutionary era; see Nash, *Race and Revolution*, Chapter 2. Also see Gregory D. Massey, "The Limits of Antislavery Thought in the Revolutionary Lower South: John Laurens and Henry Laurens," *Journal of Southern History*, 63 (1997), 531–52. Richard S. Dunn, on the other hand, believes that the commitment to slavery during the period was so strong that "even if Washington, Jefferson, Madison and Monroe had devoted all their leadership skills to the single cause of black freedom, they still would have failed utterly, for their society was moving inexorably in the opposite direction"; Dunn, "Black Society in the Chesapeake, 1776–1810," 81. Perhaps, but what is significant is that the revolutionary leadership failed devote significant energy to the cause of emancipation. Assuming Dunn is correct, then the "Founding Fathers" were followers on the issue of slavery, not leaders.

18 Randolph quotation in Willie Lee Rose, ed., *A Documentary History of Slavery in North America* (New York: Oxford University Press, 1976), 65. Figures on free blacks are from Duncan J. MacLeod, "Toward Caste," in Berlin and Hoffman, *Slavery and Freedom*, 217–36; Dunn, "Black Society in the Chesapeake, 1776–1810," 62, 50.

19 Frey, *Water from the Rock*, 218.

20 The figure on South Carolina manumissions is from Morgan, "Black Society in the Lowcountry," 116. The information on imports to South Carolina is from Frey, *Water from the Rock*, 213. Also see Patrick S. Brady, "The Slave Trade and Sectionalism in South Carolina, 1787–1808," *Journal of Southern History*, 38 (1972), 601–20.

21 Frey, *Water from the Rock*, 223. See Chapter 7 for a detailed discussion of postwar slave resistance. Also see Jeffrey J. Crow, "Slave Rebelliousness and Social Conflict in North Carolina, 1775–1802," *WMQ*, 37 (1980), 79–102; Douglas Egerton " 'Fly Across the River': The Easter Slave Conspiracy of 1802," *North Carolina Historical Review*, 68 (1991), 87–110; Herbert Aptheker, *American Negro Slave Revolts* (New York: Columbia University Press, 1943, repr. New York: International Publishers, 1987), Chapter 9.

22 For links between the American Revolution and events in Haiti, see Frey, *Water from the Rock*, 191–2. Also see Alfred N. Hunt, *Haiti's Influence on Ante-bellum America: Slumbering Volcano in the Caribbean* (Baton Rouge: Louisiana State University Press, 1988). For the American reaction to the Haitian Revolution, see Donald R. Hickey, "America's Response to the Slave Revolt in Haiti, 1791–1806," *Journal of the Early Republic*, 2 (1982), 361–79; Tim Matthewson, "Jefferson and Haiti," *Journal of Southern History*, 61 (1995), 209–48; James

Sidbury, "Saint Domingue in Virginia: Ideology, Local Meanings, and Resistance to Slavery," *Journal of Southern History*, 63 (1997), 531–52; and Egerton, *Gabriel's Rebellion*, 45–48, 168–172.

23 Monroe quotation from Egerton, *Gabriel's Rebellion*, 47. Revolutionary black resistance was not confined to Saint-Domingue and the United States. During the 1790s slave revolts also occurred in Puerto Rico, Venezuela, Curaçao, and Grenada. Conspiracies were uncovered in Cuba as well as Louisiana, and Jamaica was the site of widespread maroonage. See Egerton, *Gabriel's Rebellion*, 45–9; and Frey, *Water from the Rock*, 228–32.

24 Egerton, *Gabriel's Rebellion*, 102.

10 AMERICAN WOMEN IN THE AGE OF REVOLUTION

1 Joan Hoff Wilson, "The Illusion of Change: Women in the American Revolution," in Alfred F. Young, ed., *The American Revolution: Explorations in the History of American Radicalism* (DeKalb: Northern Illinois University Press, 1976), 383–445, quotation from 387. Linda K. Kerber, " 'History Can Do It No Justice': Women and the Reinterpretation of the American Revolution," in Ronald Hoffman and Peter J. Albert, eds., *Women in the Age of the American Revolution* (Charlottesville: University Press of Virginia, 1989), 3–42. This essay was reprinted in Linda K. Kerber, *Toward an Intellectual History of Women* (Chapel Hill: University of North Carolina Press, 1997), 63–99, quotation from 98.

2 At least in the north, some African Americans could petition the courts and legislatures for their freedom. Similarly, black males could win their freedom by taking up arms. This is not to say that the plight of free white women was worse than that of African American slaves, only that the Revolution may have presented slaves with greater means to secure their freedom than it did to women. Such a comparison ignores the plight of African American women, who faced a double burden as both slaves and females. See Jacqueline Jones, "Race, Sex, and Self-Evident Truths: The Status of Slave Women during the Era of the American Revolution," in Hoffman and Albert, eds., *Women in the Age of the American Revolution*, 293–337.

3 Alfred F. Young, "The Women of Boston: 'Persons of Consequence' in the Making of the American Revolution," in Harriet B. Applewhite and Darline G. Levy, eds., *Women and Politics in the Age of Democratic Revolution* (Ann Arbor: University of Michigan Press, 1990), 181–226, especially 194–204.

4 See Mary Beth Norton, *Liberty's Daughters: The Revolutionary Experience of American Women, 1750–1800* (Boston: Little Brown, 1980), Chapter 6. Quotation, 160. Also see "The Female Patriots, Address'd to the Daughters of Liberty in America, 1768," *WMQ*, 34 (1977), 307; *Boston News-Letter*, November 5, 1767; *Boston Evening Post*, February 5, 12, 1770; *Boston Gazette*, February 12, 1770. Oliver quotation from Douglas Adair and John A. Schutz, eds., *Peter Oliver's Origin and Progress of the American Rebellion: A Tory View* (Stanford: Stanford University Press, 1961), 61.

5 *Boston Post-Boy*, November 16, 1767, as quoted in Young, "The Women of Boston," 197. *Peter Oliver's Origin and Progress of the American Rebellion*, 64. For domestic manufacturing as a form of political protest, see Norton, *Liberty's Daughters*, 164–70. For a recent study of home manufacturing by women during the period, see Laurel Thatcher Ulrich, "Wheels, Looms and the Gender Division of Labor in Eighteenth-Century New England," *WMQ* , 55 (1998), 3–38.

6 Kerber, " 'History Can do it No Justice'," 76. The phrase "midwives of the revolution" was suggested to me by my colleague Dr. Jane McDermid of the University of Southampton, New College.

7 Quotation in Norton, *Liberty's Daughters*, 197. For the wartime experiences of American women, see Joy Day Buel and Richard Buel, Jr., *The Way of Duty: A Woman and Her Family in Revolutionary America* (New York: Norton, 1984), Chapters 5–6; Norton, *Liberty's Daughters*, Chapter 7; Linda K. Kerber, *Women of the Republic: Intellect and Ideology in Revolutionary America* (Chapel Hill: University of North Carolina Press, 1980), Chapter 2.

8 L.H. Butterfield *et al.* eds., *Adams Family Correspondence*, 6 vols. to date (Cambridge, Mass.: Harvard University Press, 1963–), 1: 289, 297.

9 Norton, *Liberty's Daughters*, 202–4, quotation 202.

10 For estimates of the numbers of camp followers, see Walter H. Blumenthal, *Women Camp Followers of the American Revolution* (Philadelphia: G.S. MacManus, 1952), 38–9; and Linda Grant De Pauw, "Women in Combat: The Revolutionary War Experience," *Armed Forces and Society*, 7 (1981), 210 as quoted in Kerber, " 'History Can Do It No Justice'," 70–1. Also see Holly A. Mayer, *Belonging to the Army: Camp Followers and Community during the American Revolution* (Columbia: University of South Carolina Press, 1996).

11 The information in this paragraph is based on my forthcoming *William Russell and the Experience of Maritime Prisoners during the American Revolution* (Naval Institute Press: Annapolis), Chapter 1.

12 *Adams Family Correspondence*, 1: 370.

13 *Adams Family Correspondence*, 1: 382.

14 Robert J. Taylor *et al.* eds., *The Papers of John Adams*, 10 vols. to date (Cambridge, Mass., 1977–), 4: 213, as quoted in Kerber, "Paradox of Women's Citizenship in the Early Republic," 368.

15 Elias Boudinot, *An Oration Delivered at Elizabeth-Town, New-Jersey ... on the Fourth of July MDCCXCIII* (Elizabethtown, N.J., 1793), 24, as quoted in Rosemarie Zagarri, "The Rights of Man and Woman in Post-Revolutionary America," *WMQ*, 55 (1998), 203–30, quotation 210.

16 For women's voting in New Jersey, see Norton, *Liberty's Daughters*, 191–93; Gundersen, "Independence and Citizenship," 65–6; Judith Apter Klinghoffer and Lois Elkis, "The Petticoat Electors: Women's Suffrage in New Jersey, 1776–1807," *Journal of the Early Republic*, 12 (1992), 159–93; Richard P. McCormick, *The History of Voting in New Jersey: A Study of the Development of Election Machinery, 1664–1911* (New Brunswick: Rutgers University Press, 1953), 97–111.

17 *Centinel of Freedom* quoted in Zagarri, "Rights of Man and Woman in Post-Revolutionary America," 220; Legislature quoted in Norton, *Liberty's Daughters*, 193.

18 The seminal work on the subject is Linda K. Kerber, "The Republican Mother: Women and the Enlightenment – An American Perspective," *American Quarterly*, 28 (1976), 187–205, quotation 202, repr. in Kerber, *Toward an Intellectual History of Women*, 41–62. Also see Norma Basch, "From the Bonds of Empire to the Bonds of Matrimony," in David Thomas Konig, ed., *Devising Liberty: Preserving and Creating Freedom in the New American Republic* (Stanford: Stanford University Press, 1995), 217–42; Ruth Bloch, "The Gendered Meanings of Virtue in Revolutionary America," *Signs: Journal of Women in Culture and Society*, 13 (1987), 37–58; Kerber, *Women of the Republic*, Chapter 9; Jan Lewis, "The Republican Wife: Virtue and Seduction in the Early Republic," *WMQ*, 47 (1987), 689–721; Rosemarie Zagarri, "Morals, Manners, and the Republican

Mother," *American Quarterly*, 44 (1992), 192–215; Zagarri, "Rights of Man and Woman in Post-Revolutionary America."

19 Joel Perlman and Dennis Shirley, "When Did New England Women Acquire Literacy?" *WMQ*, 48 (1991), 50–67.

20 For women's education during the period, see Kerber, *Women of the Republic*, Chapter 7; and Linda K. Kerber, "Daughters of Columbia: Educating Women for the Republic, 1787–1805," in Stanley Elkins and Eric McKitrick, eds.. *The Hofstadter Aegis: A Memorial* (New York: Knopf, 1974), 36–59, repr. in Kerber, *Toward and Intellectual History of Women*, 23–40. For women's reading, see Kerber, *Women of the Republic*, Chapter 8; Cathy N. Davidson, *Revolution and the Word: The Rise of the Novel in America* (New York: Oxford University Press, 1986); and Cathy N. Davidson, "The Novel as Subversive Activity: Women Reading, Women Writing," in Alfred F. Young, ed., *Beyond the American Revolution: Explorations in the History of American Radicalism* (DeKalb: Northern Illinois University Press, 1993), 283–316.

21 Kerber, " 'History Can Do it No Justice'," 95.

CONCLUSION: WE THE PEOPLE

1 The debate over the nature of the American Revolution was recently revived when Gordon S. Wood's *The Radicalism of the American Revolution* (New York: Knopf, 1992) was awarded the Pulitzer Prize in 1993. As implied in his title, Wood argued that the creation of republican governments in the United States was indeed a revolutionary step. For criticism of Wood's argument, see Gordon S. Wood *et al.*, "Forum: How Revolutionary was the American Revolution? A Discussion of Gordon Wood's *The Radicalism of the American Revolution*," *WMQ*, 51(1994), 677–716. Also see Alfred F. Young, "How Radical was the American Revolution?" in Alfred F. Young, ed., *Beyond the American Revolution: Explorations in the History of American Radicalism* (DeKalb: Northern Illinois University Press, 1993), 317–64.

2 Aaron S. Fogleman, "From Slaves, Convicts, and Servants to Free Passengers: The Transformation of Immigration in the Era of the American Revolution," *JAH* 85 (1998), 43–76. Also see Michael Durey, *Trans-Atlantic Radicals and the Early American Republic* (Lawrence: University Press of Kansas, 1997).

3 This interpretation is made most eloquently and persuasively by Gordon S. Wood in *The Radicalism of the American Revolution*.

4 Edward Countryman has argued that the displacement of Native Americans and the remaking of map of North America at the conclusion of the war was among the most revolutionary consequences of independence. See Edward Countryman *et al.*, "Rethinking the American Revolution," *WMQ*, 53 (1996), 341–86.

BIBLIOGRAPHIC ESSAY

Students of the American Revolution are blessed with an astounding amount of primary source material which is available in print. These sources are a crucial starting point for any serious study of the Revolution. The first substantial effort to compile a documentary history of the Revolution was Peter Force's *American Archives*. Force's wordy subtitle was an ambitious mission statement: "consisting of a collection of authentick records, state papers, debates, and letters and other notices of publick affairs, the whole forming a documentary history of the origin and progress of the North American colonies; of the causes and accomplishment of the American revolution; and of the Constitution of the government of the United States, to the final ratification thereof." Force intended to prepare six series of documents. He only completed one, *American Archives*, 4th Series, 6 vols. (Washington: St. Clair and Force, 1837–46) and a portion of the fifth series, 3 vols. (Washington: St. Clair and Force, 1848–53). The published volumes cover the years from 1774 to 1776. Although he never completed his project, and the volumes which appeared are poorly organized, they remain of value, particularly for the origins and early days of the Revolution. Force, lacking significant editorial and publishing assistance, produced nine massive volumes that demonstrated the scholarly value of such documentary collections. Modern editors of primary sources must look to Peter Force as their own founding father. Students of the Revolution can still profit by struggling with his dusty oversized volumes and their minute nineteenth-century type.

Fortunately, Peter Force's efforts presaged a plethora of twentieth-century documentary collections relating to the Revolution and the early republic. For the intellectual background and origins of colonial discontent, see Bernard Bailyn ed., *Pamphlets of the American Revolution, 1750–1776* (Cambridge, Mass.: Harvard University Press, 1965). Also of use for the origins of the Revolution as well as the conduct of the War of Independence are Gaillard Hunt and Worthington C. Ford, eds., *Journals of the Continental Congress, 1774–1789*, 34 vols., (Washington: Government Printing Office, 1904–37), and Paul H. Smith *et al.* eds., *Letters of the Delegates to Congress, 1774–1789*, 25 vols. (Washington: Library of Congress, 1976–98). Of value for the study of the postwar struggle over the Constitution are James Madison, *Notes of the Debates in the Federal Convention of 1787* (New York: Norton, 1987); Max Farrand, ed., *The Records of the Federal Convention of 1787*, 4 vols. (New Haven: Yale University Press, 1911–37); and Bernard Bailyn, *The Debate on the Constitution: Federalist and Antifederalist Speeches,*

Articles, and Letters during the Struggle over Ratification, 2 vols. (New York: Library of America, 1993). The definitive collection concerning ratification is Merrill Jensen, John P. Kaminski, and Gaspare J. Saladino, eds., *The Documentary History of the Ratification of the Constitution*, 18 vols. to date (Madison: State Historical Society of Wisconsin, 1976–).

The nineteenth century saw the early editing and publication of the papers of most of the more prominent statesmen among the revolutionary generation. The editors of these works, often descendants of the men in question, frequently adopted a filiopietistic editorial voice. Although of considerable value, most of the nineteenth-century documentary collections have been (or are being) replaced by modern editions which are more scholarly and accessible to readers and researchers. University presses, often with the support of the National Endowment for the Humanities, have undertaken a commitment to produce very long runs over decades to complete these series. The result is a body of sources which is of inestimable value to students of the American Revolution. Indeed, the publication of these papers is the most important scholarly advance in early American history during the twentieth century. Among these one of the first and most valuable series is Julian Boyd *et al.* eds., *The Papers of Thomas Jefferson*, 24 vols. to date (Princeton: Princeton University Press, 1950–). The papers of the Adams family represent one of the United States's national treasures. The Massachusetts Historical Society in conjunction with Harvard University Press, in a project which will take decades to complete and run to hundreds of volumes, has undertaken to publish the entire body of the papers. Among those which were useful for this study were: L.H. Butterfield, ed. *Diary and Autobiography of John Adams*, 4 vols. (Cambridge, Mass.: Harvard University Press, 1962); L.H. Butterfield *et al.* eds., *The Adams Family Correspondence*, 6 vols. to date (Cambridge, Mass.: Harvard University Press, 1963–); Robert J. Taylor *et al.*, eds., *The Papers of John Adams*, 10 vols. to date (Cambridge Mass.: Harvard University Press, 1977–); L. Kinvin Wroth and Hiller B. Zobel, eds., *The Legal Papers of John Adams*, 3 vols. (Cambridge, Mass.: Harvard University Press, 1965). Since Jefferson and Adams were so long-lived (they both died on July 4, 1826) and articulate, and were key players in many of the crucial events associated with the Revolution and the early republic, their papers constitute a vital source for all serious students of the period. The two-volume edition of their correspondence edited by Lester J. Cappon, *The Adams Jefferson Letters: The Complete Correspondence between Thomas Jefferson and Abigail and John Adams* (Chapel Hill: University of North Carolina Press, 1959), is an enlightening collection with respect to a key relationship between two of the central figures of the revolutionary period.

George Washington, of course, played a decisive role in the American Revolution and the early republic. Early in this century a fairly complete edition of his papers appeared. See John C. Fitzpatrick, ed., *Writings of George Washington*, 39 vols. (Washington: Government Printing Office, 1931–44). This edition, which lacks extensive editorial commentary, is being replaced and superseded by a more comprehensive *Papers of George Washington* published by the University Press of Virginia. This project, published under the auspices of the Mount Vernon Ladies Association and the University of Virginia, will eventually comprise approximately eighty-five volumes. It is divided into five components: The Colonial

Series (10 vols.); The Revolutionary War Series (7 vols. to date); The Confederation Series (6 vols.); The Presidential Series (8 vols. to date); and The Retirement Series (4 vols. to date). The Virginia edition, which comprises all the letters written *to* Washington as well as those written by him, will be far superior to the Fitzpatrick edition when it is complete. For the purposes of my references I have used the Fitzpatrick edition because it is, at the moment, more readily available than the Virginia edition. Appropriately for a documentary collection which will not be completed until well into the next century, the *Papers of George Washington* has an excellent website which can be found at *www.virginia.edu/gwpapers/*.

Other documentary sets consulted in the preparation of this book include Harold C. Syrett *et al.* eds., *The Papers of Alexander Hamilton*, 27 vols. (New York: Columbia University Press, 1961–87); Henry Johnston, ed., *The Correspondence and Public Papers of John Jay*, 4 vols. (New York: Putnam, 1890–3); Richard B. Morris, *John Jay*, 2 vols. (New York: Harper and Row, 1975–80); Leonard W. Labaree *et al.* eds., *The Papers of Benjamin Franklin*, 33 vols. to date (New Haven: Yale University Press, 1959–); E. James Ferguson *et al.* eds., *The Papers of Robert Morris, 1781–1784*, 9 vols. to date (Pittsburgh: University of Pittsburgh Press, 1973–); William T. Hutchinson and William M.E. Rachal, eds., *The Papers of James Madison*, 17 vols. to date (Chicago: University of Chicago Press, 1962–); Philip M. Hamer *et al.* eds., *The Papers of Henry Laurens*, 14 vols. to date (Columbia: University of South Carolina Press, 1968–); Richard K. Showman *et al.* eds., *The Papers of Nathanael Greene*, 10 vols. to date (Chapel Hill: University of North Carolina Press, 1976–); Dagobert Runes, ed., *The Selected Writings of Benjamin Rush* (New York: Philosophical Library, 1947); L.H. Butterfield, ed., *Letters of Benjamin Rush*, 2 vols. (Philadelphia: American Philosophical Society, 1951); and George W. Corner, ed., *The Autobiography of Benjamin Rush* (Princeton: Princeton University Press, 1948).

For the British perspective on events, the most important source is R.C. Simmons and Peter D. G. Thomas, eds., *Proceedings and Debates in Parliament Respecting North America, 1754–1783*, 6 vols. to date (Millwood, New York: Krauss International, 1982–) Also see Bonamy Dobrée, ed., *The Letters of George III* (London: Cassell, 1935, repr. New York: Funk and Wagnalls, 1968); Clarence Edwin Carter, *The Correspondence of General Thomas Gage with the Secretaries of State and with the War Office and the Treasury, 1763–1775*, 2 vols. (New Haven: Yale University Press, 1933).

These titles scratch the surface of a vast literature. In addition to such series, a large number of single-volume diaries and memoirs have been published as well. There are also several works which anthologize primary sources. Among the best of these is Henry Steele Commager and Richard B. Morris, eds., *The Spirit of Seventy-Six: The Story of the American Revolution as Told by Participants* (New York: Harper and Row, 1958; repr. New York: Da Capo, 1995). Unfortunately, no comparable reader exists for the period from 1789 to 1815.

Many of the proponents and opponents of the American Revolution were remarkably articulate and perceptive men and women. Thanks to the generosity of numerous funding bodies and university presses as well as the superb efforts of hundreds of scholars who have edited and preserved their works, their words are widely available to posterity. There is no better or more enjoyable way to study the Revolution than through the eyes and thoughts of those who experienced it.

The secondary literature on the Revolution and early republic is also vast. A classic work which sought to place events in a trans-Atlantic perspective is R.R. Palmer's *The Age of Democratic Revolution: A Political History of Europe and America, 1760–1800*, 2 vols. (Princeton: Princeton University Press, 1959–64). For a work which is similarly ambitious but which places events in a hemispheric rather than a trans-Atlantic context, see Lester D. Langley, *The Americas in the Age of Revolution, 1750–1850* (New Haven: Yale University Press, 1996). For works in the "British" tradition, see George Otto Trevelyan, *The American Revolution*, 14 vols. (London: Longman, 1880–14); Marcus Cunliffe, *The Nation Takes Shape, 1789–1837* (Chicago: University of Chicago Press, 1959); Esmond Wright, *Fabric of Freedom, 1763–1800* (New York: Hill and Wang, 1961, revised 1978); Edward Countryman, *The American Revolution* (New York: Hill and Wang, 1985); Michael J. Heale, *The American Revolution* (London: Methuen, 1986 (Lancaster Pamphlets)); and Colin Bonwick, *The American Revolution* (London: Macmillan, 1991).

Perhaps the most valuable single discussion of the colonial origins of the Revolution is Jack P. Greene, "An Uneasy Connection: An Analysis of the Preconditions of the American Revolution," in Stephen G. Kurtz and James H. Hutson, eds., *Essays on the American Revolution* (Chapel Hill: University of North Carolina Press, 1973), 32–80.

One of the remarkable features of the British North American colonies on the eve of independence was the steady growth and increasing diversity of their population. See Bernard Bailyn, *Voyagers to the West: A Passage in the Peopling of America on the Eve of the Revolution*, with the assistance of Barbara DeWolfe (New York: Knopf, 1987), 25–6. Aaron S. Fogleman, Migration to the Thirteen British North American Colonies, 1700–1775: New Estimates," *Journal of Interdisciplinary History*, 22 (1992), 691–709 and Aaron S. Fogleman, "From Slaves, Convicts, and Servants to Free Passengers: The Transformation of Immigration in the Era of the American Revolution," *JAH*, 85 (1998), 43–77, provide the most current and accurate estimates of the numbers of immigrants as well as their places of origin.

The largest single migrant group in eighteenth-century America were enslaved Africans. For an excellent discussion of the literature on the origins of slavery in North America, see Betty Wood, *The Origins of American Slavery: Freedom and Bondage in the English Colonies* (New York: Hill and Wang, 1997). Winthrop Jordan's *White Over Black: American Attitudes toward the Negro, 1550–1812* (Chapel Hill: University of North Carolina Press, 1968) is a classic study of the racial attitudes prevalent among European Americans. Also see David Eltis, "Europeans and the Rise and Fall of African Slavery in the Americas: An interpretation," *AHR*, 98 (1993), 1399–1423. For the trans-Atlantic slave trade, see Philip D. Curtin, *The Atlantic Slave Trade: A Census* (Madison: University of Wisconsin Press, 1969); Daniel P. Mannix and Malcolm Cowley, *Black Cargoes: A History of the Atlantic Slave trade, 1518–1865* (Madison: University of Wisconsin Press, 1963) and Paul E. Lovejoy, "The Volume of the Atlantic Slave Trade," *Journal of African History*, 23 (1982). For more recent interpretations see Joseph E. Inikori and Stanley L. Engerman, eds., *The Atlantic Slave Trade: Effects on Economies, Societies, and Peoples in Africa, the Americas, and Europe* (Durham: Duke University Press, 1992); Hugh Thomas, *The Slave Trade: The History of the*

Atlantic Slave trade, 1440–1870 (London: Picador, 1997); and David Eltis and David Richardson, eds., "Routes to Slavery: Direction, Ethnicity and Mortality in the Trans-Atlantic Slave Trade," a special issue of *Slavery & Abolition: A Journal of Slave and Post-slave Studies*, 18 (1997).

The literature on colonial slavery is immense. A very good starting point is Ira Berlin, *Many Thousands Gone: The First Two Centuries of Slavery in North America* (Cambridge, Mass.: Harvard University Press, 1998). Also see Kenneth Morgan, *Slavery and Servitude in Colonial America* (Edinburgh: Edinburgh University Press, 1998). For a very useful overview of slavery in colonial America which is sensitive to both chronological and regional variations, see Ira Berlin, "Time, Space, and the Evolution of Afro-American Society in British Mainland North America," *AHR*, 85 (1980), 44–78. For slavery in the northern colonies, see William D. Piersen, *Black Yankees: The Development of an Afro-American Subculture in Eighteenth-Century New England* (Amherst, Mass.: University of Massachusetts Press, 1988), and Gary Nash, *Forging Freedom: The Formation of Philadelphia's Black Community, 1720–1840* (Cambridge, Mass.: Harvard University Press, 1988). For the Chesapeake colonies, Rhys Isaac, *The Transformation of Virginia, 1740–1790* (Chapel Hill: University of North Carolina Press, 1982); Allan Kulikoff, *Tobacco and Slaves: The Development of Southern Cultures in the Chesapeake, 1680–1800* (Chapel Hill: University of North Carolina Press, 1986); and Philip D. Morgan and Michael L. Nicholls, "Slave Life in Piedmont Virginia, 1720–1800," in Lois Green Carr, Philip D. Morgan, and Jean B. Russo, eds., *Colonial Chesapeake Society* (Chapel Hill: University of North Carolina Press, 1988), 433–84, are appropriate places to begin. For the colonies of the lower south, see Betty Wood, *Slavery in Colonial Georgia* (Athens, GA.: University of Georgia Press, 1984); Peter H. Wood, *Black Majority; Negroes in Colonial South Carolina from 1670 through the Stono Rebellion* (New York: Knopf, 1974); Philip D. Morgan, "Work and Culture: The Task System and the World of Lowcountry Blacks, 1700 to 1880," *WMQ*, 39 (1982), 563–99; and Jon F. Sensbach, *A Separate Canaan: The Making of an Afro-Moravian World in North Carolina, 1763–1840* (Chapel Hill: University of North Carolina Press, 1998).

American slaves worked to supply the labor requirements of the trans-Atlantic economy. For current thinking on the early American economy, see John J. McCusker, ed., "The Economy of British North America," a special issue of the *WMQ*, 56 (1999), 3–181. See especially Lance Davis and Stanley Engerman, "The Economy of British America: Miles Traveled, Miles Still to Go," 9–22. For the trans-Atlantic trade, see John J. McCusker and Russell R. Menard, *The Economy of British America, 1607–1789* (Chapel Hill: University of North Carolina Press, 1985); James D. Tracy, ed., *The Rise of Merchant Empires: Long Distance Trade in the Early Modern World, 1350–1750* (Cambridge: Cambridge University Press, 1990); David Hancock, *Citizens of the World: London Merchants and the Integration of the British Atlantic Community, 1735–1785* (Cambridge: Cambridge University Press, 1995); T.H. Breen, "Narrative of Commercial Life: Consumption, Ideology, and Community on the Eve of the American Revolution," *WMQ*, 50 (1993), 471–501. Most Americans labored to supply domestic needs. For this sector of the economy, see Richard L. Bushman, "Markets and Composite Farms in Early America," *WMQ*, 55 (1998), 351–74. Also see Joyce Appleby, "Commercial Farming and the 'Agrarian Myth' in the Early Republic,"

JAH, 68 (1982), 833–49, repr. in Joyce Appleby, *Liberalism and Republicanism in the Historical Imagination* (Cambridge, Mass.: Harvard University Press, 1992), 253–76; Christopher Clark, *The Roots of Rural Capitalism: Western Massachusetts, 1780–1860* (Ithaca: Cornell University Press, 1990); James A. Henretta, "Farmers and Families: Mentalité in Preindustrial America," *WMQ*, 35 (1978), 3–32; James A. Henretta, "The Market in the Early Republic," *Journal of the Early Republic*, 18 (1998); James A. Henretta, *The Origins of American Capitalism* (Boston: Northeastern University Press, 1991); Allan Kulikoff, *The Agrarian Origins of American Capitalism* (Charlottesville: University Press of Virginia, 1992); Allan Kulikoff, "Households and Markets: Towards a New Synthesis of American Agrarian History," *WMQ*, 50 (1993), 342–355; Allan Kulikoff, "The Transition to Capitalism in Rural America," *WMQ*, 46 (1989), 120–44; Michael Merrill, "Cash is Good To Eat: Self-Sufficiency and Exchange in the Rural Economy," *Radical History Review*, 3 (1977), 42–71; Betty Hobbs Pruitt, "Self-Sufficiency and the Agricultural Economy of Eighteenth-Century Massachusetts," *WMQ*, 41 (1984), 333–64; and Winifred Rothenburg, *From Market-Places to a Market Economy: The Transformation of Rural Massachusetts, 1750–1850* (Chicago: University of Chicago Press, 1992).

For a sample of the literature on local politics in eighteenth-century America, see Edward M. Cook, Jr., *The Fathers of the Towns: Leadership and Community Structure in Eighteenth-Century New England* (Baltimore: Johns Hopkins University Press, 1976); Stanley N. Katz, *Newcastle's New York: Anglo-American Politics, 1732–1753* (Cambridge, Mass.: Harvard University Press, 1968); Francis Jennings, *Benjamin Franklin, Politician* (New York: Norton, 1996); Charles Sydnor, *Gentlemen Freeholders: Political Practices in Washington's Virginia* (Chapel Hill: University of North Carolina Press, 1952); John G. Kolp, "The Dynamics of Electoral Competition in Pre-Revolutionary Virginia," *WMQ*, 49 (1992), 652–74; Robert M. Weir, " 'The Harmony We Were Famous For': An Interpretation of Pre-revolutionary South Carolina Politics," *WMQ*, 26 (1969), 473–501. In a hotly contested thesis, Robert E. Brown in *Middle Class Democracy and Revolution in Massachusetts* (Ithaca: Cornell University Press, 1955) argued that New England's pre-Revolutionary politics were democratic. Also see Robert J. Dinkin, *Voting in Provincial America: A Study of Elections in the Thirteen Colonies, 1689–1776* (Westport, Conn.: Greenwood, 1977).

For the role of the assemblies in colonial politics, see Jack Greene, *The Quest for Power: The Lower Houses of Assembly in the Southern Royal Colonies, 1689–1776* (Chapel Hill: University of North Carolina Press, 1963); Jack P. Greene, "The Role of the Lower Houses of Assembly in Eighteenth-Century Politics," *Journal of Southern History*, 27 (1961), 451–74, recently reprinted in Jack P. Greene, *Negotiated Authorities: Essays in Colonial Political and Constitutional History* (Charlottesville: University Press of Virginia, 1994), 163–84. For the experiences of one governor who served in Massachusetts and New Jersey, see Michael C. Batinski, *Jonathan Belcher, Colonial Governor* (Lexington: University Press of Kentucky, 1996). Also see Leonard W. Labaree, *Royal Government in America: A Study of the British Colonial System before 1783* (New Haven: Yale University Press, 1930). A dated but still useful work is Evarts B. Greene, *The Provincial Governor in the English Colonies of North America* (New York, 1889). Also see James A. Henretta, *"Salutary Neglect": Colonial Administration under the Duke of Newcastle*

(Princeton: Princeton University Press, 1972). On the problems of imperial administration, see Jack P. Greene, "Negotiated Authorities: The Problem of Governance in the Extended Polities of the Early Modern Atlantic World," in Jack P. Greene, ed., *Negotiated Authorities*, 1–24. For colonial agents and interest groups in British politics, see Alison G. Olson, *Making the Empire Work: London and American Interest Groups, 1690–1790* (Cambridge, Mass.: Harvard University Press, 1992); Michael Kammen, *A Rope of Sand: The Colonial Agents, British Politics and the American Revolution* (Ithaca: Cornell University Press, 1968); Michael Kammen, *Empire and Interest: The American Colonies and the Politics of Mercantilism* (Philadelphia: Lippincott, 1970); Andrew J. O'Shaughnessy, "The Formation of a Commercial Lobby: The West India Interest, British Colonial Policy and the American Revolution," *The Historian*, 40 (1997), 71–95.

The seminal work on the intellectual origins of the Revolution subject remains Bernard Bailyn, *The Ideological Origins of the American Revolution* (Cambridge, Mass.: Harvard University Press, 1967, repr. 1992). For recent works which take exception with Bailyn's emphasis on the "Real Whig ideology," see T.H. Breen, "Ideology and Nationalism on the Eve of the American Revolution: Revisions once More in Need of Revising," *JAH*, 84 (1997), 13–39; and Jack P. Greene, "Pride, Prejudice and Jealousy: Benjamin Franklin's Explanation for the American Revolution," in Jack P. Greene, ed., *Understanding the American Revolution: Issues and Actors* (Charlottesville: University Press of Virginia, 1995), 18–47. Also see Joyce Appleby, "The Social Origins of American Revolutionary Ideology," *JAH*, 64 (1978), 935–58. For historiographical reviews of the subject, see Robert E. Shalhope, "Toward a Republican Synthesis: The Emergence of an Understanding of Republicanism in American Historiography," *WMQ*, 29 (1972); Robert E. Shalhope, "Republicanism in Early American Historiography," *WMQ*, 39 (1982); Daniel T. Rogers, "Republicanism: The Career of a Concept," *JAH*, 79 (1992), 11–38. Enlightenment thought had a crucial influence on the American Revolution. For an excellent treatment of this topic see Henry F. May, *The Enlightenment in America* (New York: Oxford University Press, 1976). Also see Henry Steele Commager, *The Empire of Reason: How Europe Imagined and America Realized the Enlightenment* (Garden City, N.Y.: Doubleday, 1977). For popular expressions of political ideology, see Pauline Maier, "Popular Uprisings and Civil Authority in Eighteenth-Century America," *WMQ*, 27 (1970), 3–35; Jesse Lemisch, "Jack Tar in the Streets: Merchant Seamen in the Politics of Revolutionary America," *WMQ*, 25 (1968); Gary Nash, "Social Change and the Growth of Prerevolutionary Urban Radicalism," in Alfred F. Young ed., *The American Revolution: Explorations in the History of American Radicalism* (DeKalb: Northern Illinois University Press, 1976), 3–36.

For the adoption of the Stamp Act, see Peter D.G. Thomas, *British Politics and the Stamp Act Crisis; The First Phase of the American Revolution, 1763–1767* (Oxford: Clarendon, 1975); John Bullion, *A Great and Necessary Measure: George Grenville and the Genesis of the Stamp Act, 1763–1765* (Columbia: University of Missouri Press, 1982); and Philip Lawson, *George Grenville: A Political Life* (Oxford: Clarendon, 1984). For American resistance to the Stamp Act, see Edmund S. Morgan and Helen M. Morgan, *The Stamp Act Crisis: Prologue to Revolution* (Chapel Hill: University of North Carolina Press, 1953, repr. 1995) and Pauline Maier, *From Resistance to Revolution: Colonial Radicals and the Develop-*

ment of American Opposition to Britain, 1765–1776 (New York: Vintage, 1972). For the ideological implications of the nonimportation movement, see T.H. Breen, "Narrative of Commercial Life: Consumption, Ideology, and Community on the Eve of the American Revolution," *WMQ*, 50 (1993), 471–501. For the repeal of the Stamp Act, see John L. Bullion, "British Ministers and American Resistance to the Stamp Act, October-December 1765," *WMQ*, 49 (1992), 89–107. For the Stamp Act crisis in areas outside of the thirteen colonies, see Andrew J. O'Shaughnessy, "The Stamp Act Crisis in the British Caribbean," *WMQ*, 51 (1994), 203–26; W.B. Kerr, "The Stamp Act Crisis in Quebec," *English Historical Review*, 47 (1932), 648–51; and W.B. Kerr, "The Stamp Act Crisis in Nova Scotia," *New England Quarterly*, 6 (1933), 552–66.

For the adoption of Townshend's program, see P.D.G. Thomas, *The Townshend Duties Crisis: The Second Phase of the American Revolution, 1767–1773* (Oxford: Clarendon, 1987) and Robert J. Chaffin, "The Townshend Acts of 1767," *WMQ*, 27 (1970), 90–121. For resistance to the duties which culminated in deadly conflict on the streets of Boston, see Hiller B. Zobel's *The Boston Massacre* (New York: Norton, 1971). For the committees of correspondence, see Richard D. Brown, *Revolutionary Politics in Massachusetts: The Boston Committee of Correspondence and the Towns, 1772–1774* (Cambridge, Mass.: Harvard University Press, 1970). For the Tea Act, see P.D.G. Thomas, *Tea Party to Independence: The Third Phase of the American Revolution, 1773–1776* (Oxford: Clarendon, 1991), and Philip Lawson, *The East India Company: A History* (London: Longman, 1993). For the Boston Tea Party, the standard work remains Benjamin Woods Labaree, *The Boston Tea Party* (New York: Oxford University Press, 1964).

The best account of the drafting and editing of the Declaration of Independence is in Pauline Maier, *American Scripture: Making the Declaration of Independence* (New York: Knopf, 1997). Also see Carl Becker, *The Declaration of Independence: A Study in the History of Political Ideas* (New York: Knopf, 1922); Julian Boyd, *The Declaration of Independence: The Evolution of a Text* (Princeton: Princeton University Press, 1945). For a study of the intellectual origins of Jefferson's draft as opposed to the Congressional document, see Garry Wills, *Inventing America: Jefferson's Declaration of Independence* (New York: Doubleday, 1978). Jay Fliegelman argues that the declaration can only be understood in the context of eighteenth-century theories of rhetoric; see his *Declaring Independence: Jefferson, Natural Language & the Culture of Performance* (Stanford: Stanford University Press, 1993).

Stephen Conway's *The War of American Independence, 1775–1783* (London: Edward Arnold, 1995) is an excellent one-volume overview of the War of Independence. Also see Don Higginbotham, *The War of American Independence: Military Attitudes, Policies, and Practice* (New York: Macmillan, 1971, repr. Boston: Northeastern University Press, 1983). For a collection of perceptive essays on the war, see John Shy, *A People Numerous and Armed: Reflections on the Military Struggle for American Independence* (University of Michigan Press, 1993). For an overview which considers the conflict mainly from the British perspective, see Piers Mackesy, *The War for America, 1775–1783* (Cambridge, Mass.: Harvard University Press, 1964). Also see Stephen Conway, "The Politics of British Military and Naval Mobilization, 1775–1783," *English Historical Review*, 112 (1997), 1179–1201.

On the development of the Continental Army, see Robert K. Wright, " 'Nor is Their Standing Army to Be Despised': The Emergence of the Continental Army as a Military Institution," in Ronald Hoffman and Peter J. Albert, eds., *Arms and Independence: The Military Character of the American Revolution* (Charlottesville: University Press of Virginia, 1984), 50–74; Charles Royster, *A Revolutionary People at War: The Continental Army and American Character, 1775–1783* (Chapel Hill: University of North Carolina Press, 1979), especially Chapters 1–2; and Charles P. Neimeyer, *America Goes to War: A Social History of the Continental Army* (New York: New York University Press, 1996). For a recent study which argues that Washington made greater use of militia and irregular partisans than is normally supposed, see Mark V. Kwasny, *Washington's Partisan War, 1775–1783* (Kent, OH.: Kent State University Press, 1996). On the logistical problems which faced the rebels, see E. Wayne Carp, *To Starve the Army at Pleasure: Continental Army Administration and American Political Culture, 1775–1783* (Chapel Hill: University of North Carolina Press, 1984).

For a detailed consideration of Britain's "southern strategy," see Ira D. Gruber, "Britain's Southern Strategy," in W. Robert Higgins, ed., *The Revolutionary War in the South: Power, Conflict, and Leadership* (Durham: Duke University Press, 1979), 205–38. For the war in the south, see Jeffrey J. Crow and Larry E. Tise, eds., *The Southern Experience in the American Revolution* (Chapel Hill: University of North Carolina Press, 1978); Ronald Hoffman, "The 'Disaffected' in the Revolutionary South," in Alfred F. Young, ed., *The American Revolution: Explorations in the History of American Radicalism* (DeKalb: Northern Illinois University Press, 1976), 273–316; and John S. Pancake, *This Destructive War: The British Campaigns in the Carolinas, 1780–1782* (University, Ala.: University of Alabama Press, 1985). On partisan warfare in the south, see Clyde R. Ferguson, "Functions of the Partisan-Militia in the South during the American Revolution: An Interpretation," in Higgins, ed., *The Revolutionary War in the South*, 239–58. Also see Don Higginbotham, "Daniel Morgan: Guerrilla Fighter," in Don Higginbotham *War and Society in Revolutionary America: The Wider Dimensions of the Conflict* (Columbia: University of South Carolina Press, 1988), 132–52; Hoffman, "The 'Disaffected' in the Revolutionary South," 290–8; and Ronald Hoffman, Thad W. Tate, and Peter J. Albert, eds., *An Uncivil War: The Southern Backcountry during the American Revolution* (Charlottesville: University Press of Virginia, 1985).

For the experience of frontier settlers during the Revolution, see John Mack Faragher, *Daniel Boone: The Life and Legend of an American Pioneer* (New York: Henry Holt, 1992), Chapters 4–6. A dated but still useful overview is Jack M. Sosin, *The Revolutionary Frontier, 1763–1783* (New York: Holt, Rinehart and Winston, 1967). For the Native American experience during and immediately after the War of Independence, see Colin Calloway, *The American Revolution in Indian Country: Crisis and Diversity in Native American Communities* (Cambridge: Cambridge University Press, 1995); Gregory Evans Dowd, *A Spirited Resistance: The North American Indian Struggle for Unity, 1745–1815* (Baltimore: Johns Hopkins University Press, 1992); and Francis Jennings, "The Indians' Revolution," in Alfred F. Young, ed., *The American Revolution: Explorations in the History of American Radicalism* (DeKalb: Northern Illinois University Press, 1976), 319–48. Wiley Sword, *President Washington's Indian War: The Struggle for the Old*

Northwest, 1790–1795 (Norman: University of Oklahoma Press, 1993) considers the struggle between Native Americans and the new Federal government. Edward Countryman, "Indians, the Colonial Order, and the Social Significance of the American Revolution," *WMQ*, 53 (1996), 342–362, argues that changing power relations between Indians and the new United States was among the most significant and radical consequences of the revolution. Two works which place these events in a broader regional and chronological context are Eric Hinderaker, *Elusive Empires: Constructing Colonialism in the Ohio Valley, 1673–1800* (New York: Cambridge University Press, 1997), and Richard White, *The Middle Ground: Indians, Empires and Republics in the Great Lakes Region, 1650–1815* (Cambridge: Cambridge University Press, 1991).

After years of neglect, the loyalists began to receive serious scholarly attention during the 1960s. William H. Nelson's *The American Tory* (Oxford: Clarendon, 1961) is indispensable. For a first-rate biography of a leading New England Loyalist, see Bernard Bailyn, *The Ordeal of Thomas Hutchinson* (Cambridge: Harvard University Press, 1974). Wallace Brown's *The Good Americans: The Loyalists in the American Revolution* (New York: Morrow, 1969) and *The King's Friends: The Composition of the American Loyalist Claims* (Providence: Brown University Press, 1965) are perceptive analyses of Loyalism. For specific case studies of Loyalism, see Robert M. Calhoon, *The Loyalist Perception and Other Essays* (Columbia: University of South Carolina Press, 1989); Jeffrey J. Crow, "Liberty Men and Loyalists: Disorder and Disaffection in the North Carolina Backcountry," in Hoffman, Tate and Albert, eds., *An Uncivil War*, 125–78. Janice Potter, *The Liberty We Seek: Loyalist Ideology in Colonial New York and Massachusetts* (Cambridge, Mass.: Harvard University Press, 1983) presents a cogent analysis of Loyalist ideology. Paul H. Smith, "The American Loyalists: Notes on Their Organization and Numerical Strength," *WMQ*, 25 (1968) is a valuable study. Mary Beth Norton, *The British Americans: The Loyalists Exiles in England, 1774–1789* (Boston: Little Brown, 1972); Richard D. Brown, "The Confiscation and Disposition of Loyalists' Estates in Suffolk County, Massachusetts," *WMQ*, 21 (1964), 534–50; and Robert S. Lambert, "The Confiscation of Loyalist Property in Georgia, 1782–1786," *WMQ*, 20 (1963), 80–94 consider the treatment meted out to loyalists.

The definitive study of the peace negotiations remains Richard B. Morris, *The Peacemakers: The Great Powers and American Independence* (New York: Harper and Row, 1965, repr. Boston: Northeastern University Press, 1983). A more recent assessment by Morris which is generally positive about the achievements of the American negotiators is his essay, "The Durable Significance of the Treaty of 1783," in Ronald Hoffman and Peter J. Albert, eds., *Peace and the Peacemakers: The Treaty of 1783* (Charlottesville: University Press of Virginia, 1986), 230–50. For a more critical view, see Bradford Perkins, "The Peace of Paris: Patterns and Legacies," in the same volume, 190–229. The best overview of the diplomatic history of the War of Independence is Jonathan R. Dull, *A Diplomatic History of the American Revolution* (New Haven: Yale University Press, 1985).

For the social consequences of the war see Royster, *Revolutionary People at War*; Neimeyer, *America Goes to War*; Holly A. Mayer, *Belonging to the Army: Camp Followers and Community during the American Revolution* (Columbia: University of South Carolina Press, 1996); Steven Rosswurm, "The Philadelphia Militia,

1775–1783: Active Duty and Active Radicalism," in Hoffman and Albert, eds., *Arms and Independence*, 75–118; Steven Rosswurm *Arms, Country and Class: The Philadelphia Militia and "Lower Sort" during the American Revolution, 1775–1783* (New Brunswick: Rutgers University Press, 1987); and James Kirby Martin, "A 'Most Undisciplined and Profligate Crew': Protest and Defiance in the Continental Ranks, 1776–1783," in Hoffman and Albert, eds., *Arms and Independence*, 119–40.

The state constitutions have been the subject of some excellent scholarship. See Willi Paul Adams, *The First American Constitutions: Republican Ideology and the Making of the State Constitutions in the Revolutionary Era* (Chapel Hill: University of North Carolina Press, 1980); Marc W. Kruman, *Between Authority and Liberty: State Constitution Making in Revolutionary America* (Chapel Hill: University of North Carolina Press, 1997); Donald S. Lutz, *Popular Consent and Popular Control: Whig Political Theory in the Early Constitutions* (Baton Rouge: Louisiana State University Press, 1980); Donald S. Lutz, *The Origins of American Constitutionalism* (Baton Rouge: Louisiana State University Press, 1988); and Gordon S. Wood, *The Creation of the American Republic, 1776–1787* (Chapel Hill: University of North Carolina Press, 1969), especially Chapters 4–6.

Merrill Jensen remains the pre-eminent historian of the Confederation period. His *The Articles of Confederation: An Interpretation of the Socio-Constitutional History of the American Revolution, 1774–1781* (Madison: University of Wisconsin Press, 1940), and *The New Nation: A History of the United States during the Confederation, 1781–1789* (New York: Knopf, 1950), remain essential starting points for any serious study of the period. Also see Jackson Turner Main, *Political Parties before the Constitution* (Chapel Hill: University of North Carolina Press, 1973), and *Sovereign States in an Age of Uncertainty* (Charlottesville: University Press of Virginia, 1981), a collection of essays on the period edited by Ronald Hoffman and Peter J. Albert. For the fiscal troubles which confronted the United States during the Confederation, see William G. Anderson, *The Price of Liberty: The Public Debt of the Revolution* (Charlottesville: University Press of Virginia, 1983); and E. James Ferguson, *The Power of the Purse: A History of American Public Finance, 1776–1790* (Chapel Hill: University of North Carolina Press, 1961). For the political implications of the financial difficulties, see Cathy D. Matson and Peter S. Onuf, *A Union of Interests: Political and Economic Thought in Revolutionary America* (Lawrence: University Press of Kansas, 1990). On the broader implications of taxation during the period, see Roger H. Brown, *Redeeming the Republic: Federalists, Taxation, and the Origins of the Constitution* (Baltimore: Johns Hopkins University Press, 1993).

On rural unrest in the aftermath of the war, see Alan Taylor, "Agrarian Independence: Northern Land Rioters after the Revolution," in Alfred F. Young, ed., *Beyond the American Revolution: Explorations in the History of American Radicalism* (DeKalb: Northern Illinois University Press, 1993), 221–5; Michael A. Bellesiles, *Revolutionary Outlaws: Ethan Allen and the Struggle for Independence on the Early American Frontier* (Charlottesville, 1993); Robert E. Moody, "Samuel Ely: Forerunner of Daniel Shays," *New England Quarterly*, 5 (1932), 105–34; Alan Taylor, *Liberty Men and Great Proprietors: The Revolutionary Settlement on the Maine Frontier* (Chapel Hill: University of North Carolina Press, 1990). There is an extensive literature on Shays's rebellion. The best place to start in approaching the rebellion is Robert A. Gross's excellent review of that literature, "White Hats and Hemlocks: Daniel Shays and the Legacy of the Revolution," in Ronald Hoffman and Peter J. Albert, eds., *The Transforming Hand of Revolution: Reconsidering the American Revolution as a Social Movement* (Charlottesville: University Press of Virginia, 1995), 286–345. Also see Robert A. Gross, ed., *In Debt to Shays: The Bicentennial of an Agrarian Rebellion* (Charlottesville: University Press of Virginia, 1993); David P. Szatmary, *Shays' Rebellion: The Making of an Agrarian Insurrection* (Amherst: University of Massachusetts Press, 1980); Jonathan Smith, "The Depression of 1785 and Daniel Shays' Rebellion," *WMQ*, 5 (1948), 77–94; Richard D. Brown, "Shays' Rebellion and its Aftermath: A View from Springfield, Massachusetts, 1787," *WMQ*, 40 (1983), 598–615; and John L. Brooke, "To the Quiet of the People: Revolutionary Settlements and Civil Unrest in Western Massachusetts, 1774–1789," *WMQ*, 46 (1989), 425–62.

The Constitution seems to have been the cause of more active historiographical debate than any other revolutionary topic. For a review of the literature, see Peter S. Onuf, "Reflections on the Founding: Constitutional Historiography in Bicentennial Perspective," *WMQ*, 46 (1989), 341–75. Perhaps the most important early scholarly critics of the Constitution were the Progressive historians of the early twentieth century. The most famous work in this tradition is Charles A. Beard's *An Economic Interpretation of the Constitution of the United States* (New York: Macmillan, 1913), which argued that the framers of the Constitution sought to safeguard their personal property interests which had been endangered by the financial policies of the states under the Articles of Confederation. A major precursor of Beard is J. Allen Smith's, *The Spirit of American Government* (New York, 1907, repr. Cambridge, Mass.: Belknap Press, 1965). For a critique of Beard's thesis, see Forrest McDonald, *We the People: The Economic Origins of the Constitution* (Chicago: University of Chicago Press, 1958).

An indispensable work on the Constitution remains Gordon S. Wood's *The Creation of the American Republic, 1776–1787* (Chapel Hill: University of North Carolina Press, 1969). A recent work is Jack N. Rakove, *Original Meanings: Politics and Ideas in the Making of the Constitution* (New York: Knopf, 1996). Rakove presents an excellent account of the drafting of the Constitution. He also attacks those who seek to divine the original intent of the framers of the Constitution by demonstrating that the views of key figures such as Madison evolved rapidly during the early years of the Constitution. For other works on the Constitutional Convention, see Thornton Anderson, *Creating the Constitution: The Convention of 1787 and the First Congress* (University Park, Pennsylvania State University Press, 1993); William Lee Miller, *The Business of May Next: James Madison and the Founding* (Charlottesville: University Press of Virginia, 1992); and Clinton Rossiter, *1787: The Grand Convention* (New York: Norton, 1966, repr. 1987). Also see James H. Hutson, "Riddles of the Federal Constitutional Convention," *WMQ*, 44 (1987), 411–23, and Jack N. Rakove, "The Great Compromise: Ideas, Interests, and the Politics of Constitution Making," *WMQ*, 44 (1987), 424–57. For the question of slavery in the drafting of the Constitution, see Paul Finkelman, "Slavery and the Constitutional Convention: Making a Covenant with Death," in Richard Beeman, Stephen Botein, and Edward C. Carter, eds., *Beyond Confederation: Origins of the Constitution and American National Identity* (Chapel Hill: University of North Carolina Press, 1987), 188–225; John

Kaminski, ed., *A Necessary Evil? Slavery and the Debate over the Constitution* (Madison: Madison House, 1995); and Mark E. Brandon, *Free in the World: American Slavery and Constitutional Failure* (Princeton: Princeton University Press, 1998).

For the Antifederalist critique of the Constitution, see Jackson Turner Main's excellent, *The Antifederalists: Critics of the Constitution, 1781–1787* (Chapel Hill: University of North Carolina Press, 1961; repr. New York: Norton, 1974). Also see Cecelia M. Kenyon, "Men of Little Faith: The Anti-Federalists on the Nature of Representative Government," *WMQ*, 12 (1955), 3–43. A more recent study which places the contributions of the Antifederalists in the broader context of early American politics is Saul Cornell, *The Other Founders: Anti-Federalism and the Dissenting Tradition in America, 1788–1828* (Chapel Hill: University of North Carolina Press, 1999).

For the Federalist case in favor of the Constitution, see Wood, *Creation of the American Republic*, Chapters 12–13. Also see Rakove, *Original Meanings*, Chapters 6–7. Perhaps the best modern edition of *The Federalist* is Isaac Kramnick, ed., *The Federalist Papers* (New York: Penguin Books, 1987). Kramnick's introduction is an excellent and elegant precis of the issues related to the background, drafting and ratification of the constitution. Also see Douglass Adair, "The Authorship of the Disputed Federalist Papers," Parts 1 and 2, *WMQ*, 1 (1944); Douglass Adair, "The Tenth Federalist Revisited," *WMQ*, 8 (1951), 48–67; Elaine F. Crane, "Publius in the Provinces: Where was *The Federalist* Printed Outside of New York City," *WMQ*, 21 (1964), 589–92; Daniel W. Howe, "The Political Psychology of *The Federalist*," *WMQ*, 44 (1987), 485–509; and Isaac Kramnick, "The Great National Discussion: The Discourse of Politics in 1787," *WMQ*, 45 (1988), 3–32.

For the ratification contest see, John P. Kaminski and Richard Leffler, eds., *Federalists and Antifederalists: The Debate over the Ratification of the Constitution*, 2nd edn. (Madison: Madison House, 1998); Murray Dry, "The Debate over Ratification of the Constitution," in Jack P. Green and J. R. Pole, eds., *The Blackwell Encyclopedia of the American Revolution* (Oxford: Blackwell, 1991), 471–86; Michael Gillespie and Michael Liensch, eds., *Ratifying the Constitution* (Lawrence: University Press of Kansas, 1989); Main, *The Antifederalists*, Chapters 9–10; and Robert A. Rutland, *The Ordeal of the Constitution: The Anti-Federalists and the Ratification Struggle of 1787–1788* (Norman: University of Oklahoma Press, 1966). For the Bill of Rights, see Ronald Hoffman and Peter J. Albert, eds., *The Bill of Rights: Government Proscribed* (Charlottesville: University Press of Virginia, 1998); Irving Brant, *The Bill of Rights: Its Origin and Meaning* (Indianapolis: Bobbs-Merrill, 1965); Leonard W. Levy, *Constitutional Opinions: Aspects of the Bill of Rights* (New York: Oxford University Press, 1986); and Robert A. Rutland, *The Birth of the Bill of Rights, 1776–1791* (Chapel Hill: University of North Carolina Press, 1955).

The best overview of the Federalist era from the perspective of high politics is Stanley Elkins and Eric McKitrick, *The Age of Federalism: The Early American Republic, 1788–1800* (New York: Oxford, 1993). Also see Ronald Hoffman and Peter J. Albert, eds., *Launching the Extended Republic: The Federalist Era* (Charlottesville: University Press of Virginia, 1996) for a collection of recent essays on the period. Simon P. Newman has provided a superb analysis of popular politics during the period; see his *Parades and the Politics of the Street: Festive Culture in the Early American Republic* (Philadelphia: University of Pennsylvania Press, 1997). Also see Len Travers, *Celebrating the Fourth: Independence Day and the Rites of Nationalism in the Early Republic* (Amherst: University of Massachusetts Press, 1997); and David Waldstreicher, *In the Midst of Perpetual Fetes: The Making of American Nationalism, 1776–1820* (Chapel Hill: University of North Carolina Press, 1997). Taken together, these three works show that the popular political culture of the early republic is a vibrant area of exciting research. Each demonstrate that the legacy of the Revolution can only be properly appreciated in a chronological context which is broader than that which has been adopted traditionally by historians.

For Washington's presidency and his place in early republic, Marcus Cunliffe's *George Washington: Man and Monument* (Boston: Little Brown, 1958) remains an indispensable work. For a more recent treatment, see Richard Brookhiser, *Founding Father: Rediscovering George Washington* (New York: Free Press, 1996). Also see John Ferling, *The First of Men: A Life of George Washington* (Knoxville: University of Tennessee Press, 1988), Chapters 15–18; Forrest McDonald, *The Presidency of George Washington* (Lawrence: University Press of Kansas, 1974); James Thomas Flexner, *George Washington*, 4 vols. (Boston: Little Brown, 1959–1972), vol. 3; and Douglas Southall Freeman, *George Washington: A Biography*, 7 vols. (New York: Scribners, 1948–1957), vol. 6.

For Alexander Hamilton's ideas and policies, see Richard Brookhiser, *Alexander Hamilton: American* (New York: Free Press, 1999); Gerald Stourzh, *Alexander Hamilton and the Idea of Republican Government* (Stanford: Stanford University Press, 1970); Nathan Schachner, *Alexander Hamilton* (New York: Barnes, 1961); Clinton Rossiter, *Alexander Hamilton and the Constitution* (New York: Harcourt, Brace and World, 1964); Broadus Mitchell, *Alexander Hamilton*, 2 vols. (New York: Macmillan, 1957–62); Forrest McDonald, *Alexander Hamilton: A Biography* (New York: Norton, 1979); Carl Lane, " 'For a Positive Profit': The Federal Investment in the First Bank of the United States, 1792–1802," *WMQ*, 54 (1997), 601–12; Doron Ben-Atar, "Alexander Hamilton's Alternative: Technology, Piracy, and the Report on Manufactures," *WMQ*, 52 (1995), 389–414; and John R. Nelson, Jr. "Alexander Hamilton and American Manufacturing: A Reexamination," *JAH*, 59 (1972), 567–84; John R. Nelson, Jr., *Liberty and Property: Political Economy and Policy-making in the New Nation, 1789–1812* (Baltimore: Johns Hopkins University Press, 1987); and Jacob E. Cooke, "Tench Coxe, Alexander Hamilton, and the Encouragement of American Manufactures," *WMQ*, 32 (1975), 369–92. Also see Jacob E. Cooke, *Tench Coxe and the Early Republic* (Chapel Hill: University of North Carolina Press, 1978), especially Chapters 8–10.

There is a vast literature on Jefferson's political and economic philosophy. Perhaps the best starting point is Lance Banning, "Jeffersonian Ideology Revisited: Liberal and Classical Ideas in the New American Republic," *WMQ*, 43 (1986), 3–19. Drew McCoy's *The Elusive Republic: Political Economy in Jeffersonian America* (Chapel Hill: University of North Carolina Press, 1980) is a concise, elegant volume which perceptively discusses the correlation between Jeffersonian political economy and geographic expansion. Jefferson's opposition to government intervention in the economy has led some historians to argue that he was a proponent of liberal capitalism as it developed in nineteenth-century America; see Joyce Appleby, *Capitalism and a New Social Order: The Republican Vision of the 1790s* (New York: New York University Press, 1984). Also see Appleby's "Commercial Farming and the 'Agrarian Myth' in the Early Republic," *JAH*, 68 (1981–82), 833–49, and "What is Still American in the Political Philosophy of Thomas Jefferson?" *WMQ*, 43 (1986), 2–34. Both of these are reprinted in *Liberalism and Republicanism in the Historical Imagination.*

For the rise of partisanship, see Norman K. Risjord, ed., *The Early American Party System* (New York: Harper and Row, 1969), and Richard Hofstadter, *The Idea of the Party System: The Rise of Legitimate Opposition in the United States, 1780–1840* (Berkeley: University of California Press, 1969), Chapters 1–3; both are useful starting points. Also see James Roger Sharp, *American Politics in the Early Republic: A New Nation in Crisis* (New Haven: Yale University Press, 1993), and Joseph Charles, *The Origins of the American Party System: Three Essays* (Williamsburg: Institute for Early American History and Culture, 1961). For the emergence of partisan divisions in Congress, see David P. Currie, *The Constitution in Congress: The Federalist Period, 1789–1801* (Chicago: University of Chicago Press, 1997); Mary P. Ryan, "Party Formation in the United States Congress: A Quantitative Analysis," *WMQ*, 28 (1971), 523–42; Norman K. Risjord, "Partisanship and Power: House Committees and the Powers of the Speaker, 1789–1801," *WMQ*, 49 (1992), 628–51; and Eugene Sheridan, "Thomas Jefferson and the Giles Resolutions," *WMQ*, 49 (1992), 589–607.

For a seminal analysis of the political rhetoric of the period, see John R. Howe, "Republican Thought and the Political Violence of the 1790s," *American Quarterly*, 19 (1967), 147–65. For a recent consideration of journalism during the period from the perspective of the Republicans, see Richard N. Rosenfeld, *American Aurora: A Democratic-Republican Returns: The Suppressed History of Our Nation's Beginnings and the Heroic Newspaper that Tried to Report It* (New York: St. Martins, 1997). Rosenfeld presents the history of the Federalist period from the perspective of Benjamin Franklin Bache, a Philadelphia printer who was extremely critical of the Washington and Adams administrations. In a controversial methodological approach, Rosenfeld adopts the first-person voice of Bache and reprints long extracts from Bache's *American Aurora*. Also see Donald H. Stewart, *The Opposition Press of the Federalist Period* (Albany: State University Press of New York, 1969).

The Federalists have made up for their lack of popular support by the attention they have received from historians. For a recent collection of essays on the Federalists, see Doron Ben-Atar and Barbara Oberg, eds., *Federalists Reconsidered* (Charlottesville: University Press of Virginia, 1999). Also see Gary K . Kornblith, "Artisan Federalism: New England Mechanics and the Political Economy of the 1790s," in Hoffman and Albert, eds., *Launching the Extended Republic*, 249–72; James M. Banner, Jr., *To the Hartford Convention: The Federalists and the Origins of Party Politics in Massachusetts, 1789–1815* (New York: Knopf, 1970); James Broussard, *The Southern Federalists, 1800–1816* (Baton Rouge: Louisiana State University Press, 1978); David Hackett Fischer, *The Revolution in American Conservatism: The Federalist Party in the Age of Jefferson* (New York: Harper and Row, 1965); Richard G. Miller, *Philadelphia – The Federalist City: A Study in Urban Politics, 1789–1801* (Port Washington, N.Y.: Kennikat Press, 1976);

Ulrich B. Phillips, "The South Carolina Federalists," *AHR*, 14 (1909), 529–43; and Linda K. Kerber, *Federalists in Dissent: Imagery and Ideology in Jeffersonian America* (Ithaca: Cornell University Press, 1970).

For the early Republican party, see Lance Banning, *The Jeffersonian Persuasion: Evolution of a Party Ideology* (Ithaca: Cornell University Press, 1978); Noble E. Cunningham, Jr., *The Jeffersonian Republicans: The Formation of Party Organization, 1789–1801* (Chapel Hill: University of North Carolina Press, 1957); Paul Goodman, *The Democratic Republicans in Massachusetts: Politics in a Young Republic* (Cambridge, Mass.: Harvard University Press, 1964); Alfred F. Young, *The Democratic Republicans of New York: The Origins, 1763–1797* (Chapel Hill: University of North Carolina Press, 1967). For the Democratic-Republican Societies which were crucial in establishing the party at the grassroots level, see Eugene Perry Link, *The Democratic-Republican Societies, 1790–1800* (New York: Octagon Books, 1942) and Matthew Schoenbachler, "Republicanism in the Age of Democratic Revolution: The Democratic-Republican Societies of the 1790s," *Journal of the Early Republic*, 18 (1998).

The most complete work on the Whiskey Rebellion is Thomas P. Slaughter, *The Whiskey Rebellion: Frontier Epilogue to the American Revolution* (New York: Oxford University Press, 1986). Also see Richard H. Kohn, "The Washington Administration's Decision to Crush the Whiskey Rebellion," *JAH*, 59 (1972), 567–84; and Steven R. Boyd, ed., *The Whiskey Rebellion: Past and Present Perspectives* (Westport: Greenwood Press, 1985). For resistance to the excise beyond Pennsylvania, see Mary K. Bonsteel Tachua, "The Whiskey Rebellion in Kentucky: A Forgotten Episode of Civil Disobedience," *Journal of the Early Republic*, 2 (1982), 239–59; Jeffrey J. Crow, "The Whiskey Rebellion in North Carolina," *North Carolina Historical Review*, 66 (1989), 1–28.

On the complex foreign policy questions which faced the United States during the 1790s, see Alexander DeConde, *Entangling Alliance: Diplomacy and Politics under George Washington* (Durham: Duke University Press, 1958); James L. Lewis, *The American Union and the Problem of Neighborhood: The United States and the Collapse of the Spanish Empire, 1783–1829* (Chapel Hill: University of North Carolina Press, 1998); and Charles M. Thomas, *American Neutrality in 1793: A Study in Cabinet Government* (New York: AMS Press, 1967). For the Jay Treaty, see Samuel Flagg Bemis, *Jay's Treaty: A Study in Commerce and Diplomacy*, revised edn. (New Haven: Yale University Press, 1962); Jerald A. Combs, *The Jay Treaty: Political Battleground of the Founding Fathers* (Berkeley: University of California Press, 1970); Charles R. Ritcheson, *Aftermath of the Revolution: British Policy toward the United States, 1783–1795* (Dallas: Southern Methodist University Press, 1969); Bradford Perkins, *The First Rapprochement: England and the United States, 1795–1805* (Berkeley: University of California Press, 1955, repr. 1967). For the difficulties in Franco-American relations after the Jay Treaty, see Alexander DeConde, *The Quasi-War: The Politics and Diplomacy of the Undeclared War with France 1797–1801* (New York: Scribners, 1966); William Stinchcombe, *The XYZ Affair* (Westport: Greenwood, 1980). For Adams's actions during the crisis, see Stephen G. Kurtz, *The Presidency of John Adams and the Collapse of Federalism* (Philadelphia: University of Pennsylvania Press, 1957), and John E. Ferling, *John Adams: A Life* (Knoxville: University of Tennessee Press,

1992), Chapter 17. Also see William G. Anderson, "John Adams, the Navy, and the Quasi-War with France," *American Neptune*, 30 (1970), 117–32.

On the role of foreign immigrants in domestic politics during the 1790s, see Michael Durey, *Trans-Atlantic Radicals and the Early American Republic* (Lawrence: University Press of Kansas, 1997) and David Wilson, *United Irishmen, United States Immigrant Radicals in the Early Republic* (Ithaca: Cornell University Press, 1998). Each of these studies superbly places American political developments in a trans-Atlantic context. For the Alien and Sedition acts, which were adopted to stifle dissent among immigrant radicals, see James Morton Smith, *Freedom's Fetters: The Alien and Sedition Laws and American Civil Liberties* (Ithaca: Cornell University Press, 1956), and John C. Miller, *Crisis in Freedom: The Alien and Sedition Acts* (Boston: Little, Brown, 1951).

On Jefferson's interest in the west, see Stephen Ambrose, *Undaunted Courage: Meriwether Lewis, Thomas Jefferson and the Opening of the American West* (New York: Knopf, 1996); Donald Jackson, *Thomas Jefferson and the Stony Mountains: Exploring the West from Monticello* (Urbana: University of Illinois Press, 1981); and Lawrence S. Kaplan, *Thomas Jefferson: Westward the Course of Empire* (Wilmington, Del.: Scholarly Resources, 1998). Also see Frank Lawrence Owsley, Jr., and Gene A. Smith, *Filibusters and Expansionists: Jeffersonian Manifest Destiny, 1800–1821* (University: University of Alabama Press, 1997). The most complete treatment of the Louisiana Purchase is Alexander DeConde, *This Affair of Louisiana* (New York: Scribner, 1976). Also see Dumas Malone, *Jefferson the President: The First Term, 1801–1805* (Boston: Little, Brown, 1970), Chapters 14–19. For the Lewis and Clark expedition, see Ambrose, *Undaunted Courage*; Bernard DeVoto, *The Course of Empire* (Boston: Houghton Mifflin, 1952); Richard H. Dillon, *Meriwether Lewis: A Biography* (New York: Coward-McCann, 1965); and James P. Ronda, *Lewis and Clark among the Indians* (Lincoln: University of Nebraska Press, 1984). Contrary to popular belief, Lewis and Clark were not the first Europeans or Euro-Americans to cross the continent. In 1793 the Scot Alexander Mackenzie crossed Canada and reached the Pacific on behalf of the North West Company. Unlike the Lewis and Clark expedition, Mackenzie did not discover a commercially viable route to the Pacific. Nor did he gather as much information on the west as the Corps of Discovery. For MacKenzie, see Barry M. Gough, *First Across the Continent: Sir Alexander MacKenzie* (Norman: University of Oklahoma Press, 1997).

For general works on the embargo, see Louis M. Sears, *Jefferson and the Embargo* (Durham, N.C.: Duke University Press, 1927); Walter W. Jennings, *The American Embargo, 1807–1809* (Iowa City: University of Iowa Press, 1921); Burton Spivak, *Jefferson's English Crisis: Commerce, Embargo and the Republican Revolution* (Charlottesville: University Press of Virginia, 1979); and Amy Bass, "A Matter of Customs," *American Neptune*, 58 (1998), 25–37. For resistance to the Embargo, see Robin D. S. Higham, "The Port of Boston and the Embargo of 1807–1809," *American Neptune*, 16 (1956), 189–208; J.D. Forbes, "Boston Smuggling, 1807–1815," *American Neptune*, 10 (1950), 144–149C; Norman Guice, "Trade Goods for Texas: An Incident in the History of the Jeffersonian Embargo," *Southwestern Historical Quarterly*, 60 (1956–57), 507–19; James Duncan Phillips, "Jefferson's 'Wicked Tyrannical Embargo'," *New England Quarterly*, 18 (1945), 466–78; Thorp Lanier Wolford, "Democratic-Republican

Reaction in Massachusetts to the Embargo of 1807," *New England Quarterly*, 15 (1942), 35–61; and Reginald C. Stuart, *United States Expansionism and British North America, 1775–1871* (Chapel Hill: University of North Carolina Press, 1988), Chapter 2.

On the coming of the War of 1812, see Harry W. Fritz, "The War Hawks of 1812," *Capitol Studies*, 5 (1977), 25–42; Ronald L. Hatzenbuehler, "The War Hawks and the Question of Congressional Behavior," *Pacific Historical Review*, 65 (1976), 1–22; Reginald Horsman, "Who were the War Hawks?" *Indiana Magazine of History*, 60 (1964), 121–36; and Norman K. Risjord, "1812: Conservatives, Warhawks, and the Nation's Honor," *WMQ*, 18 (1961), 196–210. For the origins of the War of 1812, see Warren Goodman, "The Origins of the War of 1812: A Survey of Changing Interpretations," *Mississippi Valley Historical Review*, 28 (1941–42), 171–86; Reginald Horsman, *The Causes of the War of 1812* (New York: Octagon Books, 1972); Lawrence S. Kaplan, "France and Madison's Decision for War, 1812," *Mississippi Valley Historical Review*, 50 (1963–64), 652–69; Bradford Perkins, *Prologue to War: England and the United States, 1805–1812* (Berkeley: University of California Press, 1968); Robert A. Rutland, *Madison's Alternatives: The Jeffersonian Republicans and the Coming of War, 1805–1812* (Philadelphia: Lippincott, 1975); J.C.A. Stagg, *Mr. Madison's War: Politics, Diplomacy, and Warfare in the Early American Republic, 1783–1830* (Princeton: Princeton University Press, 1983). For the war itself, the best study is Donald Hickey, *The War of 1812: A Forgotten Conflict* (Urbana: University of Illinois Press, 1989). Also see Pierre Berton, *The Invasion of Canada, 1812–1813* (Toronto: McClelland and Stewart, 1980); Alec Richard Gilpin, *The War of 1812 in the Old Northwest* (East Lansing: Michigan State University Press, 1958); Reginald Horsman, *The War of 1812* (London: Eyre & Spottiswoode, 1969); Robert S. Quimby, The *United States Army in the War of 1812: An Operational and Command Study*, 2 vols. (East Lansing: Michigan State University Press, 1997); George C. Sheppard, *Plunder, Profit, and Paroles: A Social History of the War of 1812 in Upper Canada* (Montreal: McGill-Queen's University Press, 1994). For the emotional and intellectual impact of the war on the United States, see Steven Watts, *The Republic Reborn: War and the Making of Liberal America, 1790–1820* (Baltimore: Johns Hopkins University Press, 1987).

Sylvia Frey, *Water From the Rock: Black Resistance in a Revolutionary Age* (Princeton: Princeton University Press, 1991), is probably the best work on African Americans during the period of the American Revolution. For the contribution of African Americans to the prewar resistance movement, see Gary Nash, *Forging Freedom: The Formation of Philadelphia's Black Community, 1720–1840* (Cambridge, Mass.: Harvard University Press, 1988), 45–65. For prewar slave resistance, see Peter H. Wood, " 'Liberty is Sweet': African American Freedom Struggles in the Years before White Independence," in Alfred F. Young, ed., *Beyond the American Revolution: Explorations in the History of American Radicalism* (DeKalb: Northern Illinois University Press, 1993), 149–84; and Sidney Kaplan, "The Domestic Insurrections of the Declaration of Independence," *Journal of Negro History*, 61 (1976). For the wartime experiences of African Americans, see Benjamin Quarles, "The Revolutionary War as a Black Declaration of Independence," in Ira Berlin and Ronald Hoffman, eds., *Slavery and Freedom in the Age of the American Revolution* (Charlottesville: University Press of

Virginia, 1983), 283–301. For slaves who enlisted in the Continental Army, see Charles P. Neimeyer, *America Goes to War: A Social History of the Continental Army* (New York: New York University Press, 1996), and Frey, *Water From the Rock*. For slaves who ran away, see Billy G. Smith, "Runaway Slaves in the Mid-Atlantic Region during the Revolutionary Era," in Ronald Hoffman and Peter J. Albert, eds., *The Transforming Hand of Revolution: Reconsidering the American Revolution as a Social Movement* (Charlottesville: University Press of Virginia, 1995), 199–230. For an excellent local case study on the impact of the war on northern slavery, see Graham Russell Hodges, *Slavery and Freedom in the Rural North: African Americans in Monmouth County, New Jersey, 1665–1865* (Madison: Madison House, 1997), Chapter 3.

The most complete treatment of abolition in the north remains Arthur Zilversmit, *The First Emancipation: The Abolition of Slavery in the North* (Chicago: University of Chicago Press, 1967). Also see T.H. Breen, "Making History: The Force of Public Opinion and the Last Years of Slavery in Revolutionary Massachusetts," in Ronald Hoffman, Mechal Sobel, and Frederika Teute, eds., *Through a Glass Darkly: Reflections on Personal Identity in Early America* (Chapel Hill: University of North Carolina Press, 1997), 67–95; Nash, *Forging Freedom*; Gary B. Nash, *Race and Revolution* (Madison: Madison House, 1990), Chapter 1; William S. O'Brien, "Did the Jennison Case Outlaw Slavery in Massachusetts?" *WMQ*, 17 (1960), 219–41; Shane White, *Somewhat More Independent: The End of Slavery in New York City, 1770–1810* (Athens: University of Georgia Press, 1991).

For changing racial attitudes during the early republic, see Jordan, *White over Black*, Chapters 13–15, and Nash, *Race and Revolution*, Chapter 3. For free African Americans in the south, see Ira Berlin, *Slaves without Masters: The Free Negro in the Antebellum South* (New York: Parthenon Books, 1974); Tommy L. Bogger, *Free Blacks in Norfolk Virginia, 1790–1860: The Darker Side of Freedom* (Charlottesville: University Press of Virginia, 1997); Christopher Phillips, *Freedom's Port: The African American Community of Baltimore, 1790–1860* (Urbana: University of Illinois Press, 1997); John T. O'Brien, "Factory, Church and Community: Blacks in Ante-bellum Richmond," *Journal of Southern History*, 44 (1978), 509–36; and T. Stephen Whitman, *The Price of Freedom: Slavery and Manumission in Baltimore and Early National Maryland* (Lexington: University Press of Kentucky, 1997). For free African Americans in the ante-bellum north, see Nash, *Forging Freedom*; White, *Somewhat More Independent*, Chapter 6; and Hodges, *Slavery and Freedom in the Rural North*, Chapters 5–6. Also see W. Jeffrey Bolster, *Black Jacks: African American Seamen in the Age of Sail* (Cambridge, Mass.: Harvard University Press, 1997).

The standard accounts of the Haitian Revolution in English are T. Lothrop Stoddard, *The French Revolution in San Domingo* (Boston: Houghton Mifflin, 1914); C.L.R. James, *The Black Jacobins: Toussaint L'Ouverture and the San Domingo Revolution*, rev. edn. (New York: Vintage Books, 1963); and Thomas O. Ott, *The Haitian Revolution, 1789–1804* (Knoxville: University of Tennessee Press, 1973). For a recent account which places these events in a hemispheric context, see Langley, *The Americas in the Age of Revolution, 1750–1850*. Also see David Berry Gaspar and David P. Geggus, eds., *A Turbulent Time: The French Revolution in the Greater Caribbean* (Bloomington: Indiana University Press, 1997); and David P.

Geggus, *Slavery, War and Revolution: The British Occupation of Saint-Domingue, 1793–1798* (New York: Oxford University Press, 1982). Two studies which consider the how these events relate to aspects of American politics and policy are James Sidbury, "Saint Domingue in Virginia: Ideology, Local Meaning and the Resistance to Slavery," *Journal of Southern History*, 63 (1997), 531–52, and Tim Matthewson, "Jefferson and Haiti," *Journal of the Southern History*, 61 (1995), 209–48.

The most important works on women during the era of the Revolution and early republic are Joan Hoff Wilson, "The Illusion of Change: Women in the American Revolution," in Alfred F. Young, ed., *The American Revolution: Explorations in the History of American Radicalism* (DeKalb: Northern Illinois University Press, 1976), 383–445; Linda K. Kerber, " 'History Can do it No Justice': Women and the Reinterpretation of the American Revolution," in Ronald Hoffman and Peter J. Albert, eds., *Women in the Age of the American Revolution* (Charlottesville: University Press of Virginia, 1989), 3–42 (this essay was reprinted in Linda K. Kerber *Toward an Intellectual History of Women* (Chapel Hill: University of North Carolina Press, 1997), 63–99); Mary Beth Norton, *Liberty's Daughters: The Revolutionary Experience of American Women, 1750–1800* (Boston: Little Brown, 1980); Linda Kerber, *Women of the Republic: Intellect and Ideology in Revolutionary America* (Chapel Hill: University of North Carolina Press, 1980); Joy Day Buel and Richard Buel, Jr., *The Way of Duty: A Woman and Her Family in Revolutionary America* (New York: Norton, 1984); Harriet B. Applewhite and Darline G. Levy, eds., *Women and Politics in the Age of Democratic Revolution* (Ann Arbor: University of Michigan, 1990); and Joan R. Gundersen, *To Be Useful to the World: Women in Revolutionary America, 1740–1790* (New York: Twayne, 1996).

For the debate over the place of women in a republican polity, see Ruth Bloch, "The Gendered Meanings of Virtue in Revolutionary America," *Signs: Journal of Women in Culture and Society*, 13 (1987), 27–58; Elaine F. Crane, "Dependence in the Era of Independence: The Role of Women in a Republican Society," in Jack P. Greene, ed., *The American Revolution: Its Character and Limits* (New York: New York University Press, 1987), 253–75; Joan R. Gundersen, "Independence, Citizenship and the American Revolution," *Signs: Journal of Women in Culture and Society*, 13 (1987), 59–77; Linda K. Kerber, " 'I Have Don ... much to Carrey on the Warr': Women and the Shaping of Republican Ideology after the American Revolution," in Applewhite and Levy, eds., *Women and Politics in the Age of the Democratic Revolution*, 227–57, repr. in Kerber, *Toward an Intellectual History of Women*, 100–30; and Linda K. Kerber, "The Paradox of Women's Citizenship in the Early Republic: The Case of *Martin vs. Massachusetts*, 1805," *AHR*, 97 (1992), 349–78. The latter article was reprinted in Kerber, *Toward an Intellectual History of Women*, 261–302. Also see Rosemarie Zagarri, "The Rights of Man and Woman in Post-Revolutionary America," *WMQ*, 55 (1998), 203–30. The seminal work on Republican Motherhood is Linda Kerber's, "The Republican Mother: Women and the Enlightenment – An American Perspective," *American Quarterly*, 28 (1976), 187–205, repr. in Kerber, *Toward an Intellectual History of Women*, 41–62. Also see Norma Basch, "From the Bonds of Empire to the Bonds of Matrimony," in David Thomas Konig, ed., *Devising Liberty: Preserving and Creating Freedom in the New American Republic* (Stanford: Stanford University Press,

1995), 217–42; Ruth Bloch, "The Gendered Meanings of Virtue in Revolutionary America," *Signs: Journal of Women in Culture and Society*, 13 (1987), 37–58; Kerber, *Women of the Republic*, Chapter 9; Jan Lewis, "The Republican Wife: Virtue and Seduction in the Early Republic," *WMQ*, 47 (1987), 689–721; Rosemarie Zagarri, "Morals, Manners, and the Republican Mother," *American Quarterly*, 44 (1992), 192–215.

On the changing legal status of women during the period, see Nancy F. Cott, "Divorce and the Changing Status of Women in Eighteenth-Century Massachusetts," *WMQ*, 33 (1976), 586–614; Kerber, *Women of the Republic*, Chapters 5–6; Kerber, "Paradox of Women's Citizenship in the Early Republic"; Marylynn Salmon, " 'Life, Liberty, and Dower': The Legal Status of Women After the American Revolution," in Carol Berkin and Clara M. Lovett, eds., *Women, War and Revolution* (New York: Holmes and Meier, 1980), 85–106; and Marylynn Salmon, *Women and the Law of Property in Early America* (Chapel Hill: University of North Carolina Press, 1986), Chapter 4. For women's education during the period, see Kerber, *Women of the Republic*, Chapter 7; and Linda K. Kerber, "Daughters of Columbia: Educating Women for the Republic, 1787–1805," in Stanley Elkins and Eric McKitrick, eds., *The Hofstadter Aegis: A Memorial* (New York: Knopf, 1974), 36–59, repr. in Kerber, *Toward and Intellectual History of Women*, 23–40. For women's reading, see Kerber, *Women of the Republic*, Chapter 8; Cathy N. Davidson, *Revolution and the Word: The Rise of the Novel in America* (New York: Oxford University Press, 1986); and Cathy N. Davidson, "The Novel as Subversive Activity: Women Reading, Women Writing," in Alfred F. Young, ed., *Beyond the American Revolution: Explorations in the History of American Radicalism* (DeKalb: Northern Illinois University Press, 1993), 283–316.

INDEX